# TIMES SQUARE REMADE

# TIMES SQUARE REMADE

## THE DYNAMICS OF URBAN CHANGE

LYNNE B. SAGALYN

**THE MIT PRESS**   Cambridge, Massachusetts   London, England

The MIT Press would like to thank the anonymous peer reviewers who provided comments on drafts of this book. The generous work of academic experts is essential for establishing the authority and quality of our publications. We acknowledge with gratitude the contributions of these otherwise uncredited readers.

This book was set in Stone by the MIT Press. Printed and bound in the United States of America.

Library of Congress Cataloging-in-Publication Data

Names: Sagalyn, Lynne B., author.
Title: Times Square remade : the dynamics of urban change / Lynne B. Sagalyn.
Other titles: Dynamics of urban change
Description: Cambridge, Massachusetts : The MIT Press, [2023] | Includes bibliographical references and index.
Identifiers: LCCN 2022049792 (print) | LCCN 2022049793 (ebook) | ISBN 9780262048545 (hardcover) | ISBN 9780262376327 (epub) | ISBN 9780262376334 (pdf)
Subjects: LCSH: Times Square (New York, N.Y.)--History. | Cities and towns--Study and teaching--New York State--New York.
Classification: LCC F128.68.T55 S24 2023  (print) | LCC F128.68.T55 (ebook) | DDC 974.7/1--dc23/eng/20230307
LC record available at https://lccn.loc.gov/2022049792
LC ebook record available at https://lccn.loc.gov/2022049793

10  9  8  7  6  5  4  3  2  1

To the memory of Herb Sturz
and
all those who made possible
renewal of the city's symbolic soul

# CONTENTS

# REMADE: AN INTRODUCTION

Remade times four: Longacre Square to Times Square. Live theater to grinders and burlesque. Honky-tonk to pornography. Adult entertainment to family friendly. Each of the remakes of 42nd Street and Times Square has been legendary, a chronicle of change recorded by historians, journalists, photographers, critics, and urban scholars; times lived by producers, performers, artists, speculators, small businesses, luncheonettes and bars, neighborhood residents, tourists, out-of-sorts drifters, and grifters. What is it about the place that has inspired such attention for well over a century, commanded so many words and multitudes of photographs, and continues to evoke nostalgia for each of its era personalities? How is it that, despite its many changes of character, the place has maintained a unique hold on the urban imagination? What has made it iconic, a symbol of city life? A place demanding the homage of nearly every tourist to New York? And what might follow the pandemic-induced hollowed-out eerie desolation of shuttered movie theaters and entertainment venues on both sides of West 42nd Street, the transformed street of historic fame brought into fresh being early in the twenty-first century after 20 years of effort by public officials and private investors?

Times Square is a nexus of change. The four transformations chronicled in these pages span its formative growth, unexpected national constrictions, slow but steady decline amid a temporary economic revival, and most recent public renewal. Each era dislocated earlier conditions—physical, economic, and social—in ways that profoundly altered the built environment and experience of the place. In each era, some of the changes were evident, others may have seemed discernable in retrospect, but exactly what tipped the scales and made for a definitive inflection point was not predictable. That is the nature of urban change. Districts evolve. It takes time. Change that refashions an area in profound ways typically occurs over many years (often decades), punctuated by bold and risky visions (as well as thwarted ambitions), competitive challenges, setbacks and bottlenecks, new social norms, demographic changes, and government actions, all amid the vicissitudes of real estate markets. In the process, the tangents of change do not always lead in the same direction at the same time.

Real estate is a driving force of urban social change. Land and what is built on it order urban space. Buildings, open spaces, and pathways establish the physical framework of residential neighborhoods and economic districts; together, they define the fabric of place. In the twentieth century, real estate developers and investors became active agents of change, building at large scale and at towering densities, in contrast to the individual builders who fashioned the nineteenth-century neighborhoods of New York through smaller-scale projects, at lower densities, and incrementally over time. Speculation in real estate has been a handmaiden of growth since New York's earliest days as the nation's first capital. John Jacob Astor set the pace with his acquisitive land purchases in the first years of the nineteenth century, which were held for decades, sometimes a century or more, by his heirs, in a firm belief in the future growth and economic prosperity of New York. Real estate formed the basis of Astor inherited wealth and influence. The patriarch's example was not lost on others. Holding long, however, did not mean holding in perpetuity. As the economic value of what builders and developers could put on land changed, prospective profits far exceeded rents from existing uses of the land, triggering a repetitive pattern of speculative tearing down to rebuild.

New York's culture of commerce literally rests on this foundation of real estate—its immovability and the ambitions behind its mutability. As one of the city's well-known brokers remarked in 1930, "There is no romance any greater in New York City and no gold mine ever produced 'pay gold' such as Broadway, Fifth Avenue, Wall Street and many other centers on good old Manhattan Island have produced for its owners."[1] *Times Square Remade* draws on the city's real estate history and evolution to tell a story of how economic forces and social change first shaped and then reshaped a legendary place, a place often called the symbolic soul of New York. It is a New York story yet told in a way to illuminate the dynamic forces of change—growth, decline, and renewal—characteristic of most North American cities.

Twenty years after finishing *Times Square Roulette*, in which I chronicled the tortuous path public officials followed to transform West 42nd Street, I thought it was time to take a look at what the transformation had brought about. After all, the story of urban change is what comes after, what it leads to, how it does or does not affect the life of the city and its residents. As a born-and-bred New Yorker, I had closely studied my city's development and its politics for many decades during the years I taught real estate finance, transaction strategy, and development to graduate business and planning students and engaged in the business life of the industry as part of my professional academic responsibilities. I expected the impacts of Times Square's transformation to travel well beyond the square itself, and I wanted to explore that path of impact and its meaning. My deep engagement in the city's development issues while researching and writing *Power at Ground Zero: Politics, Money, and the Remaking of Lower Manhattan* had presented, in stark contrast, the promise and problems of rebuilding another symbolic site under deeply emotional conditions following the catastrophic 9/11 terrorist attack, a difficult story to tell. The Times Square story would, thankfully, carry none of those difficult overtones.

In once again focusing my attention on Times Square, I wanted to understand the evolution of change in the celebrated district once the deep decline and decrepitude of West 42nd Street no longer presented a bottleneck to the westward expansion of midtown, long thought by realty interests to be just a matter of time. What would it mean for Hell's Kitchen, the storied adjacent working-class neighborhood and the slumbering area of warehouses, parking lots, lumber yards, and assemblages of land waiting to be developed along the spine of 42nd Street stretching westward to the Hudson River? What were some of the hidden stories of success overshadowed by much too much commentary on what many critics considered the "Disneyfication" of 42nd Street? How would the "river-to-river" vision of this central crosstown artery of business, transportation, and culture finally evolve? As a defining feature of New York's history and its political economy, the ways in which real estate and its particular dynamic have shaped Times Square from its earliest days are a story largely untold. Researching that story promised to reveal insights into the economic and political culture of New York City. The story called for visualization, for telling images captured by photographers seeking to record history, chronicle change, or capture the energy of Times Square and the everyday character of urban life in the district. There are many such images within these pages. The trajectory of my scholarly life has been anchored in explaining the complex ways in which cities are built and rebuilt. With this sequel to the story of Times Square, I hope to shed light on the dynamics of urban change.

The story of what made Times Square a city icon begins in the late 1890s. Speculation marked its early development, starting with Oscar Hammerstein's unconventional choice of a location for his pace-setting Olympia Theatre on Broadway at 44th Street, blocks beyond the established theater district, known as the Rialto, centered around Herald Square and 34th Street. Theatrical enterprise soon attracted numerous entrepreneurial producers, the smart set, daring restaurateurs, and ever-growing troops of tourists to Longacre Square, dislocating the horse dealerships, carriage factories, and livery stables that had populated the place since the end of the Civil War. The opening of the paper of record's new headquarters gave the place a new name at the same time the inauguration of the city's first subway line with a station entrance in the Times Tower established an enduring centrality to this western section of midtown. When the two Astor cousins opened competing hotels on their inherited lands not many years after the turn of the century, their new standard of luxury for tourist accommodations, evening celebrations, and business gatherings cast an indelible mark on the development character of the burgeoning entertainment district. As I explain in chapter 1, the character of Times Square—speculation, theater, tourism, and transportation nexus—formed during these two decades would dominate its evolution. Even when it was long past its prime, Times Square's historic bones would continue to shape it.

The aspirations of city officials, planners, and realty interests for how the western section of midtown would develop were continually thwarted. In the early decades of the twentieth century, they envisioned an expansion of office development westward toward Times Square into the pulsating entertainment district, but decades would pass without such an advance. First came Prohibition, then the Depression, followed by World War II. Growth that had seemed inevitable had come to a halt for reasons beyond local control. During a postwar euphoria, the district recovered briefly, but developers saw more fertile opportunity on the east side of Manhattan, where the commercial thrust of office development flourished without the conflicting forces of entertainment and vice. A vibrant Broadway still entranced the crowds, especially at night, galvanized as most were by the blazing lights of the Great White Way, although the downward trajectory of the 1960s and '70s, laid bare in chapter 2, could not be stopped by any means city officials tried (and they tried many). Even the intense speculative activity in Hell's Kitchen during the 1950s and early '60s predicated on westward expansion abated as the decline deepened and pornography and crime took over West 42nd Street. Newly recast as the Deuce, the historic theater street morphed into vice central. The depravity of the place dramatically altered developers' ideas about the trajectory of midtown expansion, though not the aspirations of planners and city officials.

For decades beginning with the mayoralty of Fiorello LaGuardia, city officials tried every legal enforcement and regulatory approach on the books, but all, including well-publicized crackdowns on prostitution, failed to alter the depths of despair on the Deuce. By 1980, city officials believed that nothing short of radical surgery through change "of the whole" would succeed—the market on its own, they had concluded, could not effect the needed makeover. Wholesale change meant adopting an aggressive urban-renewal-style strategy designed to establish a critical mass of new economic activity on West 42nd Street, broad in scope and deep in impact. It was a strategy rooted in urban anthropology: putting good uses in place to drive out the bad. And as I explain in chapter 3, city officials' determined focus on creating opportunity for high-density office development on the four crossroads corners of Times Square made the transformation possible, economically. The office tower focus neatly aligned with Mayor Ed Koch's ambitions for revitalizing the economy of New York City, still smarting from its near-term brush with bankruptcy in the mid-1970s.

Yet the real estate strategy behind the redemption plan for "Sodom on the Hudson" represented a first on this symbolic turf. Never before had New York City employed the heavy hand of eminent domain to take private property for a commercial redevelopment project in Manhattan or relied on deals with private developers to fund the cost of doing so. This was immediately controversial. The potential upscaling impact on long-time residents of neighboring Hell's Kitchen was a clear threat as well; in response, community leaders successfully demanded millions as a quid pro quo for the community's support of the 42nd Street project. In one of those hidden stories of the project's impact I set out to reveal, those dollars went to improving hundreds of existing housing units to assure their affordability for low- and moderate-income residents to avoid displacing them. However strong the consensus among the city's vocal interest groups that cleansing the Deuce was necessary, the politics of carrying out the joint city-and-state plan for a transformation proved dicey—at one point observers gave it only a 50–50 chance of success. It took officials nearly two decades of persistent effort, aided by market forces, the winning of more than fifty lawsuits, and a revision of plans before they could hold press conferences to herald success.

The arena of change had become a contest of wills. On the one hand, nostalgia: the glorified past of 42nd Street—against the reality of decades of accumulated blight encrusted with every imaginable type of sex entertainment and porn, plus round-the-clock crime. On the other hand, ideology: government-driven redevelopment to eradicate the depravity of the Deuce and install office development that had been a shadow of opportunity—against a belief in incremental market-driven redevelopment of the theaters, one at a time. The counterfactual of the latter was not possible to prove, though it has been frequently asserted then and since.

Although the troubled path to the transformation was not what city planners and public officials had anticipated, once the new fundamentals of 42nd Street were in place, change seemed to happen overnight. The place was now safe. Popular entertainment returned. Families returned, as did teens and couples from the boroughs. Historic theaters once again hosted live entertainment. Illuminated signs flashed brighter than before. Thousands of office workers moved into four new skyscrapers, that long-hoped-for expansion of midtown's business core. Retail sales soared. Commercial property values flourished. And tourists came in record numbers, even after 9/11, powering the city's economic recovery. Beyond what was so immediately visible, the transformation set in place a new economic underpinning for West 42nd Street, one that promised ongoing returns to the entertainment legacy of the place, especially for the nonprofit theater entity, New 42, dedicated to legitimate theater for youth audiences. The revenues flowing into public coffers validated the public sector's bold gamble on transforming 42nd Street, and they would eventually support citywide economic development and policy initiatives such as the NYC Ferry system.

Success had its side effects. As the crowds in Times Square swelled exponentially, even tourists joined local voices in constant complaint about crushing congestion. Sixty-seven million tourists visited New York in 2019, the last full year before the pandemic shut down activity across the nation, and some 80 percent of them made a pilgrimage to Times Square to see for themselves what made the place an urban icon—it was a rite of passage. As an economic engine, visitors' spending power was generating billions for hotels, Broadway ticket sales, retail purchases, and food-and-drink tabs in the district's restaurants and bars, not to mention the billions the city treasury takes in tax revenues and the hundreds of thousands of direct jobs for New Yorkers. Still, the place had come to feel too touristy, less a place for New Yorkers. Safe was good, but the cultural changes in Times Square left many feeling that something authentic, if not unique, had been lost—the moxie and grit and edge that is a part of New York. As laid out in chapter 4, it has left many asking where the balance, the legacy, is—whether Times Square can reestablish itself as a place for New Yorkers. Even at the nadir of tawdriness, Times Square was an authentic New York place. It has always been a place that needs New Yorkers to be a New York place.

Success also triggered unanticipated consequences. In 2009, after the Bloomberg administration pedestrianized Times Square, the spacious plazas presented new opportunities for belligerent as well as benign behavior. As soon as work crews finished constructing the plazas, gaggles of costumed characters and seminude women showed up in ever-increasing numbers, many panhandling with ever-increasing aggression—pawing tourists and berating them for not handing over enough money for a photo-op. The human crush of Elmos, Cookie Monsters, Spider-Men, and multiples of Micky Mouse and Minnie Mouse was smothering pedestrian movement and turning a tourist snare into a quality-of-life nuisance, especially for local workers in Times Square, who were not on vacation. In a place legendary for its chaotic spontaneity, the hustling, hawking, and harassing was simply out of control, and it posed a threat to the economic engine that transformed Times Square.

Mayor Bill de Blasio said he would consider tearing up the plazas. This instantly provoked its own outcry. The plazas were popular. They were credited with relieving dangerous pedestrian overcrowding and injuries in an area teaming with tourists. The tabloid-fueled hullabaloo over the topless women pushed the mayor to create a special task force to review the situation in Times Square and make recommendations. As I explain in chapter 5, the City Council considered a number of legislative proposals to regulate the chaos of hundreds of costumed characters and held public hearings. The issues were complex, far too complex for an easy legislative fix. The new laws had to be carefully crafted to avoid treading on First Amendment rights. The Police Department upped its police presence in Times Square. New rules were eventually put in place, but they failed to completely eliminate the problem of aggressive panhandling, which has long been illegal in New York City. The challenge New York faces in figuring out how much to regulate behavior in public spaces is not unique. Las Vegas, Hollywood, San Francisco, and Seattle, among others, have been grappling with how to establish time, place, and matter restrictions over street performers, licensed and unlicensed, and costumed characters that cluster in places that attract a critical mass of tourists.

The iconic power of Times Square has made it a screen for urban anxieties. Its celebrated transformation did not wash away fears that the bad behavior of the past could reappear. Rather, it has hung there, a lurking specter no amount of success can expunge. It has made the tenor of the place vulnerable, susceptive to overreaction when forces of disorder appear to be beyond control, as in the case of the kerfuffle over the costumed characters and *desnudas*.

The star attraction of Times Square has always been the flashing, pulsating, sometimes disorienting messages radiating in all directions from the supersized signs surrounding the heart of the square. They are a magnet, a primary reason why throngs of people have flocked to Times Square year after year, decade after decade for more than a century. At night, the signs reflect the magical energy of the city, the serendipitous encounters among strangers mesmerized by the scope and vitality of New York. This illuminated theater of American commerce has shaped an imagistic personality of Times Square. Aided by continuous advances in technology, billboard entrepreneurs profiled in chapter 6 kept upping the visual spectaculars in ways that made Times Square a singular place where advertising spectacle became entertainment. It is because of this visual power to enthrall—to hold rapt all who step into the bowtie's open arena—that Times Square became iconic.

As a platform of visual power, the billboards of Times Square mirror the place's trajectory over time. Spectaculars that glowed during the decades before World War II and into the 1950s would go dark, and many were taken down when Times Square descended into pornography. Only the signs sponsored by Japanese advertisers lit up the sky until American brands came back after the transformation rooted in place. In the late 1990s, the emergence of big, bold, captivating signs employing the latest technologies signaled competition for financial information, the newest consumer product, simultaneously announcing the transformation of business conducted in the new office towers of Times Square.

The messaging market of Times Square plays host to hot-button issues along with corporate brands. Seen by millions, the vertical acres of billboards rarely shy away from the provocative. Not just in Times Square, billboards are a go-to medium for expressing advocacy on social and political issues, as revealed in the critically acclaimed film *Three Billboards Outside Ebbing, Missouri*. In our social-media world, billboards in high-trafficked locations like Times Square are a forum for turning heads in reaction to provocative content—and counting clicks. Clashes over social issues are not uncommon, especially in today's hyperpartisan environment. When it comes to accepting or rejecting an ad that might be provocative, however, what a private owner of property can do differs from the rules government must follow, as I discuss in chapter 6.

The character of urban change runs powerfully through the story of Times Square. The earliest development of Manhattan's midtown district started on the west side, in Times Square with the growth of an entertainment district. Only with the opening of Grand Central Terminal in 1913 did the east side of midtown begin to take on its premier role as the city's business center. The centrality of transportation in both instances shaped a strong spine of development along 42nd Street, but the growing concentration of office skyscrapers on the east side after 1950 turned a quadrangle of blocks into the largest and densest commercial center in the nation and fostered New York's rank as a global city.

Once the transformation of 42nd Street and Times Square eliminated the decades-long bottleneck of westward expansion, developers rushed to build, not office towers as many had once anticipated but luxury residential towers for walk-to-work professionals, hastening the seemingly inevitable gentrification of Hell's Kitchen, detailed in chapter 7. The rapid transformation of the far west reaches of 42nd Street eliminated the last vestiges of industrial uses along the western waterfront of midtown, more than half a century after they had been displaced on the east end by residential towers and the United Nations. It completed nearly a century-long modernization of New York's most famous crosstown street: 42nd Street was now built out river-to-river, anchored on both ends by residential living, as I discuss in the concluding chapter 8.

In the early aughts, the city's rezoning for the development of a large fifty-nine-block district known as Far West Midtown, now home to the mega Hudson Yards project, further stimulated Manhattan's trajectory of westward movement. The emergence of this newest commercial and residential cluster of skyscrapers, followed by the reset of development parameters for ever-higher density in East Midtown, not surprisingly intensified midtown's competitive office market—and challenged the relatively new office towers in Times Square that had undergirded revitalization success.

I started work on this book before the pandemic changed life for everyone everywhere. As successive waves of the virus swept across New York, emptying midtown and Times Square of their intense daily activity, even the most astute observers of the city's dynamic found the future return to a business "normal" unknowable. The repeated recalibration of back-to-the-office dates clouded crystal balls, as did uncertain future demand for office space given how readily businesses and hundreds of thousands of office workers had adapted to remote work. Absent the normal throngs of tourists, especially those from abroad, and with the shuttering of Broadway theaters, images of a vacant Times Square carried by the media across the globe became a metaphor for the pandemic's painful economic and social impact. A coda ties up the changes to Times Square and the storylines of this book brought about by the global pandemic.

# 1 BUILT ON SPECULATION

The effect of the passing of the property out of the hands of the Astors would be similar to that of opening the flood gate of a reservoir.
*New-York Tribune*, June 1919

He was the son disinherited, ostracized by his family for marrying beneath their immense wealth and exalted social standing. He had fallen in love with the daughter of a gardener who worked on his father's country estate, and the family could do nothing to prevent the ceremony: his brother arrived too late to enter his protest. The social scandal of that post-antebellum coupling of the rich with the poor left the upper crust of New York society chattering, but that world was of no consequence to Henry Astor, the youngest and reportedly favorite son of William B. Astor and grandson of the legendary family patriarch, John Jacob. Although cut off from his father's millions, Henry would not want; John Jacob's bequests to his three grandsons assured as much. He would live a simple life of comfort as a country gentleman from the millions in rents received from his inalienable share of the patriarch's real estate holdings in the heart of Times Square. With those millions, he built up a 200-acre farm estate and other business operations in the village of West Copake amid the rolling hills of Columbia County, more than 100 miles from New York City. He lived in a large home furnished with antiques, helped his people-in-law, and forgot his family. And they forgot him—until he died, at age 87, in June 1918, childless. Within days of his passing, attorneys acting on behalf of some forty heirs filed papers in a friendly suit to distribute the real estate holdings in the trust Henry created in 1869 among the descendants of his brothers and sister—except for descendants of one brother, John Jacob Astor III, father of William Waldorf, who had emigrated to Britain and become a viscount in the British peerage—they already had too much money.

Just days after the *New York Times* published his obituary, initial estimates of the value of Henry's realty holdings in Manhattan's celebrated entertainment district hit the newspapers—between $10 million and $20 million ($200 million to $400 million in 2022 dollars). Under a national economy weakened by the 1918 influenza pandemic and a modest recession, it was hard to be more precise. Administrators for the estate said they could not fix on a firm value because the property in the trust was of varying descriptions and widely distributed between 45th and 51st Streets running in a diagonal west of Broadway to the Hudson River—the "Astor Zone." Aside from the gossip value of the overall figure, what really mattered to both realty interests and city officials was the release of some 141 parcels of choice property in a high-demand district that had been held intact through concentrated single ownership for over a century.

Concentrated ownership was not good for any section of the city, so the thinking went, because passive ownership stifled development incentive on the part of others who might only be able to lease land for a defined period, after which whatever structures built on leased parcels reverted to the owners of the land, as was the case with the Astor holdings. The Astors' possessions were vast; the increments from annual rents on leased properties increased their wealth on a continual basis and became the source of funds for buying ever more property. In 1897—just one year before municipal consolidation of New York and Brooklyn (the first and fourth largest cities in the nation) established the modern metropolis of Greater New York—twenty individuals and great landed estates owned nearly 18 percent of the real estate in the then-City of New York; the two Astor branches—William Waldorf and John Jacob IV—held $180 million of the total of $2 billion assessed valuation, an astonishing 9 percent of the city's realty wealth. Holdings of the next two largest landed estates—Robert and Ogden Goelet ($35 million) and Amos R. Eno ($25 million)—were a mere fraction of the Astors' realty wealth. "Never sell a lot or a building" was the patriarch's policy, and his sons and grandsons generally followed his practice. "Astor real estate is unpurchasable," reported the *New York Herald*.[1] But that was about to change.

**1.1** Notice of the Henry Astor Trust Estate to be sold at auction on March 9, 1920, at the Hotel Astor. "Most of these properties should make a desirable investment for income purposes, together with the opportunity for speculation and a reasonably sure profit for the future increase in values." Collection of the author.

## SCRAMBLING FOR PROPERTY

As the March 9, 1920, date for the public auction of Henry's trust estate neared, speculative fever took hold. Enormous fortunes had grown from investments in Manhattan real estate, especially since 1845, when Broadway was first widened from 25th to 45th Streets. "Past experience proved that while real estate is the last to rise, it always increases in proportion to other commodities," said the experienced auctioneers for the sale, J. Clarence Davies and Joseph P. Day; "shrewd speculators" know this to be true, they declared in a promotional public statement. In a city where the realty annals recorded many notable auction records, the hype was hyper: the heavily promoted auction "will be one of the most successful ever held in New York City" (February 15). It was going to be "epoch making" (February 21). It was going to make "real estate history" (March 6). It was going to be "the first opportunity in the last 100 years to obtain convincing evidence of the 'rock bottom' value of the real estate in Times Square—the 'Heart of New York' purchased by the original John Jacob Astor, in the 18th Century, at a time when this outlying section of New York was known as Eden 'farm.'" The timing was "most opportune," the *Real Estate Record and Builders Guide* went on to explain, because the supply of neighborhood property available for purchase was at its lowest level in many years and demand was at a "high water mark."[2]

The cachet of the Astor name and curiosity as to what it would bring "aroused interest from hundreds of persons who have never been real estate investors and who do not expect to be." That the property to be sold tied back to the tale of a social scandal most likely intensified the general interest—every newspaper recounted the story in its report of the pending sale—but the excitement that awaited the Astor auction spoke to New York City's culture of commerce, which was intimately identified with real estate: "New York, modern, prosperous, purposeful and progressive New York," said the *Record*, "needed just a big real estate sale such as that of the Henry Astor Estate."[3]

A historic barrier to Manhattan's westward growth was about to go down. The expectation of great change near at hand was such that the *Times* could write, "it is only a question of a short time when tall industrial buildings, apartment houses and hotels will occupy every site available between Broadway and the Hudson River."[4] Commonplace houses interspersed with heavy and light industry and associated wholesalers—carpet and piano factories, sawmills, gasworks, breweries, and warehouse lofts—occupying those sites were evident tear-down targets. So too the dancehalls and brothels of the area. All were fair game in the often chaotic process of destruction and rebuilding that accompanied the growth imperative remaking the physical landscape of Manhattan.

Beginning in 1910, two forces acting simultaneously were at work reshaping Manhattan's western middle section: a push west from the entertainment businesses of Times Square and a push east from the new 1,000-foot steamship piers along the Hudson River frontage between 44th and 45th Streets. The location of Astor properties on blocks between 44th and 47th Streets fronting both sides of Eighth Avenue became a hot spot of buying interest. Sites for new theaters, stores, and offices were hard to come by there because so much of the property was owned by estates and typically held stationary. Since the opening of Pennsylvania Station (1910) and the new General Post Office (1912), both designed by the celebrated architectural firm of McKim, Mead and White in Beaux-Arts style, theatrical enterprises and business interests of all types had been marching northward. New York was "being made over" by the shift of trade centers, remarked the *Times*.[5] With unbridled optimism, investors, operators, and speculators believed that all the property lying west of Broadway would become an integral part of the Great White Way. Based on that dynamic vision of the district's future, profitable investments were bound to accrue to those buying at the Astor Estate auction.

Boosterism was running high. Reading the news of the realty trade, one could sense a palpable release from years of economic restraint due to wartime conditions, when private building had been subordinated to government demands and speculative activity nearly ceased. Even before the armistice had been signed to end World War I, some writers saw hope for realty markets in 1918. For the men in this business, the wartime quiescence of Times Square, hitherto viewed as "Speculative Centre," had been dull and boring, the dearth of transactions a sharp contrast to the vibrant market they had experienced for more than a decade since the turn of the century. Those were years of intense growth in the district, growth set in motion by three economic forces hungrily feeding off one another: a theater construction boom driven by fierce competition among theater operators, the growth of tourism and the building of big trend-setting hotels, and the location of a subway station at 42nd Street and Seventh Avenue.

In 1902, Adolph S. Ochs, owner and publisher of the *New York Times*, announced he would build a new headquarters for his newspaper on the district's most visible site, a small triangle of land at 42nd Street where

Broadway crosses Seventh Avenue principally occupied by the upscale Pabst Hotel and restaurant (1899). The news calendared a new dawn for the district soon to be named after his newspaper. Ochs's decision set off a fresh wave of land speculation. To realty interests, the surprise announcement was a harbinger of the district's future importance as a midtown business hub. Ochs demolished the three-year-old hotel and built an Italian Renaissance-style headquarters faced in limestone, terra-cotta, and brick, designed by American architect Cyrus L. W. Eidlitz. The 25-story Times Tower was the second tallest building in the city when it opened, reportedly visible from a distance of 12 miles. A booster for the growing city as well as for his paper, Ochs reversed the downtown orientation of the earlier structure; where the Pabst Hotel had looked toward downtown, the Times Tower looked uptown and its main entrance faced east toward the emerging midtown business district.

The confluence of economic forces fueled a wild scramble for property in a market where the "record" sale price lasted only until the next record. Resales of property at ever-higher prices merely furnished material for a week of real estate gossip. In unbroken degrees of amazement, the press reported on the remarkable, ever-rising values and rents, especially for ground-floor properties in the travel path of pedestrians who crowded the square day and night. Growth was adding millions to realty values in Times Square, the *Times* emphasized in a review of assessment valuations—increases of 250 percent, as determined by the Tax Department—over the decade since the IRT subway station at Times Square opened in fall 1904 and the *Times* moved into its new home at the start of 1905. A more accurate way to understand the "startling rise in realty values," the paper of record said, would be to look at just the land component of assessed valuations.[6] The true index of worth in the real estate logic of the day lay in the underlying land value of a site: in neighborhoods undergoing such radical change, antiquated buildings held little to no value; they would give way to a higher and better use once the wrecking companies finished their work.

The southeast corner of Broadway at 43rd Street occupied by the 12-story Fitzgerald Building and the Cohan Theatre (1911) was a "most striking" case, an "object lesson" of the before-and-after contrast in land values. In 1905, the land was assessed at $475,000, the "old wooden shacks standing there having no tax value"; the new assessment in 1915 was $1,675,000, 253 percent higher. Almost as impressive was the 116 percent assessment change in the land underlying the adjoining 12-story Longacre Building (1912) developed by Vincent Astor: to $2,000,000, up from $925,000.[7]

THE TIMES BUILDING, NEW YORK

**1.2** Times Square got its name upon the completion of Adolph S. Ochs's Times Tower, shown here in 1905. Built on the site of the three-year-old Pabst Hotel, circa 1900, the 25-story tower was at the time the second tallest building in the city. The prestige of the tower married with the new subway line opened up tremendous real estate opportunities in the area. Wallach Division Picture Collection, The New York Public Library (top); Arthur Vitols, Byron Company. Museum of the City of New York. MNY69503 (bottom).

**1.3** On Broadway at Times Square, circa 1910–1911: Fitzgerald Building (1911) on the southeast corner at 43rd Street; on the northeast corner at 42nd, a collection of three-story buildings covered with billboards about to be demolished to make way for development of the Longacre Building (1912). Robert L. Bracklow Photograph Collection, nyhs_pr-008_66000_657, © New-York Historical Society.

**1.4** Broadway at 42nd Street transformed into a vibrant commercial corner anchored by the Fitzgerald and Longacre Buildings, 1926. Milstein Division, New York Public Library.

The transformation appeared to happen overnight. Within one decade, Longacre Square, named after its London ancestor, was no longer. The sparsely populated, sleepy district of horse dealerships, carriage and harness factories, and livery stables that had served as the city's coach-building center since 1872 had vanished, its rollicking reputation as "Thieves Lair" now a memory. Its physical past just disappeared: wearisome open space, drab apartment houses and dowdy dwellings, and dated hotels, gone. The advent of the automobile had first taken over the carriage trade headquarters, replete with so many new salesrooms along Broadway from 42nd to 59th Streets that the expanse became known as "automobile row." Not for long, however. With the rapid expansion of theater construction and hotel establishments, land values in the vicinity became too great for ordinary business purposes and, in turn, the automobile trade was pushed farther north along Broadway from 59th to 80th Streets.

Continuous activity had turned the place inside out. Small lots had been assembled into larger holdings by speculators and builders who entertained great aspirations for the area. Today, evidence of the past remains only in archival photo collections and the occasional "ghost sign," such as the one in figure 1.5 advertising "J. A. Keal's Carriage

Manufactory. Repairing" for horse and buggy carriages painted in the era of gaslights, suddenly revealed in 1998 during demolition of the Central Theatre (1918). These signs "painted on the sides of humdrum brick buildings," wrote Joseph Berger of the *Times*, "are hieroglyphics of a bygone New York, writings on walls redolent of a time when women wore corsets, nearly every parlor seemed to have a piano and buggies could be hired for a genteel ride up the avenue once the blacksmith shod the horses."[8]

The place was now Times Square: the pulsating heart of New York City, crowded with both posh entertainment and popular amusements—the center of theater, vaudeville, music publishing, and nightlife in America, a unique place in the nation's largest and most dynamic city. Evidence of a past quiet era, of landmarks like the Hotel Barrington made from eight old dwelling houses and favored by theatrical people, had given way to "a high character" of development. The new hotels, restaurants, theaters, and shops of Times Square had the mark of "aggressive modernity." So much was new and so many more developments were in sight by 1910 that the *Times* ventured to say the transformation of Times Square "will soon be complete."[9] Much more, however, was to come: many more up-to-date theaters, ornate movie palaces, luxury

**1.5** This "ghost sign" for J. A. Keal's Carriage Manufactory on the southwest corner of Broadway and 47th Street was suddenly revealed during demolition of the Central Theatre (1918) and concealed again the next year as the W Hotel Times Square (2001) began rising on the same spot. Signs like this are preserved virtually, through the internet. Fading Ads of New York City, History Press 2011 © Frank H. Jump, Fading Ad Blog.

**1.6** Broadway at 45th Street in 1921: the Theater District aglow with marquees of the Astor, Gaiety, Globe, and Strand Theatres and brilliant electric advertising signs, including one for Marion Davies in the silent movie *Buried Treasure*. Edwin Galloway. Museum of the City of New York. 98.92.1.

hotels, and sumptuous restaurants, as well as those "high-class" office buildings considered skyscrapers in their day.

By the time of Henry Astor's passing, the stretch of Broadway cutting through the heart of Times Square would have been unrecognizable to those with visual recall of the late nineteenth-century Longacre Square. The makeover of this roughly sixteen-block area was as radical as New Yorkers had ever beheld, a set of changes that layered social and economic complexity into the physical landscape of a burgeoning midtown district. With so much new already in place, how would the release of Henry's trust estate lands in the heart of Times Square shape its future? Scores of apartment hotels fitted out for the convenience and comfort of bachelors and families who chose not to maintain a fully staffed home already lined the side streets east and west of Broadway. Operators of restaurants, nighttime amusements, and theaters had bid up rents to levels that made the building of conventional office and shopping establishments desirable but economically difficult. Still, large land parcels were relatively sparse. At a time of soaring property values in Times Square, Henry's lands presented new opportunities, especially those on West 45th Street adjoining the Astor, Bijou, and Morosco Theatres (developed under leases on lands his trust owned) and West 46th running to Ninth Avenue. Choice parcels on Eighth Avenue also would be auctioned, among others of strategic value. Would the eagerly awaited event deliver on its speculative promises? How might the release of lands impact the trajectory of Times Square's seemingly inexorable growth?

## BREACHING CONVENTION

Forty-second Street at Longacre Square was the "dead line" no one in the realty business could conceive of crossing—until Oscar Hammerstein boldly did early in 1895. "Nothing could be done in that section until the large estates which owned nearly all the avenue property showed a disposition to either improve, lease or sell their holdings," explained the *Real Estate Record and Builders Guide*, a weekly trade publication that functioned as the "oracle" of the New York real estate world from March 1868 to December 1961.[10] Few of the owners showed such a disposition. In the last decades of the nineteenth century as businesses and retail shops moved uptown, they bumped against the nearly immovable force of these landed estates, including that of the Astors.

Hammerstein was fond of kicking aside traditions and precedents, according to one biographer. He breached the barrier by purchasing a large, nearly vacant blockfront parcel on the east side of Broadway between 44th and 45th Streets previously occupied by the 71st Regiment Armory, which had burned to the ground. Having developed the Harlem Opera House (1889), the first large modern theater and music hall erected on 125th Street, followed by the Columbus Theatre (1890) on the same street, he was known to be an audacious pioneer in the selection of new sites for places of entertainment. This latest move also shunned real estate safety. It was only five blocks from the northernmost theater in the established theater district, but at the time, this was akin to being in the hinterland. Looking ahead to the time when fresh investment would trigger development growth, the *Times* considered it "the first of note to give Longacre Square a distinctive character or to infuse business life into the property on Broadway above Forty-Second Street." The Astors owned nearly all of the westerly side of the square, and they had not been "found backward in improving their holdings, once the character of the area becomes fixed," the newspaper wrote optimistically about the area's future.[11] After Hammerstein's move, only five years would pass before William Waldorf Astor announced plans for the Hotel Astor, the family's first place-making move in Longacre Square, a story told further on.

Unorthodox as they were, Hammerstein's plans for his Longacre site aligned with three rules for what he wanted to accomplish professionally: he aimed to do things no one had ever done before; whatever he chose to do should be on a larger and grander scale than ever done before; and whatever he chose to do he must do alone. For this, his third theater, he would erect a theatrical enterprise that promised to dwarf in scope and embellishment any in New York and was destined, so he believed, to become the greatest structure devoted exclusively to theatrical entertainment in the world. His not-to-be-outdone vision was a three-in-one enterprise: a theater, a concert hall, and a music hall—furnishing concerts, light operas, ballets, and vaudeville—for one general admission of fifty cents. Later he would add a rooftop garden for entertainment in the summer, when New York's sweltering heat made indoor theater intolerable. Sheathed in an immense limestone slab, the Olympia was a 10-story-tall structure on nearly an acre of ground capable of seating 6,000 patrons—"so colossal as to be its own center of gravity."[12]

The obsessive producer's ambitious plans set "tongues wagging." Within professional theatrical circles, the reactions ranged from "raised eyebrows to open derision." The neighborhood was considered seedy at best. The air was fetid with the smell of manure dumped on the side streets at night. It was dark because the neighborhood was not yet served by streetlamps; by 1895, electric lights had only reached 42nd Street. The location was all wrong, too far north of the Rialto, the historic name of theater district, and it was not respectable. At the time, no fashionable theater audience would be seen in so disreputable an area. They called it Hammerstein's folly: "To build a theater in Longacre Square was foolhardy. To build a whole block of theaters was the sheerest folly, of which only one as crazy as Hammerstein would be capable." It was a bluff, some said, designed to fight (and frighten) his soon-to-be-former partners in Koster & Bial's Music Hall. Some thought his plans for the Longacre site "farsighted," but most professionals were "completely skeptical." His timetable from construction to opening—ten months—was ridiculed.[13] Vindication on this point came when the $2 million Olympia opened on November 25, 1895, in ten months.

**1.7** Oscar Hammerstein's Olympia (1895), a $2 million limestone extravaganza replete with electric signs grandly illuminating the impresario's name in scale matching his larger-than-life personality. The neighborhood—Broadway between 44th and 45th Streets—still had no streetlamps and was a distance from the reputable theater district, centered at Herald Square, 34th Street. Robert L. Bracklow (1849–1919). Museum of the City of New York. 93.91.307.

Hammerstein's theatrical gambles carried more than a whiff of speculation. Before he became a legend in his own time during New York's golden age of theater and music, Hammerstein had been dealing in real estate in Harlem—also thought to be too far uptown for conventional investment—since the mid-1880s. Speculators, however, had earmarked Harlem as a potential middle-class enclave. In the last decades of the nineteenth century, the neighborhood became the safety valve for Jews overcrowded in the Lower East Side and seeking to improve their living conditions. "On the map of the Jewish diaspora, Harlem is Atlantis," wrote veteran *Times* reporter David W. Dunlap. That it was once the third largest Jewish settlement in the world after the Lower East Side and Warsaw—"a vibrant hub of industry, artistry and wealth—is all but forgotten. It is as if Jewish Harlem sank 70 years ago beneath waves of memory beyond recall."[14]

In Harlem, Hammerstein bought lots and sold lots, bought single-family houses and sold them, leased buildings, and built apartment houses. Ever entrepreneurial, he was simultaneously devising scores of mechanical inventions with patents in his name and publishing a tobacco trade journal. By 1893, the real estate weekly press no longer identified him as an editor of "great pluck" engaged in big building operations, but as Hammerstein "of Harlem Opera House celebrity."[15]

Hammerstein's next operatic efforts in the established Broadway Rialto did not meet with success. In 1890, he had exchanged his Kaiser Wilhelm apartment building in Harlem for an eight-lot assemblage midblock on 42nd running through to 41st east of Broadway on which he intended to build one of the finest theaters in the city, the Murray Hill Theatre for the production of German opera. He filed plans for a stone-faced theater and a four-story office building, only to sell most of the assemblage to a dry goods man less than a year later. A few months after that he transferred his aspiration for a grand opera house to a vacant site he leased on 34th Street west of Broadway, where the Manhattan Opera House opened in 1892. It didn't last long. Facing financial troubles, Hammerstein entered a partnership with Koster & Bial, who reconstructed the theater at 34th Street between Broadway and Seventh Avenue (where Macy's flagship store now stands) for vaudeville under the name of Koster & Bial's Music Hall.

For his third try at a grand theatrical venue, Hammerstein would have needed a low-cost site. The $850,000 (nearly $30 million in 2022 dollars) he paid for the former armory site and adjacent building tallied up at less than $21 for each square foot of land, only cents more than the exchange cost of his earlier small assemblage on West 42nd. The benefit from buying such a large site in "seedy" and "disreputable" Longacre Square for his newest theater venture was strategic, if not obvious to others at the time. Leapfrogging to a Longacre site afforded Hammerstein a first-mover advantage in the fast-paced field of theater expansion; there he could find a site sufficiently large to build a theater that would match his theatrical vision. If, like Al Hayman, a highly successful theater manager from San Francisco who had long wanted his own theater in New York, Hammerstein had only wanted a prominent location, he might have chosen a site in the established theater district, as did Hayman and his partner Frank Sanger, when they paid $300,000 for a site on Broadway at 40th Street across from the opulent Metropolitan Opera House for their soon-to-be-named Empire Theatre (1893), one of the last theaters to open before the Olympia.

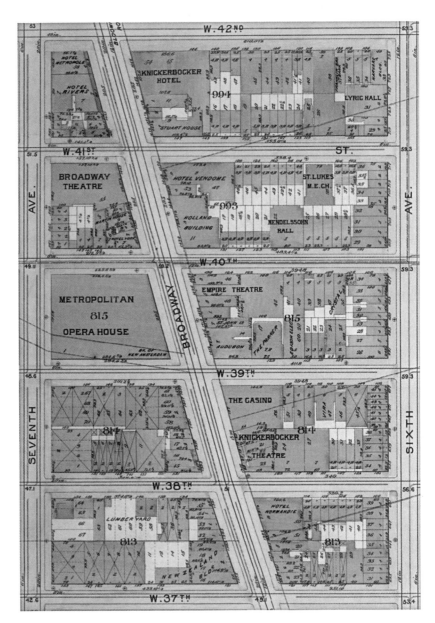

**1.8** Clustered theaters of the established Broadway Rialto, 1890s: the Casino (1882), Metropolitan Opera House (1882), Broadway Theatre (1888), Mendelssohn Hall (1891), Knickerbocker Theatre (1893), and Empire Theatre (1893). Atlas of the City of New York, 1899. Lionel Pincus and Princess Firyal Map Division, New York Public Library.

Hayman and Sanger's plot fronted Broadway for 35 feet, just enough for an entranceway that led down a corridor to the auditorium in the rear of the site. On the square-foot basis that realty people use to gauge price, the site was more costly than what Hammerstein would pay four years later for a site larger by a factor of three. More importantly, Hammerstein's Olympia site had six times the amount of frontage on Broadway—frontage especially important to such a dramatic personality. Where Broadway cuts a diagonal across Seventh Avenue it creates two inverted triangles, or bowties as they are called. The ten-block bowtie in Longacre Square presented a perfect physical platform for viewing an illuminated theatrical enterprise, which the Olympia would be. The impresario would take full advantage of this platform with an electric sign strung out in a long arch above the marquee that "gave more importance to Hammerstein's name than the theater's, reflecting the drawing power of the entrepreneur."[16] Longacre Square, however ill-lit and disreputable at the time, was nevertheless a natural crossroads of the city, destined to be ever more prominent than the city's other Broadway bowtie at 34th Street in Herald Square, the southernmost anchor of the established Rialto.

Broadway holds a special place in the history of the city. It is the "counterpoint" to the linear logic of the Manhattan street pattern. It was not part of the Commissioners' 1811 plan that laid out a grid of streets and avenues for the growing city. Rather, the boulevard represents history and circumstance. It was the main axis of the colonial city merging with Bloomingdale Road, the primary route on the island's west side. Broadway was the name given to the stretch below 59th Street; northward to 108th, it was called the Boulevard until 1899, when the whole long stretch was named Broadway. The bowtie intersection of Broadway and Seventh Avenue brought into being by the diagonal cut against the grid of streets and avenues came to define a distinctive public realm made legendary by the gravitational pull of the Times Square entertainment district. The "square" was not a square by any usual definition, only "by New York's loosely defined geometry."[17]

Opening night at the Olympia was such a grand success that it created mayhem, a near riot, as Hammerstein had oversold thousands of tickets for the evening. The Olympia did succeed in bringing amusement patrons to Longacre, but it closed less than three years later in 1898, a victim of financial operating pressures and problematic programming. Hammerstein's debt-ridden enterprise was auctioned off and its components split up, each surviving under separate management and new names, until the legacy-making place succumbed to the

**1.9** The bowtie of Times Square between 42nd and 47th Streets looking northward, 1905. This photograph was taken from the top of the Times Building, where the ball has been dropped each New Year's Eve since the tradition began in 1905. The massive building in the left foreground is the Hotel Astor; across the way, the International Casino, successor to Hammerstein's Olympia. Byron Company. Museum of the City of New York. 93.1.1.14499.

wrecking ball in 1935 to make way for the next cycle of development progress.

The real estate press said Hammerstein had been a "pioneer" when he built the Olympia, "but even he could not overcome the 'hoodoo' and the result spelt failure for him." Whether it was "hoodoo" or the consequence of poor management, the Olympia proved to be only "*slightly* ahead of its time."[18] In short order, Hammerstein would rise from the ashes to recoup his position as one of the greatest showmen in an era of great showmen, opening three more theaters in Times Square on 42nd Street: the Victoria (1899)—a name asserting triumph over the moneylenders who had foreclosed on the Olympia—the Republic (1900), and the Lew Fields (1904). At his death in 1919, Hammerstein's theater-building legacy totaled fourteen, including opera houses in Philadelphia and London.

OSCAR HAMMERSTEIN, on the way to his Victoria Theatre.
*Photograph by Lee Harrison.*

**1.10** Oscar Hammerstein in his "uniform"—Prince Albert coat, silk top hat— standing before his Victoria Theatre. Lee Harrison, Billy Rose Theatre Division for the Performing Arts, New York Public Library.

Everything Hammerstein did was an event; he was news. His cease-less ambition and irrepressible, outsized personality were a stand-in for New York's culture during a unique period of its history in which he could claim to have made a memorable difference. Would Times Square have become what it did if Hammerstein had not pioneered such a "foolhardy" location? Undoubtedly, in time, but with less bravado. "It took no special clairvoyance to predict that the broad area created by the confluence of Broadway and Seventh Avenue would be uti-lized, as had Union, Madison and Herald Squares before, by theatrical developers for the creation of a new entertainment center," wrote theater historian Mary C. Henderson. Less foreseeable was the astounding expansion of theatrical production in the city housed in a staggering number of theaters built within a limited area in the first three decades of the new century. Ahead of his time as his cherished Olympia failed, Hammerstein would earn an enduring reputation as "the man who created Times Square."[19]

## LIKE NO OTHER STREET IN THE WORLD

The bold and brilliant theater impresarios of the first two decades of the twentieth century almost to a one chose to locate their theaters on the "uptown" 42nd Street block between Broadway and Eighth Avenue, as Hammerstein did after the Olympia. The other theatrical producers who put down roots there—Klaw and Erlanger, the Shubert brothers, the Selwyn brothers, Charles Frohman, David Belasco, Al H. Woods, and Sam Harris—were "adventurers." Big personalities, more than a few named their playhouses after themselves; others like Al Woods thought the name of a star—such as the female impersonator Julian Eltinge—was best for commercial success.[20] The glamour and star power of their theatrical and musical productions made 42nd Street world-famous. As early as 1903, sites on the street were becoming scarce. Land prices were escalating so rapidly that many a theater owner, maybe aided by a specialist in assembling sites for theaters, might only be able to purchase a narrow entranceway on 42nd with a funnel-like strip of land leading to the auditorium behind on 41st or 43rd Street. Even so, they had the essential ingredient: an address on the fabled street for marketing their entertainment business.

Well into the 1890s, before it became the world's most famous theater block, there was nothing particularly notable about this 800-foot stretch of 42nd Street between Seventh and Eighth Avenues. It was lined with a nondescript collection of private homes, modest storefronts of neighborhood shops, a coal and wood supplier, the Garrick Chop House, Kings Oxygen and Dental Infirmary, Central Baptist Church, a laundry, and a branch of the N.Y. Circulating Library. Commercial but otherwise unremarkable, it had little to suggest what this entranceway to Longacre Square would become in the next 10 years. A glimmer of the future appeared in 1893, when T. Henry French opened the American Theatre on Eighth Avenue and 42nd Street, though the main façade and bulk of the theater were on 41st Street; the specialist assembling the site had procured land from seventeen different owners.

Theater cognoscenti considered the location foolhardy, but French, a theater manager and investor and son of the dramatic-prose publisher Samuel French, viewed the undeveloped district as an opportunity for productions of his family's company. (Founded in 1830, the Samuel French company would grow to become the world's leading publisher and licensor of plays and musicals.) French built a huge auditorium with 2,064 seats and room for two hundred standees; an open-air roof garden on the top of the theater offered entertainment on summer nights. He had the house entirely wired for electricity and installed ingenious stage machinery as well as the first elevators in a theater to whisk patrons to their balcony or roof garden seats.

As they multiplied—there were two in 1900, seven by 1905, ten by 1914, and twelve by 1920—the glowing array of theaters with electrically illuminated marquees on both sides of 42nd Street fashioned an extraordinary presence. The future impact of this ever-growing concentration was evident to the real estate trade as early as 1902, when four theaters were under construction. It promised to "give the Square a much more definite and peculiar character than Greeley and Madison Squares," said the *Record*, because of its devotion "to the pleasures and activities of New Yorkers, which come to the surface after dark—to the places of amusement, restaurants and the like."[21] The street's distinctive concentration of theaters came to represent close to one quarter of all the theaters built in the Times Square area since the turn of the century. Even as it was rapidly being eclipsed by expansion and movement of the theatrical business into Times Square proper between 1920 and 1930, 42nd Street would remain the world's most famous theater block. Its romantic image as the glamorous, exciting, ever-vibrant, and quintessentially New York entertainment district was firmly established in the first two decades of the twentieth century. Its reputational legacy would endure—in memory and myth—over the block's long slide into darkness and decrepitude that would come in the 1960s and '70s.

Forty-second Street was designated a crosstown thoroughfare when the commissioners laid out Manhattan's grid of streets, though the street was not officially opened until 1837, a quarter-century later. It evolved into a crossroads—shortly to become *the* crossroads of the city—only after New York City's first subway, the IRT, opened with great fanfare in October 1904, with a pivotal station at 42nd Street where Broadway crosses Seventh Avenue. In the half-century from 1850 to 1900, the city's major east-west thoroughfare had moved northward twice before, from 14th Street to 23rd Street, then to 34th Street, before settling at the 42nd Street/Broadway crossroads in 1915.

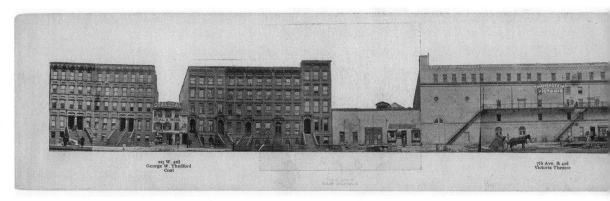

**1.11** Panorama of turn-of-the-century everyday businesses on West 42nd Street. At top right, Hammerstein's Victoria Theatre, circa 1900. Geographic Images Collection, NYC Box32, nyhs_pr_20, © New-York Historical Society.

The subway proved pivotal to 42nd Street's centrality because it brought a traffic of people to the district in its traverse across Manhattan. From City Hall in downtown Manhattan, the tracks ran straight up the East Side under Fourth Avenue to Grand Central Depot (1871, the mammoth predecessor to Grand Central Terminal) where they turned west, traveling crosstown under 42nd Street to intersect with Broadway before making another sharp turn and heading north to the Upper West Side, where they divided into two branches that continued north and terminated in the Bronx. The trip was speedy: "City Hall to Harlem in 15 Minutes." At five cents a ride, it was a bargain. New Yorkers took to the subway in the proverbial New York minute. In its first year of operation, the Times Square station accommodated almost five million customers; by 1914, twenty-seven million people were said to have passed along its platforms during the year.

By 1928, West 42nd Street was accessible to the furthest points of the city, with five subway lines, four elevated lines, five bus lines, eleven

**1.12** By the early 1920s, West 42nd Street had no rival as the world's most famous theater street. Home to twelve lush theaters of astounding variety, it anchored the Theater District (pictured in 1924). It was the place where play brokers, agents, publicists, photographers, anyone connected with show business had to be. B'Hend-Kaufman Archives, Academy of Motion Picture Arts and Sciences.

surface lines, and a ferry having stations, stops, or a terminal there. The many access modes gave Times Square an unsurpassed advantage for the mass marketing of entertainment because the location attracted three distinct groups of the metropolis: city residents, affluent suburbanites, and visitors from near and far. Superior transit gave it a lock on the Rialto and for a long time halted theater's continuous move uptown. Reluctant to locate their playhouses too far north of the subway stop, theater producers spread out into the side streets of Times Square, mostly west of Broadway. In that fashion, 42nd Street became the anchor of the Theater District, the centerpiece of the city's entertainment marketplace.

When after years of debate the Rapid Transit Commission finally fixed the route for the new subway with a turn westward at 42nd Street in 1901, the news triggered a feverish movement of speculative activity in anticipation of growth opportunities in Times Square. Land values rose about a third almost immediately. The *Record* and the *Times* avidly

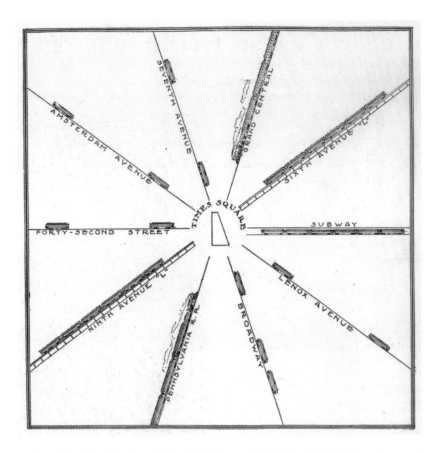

**1.13** With a pivotal station at West 42nd Street, the IRT, New York's first underground subway line, transformed Times Square into a transportation hub. The subway offered full service at five cents a ride. Private collection.

chronicled the trading of property on Broadway and its side-street tributaries. Plans were filed for hotels, apartment houses, theaters, and restaurants. The specific location of the "tunnel"—whether at 42nd Street or 46th Street and Broadway—remained uncertain as late as December 1900, but that detail did not dampen the ardor of speculators buying what they could in the area. They were marking up prices and piecing together parcels for subsequent development.

As the run-up in prices escalated, voices of skepticism emerged: the movement "contains a larger proportion of the wine of speculation than it does the meat of permanent value." New York "has all the theaters it needs at present." The *Record* was having a hard time making sense of the many plans being published for new theaters when so many others "have not been particularly successful"; the constant building, it remarked, was due to the "peculiar conditions of the theatrical business." No matter. The competitive scramble for property continued in 1902 and 1903. The trade weekly was aggrieved: "in all but very unusual instances, the speculators have pretty well squeezed out in advance any change of increases in value." Its editors were on the side of investors, who they believed had no opportunity in this market. "So far the only people who have made purchases in that vicinity for permanent possession are restaurant keepers or theatrical managers—that is people who want to use the property rather than those who want to derive income from its use by others."[22] Touché.

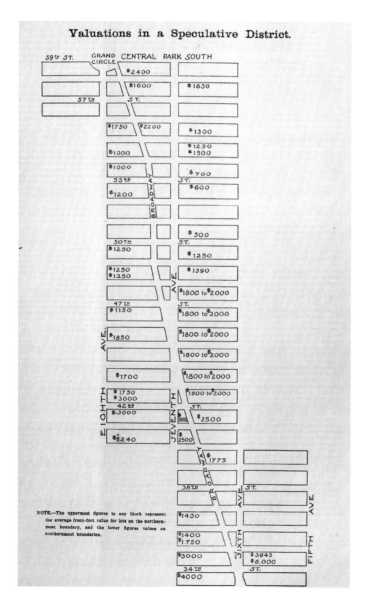

**Valuations in a Speculative District.**

NOTE.—The uppermost figures in any block represent the average front-foot value for lots on the northernmost boundary, and the lower figures values on southernmost boundaries.

**1.14** Values for land in the "speculative" district of the Times Square bowtie were highest on 42nd Street as theaters were being built one after another. As the entertainment district took shape, theaters, restaurants, and hotels continued to boost values. *Real Estate Record and Builders Guide* (September 13, 1902).

## THEATRICAL DISTRICT

The subway bolstered the burgeoning theatrical business on 42nd Street. It was key to its growth and the growth of Times Square as a whole, a structural facilitating force amid the confluence of economic and social forces shaping this midtown territory. But only in the eyes of realty men, as the real estate press kept claiming, did it generate Longacre's virtual overnight transformation. "The primal driving force," wrote historian Mike Wallace, prize-winning author of *Gotham* and *Greater Gotham*, "was the expansion, consolidation, and centralization of the theatrical industry."[23]

A fiercely competitive effort to dominate the national market for theatrical bookings, which was centered in New York City, began in the summer of 1896. Six men, theater booking agents and producers, gathered for lunch at the majestic Holland House (1891) on Fifth Avenue at 30th Street and "hammered out a plan to monopolize the country's theatrical business"—the Theatrical Syndicate. By joining forces and seeking to control the business for the distribution of plays around the nation, their goal was to bring "order out of the existing chaos," said producer Marc Klaw, and "legitimate profit out of ruinous rivalry." After assessing the historical outcome of their strategy, Wallace saw truth in this assertion, but "their tactics had also generated vigorous opposition." Sometimes this "took on an anti-Semitic quality." All of the Syndicate members were "Jews—immigrants or sons of immigrants. The theater business attracted Jews precisely because Protestant magnates wouldn't touch it—too risky, too risqué," he wrote. "Largely frozen out of the corporate and professional world, Jews found the stage appealingly open to talents."[24]

As they set out to increase the number of theaters under their respective control, the rivalry between the Syndicate and independent producers triggered a remarkable spree of theater building not just in New York but in towns and cities across the United States, at precisely the time when live theater was beginning to lose its footing to entertainment's new format: motion pictures. In 1911, a decade after it first expressed skepticism about the extraordinary extent of theater building, the *Record* reiterated disbelief: "In so much as the restaurant and theatre proprietors claim that there are already too many places of amusement in Manhattan, their multiplication must remain a matter of wonder."[25] Four theaters opened that year in the Times Square district; another twelve would open before wartime restrictions slowed the pace of private construction. Ten months later, the *Record* thought hotels might be oversupplied in Times Square, but theaters and restaurants could not be overdone.

Producers were on a tear, vying to build or lease ornate theaters to serve as showcases for their "Direct from New York" productions. They all sought national publicity for their New York productions, and to get it they built showcase theaters in Times Square. The battle for control between the Syndicate and independent producers turned into a war just between Klaw and Erlanger and the Shuberts. In 1913, the warring parties agreed to a truce that brought theater construction and acquisition under control, though it did not stop the overexpansion of theaters in New York. Needing showcases of their own to compete against the Syndicate, independent producers continued to build their own theaters. In 1916, the Shuberts' campaign of theater building broke the monopoly of the Theatrical Syndicate, but the pace of building remained torrid, even during the war years: four new theaters opened in 1917 and five in 1918.

Despite the questionable profitability of so many competing ventures and less apparent need, operators continued building theater after theater—primarily on the side-street tributaries of Broadway. By the time the Henry Astor Trust auction made realty news in 1920, forty-four new theaters (exclusive of motion picture theaters) had been built in Times Square since the turn of the century. Thirty-one of these theaters opened between 1911 and 1920. The fervor of theater expansion defied economic logic, especially in the face of a rising tide of crushing competition from motion pictures. Yet another nineteen would be built by 1928; in all, seventy-six playhouses were then offering live performance (legitimate theater), vaudeville, music revues, or first-run movies. With 264 productions playing in these houses, the year would become the busiest for Broadway theater. Then the theater construction boom came to an abrupt halt—for 45 years, until 1973, when real estate developer Sam Minskoff leveled the legendary Hotel Astor and built in its place One Astor Plaza, a 54-story office tower that hosted the 1,600-seat Minskoff Theatre, included in response to city zoning incentives for theater construction.

As they moved into the side streets of Times Square searching for theater sites, producers and builders faced the combined hegemony of the estates of John Jacob Astor's three grandsons, owners of much of the land running diagonally west of Broadway between 43rd and 46th Streets to the Hudson River. As the area's commercial future as an entertainment center became clearer and clearer, the estates had selectively released their hold on the old Medcaf Eden farm properties. In

**1.15** The concentration of theaters made Times Square the most diversified theatrical center in the history of New York. The heart of the Theater District stretching between 42nd and 50th Streets was established between 1900 and 1930, not so much by geography but by the theaters that attracted strong patronage. © Rand McNally's Geographic Atlas of Greater New York, 1938, R.L. 91-5-119. From the collection of Charles Knapp, in William R. Taylor, ed., *Inventing Times Square* (New York: Russell Sage Foundation, 1991).

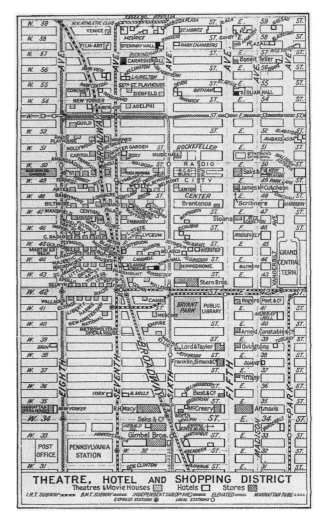

challenging the Syndicate as no one else had done, the Shubert brothers would come to control twenty-two theaters in Times Square by 1923; in the heart of their theater empire west of Broadway between 44th and 46th Streets, at least nine of them had been built on land leased from the Astors. As owners of the Shubert and Booth Theatres, their company created the through-block passage know as Shubert Alley (1913), still one of the most important gathering spaces in the Theater District.

Like an electromagnet, the compact eighteen-block area of immense theatrical talent and larger-than-life entrepreneurial personalities attracted palatial hotels, glamorous restaurants, supper clubs, and beer halls—and ready-to-spend money. Fierce competition among nighttime purveyors of food and pleasure heightened the commercial temperature of the place. During the day it was the center of all things theatrical: theatrical producers, theater managers, play brokers,

**1.16** Afternoon congestion of cars, streetcars, and pedestrians along Broadway in the heart of Times Square, 44th and 45th Streets, circa 1917. On the right is the successor theater to Hammerstein's Olympia; on the left, the Hotel Astor. William D. Hassler Photographic Collection, nyhs_pr83_4269, © New-York Historical Society.

agents and publicists, photographers, theatrical printers, scene painters, set builders, lighting companies, trunk manufacturers, transport companies, dance studios, rehearsal halls, musical-instrument shops, costumers, wig makers, makeup artists, theatrical publishers, and newspapers—whatever was needed for the production and promotion of show business. Such was the crush of pedestrians in the district that in 1924 the Police Department felt compelled to institute a new traffic plan, a "semi-military" system, of one-way streets it believed would end congestion "immediately" and allow motorists to "evacuate the theater zone within fifteen minutes."[26] A century later, congestion remained a problem in the Theater District on a typical night when performances finished—before Covid shut down Broadway.

The city's newspapers and realty press were proud, boastfully so, of the distinctive achievements that had made the entertainment district a worldwide phenomenon. The growth of "high-class amusement houses" built in Times Square was "unprecedented in any other city of the world," noted the *Times*. Nightly, more people were said to be attending performances there than in all of London and Paris combined. Seating capacity, reportedly, was almost 60,000. The pride of town extended to the architects, engineers, and builders contributing to the district's "rapid and remarkable development." The concentration of places of entertainment and amusement made Times Square unique. Its growth was adding millions to the city's taxable assessments.[27] Theaters were the economic and social life blood of the area in the early twentieth century, destined to become a major inheritance of the city.

Realty interests were ambivalent about the increasing specialization of the district, so different from the historical pattern of growth in Manhattan. The *Record* stated that the investments in the district's entertainments could not match in construction value what was being spent on a typical modern apartment house or commercial building. As early as 1901, it had argued that the only way to sustain the high values in the district was if demand for business purposes balanced out the demand for amusement purposes. Whether the district was now too richly endowed with high-class theaters was a matter of opinion. But the fervent wish for office buildings able to attract "good quality tenants" and "a better class of retail firms" to the neighborhood remained ever present among the business leadership of the industry.[28] That same sentiment would reappear in the late 1970s when city officials set out plans to reverse the decline and decrepitude that had infected the world's most famous theater block.

Commercial extravagance rather than aesthetic discipline set the prevailing tone for Times Square, and it was precisely this tone that gave the district its legendary, national distinctiveness. The distinctiveness arose not just from the success and centrality of the legitimate theater business, but from the unique role Times Square played during this period as America's great central marketplace for commercial culture. It had become a "laboratory of a new kind of popular culture."[29] As fashions in popular entertainment evolved over time in response to changes in popular tastes and the novelty of new technology, a succession of new businesses moved into Times Square: motion pictures, vaudeville, cabaret, popular music—"Tin Pan Alley" as the industry was known—then radio. Times Square evolved into a national showcase for all of it. The experimentation of popular entertainments particularly urban in form shaped the legacy of the place, and New York's position as the largest and brightest stage for the presentation and sale of commercial culture in the United States fueled the city's growing tourism business. Eager to consume the latest in popular culture, Americans were perhaps even more eager to see the syncopated dazzle of the electric spectacle on display every evening in Times Square—and to let the folks back home know what they saw when they were in New York.

## "WE'RE HAVING A FINE TIME"

So wrote M. K. Iver to a friend in Philadelphia (March 19, 1919). "This is the way we go down," Phebe scribbled on the front of a postcard to describe subway entrance and exit kiosks (October 16, 1906). "I came for one week nearly three weeks ago and am still here! Hate to leave," exclaimed Isabel Fay to her sister in Worcester, Massachusetts (February 6, 1911). "I intended writing before, but have been quite busy," Dot wrote to two friends when she got home (August 25, 1915). "Jane has nearly bought out Woolworths [sic] Store buying things for all the nieces and nephews. We have a very nice room for $1.10 each a day and running both hot water and cold" (unknown to Sara, n.d.). "Fine Table d'Hôte" at Churchill's restaurant on Broadway and 49th Street: "$1$^{00}$ dinner—with 12 orchestra specialists . . . you can sit in gallery, enjoy your meal, your perfecto, and think where to go next" (March 13, 1912).[30]

Like so many others, these postcard messages offered testimony to Times Square's commanding appeal to tourists. The color pictorial cards, hand-tinted or retouched from black and white photographs, were a way to preserve memories of a novel or exciting experience, a way to show evidence of where they stayed in the city, a way for someone on the move to say, "I've been there." And Times Square was a "must see" place, top of the list of New York's many attractions. In 1907, after Congress liberalized the rules governing postcards, messages could be written on the left half of the address side, the so-called "divided back" or "split back" card. Costing only one cent, postcards sent during the "Divided Back Period" between 1907 and 1915 reached such staggering proportions that these years are now considered the "Golden Age of Postcards." Figures from the US Postal Office for the year ending June 30, 1908, revealed that approximately seven million postcards had been mailed in the country (US population 89 million; by 1913, the number had increased to over nine million (US population 97 million), and "by this date, the craze was reportedly on the decline!"[31] "By sending postcards to friends and family at home, tourists sowed the seeds of urban tourism. They were what selfies posted on social media are today.

The postcard mania in America shaped popular expectations of what was important to see in a city. Urban postcards covered a wide landscape of possible places to visit. In New York, these possibilities seemed limitless, given the increasing numbers of skyscrapers, hotels, civic buildings and monuments, and popular places for leisure activity such as Coney Island, as well as vistas photographers could capture in the rapidly changing city. The postcards were ubiquitous and shaped the image of the city in one of New York's most formative periods of development. Their enormous circulation through the mails to cities and towns all over the nation promoted New York like no other city. They fashioned urban reputations, furthering the expansion of the tourist trade. They fulfilled a role larger than their small 3.5-inch-by-5.5-inch size would suggest because they helped tourists make sense of a rapidly changing metropolis by ordering an increasingly complex urban landscape—a landscape filled with new commercial activities and personal transactions.

Times Square's growth and prosperity as a national entertainment center directly tied into New York's newly emergent midtown business district in the early part of the twentieth century. Its development was happening at a time when, nationally, tourism was simultaneously expanding the market for entertainment and the drawing power of Times Square. For businessmen and their entourages coming to New York, the buying trips, conventions, trade shows, or financial transactions provided the pretext for visiting, but they were not the sole reason for doing so. Rather, it was the combination of business contacts and personal pleasure that brought New York so many tourists. Moreover, what tourists wanted was not always the uplifting art museums, historical monuments, and public parks, but the satisfactions of good plays, enjoyable food, jolly rides about town, memorable views from observation decks, and live music and entertainment at nightclubs and roof gardens. "This was not high culture," wrote cultural historian Neil Harris, "but in its concern for information, mundane experience, corporate celebration, and broad urban vistas, it reflected a set of metropolitan values that were easily comprehensible."[32]

Times Square was one place by day and another place by night, a dichotomy that furthered its appeal to tourists and New Yorkers alike. Of its two personalities, the nocturnal dynamic held the deepest attachment. Evident by 1920, it emerged from the rapid growth of two legacy-making trends that amounted to "a conspiracy of commerce against night." First came the clustering of ostentatious restaurants, best exemplified by Rector's, where Broadway's most glamorous celebrities and the nation's richest businessmen gathered after theater to eat and drink in theatrical style and sumptuous abandon—with a wish to be seen, definitely. As imitators followed, the trend acquired a handle, Lobster-Palace Society, so named for the foodie craze for fresh lobsters debuted at Rector's. Spectacles in themselves, these nightspots became famous for the unusual mix of fashionable elite and low-life activities in their dining rooms.[33] This was a playground after business hours had passed, but it was not the world of the heritage names of New York society—the Astors, Vanderbilts, or Goelets—who hewed to an imperative of privacy and formal decorum.

Second came the blaze of electric lights—name signs, marquee displays, promotional billboards, architectural lights outlining buildings, and animated advertising "spectaculars." With theatrical flamboyance and gigantic scale, "spectaculars" perched on rooftops around the square appeared to float in the darkness of the sky. As spectaculars evolved into more and more elaborate animated performances of flashing, moving, blinking bulbs, Broadway's nightly outdoor theater in

**1.17** The nighttime spectacle in Times Square was a common postcard image, 1918. Free to all, the syncopated dazzle of lights never ceased to enthrall visitors and locals alike. Neon replaced the electric bulb in the 1920s. © Underwood & Underwood, N.Y., collection of the author.

lights—commercial bombast with the magnetic pull of electricity and mesmerizing moving light forms—was unsurpassed by any other in the world. The exceptionally long sightlines of the square's bowtie—1,400 feet from 42nd to 47th—made a perfect showcase for these signs, as Hammerstein understood when creating the Olympia. And the show—captured in postcards sent all over the world—was open to all: locals and tourists need not pay anything to be amazed and awed at the spellbinding outdoor luminosity of the nightly ritual.

Times Square was an electric spectacle, a hypnotizing force that played an even greater role in attracting the crowds than the theaters. For many, this spectacle was why they had to bear witness to Times Square. Its visual identity, its signature aesthetic trademark, was born of a distinctively bold and brash commercial spirit created by private interests—paradoxically, in what became the city's most celebrated public place. As discussed in later chapters, proprietary control over the aesthetic stands in contrast to the lack of control over this most public of urban spaces.

## THE ASTOR FACTOR

They faced off from opposite sides of Broadway: on the west, William Waldorf Astor's 11-story Hotel Astor commanding the full face of the block running 44th to 45th Streets; and diagonally across, on the

**1.18** Rival cousins William Waldorf Astor (left) and John Jacob Astor IV (right), each a builder of a landmark Times Square hotel. The Prints Collection, New York Public Library.

southeast corner of 42nd Street, John Jacob Astor IV's 15-story Knickerbocker Hotel. Work plans on both Beaux-Arts French Renaissance hotels started in 1901, but the Astor opened first, in 1904; the Knickerbocker two years later, in 1906. Construction on the Knickerbocker had come to a stop when the out-of-town investment group holding the lease on the old Hotel St. Cloud site from Astor collapsed from dissension within. With only a steel and masonry shell completed, Astor (1864–1912) assumed control of the project and construction resumed in June 1905. William Waldorf Astor (1848–1919) was an "out-of-town" investor too, despite his heritage and birth in New York: he had forsaken the city and his country in 1890 to pursue a life and a titled position in English society. (It was his branch of the family that Henry excluded in his instructions for distribution of his trust lands because they already had too much money.) Only distant from one another by some 700 feet, the two luxurious *fin de siècle* hotels were a stand-in for the long-time rivalry between these born-of-wealth cousins whose landed actions had a formative impact on the development of Times Square.

By the end of the nineteenth century visitors of all types were coming to New York: merchants, buyers, and wholesalers to purchase fall and winter stocks of goods—often with their families; manufacturers and retail dealers to display their latest products and inventions at trade fairs—also often with their families; and sightseers and pleasure tourists to the nation's great pleasure city—who came to New York from distant places to take in as much of the city as their time would allow. Somewhat to the surprise of locals, New York had become "the greatest summer resort," *Harper's Weekly* explained, where people could enjoy the many amusements and vistas of the city from the Battery up Broadway to the theater district and its immensely popular rooftop theaters (before the advent of air conditioning and the imposition of Prohibition).[34] The construction of new hotels to meet the demand for this "floating population" typically moved in tandem with the development of the theater district; the relationship was symbiotic. By 1890 leading hotels lined the Rialto of Upper Broadway: Gilsey House (at 29th), Grand (at 31st), Imperial (at 32nd), Marlborough (at 36th), Normandie (at 38th), Oriental (at 39th), Vendome (at 41st), and at 42nd Street, where they stopped, Metropole and St. Cloud.

The news that William Waldorf Astor had entered into a lease arrangement with the experienced, ambitious hotelier William C. Muschenheim became one of the signature episodes in the development of Times Square. It was Muschenheim, along with his brother Frederick, who conceived of and convinced Astor of the idea for the development of a great first-class hotel in Longacre Square. He was said to have "a sure sense" of where the city's future lay and a vision beyond the modest accommodations typical of hotels near the Theater District.[35] Monumentally grand in the tradition of the Waldorf-Astoria, the new hotel Muschenheim and Astor had architects Clinton & Russell design would nevertheless be in tune with the commercial values and relaxed social style of the city's growing mercantile society. Instead of serving high society, the hotel aimed to serve a core clientele of tourists, businesspeople, and prosperous members of the middle class.

Although Longacre had been "a promising field" for a new hotel for several years, the collapse of earlier "schemes" left many skeptical that plans announced would materialize into actual buildings. In this instance, the *Times* reported, there would be "no occasion" to "doubt that the operation will be carried through on the lines already indicated."[36] The Astor name made the difference.

For the Astors, building first-class hotels to service the increasing numbers of tourists coming to an ever-expanding theater district presented few, if any, of the hurdles others faced. Each of the dueling Astors already owned strategic sites in Longacre Square, and their ambition could draw on unlimited funds to finance their hotel ventures. Moreover, the Astor name was synonymous with the defining development of the luxury hotel: Astor House (1836) built by the patriarch on a full block of Broadway facing City Hall Park, which gave way in fashionable style to the Waldorf (1893, built by William Waldorf) and the Astoria (1897, built by John Jacob), joined together at 33rd and 34th Streets on Fifth Avenue to become the grandest of the new hotels built in the 1890s (razed in 1929 to make way for construction of the Empire State Building). William Waldorf added the New Netherland (1893) on Fifth Avenue at 59th Street to his credit, while John Jacob did likewise with the St. Regis (1904) on 55th Street at Fifth Avenue. They were the natural first movers, equaled by none.

Realty interests appear to have been waiting to see just what "improvements" the Astors would make on their extensive holdings in the Longacre district. Progress in the area had been slow (or slower than real estate interests hoped for), but announcements by various members of the Astor family, the *Record* said, "strengthened the feeling that the square is to be improved; and a succession of similar projects may be expected within the next few years."[37] Talk about the costs of their newest hotel investments coupled with their wealth, social status, and reputation for building the most-up-to-date luxury hotels signaled investment opportunity for others and the future business growth of the district. Surely that was what Ochs was thinking during the two years after work began on the two new Astor hotels before he announced that the *Times* would be moving to a new headquarters in Longacre Square.

The story of how each cousin came into separate property holdings in Longacre Square traces back to the patriarch. Decades after John Jacob Astor (1763–1848) purchased the 70-acre Medcef Eden Farm in 1803 (with William Cutting), he partitioned his portion of the estate west of Broadway among his three grandsons: John Jacob III (1822–1890), William Backhouse Jr. (1830–1892), and Henry (1832–1918). As evident on the 1842 map of the partitioned estate (figure 1.22), the grandsons were not treated equally: 50 percent of the lands went to his namesake, son of his oldest son (William Backhouse, 1792–1875), with 25 percent going to each of the others. As the lands passed down to his great-grandsons, William Waldorf (son of John Jacob III) and John Jacob IV (son of William Backhouse Jr.; "Jack" to family and friends) became the direct players in Longacre real estate. (Henry's segment was managed by trustees of the trust he had created in 1869.) Each great-grandson controlled strategic sites fronting Broadway, but the modified primogeniture of the 1842 partition of lands had passed down to William Waldorf what was arguably the most strategic of the strategic parcels in the "Astor Zone": the full block of city lots between 44th and 45th Streets running from Broadway to Eighth Avenue, where he would build his hotel. Jack owned most, but not all, of the block immediately south, including the Broadway block face. This is where the story of the dueling landed cousins gets interesting; though we lack any direct statement of competitive intent from either, land ownership tells its own story.

In 1892, Jack purchased for $850,000 the southeast corner of 42nd Street and Broadway occupied by the St. Cloud Hotel, built in 1868, on which he would build the Knickerbocker Hotel. Along with the Rossmore Hotel (1876) on the opposite side of Broadway, the location "marked the end of the world to the sport, the tipster and the

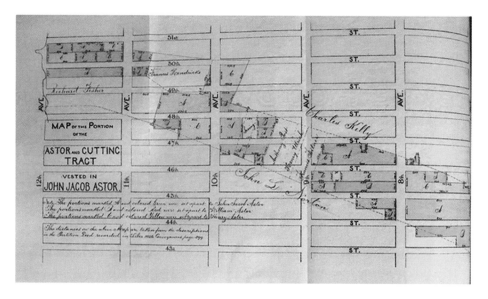

**1.19** The Astor lands in Times Square, formerly part of the Medcef Eden Farm, acquired by John Jacob Astor (with William Cutting, who deeded parcels to Astor) in 1803, through foreclosure on a mortgage note for $25,000. In 1842, John Jacob partitioned the lands among his three grandsons: parcels marked "A" to John Jacob III (in green); "B" to William Backhouse Jr. (in pink); "C" to Henry (in yellow). Abstracts of farm titles in the city of New York, between 39th and 73rd Streets, west of Common Lands. Henry Croswell Tuttle, comp. from old catalogue, 1877. hathitrust.org.

chorus-lady of *fin de siècle* Manhattan."[38] He would also come to own the northeast corner on the opposite side of 42nd Street, courtesy of inheritance from his father, William Backhouse Jr., who bought the assemblage (for $690,000) two years earlier. It is William Backhouse's purchase that sheds light on advance buying in the square years before Hammerstein bet on the location.

With these purchases, this branch of the family controlled the two strategic 42nd Street corners at the eastern entrance to Longacre Square—the logical path from which the midtown district would expand westward. These strategic corners—soon to become iconic for the structures built on them—set the frame of geography for the Astors' rival development of luxury hotels in the burgeoning theater district, yet to be named Times Square.

The significance of an Astor acquiring ever more property in the neighborhood was evident. In its weekly report to the realty trade, the *Record* remarked that the "important" St. Cloud transaction "gives material sign of an intention [of Upper Broadway] to emerge from its period of gloom." The *Record* was impressed that some of the country's "shrewdest real estate operators" had been attracted to the area by the prospect of underground rapid transit through Broadway; it was advising others "to closely investigate this district."[39]

At the time of the St. Cloud purchase, Astor was said to have no intention of rebuilding the site, and indeed, the next year he leased the St. Cloud to an operator. But Astor was not buying a hotel per se; he was buying the land underneath for future gain. "The price paid was reasonable," remarked the *Record*, "the ground alone being estimated to be worth not far short of the $850,000 paid."[40] That was the way of the Astor heritage.

Turning from global commerce in fur and trade in teas, silk, spices, and chinaware to real estate, the patriarch John Jacob Astor had become the most acquisitive landlord in New York, buying property far from the built-up sections of Manhattan. At the time of his death in 1848, he was considered one of the richest, if not the richest, man in America; estimates of his wealth ranged from $5 million to $20 million (the equivalent of $188 million to $750 million in 2022 dollars, which may not seem as impressive today but then the buying power of those millions was much greater than it is today because of the 3,650 percent change in prices). He exhorted his heirs not to sell what he had accumulated, but instead to lease land and sell only when its value had increased significantly, which generally meant when the northward flow of population caught up with it. In keeping with his wishes, the heirs were thought of as very prudent investors. Until this third generation, they had not been builders, just landlords. On hundreds of city lots leased to others who built tenements, apartment houses, theaters, churches, and commercial buildings, they collected steady ground rents with little financial risk. The terms were clear: a lease of 21 years with renewal rights (generally three terms, for a total of 84 years), and at the end of those years, the improvements reverted to the Astors, absolutely. More importantly, the unearned increment on the land along with its potential future development value belonged to the Astor estates.

This was the long-lease idea the patriarch had brought to America from England. And in that era, other large landowners commonly were doing the same; it was the way landed estates could ensure continuity of wealth for future generations as the city's growth perpetuated rising values of landed property. The timing of that growth might not be predictable, but the long-term hold on the underlying ownership of the land evidenced an abiding belief in the economic future of New York, a belief that was substantiated by time. Contrary to a well-worn myth that they never sold property, the Astors did sell—when the timing was right, that is, when an area was ripe for improvement and for harvesting the gain in accrued land value. Or they would sell when vacant parcels were not of "gilt-edged character" and use the proceeds to buy more acreage along the paths of the city's population march.

By 1900, the patriarch's fourth-generation namesake had decided the time was ripe for rebuilding the St. Cloud site. He leased it to a Philadelphia-based firm, which included the prominent hotelier James B. Regan, who had worked his way up from being a bar boy to managing prestigious hotels, as director and lessee and driving force of the project, with the stipulation that a new hotel, costing at least $2,000,000, be erected on the site. When the *Times* reported on the first set of plans for this Astor's luxurious hotel—several stories taller than his cousin's planned hotel with the added benefit of two direct entrances to the underground subway station (the door of one still visible at the eastern end of Track 1 at the Times Square Shuttle)—he managed something of a one-upmanship on his London-based rival, cousin William.[41]

As to the latter: on its impending opening in fall 1904, the *Times* described the Hotel Astor as ten stories of the latest luxury, a "pile" built at the cost of $7,000,000 ($233 million in 2022 dollars). Clinton & Russell had been able to work with a virtually unlimited budget in designing the flamboyant hotel. This was the most modern of moderns, complete with "recently invented safeguards against fire, bad air, and all forms of discomfort." Most important for its intended clientele, it had enormous dining rooms and ballrooms as well as a sumptuous roof garden. Its public lounges and restaurants were fitted out in "a catalogue of historical styles, with evocations of the past and exotic locales which reflected the influence of theme restaurants."[42] They were designed to convey a sense of the deluxe in distinct styles for men and women. The drama of the spaces aptly fit the theatricality of the district. Sheathed in brick and limestone, the French Renaissance pile was topped by an elaborate green-copper mansard roof that sheltered the hotel's lush ballrooms. Physically, it reigned over Times Square, even as taller new structures replaced the old nondescript buildings of Longacre Square.

Hotel Astor set the tone and pace for a district rapidly transitioning from one era to the next as New York City's mushrooming resident and floating populations swelled its streets, transit facilities, and open spaces. It was the place-maker marking the next era of Longacre Square, *the* place to be, the scene of countless balls, banquets, social functions, anniversary dinners, and business conventions. It hosted diplomatic missions and was the starting point for the New York-to-Paris Auto Race of 1908. The comings and goings of people seemed endless; the hotel employed a staff of many hundreds, if not thousands. After three years,

**1.20** The splendid Hotel Astor (1904) sitting astride low-slung nineteenth-century buildings heralded a new age. Built at a reported cost of $7 million, its huge success fostered Manhattan's first hotel building boom. Managed by the Muschenheim brothers, the hotel became a venerable institution in Times Square, *the* place to hold business functions. In March 1920, the Henry Astor Trust Estate auction would be held in its grand ballroom, circa 1905. George P. Hall & Sons, nyhs_pr024_b-09_f-77_004-01 © New-York Historical Society.

it had become so successful that Astor laid out several more millions to double the number of guestrooms (to 1,000) and public facilities.

The Astor was the expected first-mover investment that gave commercial definition to the amusement district—Times Square was no longer too far uptown. Yet perhaps more important for its absentee landlord, Hotel Astor served as a strategic investment, one that was sure to enhance the value of his large inherited portfolio of property in Times Square, still relatively underdeveloped. But—contrary to the conventional storyline—its success was not the provocation for his cousin's plans for the Knickerbocker. Jack had been moving forward at the same time cousin William was planning the Astor.

Designed in the same French Renaissance style as the Astor, on its exterior the Knickerbocker was more restrained. Inside, however, was another story. When its proprietor opened its doors on October 24, 1906, the Knickerbocker was far more sumptuous than the hotel that had been originally planned in 1901. The character of Times Square had become so much more commercial in the interval between the suspension of construction in 1902 and its resumption in 1904 that "to continue with the original plans was tantamount to building a dowdy dinosaur."[43] So Astor hired a new team of architects, Trowbridge & Livingston, to redo the plans, adding over $1,000,000 to the hotel's reported $3,300,000 cost.

With carte blanche to plan his hotel to suit his own ideas and with a seven-month-long trip to Europe seeking fittings, Regan set out to deliver unsurpassed services to the traveling businessmen, celebrity residents (among them Enrico Caruso), and affluent visitors staying in the hotel's 556 rooms. Among other items, he brought back solid-gold service for forty-eight for the "gold room," one of the hotel's eight private dining rooms, and 500 Paris-made clocks. Most appealing to visitors was a system of service and communication between the kitchen and pantries installed on every floor. The press highly praised the most unique character of the Knickerbocker, in particular the lavish decoration of its interior spaces, which Regan achieved by combining luxurious decorative appointments with major commissioned works of art: Maxfield Parrish's tableau *Old King Cole and His Fiddlers Three* in the oak-paneled barroom (now hanging in the St. Regis Hotel), and in the café, Frederic Remington's *The United States Calvary Charge* (now in the collection of the University of Texas at Austin).

Rather than strive for exclusivity, Regan set out to make the Knickerbocker a prominent scene for the nighttime excitement of Times Square. A popular hotel—"a Fifth Avenue Hotel at Broadway prices"—the Knickerbocker still reflected the architectural richness of the Gilded Age.[44] An elegant iron canopy graced its entrance, its lobby nightly serving as a date-rendezvous meeting place. The canopy, however, was a casualty of the street's widening in 1910, along with the marble columns on 42nd Street. The Knickerbocker "has the perfect location for a hotel," opined the *Record*, "much more accessible than the Hotel Astor, because it can be reached by crossing Broadway at a narrow point instead of by a good stretch of asphalt" across Times Square.[45]

The Knickerbocker's success as a hotel was relatively short-lived. In 1920, Regan surrendered his lease to the hotel, saying he wanted to retire. But like so many other hotels economically crippled by Prohibition, nothing could keep it afloat. In 1912, Jack went down on the *Titanic*, leaving his propertied estate to his son Vincent Astor (1891–1959), then just shy of twenty-one and a freshman at Harvard University. With property in Manhattan and the Bronx valued for inheritance

**1.21** The Knickerbocker Hotel created a sensation upon its opening in 1906. Its lavish interiors, murals by noted artists, and elegant iron canopy gracing its entrance reflected the architectural richness of the Gilded Age. With the onset of Prohibition, Vincent Astor converted the Knickerbocker to commercial and office use, and it continues to serve these purposes today. Historic blotter, circa 1906. Collection of the author.

purposes at over $63,000,000 (20 percent more than the assessment on the city's tax rolls and equivalent to nearly $2 billion in 2022 dollars), in addition to property outside the city, upon turning twenty-one Vincent would become "the wealthiest member of the Astor family." He would also hold "the unique distinction in the history of the Astor family of being the sole master of practically all of his inheritance at so early an age."[46]

With its closing, Vincent Astor announced plans to convert the Knickerbocker into an office building. After several more significant building projects, he would leave an "Astor legacy in brick and stone." Unlike William Waldorf's Hotel Astor, which was demolished in 1967, Jack's Knickerbocker lives on—declared a New York City landmark in 1988 and certified on the National Register of Historic Places in 1980. Substantially renovated twice, the building still commands attention, "as it must have when first built . . . a Beaux-Arts vision of order and high taste [that] seemed poised to remake New York."[47]

The first of the Astor dynasty to invest their fortunes in city-building projects, the cousins' activity triggered the development of other hotels, large and small, as well as assemblages for apartment hotels and bachelor apartments in the square. With the end of World War I, most of Manhattan's commercial hotels were being built in the Times Square theater district. Although sites with frontage on Broadway were generally too expensive for hotel use—a notable exception being the 19-story Hotel Rector (1911, renamed Claridge Hotel in 1913)—large sites could be easily assembled on the side-street tributaries, where land was comparatively inexpensive. On these side streets, especially those west of Eighth Avenue, a different world prevailed—a world of leasehold interests built on Astor lands.

## BEYOND THE BRIGHT LIGHTS

By the time the Henry Astor lands came to auction in 1920, Times Square's commercial economy, cultural tone, and centrality as a public place were well established. Unrestrained by the conventions of nineteenth-century social order and real estate conservatism, a new social space had evolved there. As urban historian Elizabeth Blackmar explained in her essay "Uptown Real Estate and the Creation of Times Square," the developing commercial dynamic of the district challenged conventional notions of propriety and authority. Real estate investment, typically conservative, associated the value of a neighborhood with the moral "character" of its users, and to preserve value, owners and brokers sought to control space by restricting access. But the development of Times Square cut a potent alternative pattern. It threw off "the contemporary progressive-era preoccupation with establishing social order (and value) through spatial uniformity and predictability." Theater's foothold on 42nd Street at the beginning of the century and the ancillary activities drawn to nightlife on the town—vice, corruption, and prostitution—were anything but conducive to conventional patterns of neighborhood development. The release from the past opened the "district to rapid innovation and novel definitions of its cultural identity and appeal as a social space." It created an air of excitement and endowed Times Square with an economic edge that "arose from cultural unpredictability, impulse and risk."[48] New Yorkers' own disregard for cultural boundaries also contributed to Times Square's cultural identity as a socially tolerant place where all classes mingled. In short, an emerging cultural DNA imprinted on the Rialto of Times Square something different and apart from the Rialto of Herald Square—a distinctive urban energy.

In the unstable environment of rapid growth and accelerating land values driving Longacre Square's transformation, speculation flourished. In issue after issue of the *Record*, more plans for theaters, stores, restaurants, hotels, apartment hotels were regularly announced than actually realized. Speculation, rather than development, was the most active and profitable arena of Times Square real estate investment before the 1920s. Landowners and brokers knew (and hoped to persuade buyers) that the area of midtown was valuable, even if they were less certain of what uses would best be put on that land.

With theater, restaurants, and commercial uses leading the transformation of the district, residential development faced strong competition, except for the blocks west of Eighth Avenue and beyond to the waterfront that had been home to working-class families since the mid-nineteenth century. Just one block west of the glitz and glamour of Broadway, a starkly different world prevailed, whose daily round of life only casually crossed with that of Times Square. This was Hell's Kitchen. By reputation, it was a historically rough working-class neighborhood packed full of immigrant poor attracted there by nearby jobs in manufacturing and warehousing enterprises attracted to the district's cheap land and ready access to the many working piers along the Hudson River, including uses considered nuisances intolerable in residential neighborhoods. Several explanations exist for the neighborhood's name, which surfaced sometime in the second half of the nineteenth century, but no one can pin down its exact origins. It could have been taken from that of a gang formed in the area in 1868, or adopted by local police in the 1870s, but whatever the origins, the area's history is as colorful as its name. Replete with stories of gangsters, streetwalkers, speakeasies, mysterious disappearances, and gruesome murders, it's a chronicle "troubled by violence and general disorder from an early point in its history."[49]

In the eyes of Otho G. Cartwright, a social worker of the progressive movement, it seemed strangely detached from the rest of the city and different from the city's other tenement neighborhoods, a "neglected and little known" place (except by its negative reputation). Cartwright had been charged with writing a historical overview of the "Middle West Side" as part of a large 1912 study of the area's social problems undertaken by the Bureau of Social Research of the New York School of Philanthropy with support from the Russell Sage Foundation. For the reform-minded progressives who sought policies that would improve the conditions of the urban poor, Hell's Kitchen's turn-of-the-century reputation as both a slum and a red-light district with a history of gangs made it a prime case study. "From an architectural standpoint the district has neither salient features nor real uniformity," a condition

**1.22** Brownstones on West 46th Street built as private dwellings in the 1880s under long-term lease arrangements, nine on the western end with an absolute termination date of May 1, 1920, free and clear of mortgages at the Henry Astor Trust Estate auction, circa 1920. Collection of the author.

Cartwright ascribed to "the lack of a proper building plan." On the other hand, he noted, it was homogeneous and stable. What appeared to trouble him most was "the sordid, deadly monotony and lack of picturesque life . . . no hint of quaintness or color relieves this region of slaughter houses, railway sheds, gas tanks, and piano factories."[50]

Row after row of commonplace three-story brownstones and Old Law Tenements built during the nineteenth century crowded the blocks from 44th to 50th Streets from Eighth Avenue to the Hudson River—over lands owned by the Astors and leased to others. Interspersed with the residential buildings that made up the fabric of the side streets were churches, clubs, schools, small shops, cafes; salons mixed with breweries, factories, and warehouses. This was a neighborhood of renters—an ethnically diverse but predominantly white population of native-born and immigrants—Irish, Italian, German, Greek, Polish—nearly all of whom became naturalized citizens, as census records showed. In 1920, across the eight tenement blocks closest to Times Square (Eighth to Ninth Avenues, from 42nd to 50th Streets), the density of people crowded into apartments with little light and air was high: between 294 and 359 persons per acre—not nearly as injurious as that of the worst tenement neighborhoods of the Lower East Side (650 and 636 persons to an acre) but intense nevertheless.[51]

Who were these people living so close to yet seemingly so far from the lights of Broadway? A close look at a typical block of Henry Astor's lands in 1920—46th Street between Eighth and Ninth Avenues, now the well-trod sidewalks of Restaurant Row—shows over 1,000 people living in seventy buildings (all brownstones or tenements but for one apartment building, as shown on the Bromley map based on actual surveys and official plans), more than half of whom were "lodgers." And based on a tabulation of block-level census data, in more than a few instances ten or more (sometimes many more) lodgers might be boarding with a head of household, who seemed as likely to be a widow as a husband with a family.

At number 321, on the north side of the street, in one of the four contiguous three-story brownstones that today make up the oldest restaurant on Restaurant Row, Barbetta (1906), lived Marvin Fink and his wife Carrie, their daughter, and ten lodgers; the lodgers included a doctor, dentist, music director and his wife, actor, actress, hotel clerk, hotel waitress, linotype operator, and manager in brokerage. Like those in 321, the residents on this block were working people employed in a broad range of occupations within the local economy: theater, hotels and restaurants, sales, personal and domestic service, clerical fields, journalism, music and design, film production, garment trade, financial business, real estate, medicine, law, engineering, manufacturing and repair, and shopkeeping. Notably, for the fifteen out of every hundred of these residents working in the theater industry—actors, actresses, dancers, musicians, singers, chorus girls, ushers, stage carpenters, stagehands, stage mechanics, electricians, show managers, secretaries, treasurers, ticket agents, property men—the walk-to-work location was ideal.

The adjacency of this seemingly immutable neighborhood established Times Square's mixed-class character from the outset. To realty interests, however, the neighborhood was ripe for change. The expected path of expansion triggered by Times Square's transformation was westward. As the *Record* explained just days before the Astor auction, Eighth Avenue was the locus of "a decided buying movement" for new theaters, hotels, stores, with the side streets refashioned for apartments, studios, and business structures.[52] To realty interests, conversion or demolition of existing structures that were "not up-to-date" seemed inevitable. The physical changes would be in keeping with Manhattan's tear-it-down-to-build-it-up pattern of growth.

**1.23** Barbetta, 321 West 46th Street, the oldest restaurant on Restaurant Row; the long-popular restaurant, in one the area's many former speakeasy locations, is one of New York's oldest family-owned Italian restaurants, in continuous service since 1906 (pictured in 2022). First located near the Old Metropolitan Opera House on 39th Street, in 1925 owner Sebastiano Maioglio moved it to the four contiguous brownstones where you can still dine in elegant comfort. Gary Hack.

Early in the district's transformation, Broadway sites in Times Square had quickly become too expensive for solo theater operations if not married to an office building that could command higher rents. Consequently, during the first boom in theater construction, the builders of new playhouses (other than those on 42nd Street) opted for sites on the side streets that hewed tight to the sight lines of Broadway. By 1920, the roster of these new theaters included the Gaiety, Globe, Fulton/Folies-Bergère, Little Theatre, Weber & Fields/44th Street, Shubert, Longacre, Booth, Candler/Cohan & Harris, Broadhurst, Plymouth, Morosco, and Bijou. By the end of the theater-building boom in 1928, there were an additional seventeen: Klaw, Music Box, Ritz/Walter Kerr, 49th Street Theatre, Ambassador, Imperial, Chanin's 46th Street, Biltmore, Eugene O'Neill, Mansfield/Brooks Atkinson, Edyth Totten, Erlanger/St. James, Majestic, Theatre Masque, Royale, and Ethel Barrymore. The Martin Beck (1924) would be the lone major theater to leapfrog Eighth Avenue to the 300 block of 45th Street.

In 1920, the physical fabric of the residential blocks immediately west of Eighth Avenue appeared unaffected by the transformation of Longacre Square. The blocks still housed the same row after row of tenements and high-stoop brownstones, with only minor differences evident on the Bromley map of the neighborhood: a converted storage warehouse, a small theater on Ninth Avenue, a very small hotel on Eighth Avenue, and the short-lived Amsterdam Opera House midblock on 44th. Many of the buildings had been built in the 1870s and '80s on lands owned by the Astors and had many more years to run before they hit the wall of absolute termination of their occupancy rights. The likely absentee landlords who held long-term leases on these blocks would only gradually be displaced by new commercial ventures that found redevelopment of the lots sufficiently profitable. Of course, with the public auction of Henry Astor's trust estate on the calendar, maybe that event—with its potential for fresh speculation—would change the trajectory of these blocks.

## THE AUCTION

This then was the situation when J. Clarence Davies and Joseph P. Day exercised the gavel at the landmark public auction of the "great estate" of Henry Astor, at 11 A.M. in the grand ballroom of the Hotel Astor. The auctioneers' choice of the hotel's grand ballroom with its flag-draped balconies and high ceilings contrasted sharply with the all-business décor of the Real Estate Exchange Salesroom at 14 and 16 Vesey Street,

**1.24** Advertisement for the 141 properties of the Henry Astor Trust Estate to be sold at auction in the grand ballroom of the Hotel Astor, 1920. Collection of the author.

where they customarily held property auctions (and which was soon to be the site of another eagerly awaited sale: the estate of F. W. Woolworth). A public sale of Astor lands was in and of itself a first. When the father of William Waldorf Astor died in 1890, the *Record* remarked, "Of course, none of his property will come on the market, as is usual when owners of realty pass away." Brokers wished it had "come under the hammer, for the public would then have witnessed such a scramble to buy as was never seen before," one said. "The property would have literally been 'gobbled' up, any number of millions of dollars worth of it."[53]

The Astor name had acquired a mythic dimension rooted in the patriarch's unwavering faith in rising New York land values. Leveraging the association of lineage wealth that needed no explanation, Davies and Day advertised the sale widely—their standard approach was "every day is boom day, and every site is a bonanza"[54]—employing large-font booster rhetoric to emphasize the opportunity to be had in purchases from the Henry Astor Trust Estate. First, they promoted Times Square in full-page ads: "The Heart of This Great City Is Now Settled for All Time. . . . IT IS HERE that property will become the most valuable." Next, it was Eighth Avenue, from 42nd to 59th Street: "The FUTURE GREAT WHITE WAY . . . in a few years. . . . There will, therefore, be a great increase in value of this property." And days before the auction, they made a pitch to investors in bonds and stock and depositors in savings banks: "DO YOU WANT A STEADY INCOME and ABSOLUTE SAFETY With Increase In Future and Chance for Profit? This can be had by buying a lot leased with Astor leasehold." Sixty-three such parcels would be up for sale, and the advertisement laid out the math of how you could earn a 10 percent investment on $2,100. By converting houses into multiple one- or two-bedroom apartments, the auction catalogue noted a buyer could double and triple the amount of the present rental obtained. The sale of these properties was expected to be the main factor in "completely transforming the more westerly portion of the Times Square or Astor Zone."[55]

The event reported on page one of the *Times* did not disappoint the capacity crowd said to number more than 2,500, including all the well-known realty operators, speculators, representative of estates, and brokers who were active in the market, as well as a host of interested heirs or their legal representatives. It took more than an hour to read through the terms of the sale before intense bidding began. Bids for the first parcel "came so fast from all quarters of the room," according to the *Times*, "that it was difficult to keep track of them."[56]

The bidding was fiercely spirited for three theaters under leaseholds: the Astor, Bijou, and Morosco (all of which would be infamously demolished in 1982 to make way for the Marriott Marquis Hotel); they went to one of the largest operators in the city, Robert W. Dowling, president of City Investing Company. The competing Syndicate and Shubert interests (directly or through agents), bidding furiously for lots that could make up an assemblage, "sent prices soaring." After one intense incident in which each counterbid to block the other, "both sides found they had paid a lot of money for lots disconnected and useless as theater sites," reported the *New-York Tribune*. "If ever they iron out their differences, they can piece together a fine plot."[57] They would do so only after the lots were resold. The lone lot between those of the bidding competitors would become the entrance through which patrons reached the Shuberts' Imperial Theatre (1923) on 46th Street.

Dinty Moore, owner of his eponymous restaurant (legendary for its corned beef and Irish stew), was also a noted buyer; he bought three contiguous lots, including the northeast corner of Eighth Avenue and 45th Street. The restaurant he opened in 1914 (at 216 West 46th Street) had quickly become a habitual place for prominent judges and politicians as well as celebrities. At the other end of the spectrum of buyers were tenants living in those high-stoop brownstones on West 46th, who "clutched tightly rolls of bills, Liberty Bonds and savings bank books," awaiting the chance to buy the buildings they called home. After twelve hours, Davies and Day knocked down the hammer on the last of the 141 lots. The celebrated event was over: "For 'Uncle Henry' Astor's benefit," the *New-York Tribune* said, "while he never enjoyed New York, he gave the town one really good show."[58]

The auction results—$5,159,075 ($77,589,345 in 2022 dollars)—set a record for the largest proceeds of any estate sale in the city's history, netting $633,775 above the assessed valuation for the property sold. The intake was close to what the state took in from its excise tax on liquor the prior year, a benchmark of sorts for the entertainment district only months before the start of Prohibition. The prices "surpassed the estimates of even the most optimistic speculator," remarked the *Times*. The results reportedly satisfied everyone, especially the heirs who were on the receiving end of handsome proceeds. "The prices obtained look good today," Davies said, "but they are 25 to 30 percent under what they will be two or three years from now. Everybody that bought got a bargain."[59] It only took a few weeks for two of the high-profile bidders to realize handsome profits: just days after the auction, the first resale with its profit-taking of $60,000 was announced; the next week, another with profit-taking of $48,000. Both these resales completed assemblages for theater construction that had been thwarted in the auction's intense counterbidding mentioned above. On the lots of the first resale the Shuberts would build The Music Box (1921); on the second, former Syndicate principal Marc Klaw built Klaw Theatre (1921).

A week after the event, the auction results were still the subject of talk in the realty world. The *Record* was sure that the prices realized at the sale indicated "a very firm undertone to the whole realty fabric" of New York City. The *Record* was also sure that the top of the market had not yet been reached and that improvements would be made to properties on those side streets "with the appearance of bye-gone usefulness and an absence of modern improvements."[60] That transformation would not happen for decades, but the profitable release of Henry Astor's estate lands did accelerate the changing pattern of land ownership in Times Square.

A year earlier, Vincent Astor had sold the six-story Putnam Building and Westover Court, including the land beneath, to a syndicate for twice the valuation on the city's tax books. This highly valuable Broadway blockfront from 43rd to 44th was one of the largest properties under single ownership in Times Square, and it housed Shanley's restaurant, a Tammany hangout turned lobster palace and local eatery landmark. The purchasing syndicate, in turn, sold it to the entertainment entrepreneur Adolph Zukor of Famous Players-Lasky Corporation, forerunner of Paramount Pictures. When the leases on the site expired, Zukor built a new skyscraper for the corporation's eastern headquarters which included a movie palace with seating for 3,664. At 33 stories, the Paramount (1927) was the tallest structure on Broadway north of the Woolworth Building (1912, 55 stories), the tallest building in the world from 1913 to 1930, in Manhattan's historic downtown. It towered over the pair of 12-story buildings diagonally across Broadway, the Fitzgerald and Longacre. With four giant clock faces on the tower's upper stories crowned with a glass globe, the Paramount's distinctive ziggurat profile quickly became the newest postcard icon of Times Square. As a movie palace, it was also a conspicuous harbinger of the change in popular entertainment coming to Times Square—a looming competitive threat to playhouses of legitimate theater.

Despite the unprecedented cost of materials and labor and difficulties financing real estate in New York following the end of World War I, Times Square ricocheted with the noise of constant construction activity. With at least twenty-two projects under way, the district was enjoying its greatest building boom. It was being remade physically at a rate faster than during the prewar boom. The Astor Trust sale was said to reveal the stability of the real estate market, but in the context of the times, "stability" could only imply the expectation of constant upward movement in property values. In 1919, Congress passed the Volstead Act ushering in Prohibition, which banned the sale of beverages containing more than 0.5 percent alcohol. The Eighteenth Amendment to the Constitution took effect on January 17, 1920, ushering in an era of

36 TIMES SQUARE AND PARAMOUNT BUILDING, NEW YORK CITY

**1.25** On the newest postcard icon, a view of the 33-story Paramount Building (1927) looming over Times Square's other landmarks, the Times Tower (left) and Hotel Astor (right). Collection of the author.

speakeasies and clandestine nightclubbing. It was the beginning of a death spiral for restaurants like Shanley's and Rector's, which had flourished in the alcohol-drenched nightlife of Times Square.

In three decades, the forces that gave rise to Times Square's theatrical character, cultural tone, and enterprising spirit exhausted themselves. The soaring land prices of speculative activity prompted operators and investors to prize predictability over innovation. Big corporations supplanted individual entrepreneurs. Development of large land assemblages became more commonplace, replacing an earlier building pattern of modest structures on the small and narrow city lots of the district's many side streets. New York's realty men remained resolute in their optimism for the future, even after the 1929 stock market crash. By 1930, the theatrical march uptown had slowed (even as the area north of 59th Street attracted a few new theaters), but Times Square's legacy as the city's entertainment center held firm. Nevertheless, its days of glory and glamor were passing as the district began a slide into decline triggered by nationwide social and economic trends in the decades leading to, then following, the United States' engagement in World War II. The descent was gradual yet persistent. By the end of the 1960s, the business of commercialized sex had overtaken the proud and glorious legacy of 42nd Street and the ambitions of those who had once seen a different future for the Times Square entertainment district.

# 2 THE LONG SLIDE

I'd like to walk away. But I am stuck with it, and I have to hold on. I don't see any buyers, and it's going to be a struggle for the next ten years.
Irving Maidman, January 1975

After 50 years the veteran investor in Times Square realty wanted out. At 78, his decades of optimistic purchases of property had made him one of the largest real estate operators in the area west of Broadway, Hell's Kitchen. His opportunistic bet now cast a surreal shadow on what had become a dense collection of massage parlors, topless bars, peep shows, porn bookstores, sex emporiums, and live burlesque—the trafficking of commercial sex and desperation on West 42nd Street. The 400 block between Ninth and Tenth Avenues—Irving Maidman's block—"had the seediest, dingiest massage parlors I'd ever seen in my life," recalled Milton "Mickey" Schwartz, commander of the Police Department's Midtown South precinct in the early 1970s. Sleaze apotheosis. Maidman saw no remedy for the area: "A business that does not cater to the people here cannot exist," he said.[1] The density of sex-based businesses in the orbit circling the neighborhood's decline seemed immune to the city's continual efforts to control the spread of vice and criminal activity.

During its darkest days of economic despair in the 1970s, when New York City was perched on the brink of municipal bankruptcy and *Rolling Stone* called West 42nd Street "the sleaziest block in America," Times Square appeared to the world at large as the personification of all that was diseased and rotten in big cities. The vividness of the Big Apple's metaphoric image was difficult to expunge. It stuck a dagger into the heart of the nation's largest and most vibrant city. Civic order had vanished in the spasms of chaos of the times. The trains were filthy. Graffiti was everywhere. Crime was a threatening presence. Much of what New York officials feared about their city's downward trajectory seemed intimately bound to the sordid conditions in Times Square, conditions that threatened to jeopardize the city's economic viability and global reputation. By the 1990s, when the violence and exploitation of the place had at last been expunged through aggressive public intervention, few admitted to missing the grunge and fear and crime that had pervaded the recent past. Only a more distant nostalgia remained, for Times Square's halcyon days of theatrical glamour and glory.

What the doom-and-gloom history of the 1970s in New York seems to have missed was the fact that this period was an unusually fertile period for artists. With time to reflect on the experience of that era of decline and despair, artists who lived in the Times Square neighborhood later identified the emergence of something unexpected in the era's cultural upheavals: "real freedom, not just in Times Square, but all of New York." Out of that mess, recalled the artist and photographer Jane Dickson, "came an explosion of creative freedom; old norms were challenged but new norms were not yet obvious. You could do anything you wanted." That type of freedom is what cultural commentators refer to when they speak about Times Square as a place of cultural liberalism and tolerance, a place of social experimentation. "Today, it's so corporate," Dickson added. "People are nostalgic not for the sleaze, but the laissez-faire of the times."[2]

In the early 1980s, New York was on the verge of massive cultural change. What the *Village Voice* called "the first radical art show of the '80s" opened on June 1, 1980, in a former massage parlor at 201 West 40th Street and Seventh Avenue, the run-down state of the building being part of the show. Organized by the artist members of Collaborative Projects Inc., known as Colab, the *Times Square Show*, comprised of artworks by 100 to 150 artists, was open twenty-four hours a day, seven days a week, "echoing the all-hours rhythm" of nearby 42nd Street. In its choice of venue, Colab was using the social context of the site for artistic purposes, to stage event-based exhibitions "where spontaneous interventions created a stream of unanticipated alterations—much like the unpredictable reality of the streets outside." In the illicit space of Times Square during this era, where the rules of regular society were suspended, "the former massage parlor became a zone of permissibility as much as a zone of experimentation."[3]

Over the lifetimes of five generations, the cultural landscape of the Great White Way pivoted from theatrical splendor to popular culture to commercialized sex to incessant vice to corporate renewal. In contrast to the perception that change in New York happens quickly, remarkable change as experienced in Times Square—change that erases familiar streetscapes and displaces markers of memory—is far more gradual. Small changes are often imperceptible until they reach a critical mass that makes their totality obvious. Profound change that refashions an area typically takes place over many years, punctuated by bold and risky visions, competitive challenges, setbacks and bottlenecks, changing social norms, and government actions, all amid the vicissitudes of real estate markets that shape the urban fabric. The timing of change is unpredictable, as is its scope.

## TURNING POINTS

When the first theater built expressly for showing films opened in 1914, the 3,000 seats in the handsome Strand Theatre at Broadway and 47th Street made it the largest and most elaborate moving picture house in New York, the first modern "Cathedral of Moving Picture Palaces." Two years later, the 2,000-seat Rialto at Seventh and 42nd Street, self-described "Temple of the Motion Picture," replaced Hammerstein's Victoria. Further up Broadway just above 49th Street, the 2,100-seat Rivoli opened next, also in 1916, sporting a façade that would evoke the label "Parthenon of Times Square." The stately theater was called "the direct result of the prosperity long enjoyed by the Strand and the Rialto."[4]

The fast-paced competitive drive to build the biggest, most opulent, fantastically ornamented monuments to popular pleasure had just begun. In 1919, the new Capitol Theatre—with 5,320 seats, possibly the largest and surely the most lavish movie palace in the world—overshadowed the Strand, the Rialto, and the Rivoli. Still other challengers soon appeared on Broadway: Loew's State Theatre in 1921 (3,400 seats at 45th Street), Colony Theatre in 1924 (1,761 seats at 53rd Street), Embassy Theatre in 1925 (556 seats at 46th Street), Warners' Theatre in 1925 (1,322 seats, converted out of the Piccadilly Theatre between 51st and 52nd Streets), and Paramount Theatre in 1927 (3,664 seats between 43rd and 44th Streets, built on the Astor site of the former Putnam Building). The opulence of each new theater kept upping the ante in a competitive dynamic. Before the Paramount even opened, it was eclipsed by the 6,200-seat Roxy (at 50th Street and Seventh Avenue), which captured the latest accolades for size, opulence, and

**2.1** Promotional giveaway for Samuel L. Rothafel's famous Roxy Theatre, built at a cost of $12 million. Staggering in size and opulence, the theater opened its doors on March 11, 1927, on a midblock site east of Seventh Avenue between 50th and 51st Streets. The Roxy presented major Hollywood films in programs that also featured musical performances with a 110-member symphony orchestra. Demolished 1960. Centpacrr (digital image) via Wikimedia Commons.

lavish theatricality. Built by William Fox for Samuel L. Rothafel, "Roxy" as most Americans would come to know of him, the most inventive motion-picture showman of his time, this "Cathedral of the Motion Picture" marked the apogee of entertainment in Times Square—just as "talkies" appeared on the scene.

Visually elaborate spectacles, the movie palaces were unlike anything the working-class throngs of laborers, clerks, mechanics, tradesmen, secretaries, and housewives had experienced, short of the leisure-time extravagances at Coney Island. They brought democratic splendor to the white-tie-and-tails Great White Way. Their allure was unmistakable, the nightly evidence unequivocal: "Broadway at the theater-hour belongs to the people," Will Irwin wrote in 1927, "to the unnumbered, overwhelming crowds pouring into Times Square from Hudson tube, Long Island tube, West Side tube; and there, herded by the police, distributing themselves to Roxy's Theater . . . to the Paramount, the Strand, the Rialto, the Capitol and the Rivoli." The Roxy, intellectuals were quick to point out, "was not built for the same clientele that patronizes the Metropolitan Opera House, nor decorated to please, or thrill, that clientele . . . [but] the multitude who as yet are rather unsophisticated in matters of architecture and decoration, and who probably gaze upon it with awe, and name it 'grand.'"[5] And they did. The general public adored the Roxy, filled its thousands of seats night after night, reportedly drawing six and a half million patrons its first year in operation.

As physical manifestations of popular culture, the movie palaces were a powerful instrument of the theatrical fantasy. As distribution outlets for a single-picture studio, the managers of these palaces were selling the place, developing patronage. The escapist environment the studios created was designed to ensure the return of their mass-market audience week after week. Without sound, the technically crude films of these early cinematic years were only part of an "eclectic repertory" of live performances and musical concerts interwoven with the feature presentation. Besides their opulence, many of the palaces offered grand spaces for socializing, multistory rotundas and mezzanines that added to the theater experience, enabling patrons to meet and chat during intermissions. And in the competitive battle for the mass audience, motion pictures brought in special effects that were impossible or impractical in theater plays. While the Great White Way was still "the place where Somebodies and the Nobodies from Everywhere rub shoulders for an evening,"[6] its audiences were dividing themselves between movies and legitimate theater.

The Depression would severely challenge both entertainments. Even before the stock market crashed on October 29, 1929, Broadway's legitimate theaters were a threatened species. The decade's theater-building boom had greatly increased their numbers beyond audiences' ability to sustain the theater business, consigning the oldest theaters to darkness and obsolescence. One month before the crash, one of Broadway's most successful producers, Al Woods, told the *Times* that there were forty too many legitimate theaters on Broadway, and of the eighty-five first-class theaters in New York, he expected at least thirty to close on and off during the season. It wasn't just New York that possessed too many theaters, he said; the problem was national. And the motion-picture houses were overseated as well: "when the novelty of the 'talkies' dies, and the picture companies have to have at least four hundred 'talkies' to keep the different circuit open, where are they going to get the material from?"[7]

Juiced by business opportunity presented by the omnipotent crowds jamming the streets day and night, property values in the district were running high, and enthusiasts expected them to go higher. Three of the ten most valuable sites in Manhattan were on West 42nd Street, according to a *Times* ranking; Broadway at 42nd Street—known as "the 24-hour corner"—ranked third on the list. The most valuable block in the ten-block bowtie area—that between 43rd and 44th Streets west of Broadway, where the Paramount Building and theater had opened in 1927—registered a 720 percent increase in assessed value between 1905 and 1930, twice that for the bowtie blocks as a whole. "Every Hour Busy in Times Square" was the headline heralding Times Square as the busiest location in the city's entire rapid transit system.[8] More new mass transit connections were coming, in particular with the completion of the Eighth Avenue subway (1932), which was bound to further intensify land speculation.

Theaters whose underlying land carried a value greater than the theatrical operations remained in place only as prime candidates for replacement. Some replacements were already in motion. On a narrow 42nd Street frontage, the Uris brothers were developing the 22-story Dixie Hotel (completed in 1930, renamed Carter Hotel in 1976). Other developers were working on plans to replace at least two 42nd Street theaters, the Lyric and American, with 30-story office buildings. The stock market crash foiled these incipient plans, though it did little to dampen realty interests' optimism for the city's westward growth trajectory. By nature, realty interests tend to be bullish on the market. Optimism could not, however, forestall the slow but inexorable toll of the Depression.

Before the Depression darkened Broadway's legitimate theaters in 1932, a cascade of conversions to film houses or radio broadcasting or television studios was already in the works; several others would convert into elaborate restaurant-theaters. More than a few became burlesque houses. But many remained dark for years. The Shubert Organization, Broadway's largest landlord, was thrown into receivership. Al Woods declared bankruptcy, as would Arch Selwyn. The Chanin brothers had six Broadway theaters by 1927, but lost control of all of them. In mid-1935, forty-seven of the sixty-eight theaters in the district—with

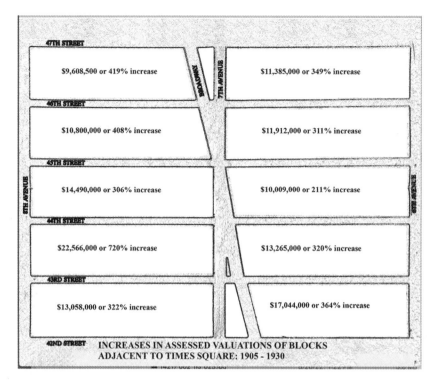

2.2 Twenty-five years of rising valuations on the ten blocks surrounding the Times Square bowtie. The block where the 33-story Paramount Building rose in 1927 registered the highest valuation—a sevenfold increase between 1905 and 1930. Research and graphic by the author.

a combined seating capacity of 55,000—originally built to house legitimate theatrical productions were owned by banks, other lenders, or estates. Of those forty-seven, only nine had been used for live productions in the previous season. More telling, Maidman told the *Real Estate Record*, the land underlying these sixty-eight theaters accounted for nearly 80 percent of their aggregate 1935 assessed values. Even though the future for theater was hard to predict, he believed that theater owners "may have seen their worst days."[9]

Well, time was not on their side. Demolition had already taken the landmarks of a former theater era: the Casino (1930), Knickerbocker (1930), American (1930), and New York and Criterion Theatres (1935) fashioned out of Hammerstein's Olympia. A few years later, two more would fall: the George M. Cohan (1938) and Hippodrome (1939). When the banks began to sell their repossessed theater holdings in the late 1930s and early '40s, there was no guarantee that theater operations would resume, even if those in theater business purchased the theaters.

As the land beneath these low-rise theaters continued to escalate sharply in value, more of them were destined to be replaced by higher-value, higher-density offices or hotels. In the 1940s, the wrecker's ball claimed another ten Times Square theaters.

Although the Depression dealt a heavy blow to the theater industry in New York, it was not fatal. The Shuberts recovered their choicest theatrical properties, if only by feats of legal legerdemain. The Chanins, commanding builders of quality eye-catching structures with a sense of theatrical style, also recovered financially and left an extraordinary building legacy validated decades later by the New York City Landmarks Preservation Commission, including six legitimate theaters (the 46th Street, Biltmore [now the Samuel J. Friedman], Mansfield [now the Brooks Atkinson], Theatre Masque [now the Golden], Royale, and Majestic) as well as the Art Deco 56-story Chanin Building on the eastern end of 42nd Street across from Grand Central Terminal, and the twin-towered Century Apartments and Majestic Apartments, two of a small set of apartment buildings that define the skyline of Central Park West. In the decades ahead, legitimate theater productions would continue to define a core element of a more diverse set of entertainments in Times Square, although the total number of productions could not sustain the height of earlier seasons.

On the 42nd Street Rialto, the death throes had started earlier, when Prohibition took effect in 1920. During that decade, as land values soared to reflect the street's business potential, rising rents led to more intense uses. The legitimate theaters, low in density and dedicated to a single use that had a short season of nine or ten months and a schedule of nine plays a week, found it difficult to generate sufficient revenues to retain command over the street. High production costs further exacerbated the economic squeeze. Raising the price of theater tickets would only go so far before it cut into the theater audience. At first, theater owners found a solution in leasing part of their space to restaurants, roof gardens, and nightclubs, but those businesses could not survive without the sale of liquor. Speakeasies—so abundant in New York that they were usually the subject of ironic jest—were seen as an economic liability to some in the realty industry who claimed they were "ruining midtown property values."[10] Even the ending of Prohibition in 1933 could not help those restaurants, hotels, and roof gardens that had already closed.

The 1930s proved to be the turning point for the famous theater street as a "class" entertainment district. The new economic formula for popular entertainment demanded continuous play and large turnover, a business strategy based on volume and lower prices and an emphasis on off-the-street trade—the motion picture model. Movies also found an economic and demographic niche in audiences for whom theater was too expensive, vaudeville too crude, and nickelodeons too dark, dirty, and cheap. Priced for a "middling" audience, David Nasaw wrote in *Going Out: The Rise and Fall of Public Amusements*, movies also had tremendous success in attracting the female audience, which testified to their newfound reputation as respectable entertainment for a broad range of city folk.[11] To the elites, the "subway crowd" had taken over Times Square.

Once the choice live venue for shows by noted playwrights, the theaters on 42nd Street converted to motion pictures, burlesque, or vaudeville beginning in 1930. The first to go was Wallack's, a Hammerstein theater, which had opened in 1904 under the name Lew M. Fields. The next year, Billy Minsky converted the Republic, another Hammerstein theater, into the street's first burlesque house, and others were soon to follow. After Woods's bankruptcy, the new operator of the Eltinge also turned to burlesque. Within two years of the Minsky brothers' move into Times Square—they had been pioneers in burlesque when they acquired the National Winter Garden Theatre on the Bowery in 1913— four continuous-performance "grind" houses showing male-oriented action films occupied the famous theater block. The New Amsterdam was the last to shut its lights on legitimate theater on West 42nd Street with a production of Shakespeare's *Othello* in 1937. An era in entertainment history had ended.

Theaters converted to movies soon discovered that they could no longer command important first-run movies and resorted to showing grinders—reruns of older movies emphasizing action and violence that

**2.3** The New Gotham Chorus at Minsky's Burlesque in New York City. Etching by Reginald Marsh, 1936. Granger.

appealed to a male rather than a family audience. The grinders brought a new kind of commercial promotion to the street: garish marquees, sexually suggestive posters, bizarre devices to lure crowds, and gravel-voiced "barkers" to induce passersby into the movies. This more than the movies per se was what detracted from the reputation and appearance of the street, turning it into a low-status honky-tonk locale and setting in motion a chain of declining fortunes. During the Depression, street crime, with its cascading impact, became a major problem as well. The decline forced hotels to lower their prices to attract patrons, as was the case with restaurants. Long considered colorful and uninhibited, West 42nd Street turned tawdry, a down-at-the-heels former star performer perceived by many as unsafe and indecent as well. It was not yet infiltrated by the drug trade, but that would come later.

The one bright spot on the street emerged in 1935, when despite conditions earlier described by the *Times* as "disturbed," the Italian-born developer Arthur Campagna[12] erected a new Rialto Theatre on the 100 percent corner of Times Square, long regarded as one of the most valuable sites in the city, that had been the site of Hammerstein's Victoria Theatre. The Art Moderne Rialto made news because of the large new electrical advertising display built on top of the theater, which featured a triangular tower 80 feet high made of milky-white glass tile, flood-lighted to advertise the distilling giant's name, Schenley, then the largest liquor company in the United States. In addition to the distiller's name, a moving sign carried nightclub and theater news. Built after the end of Prohibition, the building boasted the largest glass-block façade in New York City colored in terra-cotta and blue and gold mirrored glass sporting streamlined aluminum fins.

Designed exclusively for movies by theater design specialist Thomas Lamb and architect Rosario Candela, the new Rialto included "high-class" stores on the ground floor, a special subway entrance, offices, and a restaurant above with a circular dance floor. It opened for Christmas with Texas-born big-game hunter Frank Buck staring in the film *Fang and Claw*, an idea picture distinctly masculine in tone in keeping with the policy of theater manager Arthur Mayer. The house, Mayer explained in a newspaper interview after the opening, both in styling and choice of films, sought to satisfy the "ancient and unquenchable male thirst for mystery, menace and manslaughter." Soon called the "merchant of menace," Mayer set a price scale—25 cents in the morning, 40 cents during matinee hours, and 65 cents at night—catering to all budgets of the masses. Curiously, the 750-seat theater was relatively modest in size compared to its 2,000-seat predecessor. Also curiously,

**2.4** Mystery and melodrama films advertised on the billboard in front of a midblock theater on 42nd Street in the 1930s, a time when movies had taken over on 42nd Street. Billy Rose Theatre Collection, The New York Public Library.

**2.5** The new Rialto (with Schenley Tower) in 1936, erected on the site of Hammerstein's Victoria by real estate developer Arthur Campagna the year before. Designed exclusively for movies, the Rialto featured films distinctly masculine in tone. Fox Photos via Getty Images.

it rose only three stories on a theater location that, as the *New York Herald Tribune* noted, "probably is redolent of more show history than any other Broadway spot." The assessed worth of that historic location had risen fifteenfold since 1900. In realty terms, the new Rialto Theatre was a gussied-up "taxpayer" biding its time until hoped-for more prosperous times brought opportunities for higher-value development. It would be a very long wait. In the decades-long interregnum, the theater declined in parallel with West 42nd Street, and in the 1960s it was "satisfying another seemingly 'ancient and unquenchable thirst' for pornographic movies."[13]

By the eve of World War II, the physical changes that had taken place on West 42nd Street during the 1930s came to tarnish Broadway as well. The lobster palaces were long gone, replaced by cheap luncheonettes. The cabarets were gone, replaced by cheap dance halls. The past glamour of an era of exclusivity, of Rector's and its cohort of nightclubs and blithe restaurants, was gone. The moneyed class bemoaned the garish carnivalesque playground that Times Square had become with its shooting galleries, palm readings, flea circus, countless street pitchmen, and grifters. "The area was not simply in decline," remarked theater historian Brooks McNamara, "but in the process of redefinition," a transition to an entertainment district aimed at the broad, popular audience.[14] The wage-earning working class had taken over.

## INTERMEZZO

The outbreak of World War II brought a renewed sense of prosperity to Times Square. Despite aging theaters and tarnished glamour, it was the nation's place for entertainment, and each week more than six million military visitors and civilians flooded into Times Square. The district, declared the Broadway Association, was experiencing the "greatest boom in its history." Founded in 1911 by a group of prominent businessmen in Times Square to further the betterment of West Midtown, the not-for-profit interest group was keeping close tabs on conditions in its vested territory. Based on a four-month survey reported out in the fall of 1943, restaurants in the district served five million meals a week; weekly patronage at the forty-four motion-picture houses exceeded 1.5 million and at the thirty-nine legitimate theaters 220,000; the fifty-three nightclubs and cabarets saw 225,540 patrons.[15]

As before, people came for fun and entertainment, to consume the abundant mix of movies, dance halls, arcades, popular shows, nightclubs, shooting galleries, and all-night restaurants. The uniforms of servicemen from the Allied nations showed the crowd to be made up of the friends and families of the soldiers and sailors, a fusion of nations seeking amusement and respite from the strain of war and war work. For many, the whole scene—bright lights, shops, restaurants and nightclubs, and the extraordinary vitality of street life—was the first experience of big-city life. And when celebration was the order of the day, Times Square was the place to be, as on August 15, 1945, when, in anticipation of the war's ending, crowds gathered beneath a miniature version of the Statue of Liberty and the Times Tower's news ribbon to rejoice in the announcement of peace. By seven o'clock, the crowd had swelled to 750,000 when the message came across in lights: "Official— Truman Announced Japanese Surrender." As it grew into the evening, the celebratory crowd of an estimated two million packed the area from 40th to 48th Streets between Sixth and Eighth Avenues. Times Square had reached the peak of its national prominence, which Alfred Eisenstaedt captured in his iconic image of a US Navy sailor embracing and kissing a white-clad nurse in Times Square on V-J day.

The brief prosperity of the wartime boom could not, however, reverse the cultural changes that had transformed 42nd Street and Times Square during the decade-long Depression. Once the Broadway Association

**2.6** Crowds gathered in Times Square awaiting news of the end of World War II, August 15, 1945. A six-story replica of the Statue of Liberty in the background had been recording the dollar amount of each issue of war loans. Hulton Archives via Getty Images.

realized that the seedy boardwalk-type enterprises would not disappear on their own, the business group began a campaign against the "carnival atmosphere" and honky-tonk establishments of Times Square. The shooting galleries and souvenir photograph places were a problem. Penny arcades and "sucker-auction" establishments were a problem. Gift shops selling shoddy merchandise and factory rejects baiting gullible out-of-towners were a problem. Illicit peddlers and professional vendors who set up displays in suitcases in the middle of the sidewalk offering everything from nylons to live turtles were street nuisances, and their pampering by city magistrates a problem. Blaring music out into the streets, another problem. Midtown property owners concerned about property values worried about "midway" cheapening of the district. Commercialism they understood, but it should be respectable. The association's president said the steady deterioration of Times Square was bad for the city because it reflected New York City's image in the eyes of the world, poorly. In short, Times Square was a reputational problem.

The association wanted the whole area purged of "objectionable" enterprises that created a boardwalk-type environment, and in 1948,

**2.7** Honky-tonk amusement center at 242 West 42nd Street, home to Hubert's Museum and Flea Circus (1925–1969), 1954. Peep booths took over in the 1970s, and the building was demolished in 1996 to make way for Madame Tussauds Wax Museum. Angelo Rizzuto, Library of Congress Prints and Photographic Division.

and again in 1954, it asked the City Planning Commission and Board of Estimate for zoning changes to upgrade Times Square. "It was within the Planning Commission's province," argued the *Times* in the first of five editorials on the issue, "to try to stem the tide of degradation of our Great White Way."[16] As evidenced by the unusual number of editorials on the issue, the *Times* had a vested interest in the social and economic state of its eponymous home. Having quickly outgrown the space in its flagship Times Tower after six years with no possibility for expansion on an adjoining site, in 1912 the newspaper of record built a larger 11-story headquarters building, the Annex, about 200 feet away on the north side of West 43rd Street between Seventh and Eighth Avenues, for its editorial and executive departments and production facilities. A staff of six hundred persons who worked in the Annex would pass through the district every day.

Mayor Robert F. Wagner Jr.'s administration delivered with revisions to the zoning code designed to "drive the honky-tonks from Times Square." The new rules prohibited the opening of any new so-called open-door nuisance establishments—freak shows, wax museums, shooting galleries, games arcades, open-front stores, sidewalk cafés, and ground-floor auction rooms—but they did not force those already in operation to close. In time, the new codes would work to a perverse and unintended effect: by driving out competitors for space on the street, "they gave a leg up to dirty-book dealers looking for storefronts . . . not the self-proclaimed 'adult' bookstores of the 1970s," wrote Anthony Bianco in *Ghosts of 42nd Street*, "but general-interest shops that kept the risqué stuff in the back room and also appealed to a hipster clientele by stocking avant-garde literary works that ran afoul of censors."[17]

It was during this period of the early 1950s that the character of Nathan Detroit, the crap-game promoter of *Guys and Dolls*, and his crowd of gamblers, nightclub entertainers, and street-corner salvationists in a fictional New York City captured the attention of a national audience. More than three million people saw the musical hit during its three-year run on Broadway before Samuel Goldwyn brought the movie version to many more millions. The raffish characters of this musical fable of Broadway, based on a story and characters invented by Damon Runyon, acted in front of scenery designed to evoke the Great White Way. There was more than a whiff of resemblance to reality in the amicable grifters of this fast-paced world of fun and fraud, who operated in a half-world between respectability and crime never more than a jump or two ahead of the law. The world of Times Square in the 1950s idealized in the tinsel fantasy was edgy, but it was not yet terribly dangerous. The sexual revolution of the 1960s had not begun, nor had drugs deeply infiltrated the place. Families were still coming to Times Square. People of a certain age, the baby boom generation, remember this period in a positive light.

## MARKET MESSAGES

West Side property owners had reason to hope that Times Square would benefit from a midtown building boom, but when commercial development in New York resumed after the war—there was no office development after 1933, other than Rockefeller Center—it bypassed Times Square. Commercial developers were focused on the eastern side of midtown in the district around Grand Central Terminal, picking up where the 1920s building boom left off and pioneering a new corridor on Park Avenue for the expansion of corporate headquarters and large-scale speculative office towers. Nineteen office towers were built on Park Avenue between 1947 and 1964, and although only five were home to corporations (Lever House, Seagrams, Pepsi-Cola, Union Carbide, and Citicorp), their choice of Park Avenue, on a tony stretch of the then-residential avenue where the wealthy had built their mansions and swank apartment houses reigned, conferred status and validated the centrality of East Midtown as the city's premier office district. In the years ahead, developers pursued the opportunity there en masse.

It no longer seemed likely that change would reshape Times Square along the corporate lines of Rockefeller Center. During the 1960s, when the building boom remodeled Sixth Avenue into a 14-block stretch of office towers—over 20 million square feet of new space erected in 18 towers between 56th and 42nd Streets from 1959 to 1974—Broadway found builders scarce. Building speculative office towers on the more prestigious Park, Madison, and Fifth Avenues and their tributaries, all close to commuters coming from northern suburbs into Grand Central Terminal, or on Sixth, Third, or Lexington Avenues was far less risky than venturing into Times Square, where social conditions were fast growing more difficult.

Seventeen years of furious commercial development delivered 169 new office buildings with more than 61 million square feet—equivalent to the combined office inventory of the nation's third and fifth largest central-city office markets, San Francisco and Houston, in 1974. All but eleven were built in the propertied quadrangle bounded by 40th Street to the south and 59th Street to the north, Third Avenue to the east and Sixth Avenue to the west. The scope and pace of this postwar office construction transformed the face of midtown and established its hegemony as the city's modern business district, surpassing in importance the city's historic business center in downtown Manhattan.

The Uris brothers, builders of the pre-Depression Dixie Hotel in Times Square and among the very first to develop in midtown after the war, built fourteen office towers between 1949 and 1972, all but three on the East Side. Only in the late 1960s did they travel crosstown to Times Square to erect the 48-story Paramount Plaza (1971), a 2.2-million-square-foot behemoth (housing the Gershwin and Circle in the Square theaters), on Broadway at 50th Street on the site of the large and lavish Capitol Theatre movie palace (1919), which had dominated the film exhibition business for decades. The new building, a harbinger of what was to come, did not inspire: years later writing in the *Times*, architectural critic Paul Goldberger called the 1633 Broadway building "a black box that may be the worst tower in midtown Manhattan." Another new office building in the district, 1500 Broadway, a 34-story tower (1972) developed by Arlen Realty and Development, replaced the 16-story stately Beaux-Arts-style Claridge (formerly the Rector) Hotel at

44th Street. When the character of the Times Square district was being debated in the mid-1980s, Goldberger warned that these huge office buildings were "essentially incompatible" with the physical essence that has long characterized Times Square—the "light, the energy, the sense of contained chaos . . . they squash it, as firmly as a shoe might flatten an ant."[18]

Once again, speculators eyed the unfulfilled potential of Eighth Avenue and its tributary streets abuzz with activity—but again it became a case study of frustrated realty ambitions. After the war ended, but before the 1970s contagion of social conditions on 42nd Street and in Times Square squashed development plans, investment syndicates and private interests had taken to betting on a future of hotel, office, and residential towers stretching north from 42nd Street to Columbus Circle at 59th Street. A new cohort of speculators following the same ambitions pursued by others in the late 1920s started buying block-front parcels of walk-up tenements and small business buildings on or adjacent to Eighth Avenue, assembling parcels into larger holdings that someday, they hoped, would give way to modern structures. Active buying and selling of property, particularly around the then-location of Madison Square Garden in the low West 50s, continued unabated throughout the 1950s, leading the *Times* to say, "Eighth Avenue may be on its way to losing its label as a white elephant of the midtown real estate world."[19]

Irving Maidman was in the forefront of this activity, but he was not alone in hoping to see "the shabby decadence of the area . . . transformed to one of sparkling, tax-producing modernity," as the *Times* put it.[20] Two other speculators had even larger accumulated holdings, and many others had smaller holdings. Seymour Durst, one of the city's experienced assembly experts before he became a prominent commercial developer, was also active in Hell's Kitchen. He was buying on a block that was almost entirely residential and yet had the highest commercial zoning allowed, which would have allowed him or another developer to transform it with office towers as of right, without seeking special zoning adjustments. After the better part of a decade and scores of separate transactions, Durst succeeded in acquiring the entire block from 42nd all the way to 43rd from Ninth to Tenth Avenues, some seventy different parcels, including several owned by Maidman, on which he tentatively planned to build an office tower. In the early 1970s, he sold the block to another developer, Richard Ravitch, who built Manhattan Plaza (1977), a large federally subsidized residential complex that became home to many performing artists and others in the entertainment business and helped start a process of change on the further reaches of West 42nd Street, as I discuss in later chapters.

Increasing signs of activity prompted the irrepressible president of Webb & Knapp, William Zeckendorf Sr., "Big Bill" of realty fame, to describe the district as "the only remaining area in Manhattan where property was available for massive developments."[21] He had reason to be promotional. As manager for Vincent Astor's properties during the war, Zeckendorf was likely to be more familiar than most with the west side of midtown, and after the war he had begun buying properties in the Times Square district for his own account. In 1956, he purchased the Hotel Lincoln on Eighth Avenue between 44th and 45th Streets (originally built by Chanin, 1928), which he was remodeling into the Hotel Manhattan. Several years earlier, he had taken control of the Hotel Astor but flipped it to Sheraton, only to reacquire it in 1958. (Years later he would acquire the Taft Hotel, Roxy Theatre, and Paramount Building.) Zeckendorf had an uncanny skill at recognizing hidden land value, but his view of Times Square as ripe for change was shared by others. Land prices were reportedly far below those on the east side of Manhattan, where prices were skyrocketing, and on the west side sites strategically located for both residential and commercial construction were more readily available.

Realty optimism was brewing in early transactions, foreshadowing a trend that would alarm theater interests and preservationists in the mid-1960s. In 1953, the Empire Theatre at Broadway and 40th Street was demolished to make way for an office building (1430 Broadway, 1956) in an expanding Garment District. In 1954, wreckers took down Marc Klaw's theater, which had long been operating as a radio studio but whose new owners thought they might construct a hotel above the theater. Maidman's Vanderbilt Theatre also went down that year. Both theaters were replaced with parking lots, as was the 48th Street Theatre the following year. In 1960, the opulent Roxy was replaced with a 23-story office tower (1963).

When the Roxy went down, it was enough of an event for a performance by Gloria Swanson, actress and one of the film industry's pioneering women filmmakers, to memorialize the demolition. (Swanson's production *The Love of Sunya* had opened with great fanfare at the theater on March 12, 1927.) Dressed in a black Jean Louis sheath and $170,000 worth of jewels complete with elbow-length black gloves and a long fuzzy red scarf, the great star posed for *Life* magazine photographer Eliot Elisofon on October 16, 1960, amidst the rubble of the once-majestic Roxy lamenting its loss. "The image is wildly dramatic,

**2.8** Postcard view of the 1,400-room Hotel Lincoln (1928), renamed Hotel Manhattan after a $13 million makeover by William Zeckendorf Sr. and Jr. Reported to be New York's first "new" hotel in 25 years, its phoenix-like renewal in the mid-1950s was seen as a harbinger of better times for Eighth Avenue. Collection of the author.

appropriately theatrical, but also highly resonant emotionally because it is loaded with symbolism for the end of the studio system in its last stages of collapse and for the end of the era of the 'great movie star' that Swanson represented."[22]

Four years later, another shock: the showcase Paramount Theatre closed. Then in 1967, its newest owners announced plans to convert its vast ornate space, where the greatest bandsmen of an era had played, into eight floors of offices. That same year, wreckers took down the Metropolitan Opera House, occupying a full block bounded by Broadway and Seventh Avenue, 39th and 40th Streets, to make way for Chanin's 22-story banal box of an office building (1411 Broadway, 1969). Impending dramatic change in Times Square was undeniable, if not immediate.

Members of the West Side Association of Commerce pushed the city to rezone sixty-four blockfronts in the area for commercial uses, hoping that builders' plans for extensive development of the area would make it a rival of East Midtown. "Once developers set their sights on the West Side, it will only be a matter of time before this once ugly duckling area is upgraded to the point where all its latent potential is fully realized,"

Maidman optimistically remarked in 1960.[23] Other investors would likewise come to assume that the West Side was the next logical area to search for development sites. Reading the signs of change, realtors and city planners did not believe Times Square could survive solely as an entertainment district. Competition threatened—from the rise of television and family-oriented suburban living as well as the development of Lincoln Center (new home for the Metropolitan Opera and other cultural institutions) just north of Columbus Circle on the Upper West Side of Manhattan, built as part of Robert Moses's program of urban renewal in the 1950s and '60s.

When, in 1963, Allied Chemical Corporation purchased the namesake Times Tower with the aim of transforming the icon into a "showcase for chemistry," *Business Week* heralded the move as the "promise that Times Square, which had become a decaying travesty of its once proud self, was in for a change." The irony, of course, was that Allied Chemical's chief executive was "binding his company's image to a place where the established interest in chemistry was notoriously of the sexual sort." Boldly promoting the tower and its presence in Times Square, Allied declared: "it's new! it's colorful! it's fashion-full! it's open now!" The $10 million facelift (nearly $98 million in 2022 dollars) had produced a bland façade—what Ada Louise Huxtable called "a no-style skin of lavatory white marble with the look of cut cardboard."[24] Long considered the symbolic heart of the area, the tower's renovation appalled preservationists and seemed to make no sense to those outside realty circles. Inside those circles, however, the corporation's purchase of the Times Tower appeared to be the long-awaited watershed moment validating Times Square as a corporate location.

Just a year earlier, the *Times* had been asking why the "building boom that is transforming the face of midtown Manhattan failed to advance on Broadway," where only one significant structure had been built since the end of World War II. The reasons were many, but the lack of activity boiled down to the real estate industry's opinion that Broadway wasn't a business neighborhood. Corporate tenants did not want to be in the Theater District; their desire for prestige did not fit with the entertainment image of the district. Straightaway, Allied Chemical's decision reversed that prevailing presumption. It convinced some of the city's developers that it was only a matter of time until office development moved beyond the Sixth Avenue corridor.

A flurry of speculative purchases of blockfronts on Broadway followed, if not so immediately new skyscrapers. The area was not yet "ripe," according to Durst. Opinions were varied. Some realty men were

**2.9** Postcard image of the Times Tower reclad in a thin skin of "lavatory white marble"—still an icon, still a symbol, however much debased. Collection of the author.

sufficiently optimistic to think that in the coming years, land values and rentals in Times Square buildings would soar to levels being realized in the prime East Side locations. With nine office projects built or planned, the *Times* prospectively saw an office-building boom on Broadway "showing that it has stepped in as understudy to Park Avenue and the Avenue of the Americas."[25] The momentum of change seemed to be growing.

The sale of the Hotel Astor to commercial developer Sam Minskoff & Sons in 1966 set the stage for the anticipated Broadway office boom. Minskoff was one of Manhattan's oldest and richest real estate families, one of the storied cohort that held remarkable sway over Manhattan development. With nary a credit to the Astor's place-making legacy, Sam Minskoff announced plans to tear down what had been an icon of Times Square since the hotel's opening in 1904. The glamorous Astor had been built solidly like a fortress, her exterior brick walls two feet thick and structural steel beams and upright columns of an unusually heavy gauge. "Taking this building down," remarked the job supervisor for the wrecking company, "is a feat of engineering, not demolition." In its place Minskoff would construct One Astor Plaza, a 54-story tower containing 1.4 million square feet of office space. Others who made speculative purchases in the district would wait to see how the Minskoff tower, scheduled to begin construction in 1968, fared before moving forward with their plans. As the first new office tower on Broadway since the 33-story Paramount Building opened nearby in 1927, One Astor Plaza "marked the dramatic acceleration in the shift from Times Square's principal role as a nighttime world of entertainment to its hitherto secondary daytime role as an office district."[26]

Tucked into the new tower were two theaters: the 1,621-seat Minskoff Theatre suitable for large theatrical productions and a 1,500-seat movie theater. Both were products of the city's Special Theater District ordinance passed in December 1967, after arduous negotiations between city officials and the Minskoffs. In exchange for including theaters and other amenities, developers were allowed to build 20 percent more office space than the zoning would have otherwise allowed. The policy was designed to direct market forces and support the theater industry through new construction; it was not designed to preserve Broadway's existing theaters. At the time, "city planners were not sensitive to the precarious future that New York's entertainment industry faced," Robert A. M. Stern and his colleagues wrote in their history of architecture and urbanism of the development era. "Moreover, few people, even those who struggled to preserve the theater district, saw the existing theaters as inherently worth saving."[27] Designed in a different era, many theaters were considered passé as well as uncomfortable. Planners in the city's Urban Design Group envisioned the area's future as a mixed-use district of new office buildings that included theaters, which would make Times Square a round-the-clock neighborhood of both work and pleasure. With a near-term construction boom looking likely, city officials believed that the westward expansion of the midtown office district would be beneficial for New York. In a historic sense, the marriage of theaters and offices was a page taken from how builders in the 1920s coped with rising land values on Broadway when developing the Paramount, Loew's State, and Embassy Theatres.

Mayor John V. Lindsay also believed that economic development in the form of office development would drive the crime, drugs, and sex industry out of Times Square. The thrust of the innovate zoning policy, recalled Norman Marcus, general counsel to the City Planning Commission and author of the legal language of this and subsequent special districts, aimed to "preserve New York City's position as the national theater capital without curtailing construction of high-rise office buildings that were steadily replacing the old, uneconomic, two- and three-story theaters." The incentive plan "reflected more than just sentiment and nostalgia," he wrote. "There were compelling findings linking New York's pre-eminence as a national corporate headquarters to its theaters around which so many related activities, such as radio and television, shopping, dining and tourism clustered."[28]

At the groundbreaking for One Astor Plaza in October 1968, the mayor, city officials, and business leaders celebrated what they saw as "a new era of economic stability for Times Square as an entertainment center." The new Special Theater District Zoning Amendment worked: it did what it was designed to do—it brought about new legitimate theaters in two other office buildings before the collapse of the city's office market in the mid-1970s. Unfortunately, as Stern and his colleagues emphasized, "There was little to admire about any of the new theaters except that they existed at all."[29]

Broadway was vulnerable, as One Astor Plaza and Paramount Plaza had made clear. Economic events may have thwarted redevelopment of theater sites in the past, but the vicissitudes of the real estate cycle rarely alter the path of market growth, only its timing. In a market economy, the forces of economic change, however slow to manifest themselves, dominate in the long run. Broadway was where the competitive race for new skyscraper development would be staged. It was where land assemblages were proceeding quietly with the expectation of an expanding

**2.10** Scaffolding surrounds the formerly glamorous Hotel Astor in preparation for its demolition, 1967. It was replaced by a 54-story office tower, One Astor Plaza; in response to zoning incentives for a taller tower, the tower tucked two theaters within that were not much admired. Bettmann via Getty Images.

midtown office district. It was where the underused zoning capacity of the district's low-density theaters and five-to-seven-story buildings created "soft spots"—parcels of land awaiting redevelopment. Not just theaters were at risk; the building health of the whole area was tenuous. Old-time businesses—a Liggett's, a Woolworth's, restaurants, backstage suppliers of Broadway—were closing as rents and expenses went up; even Chemical Bank closed its branch in Times Square.

Medium-sized office buildings fronted and interspersed with great theater marquees and smaller-scale low-rise buildings had defined the image of Times Square. The open space in the middle, the bow-tie framed by the openness of the sky, what author Tony Hiss labeled "the bowl of light," had been the experience of the square. This would change dramatically. Following the dictates of market opportunities in the postwar era abetted by zoning incentives, the speculative high-rise office towers on Broadway built between 1971 and 1990 would dwarf in scale the low- and modest-height buildings of the past. Although the future could not recover the glamour of a different era, a buttoned-down corporate enclave such as was emerging nearby on Sixth Avenue and further east on the other side of midtown did not square with the colorful commercial-aesthetic image of Times Square. The threat to the urban fabric of the Theater District lay not in the new office buildings per se, but in the loss of existing theaters and the urban-design implications of a Broadway fashioned by high-density office buildings. Before this could happen, the city's fiscal crisis brought commercial development to a standstill throughout the city, not just in Times Square, where it brought "the indefinite postponement of office construction on sites painfully, lengthily and expensively assembled for that purpose a decade or more ago."[30] At the same time, commercialized sex was rapidly permeating Times Square.

## SPECULATIVE CASUALTY

Irving Maidman was an early believer in the real estate potential of the lands west of Times Square, especially 42nd Street, where in 1944 he started accumulating parcels on the 400 block between Ninth and Tenth Avenues. The commonplace nineteenth-century buildings and tenements on small lots were indistinguishable from those on many other side streets where a mix of street-level businesses and upper-floor apartments prevailed. Years later, he leased a bigger site on the block (no. 416–418) that once housed a branch of the defunct Bank of United States, the bank that was for many a symbol of the Depression, a bleak era that had much to do with the decline of legitimate theater on West 42nd Street. From these real estate beginnings, he would gamble on a return of legitimate theater to 42nd Street. In 1960, at a cost of $100,000 (over $1 million in 2022 dollars) in the shell of that bank building, he opened the 199-seat Maidman Playhouse, the first of a series of small theaters he would open in the next two years on a block widely considered too far from Broadway to attract theatergoers. It was a quixotic venture.

Theater columnists noted his bold initiative, and realty interests commended him for erecting a playhouse that called attention to a hoped-for resurgence of the area. Maidman's new theater saw the first opening of a legitimate theater play in the district since *Othello* opened in January 1937 in The New Amsterdam Theatre, 42nd Street's Art Nouveau crown jewel. Although this first offering, Russell Patterson's nostalgic review *Sketchbook*, was a flop, the theater itself received a rave review from the *Times* theater critic: "The seats and carpets are plush, the sight-lines excellent, the L-shaped foyer is smartly decorated with paintings, the bar is strategically situated and the over-all theater design by Mr. Patterson is tasteful."[31] As in the three more theaters he would develop, the Playhouse also included rehearsal halls and workshops for building and storing sets, props, and costumes—critically important space in short supply throughout the Theater District.

Maidman's vision was based on real estate logic. A frequent "angel" of Thespis, Maidman was boldly betting on the future of Off-Off-Broadway (theaters with less than 100 seats) by developing new intimate theaters a class above the typical converted stores, lofts, or basements of playhouses in Greenwich Village. Building fully equipped houses for professional productions, he believed, could reconstitute the historic legacy of West 42nd Street, off Broadway. While he hoped his vision would showcase the theaters, in line with classic real estate reasoning he believed theatrical success would boost the value of his considerable other real estate holdings west of Eighth Avenue, which included the West Side Airlines Terminal (1955) and the Rivera Congress Motor Inn (1961), the first of five motels he was planning. And building not just one but a complex of theaters also fit with realty notions of creating value by drawing scores more patrons.

As bold as his theater development ambitions were, his timing suffered, badly. Although the early 1960s was an exciting time for experimental productions in small Off-Off-Broadway theaters, the business was volatile. After only five years, Maidman shuttered all four of his theaters, pushed by a dwindling supply of sufficient theatrical material, the difficulties of making small theaters pay, and a suffocating concentration of sex establishments that had infiltrated the block. At first, he put the theaters to use as film houses and planned to put two up for auction, but if he did, there were no takers. He advertised for "legit theater groups for dramatic or musical comedy presentations," but the results indicate there were no takers. As the darkness of decline grew, the tenants he rented to supplied what the adult-entertainment market wanted: sex entertainment. He said he pursued rounds of litigation to evict deadbeat tenants and those in properties supposed to be free of live burlesque and sex films but were not. "I've spent so much money on the courts here," he told *Times* reporter Ralph Blumenthal, after discovering that sex shows were still operating at his properties. "And they laugh at you. It's sickening." He was, as Gail Sheehy noted in her eye-popping 1972 exposé of the landlords of Hell's Kitchen, "one of the self-made casualties of our flourishing pross and porno industries."[32]

**2.11** Former Maidman Playhouse (1960) tenanted by "Live Burlesk" on the 400 block of West 42nd Street. In 1976, Robert Moss would turn this decaying building into a home for his Playwrights Horizons, in what was to become the raw beginnings of Theatre Row. Courtesy of Building for the Arts NY, Inc.

Theater people looked at it differently: "He was trying to run a theater as a real estate business, and you can't do that," remarked Broadway producer Norman Twain.[33]

Nearly ten years after Maidman's theaters ceased offering legitimate theater, the prolific director and founder of the not-for-profit Playwrights Horizons, Robert Moss, appeared at Maidman's seventh-floor office in the Crossroads Building, a curious building at the end of a narrow tapered-rectangular block facing the south side of 42nd Street. "We came here because it was the only theater we could find, and we desperately needed a theater," Moss wrote in a letter to the editor of the *Times* that year, 1975. "Now we are excited about the cultural possibilities of the area. We think that our block . . . could be a cultural catalyst for the whole area."[34] Wild optimism, but he would prove prescient.

On his first look into Maidman's old theater at 422 West 42nd, he was appalled at what was "a garbage dump enclosed by walls."[35] Working against the sleaze of this commercial wasteland—whose sidewalks bustled with winos, derelicts, and prostitutes, drug dealers and their customers—Moss succeed in bringing theatrical life back to a block in no-man's land he had first known by reputation as "wildly dangerous."

Working with only volunteer labor, they gutted and rebuilt Maidman's old porno movie house and turned it into a 100-seat theater. In time, with Fred Papert and the help of the New York State Urban Development Corporation, they would become a cultural catalyst for the area and exceed, by a wide margin, Maidman's real estate vision for a theatrical block too far from the core of Times Square. They would create what we now know as Theatre Row, a story told in chapter 8.

Maidman possessed deep knowledge of Times Square. His zest for wheeling and dealing had been honed over many years, beginning as a broker in the area in 1920 and later, in 1940, as an independent operator and investor, then builder. A self-made man who had grown up in a cold-water flat with an outhouse in the back yard on the Lower East Side, he was known in the industry as "a clever and patient businessman." In addition to owning scores of parcels west of Eighth Avenue stretching all the way to the Hudson River, at various times he owned the Biltmore and Vanderbilt Theatres, the Candler Building and Harris Theatre, the Crossroads Building, the former Remington Typewriter Building, property in East Midtown, as well as real estate outside New York City.

"For almost every deal he made," Carter B. Horsley wrote in the developer's obituary in the *Times*, "Mr. Maidman had another dream."[36] His plans ran the gamut of possibilities: office buildings, apartment houses, motor hotels ("a new facet of the city's hotel life"), car garages, even a glass showcase for cars (displayed on a huge revolving oval belt) on the site of the Crossroads Cafe. Some plans materialized; others fizzled. He wanted to make a mark. The project in which he took the most pride was the West Side Airlines Terminal, at 42nd and Tenth Avenue, for which he painfully assembled the site and set the wreckers' ball to work on sixteen tenement buildings. The terminal opened in 1955 but was abandoned by the airlines in 1972, after serving for 17 years as the starting point for New York travelers flying out of Newark Airport. Maidman walked away from his investment; the terminal was taken over by the Port Authority of New York and New Jersey (which operated a bus terminal around the corner) and turned over to Papert's 42nd Street Development Corporation. By 1982, it was home to the second phase of Theatre Row. Fitting.

Maidman's real estate activities on the far side of 42nd Street, as optimistic investor at first and later as agent to the area's sex business, mirror a particular period of ferment in the city's development history. In Times Square, his dealings straddled the highs and lows of the district's most dynamic and depressed eras: the exuberance of the 1920s when twenty-two new legitimate theaters opened their doors; the

**2.12** Maidman took great pride in his development of the West Side Airlines Terminal on West 42nd Street, shown here circa 1970s, before its transformation into the second phase of Theatre Row housing five theaters, a recording studio, a news service, and two restaurants. Courtesy of Building for the Arts NY, Inc.

conversions and demolitions of scores of theaters under severe distress during the 1930s; the hope-filled recovery of the 1940s following the Depression; and the rekindled zeal among realty interests in the 1950s for mapping a new West Side—until the lights of possibility dimmed in the mid-1960s and the lurid but profitable enterprises of commercial sex engulfed the district in the 1970s. Nowhere was the decline more apparent and appalling than on the world-famous theater block, known by its newest nickname, the Deuce.

## VICE CENTRAL

By 1960, the once-proud public playground was now infamous as the home of vice, crime, and seemingly uncontrollable social behaviors. Prostitution of all gender affiliations, hustling of all kinds, open drug trade, alcoholism, vagrancy, and con games like three-card monte and clio ruled West 42nd Street. Criminal activity thrived nearby, inside the underground corridors of the subway stations in Times Square and on the corners of the nearby Port Authority Bus Terminal (inside too), where runaway teenagers exited into a rough life on the street, traveling across the same path as the hundreds of commuters from New Jersey starting their workday. When in 1961 the administration of Mayor Robert F. Wagner, urged on by the press, sealed up the entrance to the IRT subway through the Rialto Arcade—"the Hole," notorious as a pickup point where adult homosexuals found complicitous teenagers—the action amounted to a tacit admission that the city's Police Department was unable to control the sex-for-sale in the district. More than a few patrolmen considered it the "worst block in New York." "Life on W. 42d Street" was "A Study in Decay," declared the *Times* in an influential front-page article in 1960.[37]

Known in police circles as Midtown South, this hard-edged area ranked first in the city for felony and net crime complaints by the late 1970s. Forty-second Street between Seventh and Eighth Avenues recorded more than twice as many criminal complaints as any other street in the precinct, with dangerous drugs, grand larceny, robbery, and assault topping the list. Criminal activity on the street was out of proportion to its size measured by linear frontages in the precinct.[38] This malignancy, so disturbing to authorities, grew rapidly, notwithstanding significantly heightened protection from the presence of the city's greatest concentration of law enforcement officers: foot and car patrols of uniformed police officers, mounted police, plainclothes and anticrime units, and special forces, including the Police Department's Public Morals Squad and its Pimp Squad for Midtown South, plus the police patrols of the Port Authority and the Transit Authority. On West 42nd Street, even the police did not walk alone.

Illicit sexual activity was not limited to any one neighborhood in New York, but during the 1970s and '80s the Deuce became synonymous in the minds of a worldwide public with violence and crime, flaunted deviance, pornography, and urban decay. "The Great White Way is now a byword for ostentatious flesh-peddling in an open-air meat rack," theater historian Laurence Senelick wrote in an influential retrospective review of the city's sexual underground. The libertarianism of the '60s, instructed by a series of US Supreme Court rulings narrowing the definition of "obscene," broke the physical constraints on what had been a subterranean world of hustling. Sex became an industry "as entrepreneurs began purveying allurements to the libido on a grand scale," and massage parlors, live-nude shows, peep shows, topless bars, hard-core sex films, porn emporiums, and bookstores now called "adult" turned the street into a supermarket for sex and sleaze.[39]

In 1966, Marty Hodas, the legendary "King of Peeps," introduced the twenty-five-cent peep show with "girlie films" to Times Square. An instant success that made Hodas millions, peep shows altered the dynamic of 42nd Street. "A trip to a Peep Show is cheap, and unenlightening. The doorway is a festival of neon: 'All live girls,' 'Non-stop multi video,' 'All private booths,' '25c. only'"—a rare bargain in an expensive city. The commercial success of the peep show showed the way for small businesses to convert to arcades featuring film loops and explicit magazines. Higher profits sent the cost of leases skyward and attracted the mob, which muscled in around 1968. By the late 1970s, the best-known parcel of real estate in America was, depending upon one's perspective, "a bazaar for human ungodliness," "an Evangelical Combat Zone," "a headquarters for crime," a lawless "area of violent contrasts," "a mixture of Dante and Fellini," "'porn' thorn in midtown's side," or a "nether world" of drugs and sex.[40] It was a sad place, often a repository of runaway and forgotten youth, where life seemed hard, fast, uncompromising, and dangerous.

Vice had its own GPS pathway. Its positioning point was in an irregular L-shaped track on both sides of 42nd and 43rd Streets between Seventh and Eighth Avenues, flowing north along Eighth Avenue to 51st Street. From there it jumped to the street fronts surrounding the islands on Broadway between 47th and 49th Streets, where the Pussycat Lounge and Cinema and Kitty Kat and Mardi Gras Topless Disco did a booming XXX-rated business. In the early 1970s, the heaviest concentration of heterosexual prostitution activity clustered between 49th and 51st Streets on Eighth Avenue, conveniently right across from the "pross" hotels of "Hell's Bedroom," among them the Lark, Radio Center, Raymona, and Elite Hotels, plus two pimp bars (Tommy Small and Angel's West); further up Eighth Avenue were Cleo Hotel, Woody's pimp bar, and Westerly Apartments ("pimp headquarters of the Western World"). This was the territory Gail Sheehy described so vividly in her 1972 exposé of the city's perpetual efforts to clean up midtown's sex industry. As heterosexual prostitution shifted northwest, West 42nd Street became primarily a center for male prostitution, its stomping ground since the 1930s.

Times Square had an active, moderately open gay scene beginning in the 1920s, becoming one of the city's most significant centers of male prostitution. Many men working in the amusement district as actors, stagehands, costume designers, publicity people, waiters, and

**2.13** "Adult Peep Show with *Sound*, 25¢," on 42nd Street. During the 1970s, the City Planning Commission estimated that the city had about 245 stores catering to adult uses: adult movie theaters, massage parlors, adult bookstores, and peep shows. This is one that remained at the tail end of a decades-long run on the Deuce, 2002. New York Daily News Archive via Getty Images.

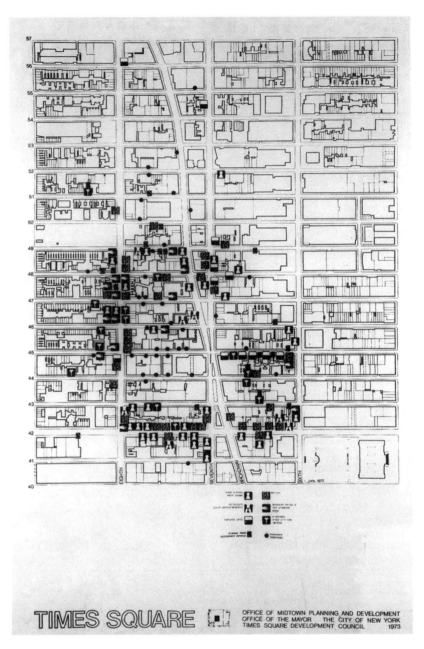

**2.14** This map of vice locations in Times Square was prepared in 1973 during Mayor Lindsay's administration to aid in its crackdown on prostitution. It was used to identify the massage parlors, hotels where prostitution was practiced, purveyors of pornographic materials, peep shows, and adult movie theaters. New York City Office of Midtown Planning and Development.

performers in restaurants and clubs, or busboys in hotels, lived there; others were attracted there by the district's many rooming houses, theatrical boardinghouses, short-let hotels, and late- or all-night businesses, gay bars, and restaurants. "As the Depression deepened, growing numbers of young men—many of them migrants from economically devastated cities . . . and some servicemen—began to support themselves or supplement their income by hustling. . . . [M]any became prostitutes for the same reason some women did: the work was available and supplied a needed income."[41] With the nightly closing of Bryant Park to the public in 1944—to curtail the gathering of "undesirable types"—the cruising moved into the all-night grinder houses and "the Hole," the arcade leading to the subway from the Rialto Theatre on 42nd Street.

Day or night, West 42nd Street was "male turf," a world of sex shops, action movies, and retail stores that catered to male tastes. The street's sexist and pornographic visual imagery provided a prime site for a field visit for the 1970s activist group Women Against Pornography, which ran twice-weekly bus tours of the Deuce. For New Jersey commuters or New York subway riders with jobs in midtown Manhattan, the street was simply the most efficient route to work, a place to pass through quickly—in the 1960s. The street could be easily avoided by walking one block south to 41st or north to 43rd, but many chose not to. The street's human street bazaar was galvanizing. By the 1970s, however, the street had become a menacing experience, and even a quick walkthrough failed the test of urban smart. The flow of commuters from the Port Authority Bus Terminal took 41st or 43rd Street to avoid the Deuce.

Vice in Times Square dates back to the turn of the century. As hotels and theaters moved up Broadway into Longacre Square, so did the brothels. The sidewalks were thick with streetwalkers prowling 42nd Street between Sixth and Ninth Avenues. Decades later, "The economic pressures of Prohibition deprived the hotel industry of liquor-related profits, which led some of the second-class hotels in the area to allow prostitutes and speakeasies to operate out of their premises."[42] As people would come to say about the real estate of Times Square, "the stories dirt could tell." One notable, the Hermitage Hotel (1907), a 13-story bachelor hotel on Seventh Avenue between 41st and 42nd Streets, was renamed the National Hotel after its owner was convicted on prostitution charges in 1943. The infamous hotel would later be torn down, along with several other parcels on the blockfront, as part of the 42nd Street Development Project to make way for an office tower.

In the 1970s, Times Square remained "a study of incredible contrasts." Amid the prostitutes, drug pushers, hustlers, derelicts, junkies,

**2.15** On April 9, 1984, nearly two hundred women marched through Times Square to protest pornography, past various peep-show parlors and X-rated theaters, speaking out against the indignity toward women in pornographic films and publications. AP Photos/ Nancy Kaye.

and pimps—the regulars who gave the Deuce its notoriety as a sexual playground—were scores of transient youth, runaways, and adults with children in welfare hotels. (Among the most squalid of these, Holland Hotel at 351 West 42nd Street at times housed more than 273 families on welfare in a structure built around 1919 as an elegant residence for young women, with a swimming pool in the basement.) Daytime brought a cross section of city workers and urban commuters—office workers, garment-center employees, local merchants, waiters, waitresses, restaurateurs, journalists, television people, and theater employees—along with area residents, tourists, matinee patrons, and street peddlers to the square. The juxtaposition of these worlds could be jarring: "The splendid facades of the district's theaters . . . stand just around the corner from the blaring music advertising live sex shows. Theater patrons hail cabs and hurry to parked cars through a sea of hustlers, drug peddlers, and prostitutes." You could find one of New York's largest religious bookstores in Times Square, as well as the legendary Colony Music, which sold classical, pop, and Broadway sheet

**2.16** The Hermitage Hotel as it first appeared on opening in 1907. In 1914, the Stanley Theatre opened next door (left) and billboards soon plastered its other neighboring building (right); across the street, Hammerstein's Victoria Theatre is visible. By 1936, a double room in this former bachelor hotel was only $3.50 a night, or $2.50 if a bathroom was shared. Demolished in the early 1990s as part of the 42nd Street Development Project. Irving Underhill. Museum of the City of New York. X2010.28.115.

**2.17** A bright spot appeared in 1977 atop the Rialto movie theater on 42nd Street: *Nine Women*, a frieze of twenty-three portrait heads each measuring 20 feet high extending along two sides of the building by artist Alex Katz. The work was realized through the cooperation of the Public Arts Council of the Municipal Art Society, Marlborough Gallery, and RKO General, Inc., owner of the billboard space. Photo by Chuck DeLaney, Courtesy of Public Art Fund, NY. © 2023 Alex Katz / Licensed by VAGA at Artists Rights Society (ARS), NY.

music and cast recordings in its jam-packed store in the Brill Building on Broadway. (Until 2012, that is, when after 64 years as a destination, it was the last of Times Square's "character" stores to fall victim to the twin forces of high rent and new technology that made it easier for records and sheet music to be brought on the internet.) "The mix of human elements is incongruous," journalist Jill Stone wrote in her pictorial history of Times Square, "but it does reflect the range of attractions that draw people to Times Square, and it does speak for the glamor and garishness that Times Square symbolizes in the public mind."[43]

The draw also came from the fact that West 42nd Street functioned as a unique movie center for the city. With ten of its fourteen movie theaters showing first-run releases of general movies and the newest kung fu, action, and horror films at low prices several times a day, the street drew teenagers and adults from all five boroughs of the city. Action movies were probably the largest single attraction of the street in the late 1970s, as a group of CUNY sociologists discovered in their comprehensive field work. The diverse draw, in concert with the equally diverse fare, made for a "cross-cultural event," journalist Mark Jacobson wrote in *Rolling Stone* a decade later. "And that's why you have to have grind theaters on Forty-second Street," he told Carl Weisbrod, then head of the Mayor's Office of Midtown Enforcement. "It's New York's drive-in circuit. You can't make every movie theater like Cinema One. If the city is really interested in the occult vibe in this country, they ought to nationalize Forty-second Street as a center for sleazological cinema studies."[44]

Though seemingly exorable, Times Square's decline after World War II occurred not as a fast-paced movie clip but rather as a series of slow-motion events and market responses reducing the district's draw as a middle-class entertainment center. By the mid-1960s, the latter role had been taken over by Lincoln Center, the largest performing-arts complex

**2.18** The titles of the sex movies being shown in theaters on 42nd Street would change, but not the subject fare. By the end of the 1960s, the street was on its way to being overrun with pornographic bookstores, movies, massage parlors, and live sex shows. Yet look above the Victory theater in this 1972 photo—still visible from the past: "Welcome to 42nd Street The World's Greatest Movie Center." Bettmann via Getty Images.

**2.19** "Cooped Up? Feelin' Low? Enjoy a Movie Today," encouraged the promoters of 42nd Street. The ghost sign on the side of the entrance to the Selwyn Theatre remained in place until construction of New 42 Studios (1998–2000). Fading Ads of New York City, History Press 2011 © Frank H. Jump, Fading Ad Blog.

in the United States. Despite continual anxiety and self-interested fears among theater owners and restaurateurs throughout the 1970s, the area's sex business was not keeping Broadway dark. Historically volatile, the theater industry in New York appeared to be in relatively good shape in 1980. After a tough 1973–1974 season, when the city itself was suffering from a near-brush with bankruptcy, box office receipts soared through the rest of the decade, as did the number of total playing weeks and new productions. Tourists packed the streets at night. That would change almost as quickly after the record attendance season of 1980–1981 (eleven million seats sold), but at the time, confidence on Broadway was strong. The area's urban ills seemed only to keep people from staying longer and frequenting the restaurants after hours.

From a real estate perspective, the problem appeared obvious if also somewhat ironic: on a street long touted for its high land values in a city that constantly tore down to rebuild, a Sodom-and-Gomorrah form of social ecology inhibited new investment. Only one new building had been built on the most famous theater block after 1920, the Rialto, which was designed exclusively for movie programs, and none was built after 1937. Landowners appeared to lack the financial motive to displace tenants running highly profitable commercial-sex enterprises and replace them with some possibly higher-yielding use. Operators were taking in huge weekly gross revenues and outsized profits from the grinder houses, porn bookstores, sex emporiums, massage parlors, and peep shows. The configuration of some sixty lots on West 42nd Street looked no different from other commercially underdeveloped blocks in West Midtown. The nature and pattern of the sex industry on the block, however, cast a particular and complex imprint on the structure of property control.

In the environs of Times Square, real estate activity resembled a byzantine underworld of covert ownership. Seeking anonymity and the ability to claim "no responsibility," landlords put a lot of distance between their title to the bricks and mortar and the ultimate operator of the businesses inside those walls. The infamous Lark Hotel on 49th Street owned by Maidman is an illustrative case. Maidman leased the hotel to the Reise brothers, a pair of chain restaurant owners, who in turn leased to another who was fronting for yet another who held the operating license on the pross hotel. The chain of ownership and leasehold interests aimed to confuse, if not obfuscate. Owning this type of real estate was a business predicated on speculative profits.

Legitimate owners of the buildings housing massage parlors— "hit-and-run brothels combing the virtues of low overhead and high turnover"[45]—adult bookstores, and peep shows commonly net leased (to tenants who were responsible for all expenses) the properties for 10 years or more to others (often organized crime interests, according to the investigative work of the New York State Select Committee on Crime), who might operate the sex-related business directly but who, in turn, were just as likely to sublease the premises on a short-term basis, even month to month, to small-time, generally fly-by-night operators. Not atypically, a speculator would purchase a property because the building was likely to be demolished in the next couple of years; in the interim, nominal improvements, if any, would be made. The short-term leases made it easy to vacate tenants quickly, while the sex-related businesses generated a lucrative source of short-term income before time was ripe for demolition. "An ugly cow gives a lot of milk," was the oft-repeated refrain. The street's ten grinder movie houses drew in millions of paying customers, gallons of milk.

The economics of these businesses was compelling. A veteran dealer in Times Square real estate explained: "a new 'skin flick' theater on 42d Street west of Times Square is reportedly paying $90,000 a year in rent—in this case $4,500 per front foot—on top of a $100,000 payment to buy out a lease. For an ordinary store on 42d Street between Seventh and Eighth, rents are said to be about $2,500 to $3,000 per front foot per year."[46] Milking, in other words, was a low-cost, high-revenue holding action among speculative owners until conditions ripened for redevelopment and property sold for substantial gains. It derived, in part, from a large increase in available space in the mid-1960s as speculators bought up properties in anticipation of office redevelopment. When the speculative boom collapsed in the early 1970s, the porn shops in the area remained.

In 1970 the pornography business in midtown Manhattan had just begun to locate its best customers—the vast population of office workers proximate to West 42nd Street, who on either side of the journey to work were within striking distance of Times Square. The people count was higher than that of Rockefeller Center, by a great deal: 49,000 persons entered 42nd Street between Sixth and Eighth Avenues during the morning rush hours compared with about 12,000 at Rockefeller Center. Aware of these figures, the West Side Association of Commerce was not so sure of the oft-repeated inevitability of office towers sweeping across 42nd Street. Nor did the business group think that an increase in land value would eliminate the pornographic bookstores or movies, which, because of their exceptionally high gross revenues and expected returns, appeared to face no economic constraints. In a report, the association's consultant listed serious obstacles in the path of redevelopment: complex ownership of many small properties, the unwillingness of many small businessmen to give up the advantage of their present sites, and, most significantly, the increasing growth of the pornography industry on West 42nd Street, which could only be expected to continue since pedestrian access was so high and office employment rapidly growing. "Prestige and acceptability are very important to the office tenant," said Seymour Durst, and the ever-growing number of theaters for sex-exploitation films was "a definite detraction."[47]

Well-positioned, erotica could afford to pay high rents on a sustainable basis. Operating on a 24-hour basis, the theaters and peep shows generated enviable gross revenues. Operators garnered tremendous profit since the establishments contained only a few cheaply made booths with small film machines and needed only a few low-paid employees to run them. Meanwhile a multiplicity of small parcels made it difficult to assemble a parcel of sufficient size for redevelopment. It was true that at that time three corporations with major holdings of theater and small-shop properties in the district controlled about 80 percent of the available land and buildings on the Deuce. This concentration, however, would not necessarily make land assembly by private interests any easier or more manageable. There were still more than twenty-seven landlords and multiple layers of fragmented property interests on the street to complicate the task immensely, as city and state officials would come to understand when they took up the task of cleansing the street of its moral decay.

## BEYOND CONTROL

In the mid-1970s, the city was broken and teetering on the edge of bankruptcy. It was a scary place, brutal and unforgiving, written off by nearly everybody. "Times Square, well beyond moral bankruptcy, was the epicenter of a beautiful, dark, dirty, and steamy flower of desperation. It was a place you went to start a new life, drop an old one, or just disappear," said Jodi Doff, a writer and photographer who first showed up there in 1974. It was wild, dangerous, recalled artist Jane Dickson, who arrived in Times Square in 1978 and took a job working the night shift for Spectacolor, the first animated lightboard in Times Square, designing glowing images on a black screen. "There were muggings and gunfire on the street, and creeps breaking in from the stairwell." She was working and living with her filmmaker husband Charles Ahearn in "Sodom on the Hudson," as the square was then known, in an old office building

**2.20** Painter Jane Dickson, self-described "flâneur," looking out the window where she lived on West 43rd Street in the 1980s, trying to get "some grip on what the hell was going on." She would later paint many of the crazy and dangerous scenes of Times Square. © Peter Bellamy.

on 43rd at the corner of Eighth Avenue that was being warehoused until it was torn down as part of the redevelopment project. At both artistic and psychological levels, she was working on subjects she was trying to understand yet also wanting people to look at, to notice "what's *really* happening." She wanted to capture the small telling and overlooked everyday things that define a time and place, the common experiences that are mostly unrecognizable as they are unfolding.[48]

The common perception of Times Square among New York's mayors and governors and the majority of their middle-class constituents was aptly summed up years later by the late urbanist Marshall Berman: "a human sinkhole, a civic disgrace, a place where no decent person would willing go, and where the only helpful thing would be to blow it all away." Writing earlier, in 1975, architectural critic Ada Louise Huxtable did not mince words either: "The area is encrusted with the dark and gritty sediment of endless seasons of concentrated use and abuse that no rain or garbage removal ever touches."[49]

**2.21** The scene at the western edge of the Deuce at Eighth Avenue across from the Port Authority Bus Terminal, circa 1972: Bus Stop Cafe with a friendly barkeeper named Jersey. Next door, Pleasure Studios advertising "Girls, Girls, Girls, Complete Satisfaction, $10 1 Flight Up, Beautiful Models, Nude Photography," including several women standing in front on the sidewalk. © JackFalat.

Its police precinct, Midtown South, was commonly described as "the diseased precinct of the universe." Still, the exotic seediness kept people coming to Times Square. Pleasure-seekers and tourists came to ogle, see the bright lights of the square, say they'd been there. The allure of danger and desire for a new experience involving some degree of risk-taking or thrill-seeking also attracted many to the "night frontier" who were willing to taste the fast life, to con or to be conned. It was "a place where the laws of conventional society are suspended."[50]

By middle-class standards of behavior, the depravity and intensity of the conditions on the Deuce provided a ready consensus for a cleanup and evidence of the assemblage problems of private market-driven redevelopment: together, a strong rationale for aggressive public intervention. Throughout the 1960s and '70s, city officials tried to deal with pornography and prostitution and their associated criminal activity through vice cleanups, prostitution crackdowns, massage parlor sweeps, more stringent licensing requirements, surveillance, and law enforcement efforts, anti-sleaze laws, porn zone ordinances, anti-porn zoning amendments, special citizen councils and civic committees, and planning studies. A succession of mayors—Robert F. Wagner (1954–1965), John V. Lindsay (1966–1973), Abraham D. Beame (1974–1977)—and their city planning commissioners revisited ever-worsening conditions. Others had preceded them—Fiorello H. LaGuardia (1934–1945), William O'Dwyer (1946–1950), and Vincent R. Impellitteri (1950–1953).

The policies were legendary for their ineffectualness. Little changed. Each new attempt was greeted by increased public skepticism. Reporting in April 1977 on Mayor Beame's new campaign against vice, the *Economist* aptly interpreted it as a "clear signal that he is in the race [for mayor]." It was, the influential London weekly explained, "little more than an election gambit," the most recent in a long line of such publicity-seeking efforts no more likely to have permanent or serious impact than those of the past.[51] Cleaning up West 42nd Street was something of a long-running joke in New York City politics: everyone running for a city office promised to do "something" about the street, but little if anything changed.

Fearing that the sex industry would engulf midtown, Mayor Beame set out to clean up 42nd Street and Times Square. Signaling a new approach to the cleanup effort, he established a special task force, the Midtown Enforcement Project, in 1976, with federal funds; when the federal funding expired, city funds were used to institutionalize the agency as the Mayor's Office of Midtown Enforcement (OME). The office was set up with the goal of coordinating the efforts of a variety of city agencies on multiple levels: inspection and reporting of illegal activities, litigation of illegal activity, and planning strategies to improve conditions that could not be addressed simply by closing brothels and other public nuisances. The action lever was code enforcement, a real estate approach aimed at combatting the spread of the sex industry.

The sex business was especially dense along Eighth Avenue just west of Times Square between 44th and 48th Streets. A twenty-member legal SWAT team set out to enforce existing laws against obscenity with the use of heavy fines, and it shut down sex-related businesses that were in violation of city fire, health, and building codes and zoning laws. Under the direction of Weisbrod from 1978 to 1984, the OME succeeded in virtually banning massage parlors—so-called "adult physical culture establishments." Massage parlors were not protected under the First Amendment and were vulnerable to many code violations, but shutting them down affected only indoor activity. Weisbrod's teams worked

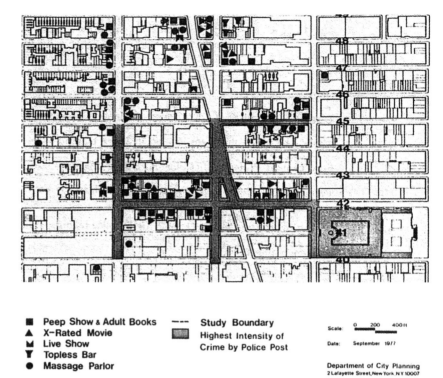

**2.22** The highest intensity of crime associated with sex-related businesses in the Times Square district, as shown on this 1977 map, was concentrated on 42nd Street between Sixth and Eighth Avenues and on Eighth Avenue between 42nd and 45th Street, with another concentration north of the bowtie between 48th and 49th Streets. Eighty-three adult-use establishments had been closed by the Mayor's Midtown Enforcement Project since January 1976. New York City Department of City Planning.

assiduously to improve street conditions on the Deuce, but the enforcement program was never successful in eliminating street prostitution, even with hyped-up arrests of prostitutes—except in terms of the optics of doing something. It was almost pointless since the prostitutes' clientele went unscathed. By law, the city could deal with prostitution only on a legal, not a moral basis, and since street prostitution was not directly connected to the real estate-based strategies of the OME, it was not susceptible to standard legal approaches.

The larger social ecology of 42nd Street and Times Square made the random-arrest-and-conviction approach to prostitution—arrests in the thousands in the early 1970s—ineffectual because as soon as the prostitutes were released from jail (typically after an overnight stay), they were back on the streets, with their pimps. In the meantime, the "morals" problems continued to worsen. In early 1978, vice in Times Square,

**2.23** Police arrest on 42nd Street in the Midtown South precinct, where efforts to control rapidly growing crime commanded the city's greatest concentration of law enforcement officers, 1979. Jill Freedman/Getty Images.

according to the Mayor's Midtown Enforcement Project, was concentrated in forty-three massage parlors, forty theaters showing hardcore pornographic films, fifty-four bookstores, thirty topless bars and live sex shows, sixty-three massage parlors, and thirty-three "prostitution-prone" hotels. It was hard to pin down the precise number of adult-use establishments in the area, however, because new ones would open and others close so often.

Crime was the most vexing problem. The spread of the sex industry, especially the illegal massage parlors, was being brought under control through legal actions and regulatory controls. By spring of 1978, the number of massage parlors had declined to forty-five from a high of about 170 two years earlier. Still prostitution persisted, "and the perception of Times Square as unsafe was also heightened by the continued presence of street hustlers and other criminals who were hanging out on the streets," said William Daly, head of the OME from 1984 to 2001, whose job included keeping track of the sex-for-sale business.[52] In 1978, the Koch administration put out the first "Times Square Action Plan" (followed by a second in 1984). The report cited the high incidence of street crime as a major impediment to further investment, job creation, and increased use by tourists and metropolitan area residents. "Individuals who perhaps may not be offended by pornography or prostitution," it said, "nevertheless fear and consequently avoid going into areas where they will be mugged, harassed, stared at, forced to accept handbills for massage parlors, and propositioned for drugs, sex or small change."[53] For city officials, reducing street crime and "street pollution" became a central goal for the economic life of Times Square and the city.

In 1978 the city had set up the Operations Crossroads Police Substation at 42nd and Broadway and added approximately one hundred additional police personnel to patrol the core area of Times Square, 40th to 50th Streets from Sixth to Ninth Avenues, from 6:00 P.M. to 2:00 A.M., the times of peak pedestrian and vehicular traffic. Notwithstanding these high-profile initiatives, law enforcement efforts to control street behaviors were of limited efficacy because constitutional safeguards and judicial practices constrained police efforts to control street traffic in drugs, remove alcoholics and vagrants, and prevent loitering in the area.

Loitering presented the police with a special problem: sorting out the "indiscernible mix of those engaged in, or about to engage in, illegal activities" and those just "hanging around" to experience the excitement of 42nd Street. The street population of the Deuce, as described in the Draft Environmental Impact Statement of the 42nd Street Development Project, was an "outdoor circus of people" made up of several groups: the regulars "in the life" at their hangouts, on their "strolls," or on their "hustles"; the winos, vagrants, derelicts, and drifters ambling about or lying in doorways in one state or another; the pedestrians on their way somewhere; moviegoers; and the tourists, joined by street-preaching revivalists, peddlers, and errant window shoppers. There were no laws against standing on public sidewalks. The police could not arrest people simply for standing around. The crowds provided "the market and the screen for the hustlers and pushers—the market in a sense of potential customers and the screen in the sense that those hanging around are often undistinguishable from criminals."[54] Just how much loitering contributed to the problems on 42nd Street was debatable, but the perception of loitering and its threatening impact on the public was real. There were genuinely threatening characters prowling the Deuce.

The arrival of crack cocaine in Times Square in 1986 triggered a dramatic increase in crime. "The overall effect of crack on Times Square during those last years of the 1980s was devastating," said Daly, "as block after block that the city had reclaimed from the prostitutes was taken over by the crack dealers, the junkies, and cardboard encampments of the homeless." The impact was especially difficult for the businesses on Restaurant Row on West 46th Street, who were frustrated by the lack of a sustained response from City Hall ("periodically, a crack-down occurs and things quiet down for a week or two, only to return to normal as soon as the pressure is off"); patrons were refusing to enter the block because of the prevalence of crack dealers and addicts "who lent an atmosphere of impending danger." In June 1988, when the block association enlisted the "quasi-vigilante group, the Guardian Angels, to patrol the block," Daly said the incident developed into a "media frenzy."[55] Reactions were mixed; some welcomed the volunteer red-bereted group since nothing else seemed to be working, others were wary of the tension between the group and the police patrolling the block using different tactics. Eventually, the police commissioner made a commitment to post uniformed officers on the block.

The mayor and the professionals he selected to lead law enforcement in Times Square were dealing with an intractable situation where the prescriptive solution needed to change public perception as well as reality. Conditions on the Deuce were a pox on this part of midtown. After years of heavy-duty but essentially ineffectual law enforcement, the conclusion was that nothing could be changed in Times Square unless 42nd Street changed, Weisbrod told me. "Most visible was the sex business, but that was only one element of a larger gestalt: crime," he said. "Sex was the springboard to bigger issues of crime, not only on 42nd Street but beyond, into Times Square. You had to deal with 42nd Street in the whole if you were ever to address the whole of Times Square."[56]

A large segment of the New York metropolitan population saw the block as dangerous and morally repulsive. Social conditions had deteriorated beyond acceptable standards, even for the most tolerant of New Yorkers hardened to a range of public behaviors others would consider unacceptable. Crime on the streets seeming increasingly random and violent. Everyday people knew of the street violence or had witnessed it; the sense of danger, of menace, was real, especially for women. Race and class also played an important part in how the middle-class perceived the area. Although whites dominated the block at all times of the day, except after midnight, the "street people" were predominately African American and Hispanic, which added considerably to the insecurity and fear of the white middle class. Beginning in the 1960s, as elsewhere, racial tensions were everywhere in the air in New York City. That the racial element affected the public's perception of Times Square was real but hardly unique to the place or the city. As the symbolic soul of the city, though, 42nd Street and Times Square seemed to represent the whole.

Across the United States, cities became identified with fear and danger. Their dark and dangerous side appeared in repeated television newscasts of big-city riots and were vividly portrayed on celluloid, with some of the most searing films cast on the mean streets of New York. John Schlesinger's Academy Award-winning *Midnight Cowboy* (1969), a shocking tale of the dark side of the Deuce's squalid subculture, was the first of a series of movies that reported on the decline of New York City to the rest of the nation. In *Taxi Driver* (1976), Travis Bickle's plight as a socially dysfunctional, mentally unstable veteran presents New York as a squalid, filthy, uncontrollable city of violence—its twentieth-century nadir—and the sidewalks of 42nd Street as plagued with pimps, prostitutes, and drifters in their recurrent strolls. The morally destitute environment of the Deuce not only offended middle-class sensibilities but offered an indelible indictment of urban depravity. In his strikingly original *Celluloid Skyline*, James Sanders captured the impactful essence of New York's darkest period: "the decline of civic order was affecting not only the poor (who had always suffered hardship), but middle-class New Yorkers, who found their relatively comfortable way of life threatened by forces that no one seemed able to reverse, or even slow. So universally recognizable was this change, in fact, that . . . filmmakers used it as the premise not of crime stories, but of *comedies*."[57] In humor lies truth.

In the late 1970s, when city officials and urban planners considered ambitious plans to renew and rehabilitate the Deuce, the public's perception of the formerly legendary but now tawdry street was clear and unambiguous. The basis for action was to deal with 42nd Street "in the whole."

# 3 THE CLEANSING

The biggest risk we perceived was that the project would fail, that it would be one more articulated plan that would go nowhere.
Herbert Sturz, 1991

The crowds had thinned out. The porn shops were mostly gone. The drug trade disappeared, and then crime dropped so fast it was stunning. Gone too were most of the old-time businesses, bar and grills, boxing clubs, and other second-floor activities, closed or relocated after the state secured title to thirty-four properties occupied by 250 businesses and a few resident individuals. The storefronts were shuttered. The movie marquees, mostly dark. The Deuce existed only as a ghostly remembrance of its former self. It was August 1992, and government officials had just formally declared their longstanding plan to clean up the street's pervasive vice to be abandoned, involuntarily. After 12 years of effort and surviving forty-seven separate lawsuits, the ambitious redevelopment plan to build four office towers and repurpose the legendary block's historic theaters had collapsed. Awash in vacant office space, the market for new skyscrapers in midtown was dead. The real estate glut had shuttered the window of market opportunity.

A few long-time critics of the project were taking a modest victory lap, calling the postponement an opportunity to reconsider the entire premise of the redevelopment project. Even before this inauspicious announcement, ever-softening office market conditions, especially in West Midtown, led some to ask whether the 42nd Street Development Project was still necessary. An enormous amount of money had already been spent over a decade on extensive predevelopment work, litigation proceedings, and condemnation awards. Some thought the planning process had gone seriously awry; others concluded that government had overreached. Still others complained that apart from the four corporate towers, the close-to-death project lacked a vision of the street renewed and went against the culture of the place known for its flamboyant high-low-brow eclecticism. Did the public sector really know what it wanted, other than to get rid of the blight? The "miscalculations in Times Square," *Times* reporter Thomas J. Lueck argued, evoked comparison with the failed massive-clearance model of urban renewal put forth aggressively by the federal government during the 1950s and '60s and reinforced the lesson that renewal needed more than wholesale clearance.[1] His conclusion was only half right, as time would reveal.

What Herbert Sturz had feared had now come to pass: the transformational project was hovering on the brink of failure. From his position as chairman of the City Planning Commission (1980–1986) during the Koch administration, Sturz had run the redevelopment project independent of the city's deputy mayors. Although he had no degree in law or urban planning and was new to the field of real estate development, he was a quick study who surrounded himself with skilled people. Early in his career he had helped found and directed the Vera Institute of Justice. "He not only has a true vision for the city," said John Zuccotti, one of the more powerful chairs of the City Planning Commission in the 1970s, "but his low-key style belies the tough and shrewd negotiator inside." He was also reported to be a wickedly good poker player. He believed in taking chances: "In order to succeed," he told a *Times* reporter, "you have to be ready to fail."[2] He was a creative and ambitious thinker who had an ability to get things done, quietly and with tenacity. In Times Square, the work and the ambition would be needed.

Before his appointment as City Planning Commission chairman at 49, Sturz had been deputy mayor for criminal justice and had dealt with the issues on 42nd Street. "We're not going to drive out every peepshow or dirty moviehouse from Times Square," he said then, "but we're going to roll things back so that the area won't be the visual blight that it is today. We'll try to bring new business into the area and try to get the porn shops out of the area through attrition." In his new city planning position, his intention was to "scatter the menacing aspect" blighting 42nd Street. This meant, he told a *Times* reporter in 1982, breaking up the sleazy element now dominating the area and scattering it elsewhere where it could be more easily controlled.[3]

**3.1** Brilliantly lit signs beckon those seeking adult entertainment on the Deuce, early 1980s. Courtesy of Jane Dickson.

Sturz was the real power behind the 42nd Street project. He had shaped its planning strategy and brought in the state's Urban Development Corporation (UDC), which had special powers and the development capability the city lacked to tackle the ambitions of such a large project. He had defined the roles of each side of the government coalition and kept control over threats to the city's sovereignty. And he was responsible for bringing in the right people who would subsequently orchestrate the build-out of the project: Carl Weisbrod and his hire, Rebecca Robertson. He publicly gave them credit and had their back.

At a projected cost of $2.5 billion (exceeding the initial projection of $1.6 billion) ($5.3 billion in 2022 dollars), it was the nation's largest redevelopment effort—and New York's most visible large-scale public development. It had benefited from consistent political support from both the governor and mayor. Still, for more than a decade, the effort to cleanse Times Square of vice had not unfolded as planned. From the outset, it was besieged by controversy. Obstacles surfaced continuously, halting progress and reducing the probability of success. Persistently troubled, the cleanup project seemed to be always hovering somewhere in the future.

But this was Times Square, the symbolic heart of New York City. Its renewal would bring national attention to a city climbing upward after a bruising fiscal crisis that had brought it to the brink of bankruptcy and "forced it to make a humiliating plea to Washington for assistance—a plea that President Gerald Ford denied at first, before reluctantly accepting on the condition that the city's finances be placed in the hands of an Emergency Financial Control Board, run by New York State and directed by a small, unelected group of corporate executives." Its successful redevelopment was perhaps the most potent way to symbolize New York's fiscal recovery and renewed vitality. To Sturz's way of thinking, the effort represented "a manhood question"—"a palpable test of whether a broken and broke city could surmount parochial concerns to be great again," Sam Roberts wrote in *A Kind of Genius: Herb Sturz and Society's Toughest Problems*.[4]

Sturz, who passed away in 2021, at 90, was a man impatient with conventional wisdom who believed in the ability of development to deliver social benefit. His long life was about making vulnerable people—the prisoners, the prostitutes, the addicts, the abused women, the underprivileged youth, the unemployed, the homeless, the poor, and the elderly—better off through the organizations he created to achieve that mission. In the 1980s, he viewed Times Square as a vehicle to help the city's poor and the immigrants who came to New York for a fresh start; it was a means to continue the city's liberal New Deal legacy crushed during the fiscal crisis, by generating the tax revenue to support it. Generating those revenues from 42nd Street would depend upon a strategy rooted in urban anthropology: putting in place good uses to drive out the bad. Before that could happen, he believed the moral mess that ruled the Deuce had to be swept clean.

By April 1990, with but two minor legal challenges left to settle, money was all that was needed for project officials to gain control over the street's real estate—though that too seemed to hang in the balance. The timing could not have been worse. New York's economy was in the middle of a protracted recession, its financial services sector hit especially hard. The office market in West Midtown was terribly overbuilt. Prudential Insurance Company, partner with Park Tower Realty to develop the four office towers, had one last chance to back out of its commitment to put up the security required for the legal gears of condemnation to move forward: $241 million of credit support (the equivalent of $555 million in 2022 dollars). To the amazement of the real estate community, the Newark-based insurance giant honored its financial commitment, thereby allowing the project to advance at a critical death juncture that would have felled any other development project. Prudential was gambling on the future development of an office market at the legendary crossroads—a gamble few others, if any, were willing to make.

**3.2** This photo circa 1992 shows the shuttered Empire Theatre on the south side of 42nd Street acquired by the New York State Urban Development Corporation in the first phase of condemnation, along with the Harris and Liberty Theatres. All three theaters would become part of a retail-and-entertainment complex, after the 3,700-ton Empire was moved along steel rails at a tortoise-like roll 168 feet closer to Eighth Avenue in 1998. Courtesy of Paul Whalen.

"We own it. It's ours," said Vincent Tese, head of the UDC.[5] For government officials, there was no turning back. To do so would have been tantamount to admitting the failure of the public sector's ambitious cleanup plan, and it was inconceivable that either Governor Mario Cuomo or Mayor Ed Koch would take that risk. The 42nd Street Development Project (42DP) was a test of political will. Despite the constant chorus of critics, there was no political need to abandon the project, especially since the state now owned nine of the project area's 13 acres. There was a need, though, to rethink how best to move forward. Knowing that redevelopment was years away, public officials privately harbored fears that the redevelopment project would become a "post-no-bills project," a reference to the ubiquitous signs put on every storefront boarded over with plywood after the state took possession of a property.

With more than a twist of irony, the indefinite suspension of office construction that precipitated the collapse of the initial cleanup plan held the seeds of a rare second chance to align vision with legend, to get the planning right. State and city officials regrouped, and for their next act they designed an entertainment strategy—42nd Street Now!—that aimed to honor the street's famous legacy and galvanize the return of the middle class, tourists and New Yorkers alike.

## THE PLAN TO INTERVENE

By the time Mayor Koch embraced the effort, cleaning up 42nd Street and Times Square had bedeviled many of his predecessors. The quest had started with Mayor Fiorello LaGuardia's ban of burlesque in 1937, when he was first up for reelection. After World War II, Mayors Robert Wagner and John Lindsay tried to clean up Times Square every four years right before election time. They would come in with police to sweep up prostitutes and clear out other "undesirables." A few sex businesses would be closed; a month after the election, whatever businesses had been closed would have reopened. The next mayor, Abraham Beame, seeking to better the city's image battered by the fiscal crisis, initiated an intense campaign to sweep Times Square clean of prostitutes, derelicts, porn shops, massage parlors, peddlers, and panhandlers before the city was to play host to the Democratic Convention in July 1976 (its first since 1924).

The most serious problem, city officials believed, was street solicitation by prostitutes—particularly in the Eighth Avenue "DMZ" area. "We're going to do our best to make sure we keep the undesirables off the streets," said Deputy Mayor Stanley Friedman. To provide a little extralegal heft, "the state legislature made arresting prostitutes easier by enacting a brand-new anti-loitering law that forbids 'beckoning' for purposes of prostitution." The law was not exact about "how a policeman is supposed to distinguish between a beckoning hooker and a beckoning hitchhiker," but even if the law—which conveniently went into effect the day before the convention—was declared unconstitutional, the convention would be over by that time. "New York is trying to demonstrate that it is just as wholesome as Kansas City," wrote a *Wall Street Journal* reporter.[6] As with previous sweeps, the cleanup achieved for those four days proved to be transitory, recalled Carl Weisbrod, who had a firsthand view of conditions in the district after Mayor Koch appointed him in the late 1970s to run the Midtown Enforcement Project and clean up Times Square.

For more than 40 years, each and every approach—policing, licensing laws, anti-sleaze legislation, anti-loitering laws, curfews, health and safety regulations, enforcement of code violations, zoning amendments

**3.3** In this July 1971 photo, two members of the newly created "Pimp Squad" of the New York Police Department escort an alleged prostitute across Broadway in Times Square shortly after 4 o'clock in the morning. Jerry Mosey/Associate Press.

restricting massage parlors, crackdowns on prostitution, and close-downs of louche bookstores, cinemas, and peep shows—had failed to alter the depth of depravity that infested the Deuce. A 1978 in-depth study of conditions on 42nd Street conducted by the Department of City Planning's Urban Design Group looked at the feasibility of implementing redevelopment of the street as a "corridor," but the report proposed no big plan or big cleanup. From his close study of the situation, Sturz concluded: "The public had lost control."[7]

Piecemeal efforts had not worked. City officials now believed that nothing short of radical surgery through change "of the whole" would succeed—the market on its own could not effect a makeover of the Deuce. In Times Square, effecting wholesale change meant adopting an aggressive urban-renewal-style strategy designed to establish a critical mass of new economic activity on West 42nd Street, broad in scope and deep in impact. City officials also wanted the down-at-heels, depressingly dilapidated Times Square subway complex renovated; it was a vital transportation nexus for the district and its refurbishment a component piece of the cleanup strategy. The corners of Broadway and Seventh Avenue might eventually have attracted new office construction without public development, Sturz believed, but the city's transformative ambitions went beyond what uncoordinated construction of tax-generating high-rise office towers could deliver.

The idea was to leverage the commercial opportunity for office development on the crossroads corners. By dealing with the block as a whole and creating value on those corners, the sites of greatest interest to developers, city officials believed they could bring back legitimate theater to the historic street and secure private proposals for the difficult western end of the block. Those western edges fronting Eighth Avenue across from the looming Port Authority Bus Terminal presented the toughest sell. Planners and real estate professionals alike deemed development of those edges absolutely necessary to stabilize Eighth Avenue and guarantee the street's physical rebirth. "Zoning alone would not have done it," Sturz told me in 1991, when I interviewed him for *Times Square Roulette*.[8] Even when done well, zoning could not serve the city's ambitions for 42nd Street. However much juiced with incentives, the zoning approach is passive, depending as it does on the initiative of developers, who are typically slow to pioneer new districts. The redevelopment project Sturz asked Koch to support called for simultaneous condemnation and comprehensive redevelopment of the 13-acre project area. It was a radical departure from local policy: never before had New York City used condemnation powers for private *commercial* redevelopment. Nonetheless, the project was an easy sell to Koch, who recognized that he would be judged, in part, by whether he was able to produce some concrete physical legacy in Times Square—in other words, accomplish what his predecessors had been unable to do—and lead a project that would symbolize recovery from New York's fiscal crisis.

The ambitions of the 42nd Street project aligned with Koch's plans to revitalize the economy of New York. Upon taking office in 1978, he had had to operate under a strict mandate to balance the budget imposed by special state authorities created to bail out the city. The changing character of the city's economy—the decline of its extensive industrial sector with its loss of job opportunities for blue-collar workers, the loss of white-collar jobs to the outlying region, and the repeated threats of corporations to relocate out of the city—weighed heavily on the mayor. Economic development emerged quickly as a top priority in the early days of his administration as Koch sensed opportunity in the growing strength and expansion of the city's financial-services sector, long recognized as the world's largest. If financial services held potential as an indispensable source of city prosperity, then commercial real estate development, the traditional stimulant of economic good fortune and the city's historic powerhouse, could be made into a turbo-charged fiscal generator for the city. "To grow and build the city-physical became

**3.4** City Planning Commission chairman Herb Sturz at the podium and Mayor Ed Koch seated during one of their many presentations on city planning policy, Board of Estimate chambers, 1981. Neil Boenzi/*The New York Times.*

the centerpiece of the mayor's program," political scientist Jewel Bellush wrote in an insightful review of the emergence of "tower power."[9]

By 1980, sanitizing clearance, the old federal formula for urban renewal, had been thoroughly discredited. Yet the clear failures of large-scale clearance seemed only to apply to "good" neighborhoods, even if poor and dilapidated, not to "bad" environments, those tolerant of sexual deviance, hustling, pornography, and drug dealing. New York officials considered their plan for effecting change on the Deuce to be more sensitive than indiscriminate bulldozing because it mixed clearance with selective preservation of three major high-rise buildings (the former Times Tower, the Carter Hotel, and the Candler Building) and restoration of the architecturally significant nine theaters in the midblock, including the legendary Art Nouveau New Amsterdam Theatre, for legitimate entertainment. Together with four office towers, a merchandise mart, a hotel, and retail, the program would put in place "good" white-collar professional uses. City officials wanted to flood the place with thousands of middle-class pedestrians—office workers, wholesale buyers, tourists, theatergoers. These were the types of people that had made Manhattan street life vibrant and abundant—and relatively safe. As described by practitioners Edward W. Wood Jr., Sidney N. Brower, and Margaret W. Latimer in a provocative and influential 1966 article, these were "planners' people," the types that habitually showed up in draftsmen's renderings of downtown redevelopment

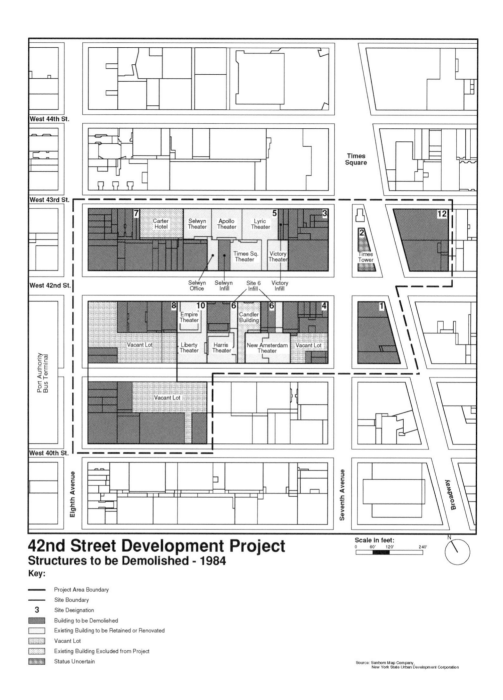

# 42nd Street Development Project
## Structures to be Demolished - 1984
**Key:**

| | |
|---|---|
| —— | Project Area Boundary |
| — | Site Boundary |
| **3** | Site Designation |
| ▓ | Building to be Demolished |
| ☐ | Existing Building to be Retained or Renovated |
| ▒ | Vacant Lot |
| ▦ | Existing Building Excluded from Project |
| ▨ | Status Uncertain |

Scale in feet:
0   60'   120'          240'

Source: Sanborn Map Company,
New York State Urban Development Corporation

**3.5** The map of the 13-acre 42nd Street project showing the structures to be demolished. Selective pieces of the block's existing fabric would be preserved—the New Amsterdam Theatre, Candler Building, Carter Hotel, and mid-block theaters. At the crossroads intersection of Broadway and Seventh Avenue, the size and placement of the four office sites illustrate their role as financial engine of the project. Morgan Fleming for the author.

schemes—stereotyped occupants of the planner's better world: the gentleman with the briefcase, the fashionable lady, mother and child, the young lovers, the viewer, and the boulevardier.[10]

The city's redevelopment plan bore a striking resemblance to a plan put forth by Fred Papert and his not-for-profit organization in the late 1970s, The City at 42nd Street. This ambitious plan aimed to transform the entire three-block area from 40th to 43rd Streets between Broadway and Eighth Avenue into a combined world's fair, theme park, and cultural showcase for New York. To meet the economic demands of financing such an ambitious agenda, Papert had to include commercial office space development and shape his plan to attract potential private investors. In addition to four million square feet of high-rise office space at the crossroads corners, the plan called for restoration of five architecturally and historically important theaters for legitimate stage house productions and façade preservation for three others, the creation of an educational entertainment and exhibit center, retail shops and restaurants, a merchandise mart for garment manufacturers, and a renovated Times Square subway station. To build support for his plan, Papert marshaled a considerable sampling of the corporate, civic, and cultural elite of the city and funding from public and private sources for professional design studies and feasibility analyses. Though ultimately rejected by Mayor Koch—who famously called for "seltzer instead of orange juice"—The City at 42nd Street was a credible piece of professional work, notwithstanding attacks on the vision from high-profile critics. Just eight months after Koch's derisive dismissal, the city and state jointly released a preliminary plan for redevelopment for 42nd Street in the form of a "Discussion Document."[11] In such a short span of time, it is doubtful that the city and state could have come up with their ambitious plan without drawing heavily on its predecessor.

Although the city's strategy for 42nd Street did not match prevailing ideas about the "right" approach to urban redevelopment, as Sturz and staff planners saw it the social environment of the Deuce held out few other options. Incremental action was unlikely to ensure the street's physical and moral turnaround. At the time, market fundamentals were not strong enough to deliver replacement uses on a scale sufficiently broad and deep to reverse the deviant social dynamic of the street (and the profitability of sex uses), where no new building had been built since 1937. Assembling enough small parcels on the block—held in balkanized ownership amid complex layers of property interests and operating businesses obfuscating the actual ground owner—to make a

**3.6** This 1978 rendering of The City at 42nd Street presents the private-sector plan for redevelopment of the Deuce promoted by Fred Papert, with support from the Ford Foundation and others, in the late 1970s. The forces behind the plan represented a significant sampling of the corporate, civic, and cultural elite of the city, with the Canadian firm Olympia & York lined up as master developer of the project. Momentum had been growing until Mayor Koch withheld support, derisively dismissing the plan as "Disneyland on 42nd Street." Famously, he called for "seltzer instead of orange juice." Chermayeff & Geismar & Haviv.

modern-day development site loomed as a formidable obstacle, even for savvy and experienced experts at assemblage.

Assemblage was a well-known obstacle for large-scale development that justified the use of the government's power of eminent domain. The financial capacity of New York City, however, was still shaky. The city did not have the money to pay property owners directly for property condemnation, whether considered from a practical or a political perspective. The 1970s fiscal crisis had exacted reductions in basic services and redistribution, cutbacks in public-sector jobs, and postponements of capital improvements. At the time, large expenditures for land condemnation to promote commercial redevelopment in midtown Manhattan would not have fit anyone's definition of a budget priority, and with the city still locked out of the bond market, it could not float bonds to finance the project, even had it wanted to. Risk aversion ruled. "Religious principle number one at the time: the city should not be at risk for buying land in midtown Manhattan," said the redevelopment project's first director, Paul Travis.[12]

To solve their financing problem, city officials devised a novel off-budget strategy that pivoted on the private sector's willingness to gamble on westward expansion of the midtown office district. Developers, designated through a competitive process and incentivized with above-average building densities and highly favorable payments in lieu of property taxes on the sites, would fund the costs of land acquisition, and this "advance" to the city would be paid back through credits against payments the developer would be making to the city over time. The approach was politically convenient: it did not draw from either the city's operating or capital budgets, so local officials could support the project without diverting funds from other projects or city services. And the extraordinarily long payback period stretched beyond the time horizon of elected officials. In concept, the device was simple; in reality, as city lawyers put the idea into draft language, it got much more complicated. The privatized financing strategy did solve the at-risk problem, an exigency given the city's fiscal condition. Without that constraint, a conventional public financing approach might have reduced some of the controversy and litigation that ensued—political risks that had to be managed adroitly. If the city had been able to issue debt directly, the economic risk of the cost of borrowing would have been tamed, as explained in the next chapter.

To see its plan to fruition, New York needed to learn how to do public development. Local capacity to implement a redevelopment project of the scale Sturz and Koch contemplated did not exist in 1980. The city's entrepreneurial arm, the Public Development Corporation (PDC), was the logical choice to lead the project, but it did not have the expertise nor the track record or credibility to do the job. Moreover, this not-for-profit corporation did not have clear statutory authority to undertake condemnation, and land use experts considered the city's process for land taking to be relatively slow. PDC also did not have the ability to customize deals for tax abatements as did the state's public-benefit corporations, particularly the New York State Urban Development Corporation. Joining forces with UDC was a purely pragmatic solution: "They have the expertise, and they know how to move fast," Koch said in making the announcement.[13]

Sturz worried about the potential loss of control accompanying such a coalition, but the combination of powers that only UDC could bring

**3.7** Mayor Koch and Governor Carey share the podium at City Hall on June 4, 1981, to announce their ambitious plan to clean out the "bad" uses of West 42nd Street and replace them with "good" uses—office towers, merchandise mart and hotel, and refurbished theaters. To the left, Richard Kahan, head of the NYS Urban Development Corporation; to the right, Harrison Golden, City Comptroller. AP Photo/Howard.

to the necessary deal-making held sway. The scope of its authority was why the agency had received uncommon attention from every governor since Nelson A. Rockefeller, who had exerted enormous pressure on state legislators for its creation in 1968, in the aftermath of the assassination of Martin Luther King Jr. Using its extraordinary powers, UDC could take title to the property, package the financial deal for the city, then transfer the development rights of each parcel to private developers through long-term lease arrangements. The agency did not need to provide any financing, just supply its tax-exempt status and real estate expertise. And it did not need a "real" economic interest in the project to justify its intermediary role in a city project. Legally, a UDC project did not even need approval from the eight-member Board of Estimate, then the city's unique executive decision-making body made up of the five borough presidents (each with one vote) and the mayor, comptroller, and president of the City Council (each with two votes).[14] But at the time that was not a feasible end-run, politically. The Board of Estimate's imprimatur was necessary and became part of the approval process, voluntarily.

The concentration of power in this city/state coalition afforded the 42DP a compelling strategic advantage. "When the mayor and governor are joined at the hip, it is a difficult powerhouse to dismantle," said

Weisbrod, whose leadership of the project spanned both sides of the coalition for five years, from 1987 through 1992, first as president of the UDC's subsidiary for the project, then as president of PDC. "Opponents find it difficult to upset that stability, that political force. The perception of opposition doesn't come across as forcefully as in other instances. Developers and others, particularly sophisticated players at the trough, like to play off the city and the state. When they are joined," he explained, "it closes off an avenue of tactical maneuver."[15] At times of tension, the governmental coalition would carry the project through many a threatening case of opposition.

## THE TOWERS THAT COULD

Office development was the linchpin of the city's financial strategy. It drove the economics of the project because it promised the most in terms of meeting private investment profitability on the road to achieving the city's economic development goals for Times Square. Only the development value of the four office sites could underwrite the privatization of the financing needs of the public agenda: land acquisition, subway station improvements, and theater acquisitions. To induce private developers to build office towers at a scale that would catalyze redevelopment, Sturz told me, "we had to create values on the corners because that was what was of interest to the developers."[16] That meant positioning the bulk of development density in the expansion path of the midtown office district, shifting over 50 percent of the eight million square feet of development rights for the entire project area eastward to those crossroads corners.

The enormous densities piled high on relatively small sites—square footage between 24.3 and 46.3 times the amount of land area of the site—far exceeded the 18 times that might have been allowed under special new zoning rules for midtown, or 21.6 times with a special-permit bonus. UDC could create those densities because under its statutory powers, it was exempt from local zoning regulations. By any standard, the densities were enormous, even for Manhattan, even in comparison with the original Equitable Building downtown built to a density 30 times its land area and conventionally credited with prompting New York's first citywide zoning ordinance in 1916.

Bulking up density was the most obvious sign that office use held a most-favored status among the project's other priorities—rejuvenation of the midblock theaters and development of the western edges of the street with a merchandise mart and hotel. When it came to negotiating

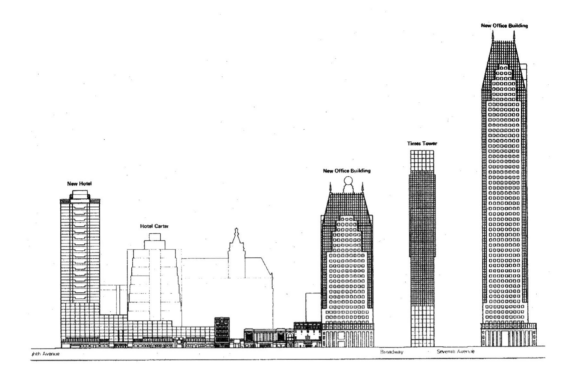

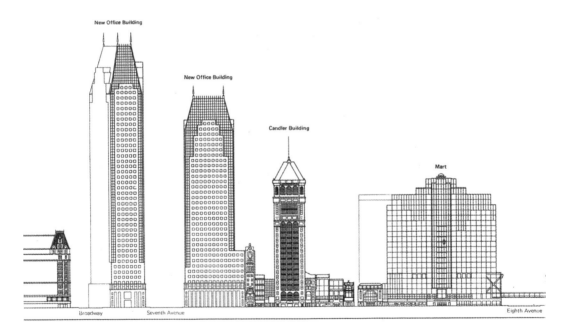

**3.8** The architectural elevations of the proposed new uses on both sides of 42nd Street, north (top) and south (bottom), show the enormous densities of the four office towers under the General Project Plan, 1984. 42nd Street Development Project.

the deals that would the transform 42nd Street, the favored position of office development stood out, with terms significantly better than those for the mart or hotel deals, as explained in *Times Square Roulette*. Even in the early 1980s, most accounts considered the office deal overly generous. The weak set of incentives in the deals for the mart and hotel sites made them nearly unworkable because the incentive pot for the mart was too skimpy, and the hotel was economically feasible only if the merchandise market could be put in place. Consequently, paying the bill for the public agenda depended more heavily than was evident on the development of the four office towers.

It was "safety driven versus maximum profits driven," said a city official in confidence about the deal for the four office sites. The amount a developer was willing to guarantee and secure with a letter of credit was the pivotal element of developer selection; the amount of base ground rent a developer was prepared to pay was almost as important to the selection, but not decisive when it came to an evaluation of the final two competing bids. The financial value of what George Klein's Park Tower Realty offered in terms of ground rent was approximately equal to the offer of the other final competitor for the office sites, but Klein's secured site acquisition payment was $25 million greater, offering the city greater financial protection from escalating site acquisition costs. Klein also agreed to provide funds for the acquisition of the five theaters of Site 5, the Harris Theatre on Site 6, and the infill area on that site, which he planned to develop for retail use.

Klein was not a player in the pantheon of big-time New York developers. He did, however, have a reputation for small, high-quality, architecturally conscious buildings, which carried significant weight with city and state officials. It did not hurt that he was politically well-connected locally and nationally. By his bidding stance and willingness to guarantee what the city wanted in terms of a large, secured site acquisition price, Klein positioned himself as more of a risk taker than New York's more seasoned developers. Except for his continuous civic and fundraising activities, he was nearly as much a real estate outsider as an out-of-town developer. Winning the designation as developer of the 42DP office towers made him the city's most prominent developer.

The importance of keeping the city's risk exposure at bay had other consequences. It pushed forward the logic of abandoning the design guidelines intended to shape the architectural vision for the new office towers in deference to the commercial dictates of marketing space to corporate tenants in such a risky location. Because the office towers could become the financial Achilles' heel of the project, all that could be done to make them maximally feasible commanded priority. When the time arrived for making the inevitable tradeoffs that accompany complex projects, decision makers ended up elevating the marketability factor, bowing to the demands of the city's financial imperative and placing less emphasis on the project's other public objectives, especially aesthetics. In the end, it became the ultimate price paid by the city for having a weak "public side of the balance sheet."[17]

Even more significant, the public benefits city officials expected from the project—revival of theater on 42nd Street and subway station improvements—were integrally tied to the timing of private development, which, in turn, depended on economic conditions of the real estate market. If the market tanked so severely that development was put on hold indefinitely—as happened just as the public sector took possession of the condemned property on the street—the promised public benefits would disappear indefinitely unless public officials found alternative sources of funds to go forward with their plans. Under the terms of the project's privatized financial equation, the gamble was not one-sided. Developers were taking on risks not typically associated with redevelopment: timing risk—not knowing when in fact they would be able to start construction (though initially they were required to start development within a period of time after the sites were delivered); the sequence of delays; funding risk—the open-ended commitment to fund land acquisition; and public-benefit risk—investment in public improvements that involved a great deal of cost. If severely overbuilt market conditions ruled out the start of construction in the foreseeable future, as happened in 1990, the developer would seek to renegotiate the deal in an effort to mitigate the negative financial consequences and public-benefit commitments of moving forward with development under highly unfavorable conditions. And this is precisely what Prudential and Park Tower did.

## PUSHING WEST

Along with its plans to redevelop the Deuce, the Koch administration was working on a zoning initiative for midtown aimed at steering future office development westward and southward, away from the overconcentration of towers in its eastern core. Without upgrading the Times Square district as a whole, the planners reasoned it would be difficult to lure development away from the preferred habitat of corporate tenants on the east side.

The push for rethinking zoning policy came from the parade of immense new towers along Madison, Park, and Third Avenues built during an unprecedented office building boom in the 1960s that stretched into the early 1970s, until the fiscal crisis shut down construction throughout the city. Size was not the irritating factor per se. Rather it was the aggregate impact of density and the "shoehorning" of so many skyscrapers "into tight sites that would have been considered unbuildable a few years ago," explained architectural critic Paul Goldberger.[18] The congestion of such density clogging the sidewalks and overburdening mass transit had generated widespread dissatisfaction among civic groups, planners, and real estate interests alike. They were questioning how the city was going to deal with increased density in the midtown area. Changes in employment patterns reshaping the economy of Manhattan were creating new pressures on the core district; strong and sustained job growth in the service economy (with continued declines in manufacturing) reflected the city's position as the center of national and international business and finance. Greater congestion from more high-rise construction seemed virtually certain to come by the mid-1980s.

The existing 1961 zoning code did not work, period, let alone in ways that fostered growth in line with any rational plan. "Zoning had become increasingly discretionary, negotiated, unpredictable," Sturz wrote in the introduction to the Department of City Planning's 1982 report *Midtown Zoning*.[19] It was functionally inoperative. Predictability and certainty had virtually disappeared, with every major new building constructed through a special permit, exception, text change, or variance. The "system" was a mess, the discretion excessive, its critics claimed. The administrative aim was to reform zoning and make as-of-right development the norm rather than the exception to zoning practice. The policy goal was to ease pressure on the crowded highly valuable East Midtown office core by shifting developers' focus west and south using zoning incentives, public projects, and tax abatement incentives.

Passed by the Board of Estimate in 1982, after three years of debate and controversy, the new midtown strategy established geographic districts, each with its own development criteria. To relieve development pressures, it downzoned the crowded East Side (the "stabilization" area) and to incentivize development elsewhere it upzoned the West Side (the "growth" area). A small preservation area of townhouses, low-scale buildings, and streetfront shops and restaurants covered several mid-blocks between Fifth and Sixth Avenues to protect the ambience of the

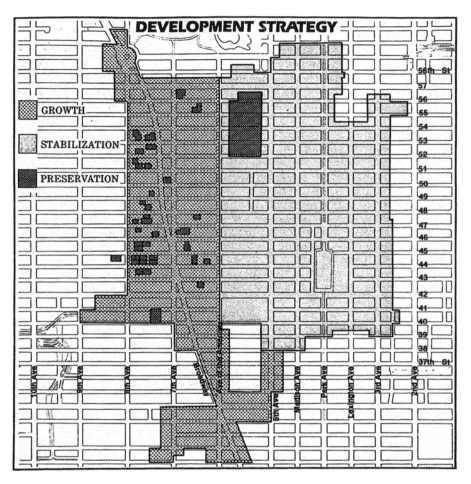

**3.9** This 1982 map of the city's 1980s development strategy for midtown shows the distinct demarcation between the growth zone of West Midtown and the stabilization zone of East Midtown, with a small preservation area in the West 50s around the Museum of Modern Art. Considered an experiment, the special bonus incentives for West Midtown would expire in six years. New York City Department of City Planning.

neighborhood around the Museum of Modern Art. The designers of the strategy made a clear distinction between midtown's east and west districts, while retaining New York City's traditional development pattern of higher density on the avenues and lower density on the side streets. Other regulations were also restructured, including special incentives for theater preservation. Midtown's new zoning marked the first time New York City had adopted an overall policy on the location of new office buildings. Considered an experiment, the new regulations for the West Midtown 50-block growth zone would sunset in six years.

As a part of the city's larger agenda to redirect commercial real estate development, transforming the Deuce was critical. The street was "the cork in the bottle of development in its move westward."[20] At the time, neither urban experts nor architectural critics questioned whether the 42nd Street Development Project was a redundant policy initiative, because few expected zoning modifications to reverse the unsavory social patterns on Eighth Avenue in the Times Square district. In the early 1980s, it was hard to view the special zoning for midtown as immediately competitive with the 42nd Street project, because developers and realty professionals did not have high expectations that the experimental zoning plan would succeed in shifting development to the west side.

Planners thought of the redevelopment of 42nd Street as happening first, as the predicate to the zoning-driven westward expansion of the midtown office district. Their skepticism underestimated developers' thirst for new development sites juiced by handsome incentives: less than five years later, a race against the clock to beat the deadline of the sunset provision threatened to oversupply the Times Square district with millions of square feet of new office and hotel projects. All the while, the 42nd Street project remained uncertain, stalled in repeated rounds of litigation and negotiation over how to proceed with the troublesome merchandise mart element of the program. Ironically, eighteen months before the pending zoning deadline of May 1988, that deluge of commercial space planned or under construction by private developers did call into question the logic of the still unbuilt 42nd Street project.

To those developers quietly focused on finding opportunity in the Times Square market in the early 1980s, the 42nd Street project signified serious public intent. The project's very promise was crucial to the private development that eventually took place in Times Square. "The project gave heart to people like me," remarked Jeffrey Katz, developer of Two Times Square, the slim building ablaze with signs anchoring the northern end of the bowtie at 47th Street. "We believed it would happen, even if it was having trouble getting started. The state's intervention," he added, "was important. The first move was so big that it couldn't be turned back; the scale of activity was terribly important to the change."[21]

Once again, Eighth Avenue seemed poised for change that would "remedy the derelict nature of much of the avenue." The city's push to close down massage parlors and a new cleanup effort were having a visible impact on the pedestrian environment. In 1979, the *Times* reported on twenty-one development projects in various stages of planning for new construction as well as rehabilitation. Hope was back, though realty people had been to that movie before, more than once.

"In a business where developers believe that location is everything, Eighth Avenue and its neighborhood represent one of the city's greatest real-estate contradictions," Carter B. Horsley wrote.[22] The stretch of real estate running from Penn Station at 31st Street to Columbus Circle at 59th Street represented the last major undeveloped area of midtown and the logical location for future expansion of the business district there, so planners had long thought. Transportation was well supplied. It was adjacent to the Times Square theater and movie center and Madison Square Garden. Yet a lengthy list of public as well as private projects over the decades of the twentieth century could have triggered renewal but did not: the public image of the place was seemingly fixed on the stroll of prostitutes and peddling of hawkers on the avenue. The push westward embedded in the new zoning incentives for West Midtown stopped at the eastern face of Eighth Avenue, 150 feet in from its western face, a boundary line aimed at preserving the low-rise residential character of the Clinton neighborhood.

In the 1970s, when the city's established developers turned to this western section of midtown, their reading of what could profitably be built on the many parking lots and assembled sites in the neighborhood ran counter to planners' expectations. The passage of time (and repeated disappointment) had invalidated the assumption that growth westward would be fueled by high-rise office development. Instead, developers were planning residential projects. And once in progress, the shift in perceptions of use shaped the district's future growth west of Eighth Avenue.

The developer Seymour Durst was the first to relinquish his property holdings on the north side of 42nd Street between Ninth and Tenth Avenues. "I started buying in that block about 20 years ago under the assumption that it would be a natural site for an office or commercial use," Durst said, but as he told the *Times*, he and other developers had come to realize that existing supply in the area east of Eighth Avenue "could handle all of the office space needed for years to come."[23] By 1971, midtown was oversupplied with office space, the result of an unprecedented speculative building binge. After the office boom collapsed, Durst lost interest in the site and in 1973 sold his assemblage, mostly consisting of parking lots, to Richard Ravitch, who had developed the residential and business complex called Waterside Plaza (1973) on the East River and owned one of the city's largest builders of middle-income housing, HRH Construction. On that superblock site, Ravitch built Manhattan Plaza (1977), an immense gutsy apartment complex for that time in a location surrounded by moral depravity.

**3.10** The scene on Eighth Avenue in Times Square on a summer evening in July 1980, a red-light district filled with peep shows, gritty bars, hustlers and their customers, and transient housing with a heavy male presence. Developers had long been eying the area for future development, however much the current scene appeared incongruous with that vision. Allan Tannenbaum/Getty Images.

Manhattan Plaza became an event, a long-running, high-stakes dispute among city, business, and neighborhood interests that ultimately had a profound impact on the neighborhood. Originally intended as upper-income housing as a way of stabilizing the dicey area, the complex consisted of twin apartment towers, one 45 and the other 46 stories tall, shops, a health club, and a parking facility occupying the block bounded by 42nd and 43rd Streets, Ninth and Tenth Avenues. Approved under the Lindsay administration and financed with a $90 million mortgage loan under the city's Mitchell-Lama program for affordable housing, Manhattan Plaza's aspirations were undercut by sharp inflation and higher financing costs stemming from the city's fiscal crisis, causing the rents to soar way beyond what was first projected. Affluent New Yorkers were not about to pioneer a marginal section of midtown when apartments in established neighborhoods were going unoccupied. So there it sat, "an empty red elephant."[24]

City officials appealed to the federal government for rent subsidies that would salvage the project by turning it into one for low- and moderate-income families. Immediately that approach evoked intense controversy. Business and community groups vigorously objected, saying it imperiled the kind of neighborhood uplift of the project's original intent. The plan was also denounced as a bail-out for developers, though city officials argued that the proposal was the only way to prevent the development from becoming an added financial drain on a city already struggling for fiscal survival; the project, they said, also had merit in its own right.

Acting on the suggestions of Fred Papert, then-president of the Municipal Art Society, and Daniel Rose, the developer retained as the project's managing agent, city officials persuaded the federal authorities to allow the subsidies to be directed to low- and moderate-income tenants engaged in the performing arts. It was an inspired move.[25] The income of arts professionals was chronically unpredictable and in conflict with the city's escalating housing costs. "Sometimes we are broke, but we are never poor," one actor remarked in a succinct statement of the condition. After nearly two years (once the subsidy program was approved in 1977), tenants began moving in: 70 percent of the 1,690 units were rented to performers, creators, and technicians in the entertainment industry, who agreed to pay 25 percent of their annual income in rent, with the remaining units rented to senior citizens from Clinton and Chelsea and other residents from those neighborhoods. Early notable residents included the playwright Tennessee Williams and such entertainment luminaries as Jane Alexander and Teresa Wright. You can listen to the stories of those who developed the project and many of its previous tenants in the New York Emmy Award documentary *Miracle on 42nd Street* (2017).

The arc of the Manhattan Plaza story—from metaphor for the city's dire plight during the 1970s to "one of the most provocative experiments in large-scale socially integrated housing ever undertaken"[26]— was a singular event of its time: more than a decade would pass before another apartment tower opened in the area.

Another prospective signal came a year or so later, when a city panel announced it had granted a 20-year property tax abatement for the $14.5 million renovation and reopening of the Royal Manhattan Hotel. The 1,300-room 27-story building (built in the shell of the old Hotel Lincoln) on Eighth Avenue between 44th and 45th Streets, and once a big-band center known as a favorite gathering spot for theatergoers, had been boarded up since closing in 1974. The huge hotel with the huge "M" on the top (figure 2.8) had become a visible casualty of the neighborhood's high crime rate and proliferation of prostitution and sex-related businesses: low occupancy and high operating costs had forced its closure, "taking with it a piece of Broadway history." Such was the sad tenor of the times that when the hotel went on the auction block the next year, it failed to bring a minimum bid of $1.8 million,

**3.11** A street view of the twin towers of Manhattan Plaza (1977, pictured in 2016), the pioneering residential project on West 42nd Street between Ninth and Tenth Avenues. Home to performers, creators, technicians in the entertainment industry, and residents from Clinton and Chelsea, after initial controversy it became a successful experiment in socially integrated housing. Michael Bednarek, CC BY-SA 4.0.

less than 25 percent of its $8 million value as assessed by the city. In 1978, an investment group led by the Milstein family purchased the building for a reported $3.5 million with the intention of converting it to apartments, but theater owners and organizations of hotel workers convinced them "that a hotel for families and tour groups would be preferable and profitable."[27] This was still, mind you, one of the worst sex-for-sale blocks in the Times Square area.

The property tax abatement for the Royal Manhattan was a "specially needed" designation, according to the city's Industrial Commercial Incentive Board. Still struggling with the fallout from its near brush with bankruptcy, New York was desperately seeking new investment. The 54-story hotel project of Atlanta-based architect John C. Portman expected to revitalize Times Square was going nowhere, stalled by the city's fiscal crisis. Now a well-known New York real estate family was willing to make a substantial investment in a dubious area. "This abatement would be an encouragement particularly for the West Side of Manhattan, where the economic risk of such development is high," said John Zuccotti, former chairman of the City Planning Commission during the Lindsay administration and then first deputy mayor in the Beame administration, in private law practice representing the Milstein family business entity before the board.[28] Renamed the Milford Plaza, the renovated hotel opened in July 1980, in time for another Democratic National Convention in August.

The biggest enticement for development on Eighth Avenue came in 1984 in the form of a four-acre parking lot that had been sitting vacant for 17 years. The availability of a full city block under single ownership in midtown Manhattan was unheard of, said the man who purchased the site, William Zeckendorf Jr. The block between 49th and 50th Streets from Eighth to Ninth Avenues had been the home of the third Madison Square Garden from 1925 through 1968. Throughout those years, the extremely popular venue, designed to hold large crowds of eighteen thousand or more, was host to numerous standout events: the first-ever televised basketball game, New York Rangers hockey club games, as well as a rally to boycott Nazi Germany, which drew a near-maximum-capacity crowd, and a pro-Nazi gathering that reportedly drew a crowd of twenty thousand. Perhaps the most famous event at this Garden was in May 1962, when Marilyn Monroe sang "Happy Birthday" to President John F. Kennedy there.

When the Garden moved to its present location atop Penn Station further south on Eighth Avenue, the old arena was torn down by its owner, the American conglomerate Gulf and Western Industries, which had at one time thought about redeveloping the site with an office tower, apartment tower, and possibly a hotel and a department store. Several earlier plans, one for a four-theater complex, another for a large commercial showroom complex, and yet another for a $30 million enclosed amusement park, had run into local opposition, financing difficulties, or a down city economy that shelved many a redevelopment project. In his posthumously published autobiography, *Developing: My Life*, Zeckendorf recalled that other developers had eyed the site, but it was an unpromising office location, not a place to which a respectable commercial tenant would consider moving. "Hell's Kitchen was the seamy underbelly of the city, overrun with prostitutes, drug deals, and addicts who roamed Eighth Avenue, with its porn theaters, peep shows, SROs [single-room-occupancy housing], and gritty bars." Like his legendary father, the son had made something of a specialty of constructing in unconventional locations. "In building my way down Broadway, I'd gotten as far as Columbus Circle and West 57th Street," he wrote, and "here was a chance to pioneer yet another undeveloped

**3.12** In 1968, the third home of Madison Square Garden was demolished after the Garden's move to its present home atop Penn Station on Eighth Avenue, 31st to 33rd Streets. The four-acre full-block site remained vacant, used as a parking lot, for 17 years until William Zeckendorf Jr. purchased it for $100 million in late 1984 and built Worldwide Plaza (1989). New York Daily News Archive via Getty Images.

area." He would build Worldwide Plaza, one of the city's largest private projects. The only other farsighted final bidder for the site at the auction was Mortimer Zuckerman, head of Boston Properties. The developers seeking to take advantage of the city's westward growth incentives were choosing to build in the less risky area between 55th and 59th Streets surrounding Columbus Circle, where there were many potential development sites. Zeckendorf was busy there too. "A lot of people are finally realizing what a great area it is," he said. "Every possible site is under some type of assemblage and development."[29]

If they weren't participating in the boomlet around Columbus Circle, developers eager to build residential projects were leapfrogging to Tenth and Eleventh Avenues, a safe distance from the sordid conditions of the Deuce and where land ripe for development was relatively inexpensive. Harry Macklowe's 44-story rental tower Riverbank West on 43rd at Eleventh Avenue on a former parking lot opened in 1987. "It's a natural extension of the Midtown West," he said. "It's an area in transition, and the development is going in fits and starts. But there are a half-dozen of us [developers] and we're continuing to acquire [in] that section."[30]

At the other end of this block, Arun Bhatia's 42-story condominium tower, The Strand, on Tenth Avenue at 43rd opened the year after. The tower replaced a cluster of six run-down two- and four-story buildings being used as video-game warehouse and repair shop and made distinctive for its diagonal placement on the half-acre site. With the building set at a forty-five-degree angle to Manhattan's gridded streets, the site afforded great views above the low-rise buildings in the vicinity. The buyers of the apartments were successful couples without children, younger than Bhatia thought they would be, and about 30 percent were affiliated with theater. As discussed in chapter 7, the area's convenient midtown location, with close proximity to cultural attractions and restaurants, would continue to attract buyers and renters of a similar demographic.

Notably, the area was free of sex shops, Bhatia emphasized, when many years later we talked about his decision to build in the area.[31] A civil engineer who came to New York in 1976 from Bombay at the age of 25, he had absorbed the lessons of real estate from James Grasskamp, the celebrated real estate professor at the University of Wisconsin-Madison, where Bhatia received a master's degree in construction administration and real estate. Grasskamp was a quadriplegic, and when things went awry with his voice enabler, Bhatia was always in the front row of the classroom, ready to help out the man who became an influential mentor for him. Starting small, Bhatia built homes in Queens, but with the ambition that drives so many other developers, he wanted to make his mark in the fast-paced realty world of Manhattan. After converting the former Bond store building on Fifth Avenue at 35th Street into cooperative apartments, he developed a string of high-rise towers on the East Side, including The Stanford near Madison Square Park. Now a premier spot, when he started the 41-story condominium tower in 1985, the park it faced was full of hookers and drug dealing.

Considering much of the land in Manhattan overpriced, Bhatia looked westward for his next project. If he could buy lower-priced sites, he said, he was willing to take more risk. The half-acre site on Tenth Avenue where he built The Strand ran the full blockface directly opposite Manhattan Plaza, just outside the Clinton preservation area, where buildings over seven stories were prohibited. "At a cost of $9 million [approximately $24 million in 2022 dollars], the site was about 60 percent less expensive than land of similar size and potential on the Upper East Side," according to the *Times*.[32]

Favorable land costs that take away the financial risk of going into edgy areas, zoning incentives and tax abatements to attract developers, and a pioneering mentality with a long-term view on returns was what it would take to push growth west beyond the psychological barrier of established midtown locations. The growth would occur in fits and starts. So too the city and state's intended transformation of the Deuce.

## "A 50–50 PROPOSITION"

Six years into the efforts to get their big redevelopment project off the drawing boards, state and city officials could not advance the 42nd Street project at anything near the pace they had hoped for. Expectations, first about the start of condemnation proceedings and construction, then about the settlement of yet another rash of lawsuits, so often failed to meet newly established deadlines that the heady optimism of early pronouncements by public officials steadily gave way to more modest press statements. Markers of time gone by were evident in the lengthening index of lawsuits, the extended timetables for groundbreaking, and the receding forecasts of completions.

The effort to clean up the Deuce suffered challenge after challenge: a political crisis when the mayor adjudged the city's autonomy to be at stake by an action of the state, barbed architectural criticism in the city's most widely circulated papers and a wide range of professional journals, pushback from community groups in Clinton and business interests in the Garment District, fallout from the city's municipal corruption scandals that led to the revocation of the designation of developers chosen to redevelop the theater sites, ever-rising land costs, and softening demand for office space.

Amidst the setbacks, there were key victories. The first came in November 1984: through compromise and promises, public officials finally succeeded in gathering the needed support for an eleventh-hour approval of the project by the city's Board of Estimate. A second, in May 1986: after twenty-five lawsuits all of which were decided in its favor, the redevelopment project advanced with the victory in *Jackson v. N.Y.S. Urban Development Corporation*, a federal decision that finalized judicial scrutiny of the General Project Plan, settling litigation on the typically contentious environmental impacts of major land use projects. That same year, Prudential Insurance Company joined Park Tower Realty as codeveloper of the four office towers, providing financial heft to the endeavor.

**3.13** In the 1980s, numerous fires made the city's fire department a regular presence on 42nd Street. Fire Department of the City of New York.

Still, even casual observers of the New York scene understood the redevelopment project to be seriously challenged and at risk of collapse. The corporate aesthetics of the designs by Philip Johnson and John Burgee for the four office towers had triggered an all-out battle for the soul of Times Square. Plans for the Eighth Avenue sites remained unresolved; the designated developers for the mart site reported that a deal was not financially feasible and that they wanted to convert the use of the site to office. The planners' goals for reviving Times Square were working at cross purposes: overbuilding stimulated by the sunset-driven construction frenzy of midtown's zoning incentives destroyed the handsome economic competitive advantage previously held by the 42nd Street office sites. The quagmire of continuing litigation was a relentless, costly headache for public officials, while the strategy of the well-funded and patient opposition was clear: "If we can prevent things from happening for any given length of time," said Brendan Gill, a preservationist who chaired the Landmarks Conservancy, "we may yet win, not on the merits but on accidents of economics." His stated dream: "if we had another year or so, people would say we don't want to invest several hundred million dollars in yet another office building."[33] George Klein was boxed in by the seemingly interminable delays, because he could not deliver the all-important date certain for occupancy for any of several potential corporate tenants who expressed serious interest in taking an anchor position in one of the towers. The saga of redeveloping West 42nd Street amounted to a recitation on the political risks of large-scale ambitious public-development projects.

By 1987, the thrust behind the city's most ambitious effort to clean up Times Square had lost momentum, and the loss of public confidence followed not far behind. "Despite cautious optimism on the part of project officials," the *Times* reported that several developers and officials who were not part of the redevelopment plan "rated the project's chance of success at about 50 percent."[34] A consistent message crossed the spectrum of news outlets: the Times Square plan was "in jeopardy," "marked by delays," "taking more twists," "a shaky step forward," "bleeding," or "endangered." When Chemical Bank, a prime prospective tenant, dropped its interest in the project a couple of years later, the mart deal finally collapsed, and with that any hope for development of the hotel site across the street disappeared. With the loss of prospects for the western edges of the project area, the plan's economic crosspieces collapsed along with any prospect for simultaneous redevelopment of the street. To have any hope of moving forward, city and state officials would have to amend their plans. It would test the political will of elected officials and would depend on the dogged persistence of those charged with the responsibility of making something happen, Weisbrod as the head of the redevelopment project, and Rebecca Robertson after he moved over to head the city's Economic Development Corporation (successor to the Public Development Corporation).

The vision that had been put forward was diametrically at odds with the inheritance of the historic theater street and the cultural symbolism of Times Square. Over decades of both prosperity and decline, Times Square had evolved as a unique urban district that numerous dedicated interests vowed to protect. Their mission was not simply to preserve the past but rather to find an accommodation with history that fit with the reality of change already transforming Times Square. To their way of thinking, the cultural fabric of the place was at stake. Would Times Square be recast as an extension of the central business district, or could some "uneasy equilibrium" between commerce and culture be maintained?

George Klein's vision of a corporate ensemble akin to Rockefeller Center came across as an ominous model for the reconstruction of the district. As the economic driver of the street's transformation, the office program had had a distorting impact on the overall redevelopment plan. Bending to the dictates of marketability to attract corporate tenants, the city had abandoned its own strong design guidelines for the project. It had even been ready to allow demolition of the former Times Tower, iconic namesake of the district. State and city officials had put time and energy into presenting and defending the proposed office tower designs, yet they failed to do the same for the culturally significant and politically important 42nd Street legacy theaters; rhetoric was all that supported the theater agenda. All these compromises had eroded public trust, and the tide of public opinion shifted against the project.

The larger planning problems of West 42nd Street were "untouched," complained Ada Louise Huxtable, who published a searing *Times* op-ed out of deep frustration with what she felt to be the continual blunders of the city's planners who failed to understand the deep complexities of Times Square. The renewal of Times Square, she wrote, was a "farce" in which the real issues—the lack of development commitment for Eighth Avenue, "where it is essential to stabilize the neighborhood"; the weak and uncertain plans for restoring and operating the historic 42nd Street theaters; and the lack of justification for the huge public subsidies—were overlooked in the "ludicrous debate about a 'suitable style.'" Change, Huxtable argued, is an important component of Times Square, a force contributing to its distinct character. What made her incessantly wary about the 42nd project was the scale and density and character of the initial proposal, which threatened to destroy the fragile urban fabric of Times Square.[35]

Flawed as the architectural vision was, the office program alone could not carry the full weight of the desired transformation. Reluctantly, in 1987, state and city officials let go of trying to redevelop the entire street simultaneously and moved forward with a plan for development of the street in distinct phases. Instead of waiting for agreements on the project's ten sites, they would proceed with the eastern portion of the site—the four office towers—and let the western portion slide until a later time. Moving forward on all fronts at once—what Weisbrod metaphorically termed "some sort of harmonic convergence"—had always been deemed necessary but was frustratingly elusive, as events had proved. In August when UDC directors amended the General Project Plan to permit the start of property condemnation and acquisition in a sequential process, the project formally lost its balance in terms of public purpose.

Simultaneous condemnation had been important, politically as well as programmatically, even though government officials expected the approach to generate controversy and spawn litigation, as it did. While the policy change to sequential condemnation signaled a reluctant concession to the practical limits of implementing the complex multibillion-dollar project all at once, much more was now at stake. Without development along the full stretch of West 42nd Street, the

**3.14** Architects Philip Johnson and John Burgee treated their commission from George Klein as an opportunity to reshape Times Square (1984). Their design for an ensemble of office towers was intended to create a sense of place through its monumentality and harmony of materials, as shown in this rendering—with a skeletal Times Tower in the foreground. Corporate in design and spirit, the vision was at odds with the commercial and cultural legacy of the place. Courtesy of Alan Ritchie. Rendering by Patrick Lopez.

singular, unambiguous, and official objective of the project for an indefinite future was office development on the four crossroads sites. To many observers and critics this meant that the state was using its public power to do little more than assemble land for the private sector's development of commercial towers. "It should have been an inviolate rule that you can't start the East Side of the project without the West Side," remarked Richard A. Kahan, head of UDC at the initiation of the 42DP.[36] It was an opinion commonly shared in certain circles.

In one of those twists of fate, the collapse of the Manhattan real estate market created an opportunity for public officials to reconceive the transformation plan for the Deuce. It compelled a reset of the project, a rare second chance to align the revitalization plan for 42nd Street with the entertainment legacy of the place—a silver lining that altered the entire dynamic of the project.

## 42ND STREET NOW!

On April 19, 1990, the day the state took title to two-thirds of West 42nd Street, Rebecca Robertson took over from Carl Weisbrod as president of the redevelopment project. The challenge she faced, once it was clear that the old plan was dead, was to get from the present half-empty, desolate street—that "post-no-bills" territory—to a future vision capable of restoring the momentum necessary to rebuild 42nd Street to its historic promise as a vibrant place of popular entertainment. Timing was important. Something needed to happen, fast; the emptiness needed to be refilled. "We had become a pariah, politically," she recalled. "We had to develop a plan that no one would think was a major plan. . . . [I]f we do a plan that just looks like interim, then we get what we want and nobody will notice it's about the whole thing."[37]

A Canadian-born professional planner, Robertson had been hired by Weisbrod in 1987 to figure out a funding plan for the renovation and operation of the theater agenda for the street, which called for at least two nonprofit performance venues. She had been deputy director of the Department of City Planning's Manhattan office and senior planner involved with the contextual rezoning of both the Upper West Side and Upper East Side. She was a veteran of the public review process and skilled in the nuances of New York's land use intricacies. By the time she left the project in early 1997 to become a senior executive at the Shubert Organization, she would be widely credited and justly praised as the mastermind behind the new vision for 42nd Street, the driving force behind its transformation. With high energy and determination, she pushed for what was both practical and "right" in terms of what she called the "good bones" that made people love 42nd Street. Ever articulate in promoting the project, for the first seven of the nine years she spent working on it Robertson needed to have what she had in abundance: optimism.

Her passion for theater, aesthetic orientation, and skill in marketing a new message shaped the revisioning process. "We hired a public relations firm, something many public development agencies might not like to do. We treated the project like a 'product.' Before, the product was four massive buildings mired in bureaucracy and controversy." That was not a very salable image to the entertainment companies she wanted to attract to the street—Disney and Viacom. "So we hired big people—Robert A. M. Stern, Tibor Kalman—made a big effort," she told me. "Then we got a favorable review from the *Times*' architectural critic Herbert Muschamp, which we broadcast everywhere; we made a lot out of this, brought it to everyone's attention. The important thing," she emphasized, "was to create a sense of activity, of movement."[38]

Working with Stern and Kalman, Robertson's vision for a reimagined West 42nd Street, which they named 42nd Street Now!, centered on creating an internationally unique place where the pulsating beat of the city never stops, and the bright lights never go out. The goal of their conceptual plan was to re-create the street's legendary luster, with razzle-dazzle honky-tonk details. They called for signs (lots of them), layered surfaces (to avoid boring flat surfaces), glass storefronts (for transparency), and bright electric lights (to entrance) everywhere. They wanted to create visual surprise and excitement of the kind that had been typical of Times Square streets in the area's heyday. The framework Stern and Kalman proposed included new and renovated buildings, restored theaters in the midblock, and for the difficult Eighth Avenue end of the project area, some type of tourist or amusement center with eye-catching architecture. While not quite sure how that vision would take its final physical form and commercial configuration, they considered the revisioning part of the new process of "unplanning," which sought to preserve the raucous traditions of the street by prohibiting uniformity and cultivating competitiveness and counting on its legacy of experimentation and revision. It was a practical and expedient approach to a redraft of the floundering Koch-era plan.

Although there was no way to foresee exactly how the street would evolve, one thing did seem clear: despite evocative verbal connections and visual linkages to its iconic past, West 42nd Street in the twenty-first century was not likely to repattern itself on an exact historic blueprint. Legitimate theater had been the signature activity of Broadway, but it had faded as a pivotal social and economic force of the area. What mattered to Robertson was programmatic flexibility—broadening entertainment options for the midblock historic theaters as well as a full range of entertainment, recreation, and retail uses for the sites at the western end of the project area. She would meld the many ideas (crazy, out-of-the box, traditional), studies, reports (theater preservation, visual aesthetics, zoning, financial feasibility, retail development feasibility), and creative thrusts proposed by Stern and Kalman into a feasible plan, then aggressively market the vision and steer the plan through various approvals that would ensure its implementation.

As with The City at 42nd Street, the first late-1970s big vision for the street, the programmatic essence of 42nd Street Now! was popular entertainment for the middle class. Both plans specified entertainment-related and tourist-oriented uses. Both would be criticized as being "Disneylike." Both called for restoration and reuse of several of the street's legitimate theaters, much retail and many restaurants, and, of course, the financially enabling office towers clustered at the eastern end of the project area. A careful tally of specifics would likely reveal other broad-brush similarities, despite the passage of more than 13 years. One glaring difference was the disappearance of the infeasible giant mart, dropped out of existence in 42nd Street Now! and supplanted by more appropriate entertainment venues and cinemas. The dramatic contrasts in approach, tone, and aesthetic vision of the two programmatic plans, however, are striking and notable. Whereas the execution outline for The City at 42nd Street was written in terms of financial feasibility, for 42nd Street Now! it was written in the code of design guidelines. It offered no formal plan per se for the new vision, rather 342 pages of detailed design, use, and operating guidelines for the individual development sites and historic guidelines for the theaters.

Robertson spent more than two years in what she termed very tortuous negotiations with the office developers and others to line up all the pieces before orchestrating the formal presentation of 42nd Street Now! The office development joint venture, Times Square Center Associates, did not take well to the frenzied, kinetic, and noisy vision put forth in the new plan and the large and varied types of signs mandated by its detailed design guidelines. They balked at the state's demands that they pay for huge neon signs during the interim years until market conditions signaled construction was feasible. "What we're being asked to do is have signs that are different than existed there before and might not make commercial sense today," said Brian Murphy, senior vice

**3.15** With this 1992 rendering of 42nd Street Now!, Rebecca Robertson promoted Robert A. M. Stern and Tibor Kalman's revisioning of 42nd Street as a street of popular entertainment: a boisterous mix of extravagant signage, high-brow and low-brow culture, and the quintessential brash commercialism of New York. © Robert A. M. Stern Architects/42nd Street Development Project.

president of Prudential's realty group. "We cannot have the tail wag the dog," he added. The glitzy neon signs were not only the antithesis of corporate culture, they were expensive. Government officials were unmovable: the developer "is tall on buildings and short on signage," said Tese; it "is a priority for us, and they've got to get real." "No way around it," said Robertson, "we are going to have glitz on 42d Street."[39] Backed by Tese, her negotiating power forced Prudential to contractually comply with what the state wanted.

The original deal for the office towers was economically untenable, so in a bow to reality and an effort to move forward, both sides agreed to renegotiate its terms. The public sector released the private office developers from an agreement to start construction on a particular timetable; instead, they could determine when market conditions were right to build. They were also relieved of their financial obligation to contribute to the renovation of the Times Square subway station complex, a concessionary loss for the public sector directed from the governor to the head of UDC to the head of the MTA and the agency's real estate director responsible for renegotiating the developer's future subway contribution. In turn, the developers would have to spend a minimum of $20 million ($42 million in 2022 dollars) in interim retail and related obligations to fill the empty spaces where the office towers would rise someday. This quid pro quo was Robertson's temporary anti-blight plan to attract pedestrian activity to the storefronts left vacant by the condemnation.

Radically different in tone and substance and aesthetics from the initial plan, the new vision won favorable reviews. Though it no longer enjoined a fight with the street's historic identity, the original high-density office program remained solidly in place. In the minds of many, 42nd Street Now! was enticing but unfortunately interim. The editors of *Newsday* advised public officials "Better rethink those office towers." The four "bulky" towers were "out of synch with market reality," and the public benefit of a renovation of the dilapidated 42nd Street subway station "was kissed goodbye." "Redeveloping Times Square is still a worthy venture," they concluded, "but what seemed feasible in 1982 may be obsolete. . . . Fifty-story boxes never did cut it in Times Square." Long-time critics of the project were quick to forcefully reiterate their objections to a "massive give-away [that] will be New York City's largest taxpayer-financed real estate boondoggle ever"; "unbelievably large subsidies . . . that never made sense for the site," said State Senator Franz Leichter, "are even worse now."[40] Veteran *Times* reporter Thomas J. Lueck questioned, "Must Show Go On?"

**Figure 3.16** Elizabeth Diller and Ricardo Scofidio's 1993 video installation *Soft Sell* in the entrance to the Rialto Theatre on 42nd Street—the mouth was a prostitute calling from the shadows—was the biggest hit in the well-publicized "42nd Street Art Project," one of Rebecca Robertson's efforts to span the gap before construction activity revitalized the street. Curated by Creative Time, Inc., a 20-year-old organization devoted to presenting performing and visual arts in public spaces throughout New York, seventeen temporary installations filled the spaces left vacant by the condemnation process, as a way to say "42nd Street is back." Michael Moran, Courtesy of Diller Scofidio + Renfro.

These criticisms of the city's financial deal with the office developer held even less political weight in the new deal-making climate than they had previously. The Dinkins administration was less friendly to real estate development than the Koch administration had been, but that distinction did not hold water. The city could not afford, as the business biweekly *Crain's* put it, "angering the company that had invested almost $300 million in the project," nor losing the 5,000 New York jobs of its subsidiary, Prudential Securities, Inc., which "not coincidentally" were in jeopardy, as *Newsday* pointed out. The reason was simple: the city and state needed Prudential to fund the anti-blight interim plan and shield the public sector from more potential failure. Although they were in a position to default the insurance giant, "A default doesn't do *us* any good," said Tese.[41]

What at first appeared to be a mistake—calling 42nd Street Now! "interim"—ceased to arouse high-pitch emotion among the civics and other long-time critics as the new plan's programmatic promises came to fruition pretty quickly, to everyone's amazement: in October 1993,

**Figure 3.17** A half-scale model of British Airways' supersonic Concorde, pictured in 1996, was erected on the roof of Hansen's brewery as part of Prudential Insurance Company's obligations under the terms of the interim retail plan. Weighing 24,000 pounds with a 42-foot wingspan, the model was in place for eighteen months until the lease on the site expired in 2001 and the site prepared for Boston Properties' construction of an office tower. As unusual as this mounted model seemed, an earlier spectacular of a three-dimensional TWA propeller-driven four-engine Super-Constellation had been mounted on the roof of Toffenetti's at the southeast corner of Broadway and 43rd Street in 1955. Gary Hack.

in a bold move, the board of the not-for-profit theater organization, known now as New 42, announced a plan to restore the Victory Theatre, previously home of some of the hottest porn films, as a theater for young people, the city's first such venue. Not long after, in February 1994, Disney announced it would restore the historic New Amsterdam Theatre and reopen it as the permanent home for Disney theatrical and musical productions on 42nd Street.

The Disney announcement created a strong momentum for the entertainment-focused plan by sparking a swift 180-degree shift in the perception of investment possibilities among private developers and brand-name corporations. It was the catalyst for other big-name commitments to West 42nd Street. Disney, however, was not the pioneer. That role belongs to New 42 with its children's theater. The timing of Disney's entrance onto the development stage, however, was near-perfect:

safety had been established on the street by the early 1990s, when negotiations with Disney began, after decades of effort and condemnation of two-thirds of the property on the block. The all-American family-oriented entertainment giant was risking its reputation by placing itself on the famously chaotic, formerly naughty, bawdy street, but it would be taking over the street's crown-jewel theater. And, importantly, under its sweetheart deal with the city-state development entity, Disney would not be taking on financial risk. Disney was questing for a Broadway theater for live performances to leverage its worldwide brand, and the choicest venues capable of mounting musical productions were all locked up by other long-running musical spectacles.[42] As discussed in the next chapter, both Disney and government officials advanced their strategic interests in lasting ways.

The announcements kept coming: in 1995, Tishman Urban Development Corporation was chosen to develop a hotel and retail-entertainment complex on the western end of the street at Eighth Avenue, and Forest City Ratner announced plans for an entertainment-retail complex, including the future home of Madame Tussauds wax museum on the south side of the street. In 1996, the Durst Organization announced its intent to buy the development rights for Site 12, and that Condé Nast would anchor the office tower. The following year, Roundabout Theatre Company announced it would renovate the Selwyn Theatre, New 42 that it would build a rehearsal building for non-profits, and the Rudin Organization with Reuters America that they would build a tower on Site 3 purchased from Prudential. In 1998, Boston Properties announced its plan to buy the last two office sites from Prudential. The next year, the *New York Times* announced its intention to move its headquarters into a new tower to be built on Eighth Avenue and 41st Street within the project area.

By 1996, after more than 16 years of effort, the last remaining adult-use stores of the Deuce had been cleared out, and with that clearance, the nostalgia stories started to appear. "It was the Pits. It'll be Missed" headlined one *Times* article.

The gap between the necessity and the invention of redevelopment, between big vision and little progress, had been bridged. While not a single appeal existed for altering the fundamental financial driver of the project, piling density on the four crossroads sites linked to an innovative financing strategy had already succeeded in doing what it was supposed to do: create the economic platform for change without directly exposing the city to financial risk. Even if the project's overall development density had not changed, the new highly detailed guidelines for each site ensured that what got built on West 42nd Street would be strikingly different from the visual image of the appropriately much-maligned Johnson/Burgee corporate towers.

By the mid-1990s, architecture no longer had to serve as a powerful instrument for the reordering of existing physical relationships on 42nd Street, as had been the case in the early 1980s. Decreasing crime and citywide efforts to improve safety, the shuttering of the street's peeps and porn shops, and the triumphs of historic preservation were reordering the space. The new tourist-based agenda pushed the pace of change by resetting the public's expectations and altering investors' perceptions with its new focus on popular entertainment. The credibility of well-known developers and clout of private investors such as Disney made the difference. Only after the psychological perceptions of 42nd Street had changed could a set of technical design guidelines allowing for small-scale internally generated transformations find acceptance as an urban reality.

# 4  SURPRISE VELOCITY

Show World is going to close in a matter of weeks. This real estate is very valuable.
Richard Basciano, Summer 2016

The winds of change had been blowing across the erotic landscape of Times Square for two decades before the undisputed king of New York porn conceded that the real estate there was more valuable than the pornography business. Richard Basciano had grown rich from a rough business he transformed into "a sort of Saks of Sleaze," offering "the absolute cutting edge in futuristic porn technologies" (so said *Screw*, the pornographic magazine). His enterprises, wrote *Newsday*, "are to porn what the Horn & Hardart Cafeterias used to be to dining—they offer something for every taste." In 1975, he opened what would become the crown jewel of his empire, Show World Center, and expanded the operation into four floors of possibly the nation's largest porn emporium of books, peeps, videotapes, sex aids, and live entertainment, including strippers on a carousel, group sex on a stage, and guest appearances from big-name porn stars. But by the late 1990s his all-things 24-hour erotic empire had been shrinking for years. Internet pornography siphoned off trade. He had lost four of his sex-related properties when New York State condemned them for the redevelopment of the Deuce, though the compensation of an estimated $14 million windfall comfortably cushioned the loss. Still, Show World Center on Eighth Avenue across from the redevelopment area hung on, albeit with a tamed-down footprint following Mayor Rudy Giuliani's 1995 anti-porn

**4.1** Richard Basciano's Show World Center (1975, pictured in 1976) was one of the last remaining pornography businesses in Times Square. After New York City passed anti-porn zoning in 1995, the sex emporium gradually transformed from all porn to part theater, leasing space to Off-Off-Broadway productions, before it finally closed in 2018. In addition to Show World, the former "sultan of smut" owned seven other properties in or bordering the 42nd Street Development Project area. AP Photo/G. Paul Burnett.

zoning restrictions. The change from what was "once all pornography" to "part theater" undoubtedly cut into the bottom line, but the value of the real estate continued to rise.[1]

The former boxer had been a "stubborn holdout" against the transformation of the neighborhood and the economic Darwinism of higher-value land uses uprooting the trade on the Deuce. He was known to be a savvy real estate investor with a pattern of selling his properties as a neighborhood gentrified, but Show World, housed in a narrow 12-story building where he had an office and a penthouse apartment with a full-size boxing ring and lived with his wife, was an exception. Proposing to close what one city official called the "flagship of the sex industry in New York" would surely mark its symbolic death in Times Square. Symbolic. Once cleansed of the four Ps—prostitutes, pornography, peep shows, and pimps—rising pressure on real estate values in the city's infamous erotic zone had been inexorable. The location was ripe, finally. But before he could capture the land value beneath his long-running sex emporium, the porn magnate aka real estate player died at age 91 in early May 2017. "Rest in Porn," the *Daily News* printed in large font on its front-page obituary. His buildings showed signs of neglect, but they were valuable, and his estate moved on, considering plans to develop an $80 million boutique office and retail property on the Eighth Avenue site.

The strip of 42nd Street that runs between Seventh and Eighth Avenues has a personality apart from that of Times Square, though the two places are often spoken of as one. It's an easy slip of the tongue (or pen) since the contiguous blocks historically have made up a world-renowned district of popular entertainment. By the 1970s, though, the cultural distinction between the two was strikingly evident: the Deuce had become sexually segregated, "closed" and "masculinized" in contrast to the "expansive, inclusive" bowtie area of the square just around the corner.[2] The extent of criminality, drug dealing, and debauchery that prevailed on 42nd Street set it apart from the down-and-out state of deterioration in Times Square. Moreover, the types of intensive law enforcement efforts that were bringing immediate changes in Times Square in the late 1970s had very little impact on the conditions on the Deuce. Forty-second Street was so out of control that the Police Department deployed its Tactical Patrol Force, otherwise known as the "Hats and Bats" for the helmets and the truncheons police would use, for several months in the summer of 1981 to calm things down.

In aggressively seeking to transform the Deuce using the government's powers of condemnation, city and state officials had undertaken a transparent gamble; the plan's visible risk could not be hidden behind opaque screens or covered up with rhetorical devices that might shield it from critics and the public at large. No matter how carefully officials maneuvered to ensure success, failure loomed as an ever-present possibility—until it wasn't. Until the infamous street of prostitutes, pimps, drug dealers, chicken hawks, and other hustlers was no longer the Deuce.

Twenty years in the making, the transformation seemed to happen overnight, astonishingly so. The critical mass of new economic activity government officials persistently pursued was at last visible. The new streetscape seemed raw, not yet inhabited, so new it had not yet acquired the patina of constant activity, which seemed out of place in the well-worn turf of Times Square. Some changes had been gradual—the one-by-one closing of street-level stores and second-level enterprises; others more immediately dramatic—the "post-no-bills" messages stenciled on vacant properties taken by condemnation. Tourist or New Yorker, if you had not been to 42nd Street since the early 1980s, the visual leap from danger zone to the "vibrant mecca of tourism" required a flight of imagination. It was a Rip Van Winkle moment. Who could have imagined 42nd Street would be safe enough for families to bring their youngsters to the city's first theater for children, a theater that once housed the raciest porn flicks? The Walt Disney Company committing to bring live theater to the disreputable street, an ungated territory it could not control? The shuttered storefronts repopulated with a wax museum, nightclub, and two multiplex movie emporiums? And who could have imagined that, "after several decades of slow decay, the transformation would be as fast as a game of three-card monte"?[3]

The place had been remade. It was safe. Evicted, porn and its adult entertainment stores moved to other places in the city and proliferated online. Crime dropped dramatically. Popular entertainment returned. Families pushing strollers replaced drug pushers. Teens and couples from the boroughs once again came for first-run movies. Historic theaters once again hosted live entertainment. New theaters were constructed, as were much-needed rehearsal studios. Illuminated signs flashed brighter than before. Thousands of office workers employed by media companies and accounting firms moved into four new office towers at the crossroads of Times Square. Occupancy at the two new hotels on the street reached robust levels, continuously. Retail sales soared. Commercial property values flourished. And tourists came in record numbers, even after 9/11, powering the city's economic recovery. The central idea behind the government's 42nd Street Development Project

**4.2** Midday on West 42nd Street, where the mix of office towers, live theaters, movies, and popular entertainments coexist with eye-catching signs in profusion. This westward view toward the Hudson River shows the new high-rise residential towers chock-a-block on both sides of the street, 2019. Gary Hack.

had been to change the market—the real estate market. That had happened, without question.

The timing of change held particular significance for those of us who chronicle the city. "By the end of the 1990s, the fiscal crisis had dwindled to a memory, and New York City seemed to have reinvented itself once again," remarked Ric Burns and James Sanders in their sweeping illustrated history of New York. "Nowhere would the city's self-transformation seem more startlingly complete than in the metamorphosis of its greatest public space—Times Square," by which they meant "42nd Street and the storied side streets off Broadway."[4]

Beyond what was so immediately visible, the transformation set in place a new economic underpinning for 42nd Street, one that promised ongoing returns to the entertainment legacy of the place. Ever since the days of Mayor Fiorello LaGuardia, moral imperative had been the driving force behind efforts to clean up the street's chronic conditions; more than 40 years later, commercial necessity became the driving force under the administrations of Mayor Ed Koch and Governor Mario Cuomo. The real estate strategy behind the redemption plan for "Sodom on the Hudson" represented a first on this symbolic turf. It was controversial. Never before had New York employed the heavy hand of eminent domain to take private property for a commercial redevelopment project in Manhattan or relied on deals with private developers to fund the cost of doing so.[5] Those deals became the foundation not just for preserving but for growing the street's legacy of live theater, as rising property values helped fund the theater agenda. The millions committed to the adjacent community of Hell's Kitchen—the political quid pro quo for supporting the project—went to improving hundreds of existing housing units that remained affordable for the neighborhood's existing low- and moderate-income residents. The outcome of the politically bold gamble was no longer uncertain.

## "AGAINST ALL ODDS"

On December 14, 2018, the New York City Economic Development Corporation released *Against All Odds*, a thirty-minute documentary film celebrating the transformation of the Deuce into a world-class entertainment district. It was time for self-congratulation. Despite continuous fateful obstacles strewn along the way, the ambitious redevelopment project had succeeded in achieving what city and state officials set out to accomplish and then some. After years and years of stalled progress, celebratory openings of renovated theaters, new office towers, hotels, and entertainment places came in rapid succession beginning in 1995, uninterrupted even by the events of 9/11.[6] This high-profile erasure of *the* symbol of the moral worst of New York was the city's first big successfully completed project since the well-known failure of Westway, the controversial project that would have replaced the collapsed West Side Elevated Highway with a new highway below ground on landfill and parkland and commercial and residential development on the land created above.

When it comes to city building, it is easier to think big than to execute on the big idea. City officials face several ever-present, well-known

**4.3** In 2018, New York City's Economic Development Corporation released *Against All Odds*, a chronicle of the transformation told in interviews with project leaders, real estate developers, architects, and law enforcement officials. The documentary's title aptly captures the trials and tribulations of the 20-year saga to transform the naughty-bawdy to family-friendly. New York City Economic Development Corporation.

problems, most with troublesome duration: Thinking big is massively expensive. Thinking big requires enormous political capital and an equal amount of persistence. Persistence is necessary to surmount the inevitable opposition from varied interest groups and the inevitable litigation, as well as the legitimate procedural demands for public reviews (absent in an earlier era when Robert Moses shaped the city with one big public work after another). If big plans call for acquiring private property through condemnation, political risk escalates exponentially. For all these reasons, big city-shaping projects typically play out over a time frame of two decades (or more), well beyond a politician's normal time horizon.

It is not easy to build big in New York City in the post-Moses era where a diffusion of power reduces the probabilities of making things happen, or happen within a reasonable time frame. New processes of participatory democracy and constraints on public officials' exercise of authority have elevated skill at process into power. Unable to power-broker from a commanding position of influence as did Moses, public officials like Carl Weisbrod and Rebecca Robertson, who managed the process of implementing the 42nd Street project, operate behind a shield of political power that only leadership from mayors and governors can provide.

The process of executing on the big plan can be grinding, fashioned as often is the case in a politicized context that imposes demands on appointed officials focused on the task at hand. This context would have been an irritation to the man who defined the definitive command-and-control style of public development. For all the just criticism of Moses's autocratic methods, he "solved a crucial dilemma for democratic societies: how to build the large public works that were essential to modern urban life but whose daunting time frame and enormous human and economic costs made them anathema to public officials, who fear alienating any segment of the electorate."[7]

Moses would have judged the institutional coalition of city and state entities needed to push forward the 42nd Street project as too diffuse a power base from which to operate because it precluded the type of unilateral decision making he exercised through personalized and consolidated control of the city's urban-renewal and building-related authorities. Having consolidated power—at the height of his career, he occupied twelve appointed positions simultaneously—Moses did not need to be patiently persevering. Nor did he need to compromise with opposing interest groups, who today through freedom-of-information laws have access to types of information he would have kept secret. And he did not need to rely on scarce local resources. The public authorities he controlled could access the weighty financial resources required, beyond the riches he was able to get from Washington, to push through his aggressive building agendas. By the mid-1980s, the monies Washington had so steadfastly supplied to cities for revitalization had dried up (except for a small amount of Urban Development Action Grant funds). Cities were on their own, forced to finance redevelopment projects with their own resources. Freed from federal rules and regulations, surprisingly, they responded with invention, devising new financial strategies that proved to be powerful alternatives to direct federal aid.[8]

Mayor Koch was hardly immune to the political risks of trying to do what so many of his predecessors had failed to do on West 42nd Street. The transformation he set in motion had not yet materialized when he left City Hall after three tumultuous terms that "encompassed the fiscal austerity of the late 1970s and the racial conflicts and municipal corruption scandals of the 1980s, an era of almost continuous discord that found Mr. Koch caught in a maelstrom day after day." But "the energy that Koch invested in the Crossroads of the World," as the *Post*'s Steve Cuozzo wrote in the former mayor's obituary, "galvanized the notion that it didn't forever have to remain the world's most brightly lit mugging and pimping ground." The template for the redevelopment Koch set in place survived, even as the architecture and land uses of the plan changed dramatically. As Koch told me in an interview for *Times Square Roulette*, "Mayors always build on the shoulders of their predecessors."[9] The final achievement is what matters, he emphasized. When it came to large-scale city-building ambitions in New York, cleansing 42nd Street broke the public curse of inhibition—an achievement evident to a worldwide audience.

City officials did not get a much-needed critical piece of their deal with the private developers who won the rights to redevelop the Deuce. Markedly, the MTA lost out on some $95 million of public improvements to the Times Square subway station ($267.3 million in 2022 dollars), the system's most heavily used station, a station complex in dire need of a complete overhaul. Developers of the four office towers had gotten the right to build towers with extraordinary density along with hefty tax abatement subsidies in exchange for direct payments dedicated to below-ground subway improvements and for financing the project's condemnation acquisitions. When the deal was cut in 1984, conditions in this complicated labyrinth of a subway station were deplorably rank, exhibiting similar social conditions to the street above. It ranked among the most dangerous stations in the system and among the most depressing public environments found anywhere. Remediating these conditions was a cost the public sector always should have borne directly; instead, it became a price for high-density development above. The city itself could do little to directly remedy the situation underground, even had it had the funds to do so, because the subway system is governed by New York State under its agent, the Metropolitan Transportation Authority (MTA), and fixing up the Times Square station was not among the MTA's highest priorities.

The initial deal to improve the experience underground in the Times Square subway station was risky because it yoked this strategic public benefit to the private-investment calculus of developers definitively going forward with construction of the four office towers. When the real estate market collapsed in 1990, indefinitely delaying a development start, the developer-funded improvements fell by the wayside; they were formally canceled in 1992. The privatized plan had been born out of financial exigency, but it was fatally flawed.[10] The public sector lost out on its side of the deal, while the developers' suffered no diminution of benefit. A revised and scaled-down plan of improvements went forward years later, but only in 2019 did the MTA announce plans for a complete $750 million overhaul and integration of work planned for the several stations along the 42nd Street corridor, with a 2022 completion date. These plans included a long overdue full reconfiguration of the Times Square Shuttle tracks and installation of handicapped-accessible elevators, two elements of the initial mid-1980s program originally intended as part of the 42nd Street project.[11]

The complex and contentious process to transform the Deuce owes its success to three essentials: the existence of vested stakeholders who could not readily walk away from the project or whose resources endowed them with staying power that could weigh in as powerfully as direct control; pragmatism on the part of both private developers and public officials, which enabled adaptive accommodation to changed circumstances; and the unwavering political commitment of three

**4.4** The Metropolitan Transportation Authority commissioned Roy Lichtenstein to create a mural for the Times Square subway station as part of its permanent art collection. Made in 1994, three years before the Pop Artist died, the enormous porcelain enamel piece (6 feet high by 53 feet long) lay in storage until it was installed in 2002, when the MTA realized that plans for the station reconstruction would not go forward as previously planned. At the far rear of this subway mezzanine, just barely visible, is the crosstown shuttle to the Grand Central subway station, 2022. Gary Hack.

mayors and two governors enhanced by an unusual continuity of leadership among the project's executive officers over its 20-year history. The 42nd Street project did not suffer the "disease of bureaucracy," nor did it collapse under the weight of continuous litigation, as did Westway. It survived because of the politics of persistence; the public sector's willingness, however reluctantly, to take risks; the ability and willingness of a private partner (Prudential Insurance Company) to live up to its financial commitment; and, in a situation of event-making opportunity, the leadership of specific individuals whose skills did more than just hold a project together: they made it happen. In surmounting a set of obstacles that had previously felled other big public ambitions, the achievement on West 42nd Street erased a brooding sense of failure and limiting scope of imagination that had shadowed City Hall in the aftermath of Westway and the setback of another large-scale project, the initial plan to redevelop the site of the Coliseum at Columbus Circle. And it definitively marked a new era of city building in New York.

## AMBIVALENCE AMID APPLAUSE

As legitimate theaters on 42nd Street opened to celebratory applause—the New Victory first followed by the New Amsterdam—the press responded with enthusiasm fused with a certain amount of disbelief. A rush of articles chronicled the "Miracle on 42nd St." and "How the City's Once Most Reviled Street Got Its Groove Back." Out-of-town travel reports gushed promotional: "respectable," "wholesome," "dazzling," "bewildering," "family friendly." In the wonder, hyperbole, photographic messages, telegenic images, and reviews, editorialists, reporters, writers, and commentators offered genuine praise for the achievement—if not complete comfort with the cultural transformation that had reduced the street's rating from XXX to G. Amid praise that was balanced and biased, realistic and nostalgic, superficial and probing, an uneasiness prevailed that something had been lost in wiping out the gritty debauched past of the epicenter of vice.

"For some, there was a price attached to the successful transformation of Times Square, which seemed to many people to have traded in its corrupt old soul for a glittering corporate veneer with nothing underneath," wrote Burns and Sanders. Was the identity of the city's iconic space "permanently betrayed" with the erasure of the old offices of press agents and talent scouts and the seedy local shops? Could the "spectacular" new structures filled with brand-name theme restaurants and chain stores and major media retail outlets capture any of the ambience of the street's vibrant history? Was Times Square in danger of becoming a historic space "neutered of all idiosyncrasy"?[12] This was not, of course, the first time corporations or their brands had made their home in Times Square, but this time it seemed like a complete takeover. The old-time places and old-time characters were gone, a ghostly presence living underneath the new, pulled up on occasion by journalists and writers fascinated by compelling stories of a vanishing New York.

Discomfort among academic commentators was widespread: The new 42nd Street was not an organic expression of New York culture. Design deliberately "edited out" the past to fit a new public, a new morality. The subsidies to developers were outsized. They allowed that the redevelopment effort was "a sophisticated, nuanced approach" and "deeply tied to the images and legacies of the area's history . . . the new spaces incorporated many of the area's old uses and remained open to new uses and appropriations by all sorts of people." But that was not a good enough scorecard for those who considered those aspects of the redevelopers' work "peripheral" to the main purpose of the redevelopment: "to create a payoff for the landlords and developers involved."[13]

From this perspective, the domineering corporate presence on the street was suspect. Well-known urban scholars voiced widespread misgiving and ultrasensitivity to the Walt Disney Company's size and power, which they took to be the prevailing influence on a tourist-oriented gestalt permeating the whole of Times Square. The theme restaurants and corporate stores were artificial because they represented marketing avenues for corporate profits (notwithstanding how consumers might feel about these places or products). The corporate decision to locate on 42nd Street was suspect as well because it was not based on New York's inherent attractiveness (left undefined) but rather on its position as a venue for global distribution (as if being a global city was a zero-sum game that precluded "intricacies of local culture"). The former theater street was "New York Land," a themed shopping area of brand identities "split among three properties owned by the Disney, Warner Brothers, and Ford corporations."[14]

In a similar vein, other critics considered Disney's brand of corporate entertainment catering to the tastes of a mass market threatening to the historic legacy of 42nd Street. "The fact that what is being offered has not just been Disneyfied but, in fact, involves Disney itself means that the sex and sophistication which once characterized the area's theatrical productions will be replaced by productions deemed acceptable for middle America." Imports like Madame Tussauds, Sony's Cinemax theaters, and London-based musicals such as *Phantom of the Opera*, *Les*

**4.5** The rock musical *Rent*, music, lyrics, and book by Jonathan Larson, played at the Nederlander Theatre at 41st Street from 1996 to 2008, one of the longest-running shows on Broadway. Loosely based on the 1896 opera *La Bohème*, the critically acclaimed and Pulitzer Prize-winning musical first appeared off Broadway at the New York Theatre in 1993. BroadwaySpain via Wikimedia Commons, CC BY-SA 4.0.

*Misérables*, and *Miss Saigon* were equally problematic because "rather than New York setting the model of artistic production emulated by the rest of the world, it is being imprinted by the standardized tourist product developed elsewhere."[15]

Were these criticisms elitism or just a clouded lens that underestimated the creative range of Broadway and the dynamic of Off-Broadway and Off-Off-Broadway theater? Did these critics factor into their calculus original productions like Jonathan Larson's Pulitzer Prize-winning rock musical *Rent*, which "upended Broadway's sense of what musical theater could be," moved from its initial home at the New York Theatre Workshop in the East Village to Broadway's larger Nederlander Theatre (National Theatre, 1921) on 41st Street, where it played 5,123 performances before closing in 2008, after 12 years as one of the longest-running shows on Broadway?[16]

Corporate approaches to theatrical advertising and marketing were nothing new to Broadway, as theater scholar Elizabeth Wollman convincingly argued: it was "the intensification, rather than the sudden introduction of trends that have existed in the theater world for decades." Was the quasi-monopolistic Theatrical Syndicate of the early twentieth century any less of a corporate presence? In terms of its financial resources and reach "back into the web of popular culture," corporatization greatly benefited the theater industry in some ways. Theater is expensive, especially in New York, and Broadway productions have been commercial ventures from their earliest beginnings. "Media conglomerates have simply made Broadway even more commercial than the Shuberts, Nederlanders, and Jujamcyns could manage on their own."[17] As for Broadway's long-term prospects, Disney shows have had an especially important impact on broadening the demographic reach of theater attendance. Moreover, Disney's presence has not chilled artistic creativity or inhibited the emergence of diversity on the Broadway stage, evident in award-winning musicals such as *The Color Purple, Spring Awakening, On Your Feet!*, and *Hamilton*, to name but a few.

The urbanist and public intellectual Marshall Berman was no cheerleader for branded environments or developer deals, but he understood the strength and nuance of New York's culture and, in particular, 42nd Street's "century-old identity as a spectacle." He believed that the force of the city's DNA and Times Square's layered meanings, what he termed a "congestion of ideas," would impact its newest corporate players rather than the other way around. Having observed the place since his parents took him there as a child and having chronicled its past and its transformation numerous times, he concluded that the old and the new could coexist, that the overflowing life on the ground proved the "hopelessness of the long crusade to kill the street." In 2007, when the street's transformation was fully evident, he wrote about the crowds being bigger than ever and more diverse, with more ethnicities, more religions, a wider spectrum of classes attracted by the bright lights. "The Scarsdale Galahads are here in force today but so are the night people; there may even be more children of the night because the night is safer now." What he loved was the essence of the place: the mixed crowds with room for everybody.[18]

Other well-known commentators were not so sure. Writers like Adam Gopnik and James Traub allowed that the transformation of the Deuce had succeeded. They did not put a false gloss on the past depravity of the place, nor did they bemoan the disappearance of the porn business or the Deuce's "predatory or just plain pitiful" denizens. It was clean now. It was safe now. It was free of the undesirables now. It was perpetually full of people now. The intense commercial festivity of the street was consistent with its entertainment legacy. The new status quo, however, was troubling. Something other than sleaze and scuzz seemed

**4.6** The crowd of pedestrians on 42nd Street as sunset nears, more interested in taking photos of the spectacle than selfies, 2018. Creative Commons CCO.

to be missing from the ensemble of glass towers, popular entertainment venues, and flashing signs that had transformed 42nd Street.

For Traub, what made the street great was that "it stood for something larger than itself—glamour, excess, sex appeal, decadence." His reference point was the street's exalted days before the downward spiral triggered by Prohibition and exacerbated by the Depression; it was not the dark days of *Midnight Cowboy*. The pervasiveness of global entertainment juggernauts crowding onto 42nd Street was sweeping out the possibility of local culture. "Perhaps what one should say of this new 42nd Street is simply that it *worked*: it drew people to the heart of the city."[19]

Gopnik considered the situation in Times Square from a more nuanced understanding of the place. He believed "you didn't have to have nostalgia for squalor and cruelty to feel that some vital chunk of New York experience has been replaced by something different, and less." On the other hand, "there was something spooky about the contemporary Times Square." The spookiness wasn't about the global branding per se, but rather the loss of a distinctively city thing: the idiosyncratic business ecology of the area. "One of the things that make for vitality in any city," he wrote, "and above all in New York, is the trinity of big buildings, bright lights, and weird stores."[20]

Weird stores are the specialized stores nurtured when "a peculiar and even obsessive entrepreneur caters to a peculiar and even an obsessive taste." Consider the sheet music emporium Colony Music (1948–2012), the celebrated Drama Book Shop (1917, reopened by Lin-Manuel Miranda in 2021 after a number of Covid-related delays), and the model train (and cars, planes, kits) mecca The Red Caboose Hobby Shop (1946). What Gopnik calls "weird stores" are the distinguishing elements of a neighborhood's commercial life. "If the big buildings and the bright signs reflect the city's vitality and density," he wrote, "weird stores refract it"; "they imply that the city is so varied that someone can make a mundane living from one tiny obsessive thing." Times Square was also distinguished by a specialized street like West 48th Street, legendary "Music Row," where since the 1930s musicians—including legends Jimi Hendrix, Eric Clapton, the Rolling Stones, and the Beatles—could find dozens of shops that sold and repaired guitars, drums, keyboards, sheet music, and accessories. Music Row thrived on the cultural calling card of Times Square until soaring rents and the conveniences offered by the Internet whittled down the shops that had lined both sides of the block. By 2016, the last of them—Sam Ash Music, Rudy's Music Stop, and Alex Carozza's accordion store—were gone. The loss of local retail variety was becoming all too ubiquitous in neighborhoods across the city (and in big cities across the nation). It was not unique to the transformation angst of Times Square. "Times Square, as so often in the past, is responding, in typically heightened form, to the general state of the city," said Gopnik. "We just feel it more on Broadway."[21]

In a thoughtful essay that stands out for its immersion in the reality of Times Square, *New York* magazine reporter Kim Velsey wrote in 2016: "The only context in which it is routinely praised is a historical one,

**4.7** Still a presence in 2022, two of Times Square's enduring specialized shops: the celebrated Drama Book Shop (1917), a cultural institution for theatrical works, at its new location on West 39th Street; and the Red Caboose Hobby Shop on West 45th Street (the last of three on that street) in a basement location on a site that has housed a hobby shop since 1946. Gary Hack.

and then usually in a misguided glorification of its former grittiness." She argued that "nostalgia clouds the ugliness of the past and conceals the vibrancy of the present, but perhaps worst of all, it offers a pass for looking at Times Square as it really is and as it should be." To ignore the square as it is now is a mistake, she said, because no other part of the city has so captured the allure and viability of the dream of New York.[22]

Most critics, though not all, judge the transformation of 42nd Street and, by extension, Times Square through the lens of memory or expectation. What the transformation symbolizes—the fears, hopes, and desires it triggers—varies with perspective and the memories the place evokes, which can depend on when one first experienced Times Square and whether that was as a child or an adult. At the same time that these reactions are personal, they are reflective of larger shifts that have been taking place in New York's creative life for decades. The currents of popular culture and creative expression that so defined the historic legacy of 42nd Street and Broadway have not disappeared in New York; they have, however, been originating in places well beyond Broadway.

Small theaters have a long history in New York City. The city's nearly 100 producing or presenting Off-Broadway and Off-Off-Broadway theaters are an especially vibrant source of cutting-edge work and a platform for theater talent that often makes its way to Broadway. The last five winners of the Tony for Best Musical, for example, came from Off-Broadway, including *Hamilton* (2016), *The Band's Visit* (2018), and *Hadestown* (2019); ditto, winners of the Tony for Best Play: *Hand to God* (2015), *The Humans* (2016), and *Oslo* (2017). Similarly, small theaters have developed Pulitzer Prize-winning plays such as *Fairview* (2019), *Between Riverside and Crazy* (2015), *The Flick* (2014), and *Clybourne Park* (2011). The sourcing of these winners has come from uncommon places; for example, *What the Constitution Means to Me*, a Pulitzer play finalist the *Times* called the most important play of the 2019 season, started in P.S. 122, a tiny performance place in Brooklyn, then moved to an alternative theater in the East Village before getting to Broadway, where it became a hit. On the popular music front, in the 1970s the boroughs of the Bronx, Brooklyn, and Queens gave birth to hip hop, Latin music, rock, and punk rock.

These wellsprings of popular culture originating in places beyond Broadway attest to New York City's historic capacity for creative innovation arising from social and ethnic diversity and its position as the nation's media capital. They are the organic, the local expressions of popular culture that had once been dominated by Times Square. They are the vital contributing force to the city's position as the world's cultural capital. Expecting a publicly driven redevelopment project or even the private market left to its devices to faithfully recapture the emotional significance of a 100-year-old cultural history in a single central place is asking too much, even for New York City's famous theater street.

"Times Square is no more Gotham's cultural crucible than it is its civic 'heart,'" remarked historian Mike Wallace. "After September 11, when New Yorkers needed to come together in public, few headed to Times Square," which surprised reporters. People were gathering in other places, "holding candlelight vigils, singing, mourning, arguing, and comforting one another in other public places in the city: Union Square, Washington Square, Central Park, the Brooklyn Heights promenade."[23] That is not so surprising considering that Times Square, first and foremost, is a place for celebration.

## BETTING LONG

Realty interests had long anticipated a westward expansion of midtown's burgeoning business district, but it would take many decades before modern office buildings finally moved onto the celebrated theater block. Real estate plays from new, higher-density office uses on 42nd Street had tantalized them during the unprecedented building boom of the roaring twenties. In 1927, when two property owners floated tentative plans to raze low-lying structures and build tall office buildings on the block, the move westward appeared imminent. Land values were soaring throughout Manhattan, especially in Times Square. Speculation was rife. Landmarks were falling to the wrecker's ball. Low-rise theaters on such prime real estate faced demolition: the "land is too valuable," the *Washington Post* informed its readers. Realty interests felt that "some of the playhouses in the theatrical block are likely to give way to commercial needs"; the question was simply when. The coming new subway line along Eighth Avenue with a station at 42nd Street connecting to the Times Square station at the east end of the street whetted the appetite of speculators; they were buying the future, buying individual parcels to assemble buildable sites out of the small, narrow lots of the city's 1811 grid.[24]

Had the Depression not intervened, commercial buildings might have replaced the theaters as developers sought to do what they do: build "higher and best uses" on land soaring in value. With the new Grand Central Terminal nearing completion, 42nd Street was experiencing a rapid transformation. In 1912, when the American business tycoon Asa G. Candler, head of the Atlanta-based Coca-Cola Company, began a

**4.8** During the 1920s building boom, realty interests expected office development to expand westward, as illustrated in this proposal for an office building on Eighth Avenue in Hell's Kitchen designed by architects Schwartz & Gross, 1925. Speculation was rife, and with the value of land under the theaters on 42nd Street soaring, commercial buildings seemed destined to replace them. Wurts Bros. Museum of the City of New York. X2010.7.1.11063.

24-story terra-cotta office tower on West 42nd Street, it was the tallest building on that section of the crosstown street (and the tallest north of the 700-foot-high Metropolitan Life Tower on East 24th Street). Even though the *Times* expected construction of the Candler and the Longacre Building to "present a totally different appearance in respect to business development than has characterized it in the past,"[25] the Candler Building was a real estate outlier, and it remained so for many more

**4.9** When the 24-story Candler Building (and Candler Theatre) opened in 1913, it was the tallest skyscraper on 42nd Street west of Fifth Avenue; its only other tower companion was the 18-story Aeolian Building. In this 1914 image, the Candler tower soars majestically over the New Amsterdam Theatre (elaborate arched entrance) to the east and the Eltinge and Harris Theatres to the west. Irving Underhill. Museum of the City of New York. X2010.28.800.

years than Candler must have expected. Irving T. Bush's Bush Terminal Company later built a taller tower, the 30-story Bush Tower (1918, originally known as the Bush Terminal International Exhibit Building and Buyers Club), a block east of the Candler, between Broadway and Sixth Avenue. After the end of World War I, a building boom between 1920 and 1931 shaped a new midtown commercial district; 132 new office buildings were constructed in the district, seventeen of which

**4.10** In 1918, Irving T. Bush built the neo-Gothic 30-story Bush Tower at 130 West 42nd Street, housing merchandise showrooms so located for the convenience of out-of-town buyers. Seen from this westward perspective in 1927, it appears to tower over the Candler, though it is only six stories taller. Wurts Bros. Museum of the City of New York. X2010.7.1.3265.

were built in Times Square, but not a one on the famous theater block. Decades would past with no new investment there.

In 1999, the Durst Organization opened its 48-story tower, the first of the 42nd Street project's office quartet at the crossroads of Times Square; though technically not on the Deuce, as the first tower of the quartet, it signaled the release of an economic stopcock that for decades had held back commercial redevelopment on the Deuce. Durst's sky-scraper occupied the complete block face of Broadway between 42nd and 43rd Streets, what the *Times* in 1930 called "one of the most valu-able realty holdings in the city." It replaced what had been built on the site before the advent of the modern skyscraper (figure 1.4): the 12-story Longacre Building (1912) and the 12-story Fitzgerald Building with the adjoining George M. Cohan Theatre (1911). Demolished in 1938, the Fitzgerald was replaced with a two-story business building that hosted the legendary 1,000-seat Toffenetti's restaurant, "Cathedral of All Restaurants." By the time the adjacent Longacre Building—home to a couple of Times Square legends: syndicated talk-show institution Joe Franklin and public-relations personality Richard Falk, known for decades as the mayor of 42nd Street—was razed in 1996 to make way for Durst's Four Times Square, what once passed for a skyscraper had endured 84 years, a venerable age for anything above ground in build-it-up-and-tear-it-down Manhattan.[26]

When city and state officials first made the economic argument for cleaning up the Deuce, only three pages in the voluminous 1,000-page Draft Environmental Impact Statement (DEIS) were needed to state the essential facts of the case: the seventy-four properties in the 13-acre area assessed at $55.1 million for the 1982–1983 tax year would deliver only $5.1 million to the city's treasury in property taxes in 1983. Build-ings nearby in midtown were generating much higher revenues for city coffers; the 40-story New York Telephone Building one block away on 42nd and Sixth, for example, assessed at $60 million was due to pay $5.6 million in property taxes. Similar stark contrasts were not hard to find. That property values in the area were "depressed," the DEIS concluded, was "a direct consequence of the lack of any substantial new constructions for decades and the deterioration of the existing improvements." Returning the area "to productive use" would bring future economic benefits accruing to "the City as a whole."[27]

The expected economic benefit behind the return "to productive use" was linked to subsidies undergirding the redevelopment project, and there was no shortage of critics who found the subsidies misguided, excessive "give-aways" to private developers. The novel funding arrange-ment for condemnation performed brilliantly in line with its political promise, protecting the city from direct exposure to escalating costs for acquiring the property slated for redevelopment. Nonetheless, the heavy subsidies grew to be a highly visible public issue, as they should have.

The developer's payment for the right to develop the four office sites had been fixed at $88 million ($247.6 million in 2022 dollars);

**4.11** As advertised in this postcard, "The Busiest Restaurant on the World's Busiest Corner," Toffenetti's was an after-theater stop "where glamour sparkles forever." It was established by the successful Italian immigrant Dario Toffenetti, who came to America in 1910. Mayor LaGuardia was on hand for the 1940 ribbon cutting of the splashy 43rd Street restaurant, which served thousands daily on its two floors before it closed in 1968, replaced by Nathan's Famous. The site is now home to Four Times Square, recently rebranded with the new address of One Five One. Collection of the author.

acquisition costs beyond that amount the city was obligated to repay; the so-called excess site acquisition cost (ESAC) was, in essence, a loan from the developer to the city. The tax benefits embedded in the arrangement had great value to whoever owned the towers because 50 percent of the below-market payment-in-lieu-of-taxes could be treated as a credit against the city's repayment obligation. Numerous studies attempted to quantify the tax subsidy, but there was no easy way to resolve the numbers controversy. Without a clear sense of how much it was ultimately going to cost to acquire the needed seventy-four parcels, public officials said they could not tell you the ultimate value of the subsidies—a discounted land cost for each development site and property tax abatements for 15 (later amended to 20) years—to the developer.[28]

The liability of the funding arrangement was not something officials worried about at the time because the redevelopment bet they were making was seen as essential to the city's economic future. They expected this "loan" to be small and easily extinguishable within a few years, as did the office developer.

In any event, the deal represented a classic public trade: upfront incentives to stimulate private investment in exchange for future tax revenues—the stakes of betting long, which is what cities do in redevelopment projects where they wish to change market signals. When considered in before-and-after terms, city officials believed, unequivocally, that the project would be a positive revenue producer for New York: "Upon reaching full taxes, the Project will provide almost *one quarter of a billion dollars annually* in taxes to the City and State treasuries," said Carl Weisbrod, then head of the redevelopment project. To support his position, he said in real estate taxes alone, the city would collect four times as much on the office tower sites during the tax abatement period as it would have received in real estate taxes if the project weren't built. According to the property owners' analysis, the four office sites alone would pay, at a minimum, $249 million in real estate taxes before going to full taxes many years later. If the project did not go forward, the downside scenario, the same sites would pay a mere $66 million in real estate taxes over the same period. As the pieces of the project finally fell into place by the new millennium, I asked Weisbrod how he thought about the subsidy issue. His answer: "Is the glass half empty or half full? Are you in favor of the project or against it?"[29] The emerging economic vibrancy of Times Square, in time, would prove that the glass was more than half full—but not before the subsidy issue once again outraged civic activists and journalists well-attuned to the issue.

By the late 1990s, Times Square real estate was hot. Land values seemed to be growing by the minute. In a complete turnaround from the 1980s, the district had become one of the most desirable locations in Manhattan for developers who were building office towers. So much so that when Prudential Insurance Company put its last two 42nd Street project sites up for sale, the bidding was "fierce," according to the *Times*. Established players and newcomers in the New York pantheon of office developers were expected to submit bids. The tax subsidies accompanying both sites—the southwest corner of 42nd Street and Seventh Avenue (Site 4) and the small block bounded by Seventh Avenue and Broadway between 41st and 42nd Street (Site 1)—were rich: "According to a sale document issued by Prudential, a builder would get property tax breaks worth $9.5 million a year, or $262.6 million over twenty years, on a planned 40-story office tower [Site 4] . . . and tax breaks valued at $236 million over twenty years for a proposed 49-story tower [Site 1]." Both sites went to Boston Properties, a publicly traded real estate investment trust with deep development expertise. When Boston Properties sold Five Times Square, the full-block trophy tower built on Site 4 ten years later in 2007, the sales brochure provided a schedule of fixed-base ground rent, from which I could estimate the expected savings from the 20-year tax abatement: $312 million—rich indeed. The transactions confirmed what Prudential's development partner George Klein had long believed: the tax deals on the 42nd Street towers were "vastly superior" to those being offered on other west side buildings.[30]

Klein also proved to be right about the city's liability for the "loan" that financed the acquisition of the four office sites and midblock theaters. During the latter half of the 1980s, condemnation costs increased dramatically as property values in Times Square escalated; litigation-driven delays postponing office construction exacerbated the cost equation and invalidated government officials' initial assumptions about the prospectively modest size of the "loan." When the state began its accounting, the initial excess site acquisition cost was $245 million. By the end of 2020, with the accrual of interest on the "loan," what the city would eventually have to repay was considerably higher, $302.9 million, even after various offsets. It was being paid down from previous years' outstanding balance, but ever so slowly. The open tab for site acquisition had become what George Klein always said it would be: "the longest municipal bond ever issued."[31]

The deal that raised the critics' blood pressure emerged in June 2000, when city and state officials came to an agreement with the New York Times Company and Brooklyn-based Forest City Ratner Companies for development of the *Times'* new headquarters, a 52-story skyscraper (2007). The site was on "a dowdy block" of Eighth Avenue between 40th and 41st Streets facing the squat, uninspiring Port Authority Bus Terminal—what one journalist described as "a structure with all the subtlety and grace of a grimy shoebox."[32] In the parlance of the project, this was Site 8S, one of two remaining sites available for development as part of the 42nd Street project. (It was where, in 1965, Irving Maidman had opened the first new building to rise on Eighth Avenue in 25 years, a six-story brick office building on the northeast corner of 40th Street.) On the map of the project's development sites in 2000 (figure 4.12), the site, one block south of the Deuce, stands out as a curious appendage to the project area. Initially identified as part of the potential site of a huge merchandise mart, the exceptionally large footprint of nearly 80,000 square feet (1.84 acres) was double the size of the typical development site for an office tower in New York, and its perfect rectangular configuration ideal for a newsroom. When word spread within the real estate

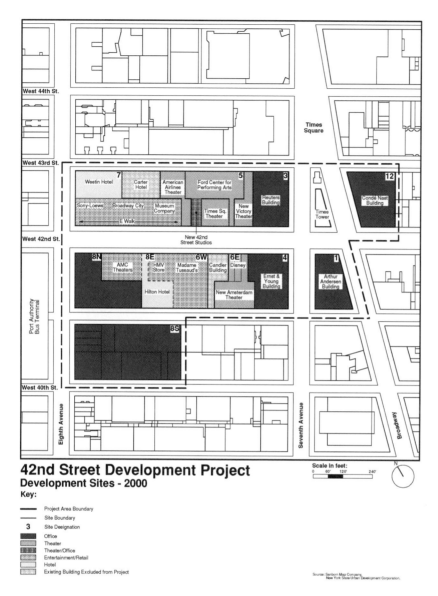

**42nd Street Development Project**
Development Sites - 2000
Key:

— Project Area Boundary
— Site Boundary
**3** Site Designation
▪ Office
▪ Theater
▪ Theater/Office
▪ Entertainment/Retail
▪ Hotel
▪ Existing Building Excluded from Project

Scale in feet:
0   60'   120'        240'

N

Source: Sanborn Map Company,
New York State Urban Development Corporation.

**4.12** Development parcels of the 13-acre transformational project as of 2000. The new uses are identified except for the former merchandise mart site, now bifurcated into two office sites, 8N and 8S, the latter the site of the future headquarters of the *New York Times*, designed by Italian architect Renzo Piano. Morgan Fleming for the author.

community that the state was preparing a request for proposals (RFP) for the site, the *Times* was in the process of exploring a move from the Annex on West 43rd Street, its home since 1913. "We'll move so long as we remain in the neighborhood, own our space, get the right floor plates, and it costs no more than staying at 229 West 43rd and renovating," said Michael Golden, vice chairman of the *Times* at the time.

Concerned that this might be the last development opportunity in the eponymous neighborhood and aware that the *Times* was unlikely to succeed in a competitive RFP process, Golden met with Charles Gargano, head of the Empire State Development Corporation, in the fall of 1999. He offered an absolute commitment to build the newspaper's new headquarters "into any market" on 8S if the ESDC would "sole source" it to the *Times*. Gargano agreed to a limited negotiation period.[33]

At a time when Times Square was booming, "some real estate executives and urban planners," wrote the *Times'* Charles V. Bagli, "complained that the city and state had given the Times Company a generous deal by selling the land at what they called a below-market price and by granting tax breaks for such prized real estate." The *Times* and its development partners would fund the acquisition costs for the development site and relocation of the existing tenants, but would be liable for only $85.6 million ($144.2 million in 2022 dollars); any costs above that number would be refunded over time with interest by the city as an 85 percent credit against annual payments in lieu of taxes, the same type of arrangement for development of the crossroads office towers, but at a substantially higher credit on the payments that substituted for property taxes. The no-bid deal included other terms favorable to the venture, "curiously attractive terms," remarked Woody Heller, a seasoned real estate professional and a managing director at Jones Lang LaSalle at the time, "particularly given the fact that The New York Times would seem to have little leverage in threatening to leave Manhattan." Gargano defended the deal for the 1.5 million square foot tower, saying officials "don't have to be as generous as we have in the past"; the deal was "'smart economics' because the *Times* was able to build a larger tower that will generate more in property taxes."[34] Left out of Gargano's response was the fact that the reduced payments in lieu of taxes would run for 29 years unless full taxes were lower, longer that the 20-year term of the crossroads towers' subsidy. And materials released in a lawsuit and freedom of information request showed "there are what even the city itself calls 'huge' additional costs to taxpayers that officials had not revealed—about $79 million," according to investigative reporting by freelance writer Paul Moses.[35]

The sole-source process and negotiated sweetheart deal for development of the site, a joint venture between the *Times* and Forest City Ratner and ING Clarion, the US investment management business of the Dutch multinational financial institution, quickly triggered several rounds of litigation by property owners at the site who opposed the government's condemnation action. Led by Gary Barnett, then president of Intell Management and Investment and owner of one of the parking lots and eleven small buildings on the site, the lawsuits challenged the state's right to condemn the property for the *Times* on constitutional grounds and as favoritism in the sole-source designation of the *Times* and a give-away of taxpayer money, amounting in law to a waste of taxpayer funds and to fraud, bad faith, and collusion.

The backdrop to the litigation began in early 1999, when Barnett and his co-litigant owners at the site told the state development corporation they were interested in developing an office tower on the site on terms that would include the payment of fair market value for the site. Instead of dealing exclusively with them, state officials rebuffed the overture, questioning whether he could deliver; Barnett reportedly responded that his company had developed the 50-story Planet Hollywood building in Times Square without subsidy. He was told the state entity would solicit offers through a competitive process, according to a court decision in the case. As had been the case in every other legal challenge to the 42nd Street project, the government succeeded in what the *Wall Street Journal* called a "David vs. Goliath battle" against the *Times*, and on August 16, 2002, the state authority was cleared to take possession of the eleven properties and start relocating some fifty-five businesses, including sex shops, trade schools, third-generation hatters, fabric dealers, and dorm rooms for students at nearby schools. At a time when the original rationale for condemnation had abated and the area was clearly on the upswing, these tenants with active small businesses reportedly did not see their block as "blighted." "Over its more than half century of use, blight had become a well-worn term of art," my colleague Martin Gold and I wrote in "The Use and Abuse of Blight in Eminent Domain." As used in takings, blight was "subjective and malleable, so much so that it can now be said to be in the eyes of the beholder."[36]

On the morning of September 12, after the terrorist attack of September 11, when the *Times*, Forest City Ratner, and ING Clarion, met as preplanned to discuss next steps, the entire project was up in the air. City and state officials and residents were in a state of shock and disbelief over the attack that brought down the iconic twin towers; everyone was extremely anxious about the city's now-uncertain future. The continued strength of the Manhattan office market was in doubt: Would tenants want to be in a market targeted by terrorists? Would employees still feel comfortable working in high-rise office towers? At the beginning of the meeting, the *Times* affirmed its commitment to build "in any market." That assured tenantry for floors two through

**4.13** The new 52-story tower for the headquarters of the newspaper of record (2007, pictured in 2008) with its gigantic Gothic blackletters greeting commuters using the Port Authority Bus Terminal every day. The tower was developed by a joint venture of Forest City Ratner, the New York Times, and ING Clarion, with speculative space for other tenants and retailers on the ground level. Under the original redevelopment plan, state and city officials had proposed a large merchandise mart for the site on Eighth Avenue. Joe Shlabotnik, 2.0 Generic CC BY 2.0.

twenty-seven, its condominium share of the proposed tower; Forest City and Clarion would have to find tenants for the upper floors which they would own and line up financing for their share of the $729 million cost of the tower. It became a tall order for a couple of years.

In the short segment of time between the collapse of the initial redevelopment plans for 42nd Street in 1990 and the recovery from the city's deep real estate downturn beginning in 1995, the implications of the city's intervention strategy were far from what was initially anticipated. The economic logic of the office towers subsidy had been overtaken by a bust-to-boom real estate cycle. What officials saw as necessary in early 1980, when investment in the area was anemic, looked very different in 1998, when conditions in Times Square were possibly stronger than in the roaring twenties. In 1980, it was not possible to guess the trends that would emerge two decades later or anticipate exactly how much incentive would be needed to effect such a dramatic transformation. A few critics continued to debate the necessity of government intervention on such a large scale, arguing that the private market could have accomplished a transformation on its own. In its essence, this is an ideological argument more easily made after the fact, as former head of the UDC William J. Stern did in "The Unexpected Lessons of Times Square's Comeback" in the conservative Manhattan Institute's *City Journal*.[37]

The quartet of high-density office towers at the crossroads of 42nd Street made the transformation possible, economically. That was the intention of the earliest plans, including the nearly forgotten privately initiated plan The City at 42nd Street. The quartet has contributed between $16 million and $24 million in each tax year from 2012 to 2019 to the city's Economic Development Corporation (EDC), which manages the properties. Moreover, through an annual fee imposed on each rentable square foot in these towers, the quartet underwrites ongoing support to New 42's extensive theater programs in ways that might not otherwise be possible, something discussed further on.

Once completed and open for business by 2004, the density piled high on the four office sites in this prime midtown location triggered a boom in realty values. The initial evidence arrived in 2007, with the first trade of a 42nd Street project office tower, Boston Properties' sale of Five Times Square. Completed just five years earlier and fully occupied with strong credit-quality tenants, its $1.28 billion price, approximately $1,160 a square foot, set a record for the area; separately valued, the ESAC credits were worth $76.1 million. The publicly traded real estate investment company booked a gain on sale of approximately $605.4 million (after accounting for a small minority interest in the asset).[38] In 2014, once again the 40-story skyscraper was sold—at a higher price, $1.5 billion, approximately $1,283 a square foot.

By the time the last office tower opened its doors on the southeast corner of 42nd Street and Eighth Avenue (Site 8N) in 2011, the transformation had exceeded its economic promise many times over. Assessed values, as calculated by the New York City Department of Finance, for the seventeen commercial and theater components of the project had reached $1.4 billion; by 2020, this pre-pandemic figure was $2.2 billion, 56 percent higher. Put in perspective, this aggregate assessed valuation of the 42nd Street project sites in 2020 was more than fourteen times the starting data point in 1983—$151.3 million adjusted for inflation to 2020 dollars—when the project was under review.[39] These assessed values are not the same as true market values; they are the values the Department of Finance ascribes to commercial property for tax purposes; true market values would be higher, by a lot. For example, when the Durst Organization refinanced its mortgage on Four Times Square in 2019, appraisers valued the tower at $1.8 billion

**4.14** The quartet of office skyscrapers at the crossroads corners seen "Looking up at Times Square," 2010. As the financial engine of the transformation of 42nd Street, the towers delivered on the promise to diversify the economy of Times Square and add billions in property assessments to New York City. Yogendra, CC BY-SA 2.0.

for a new $900 million mortgage, twice the value of its $901.2 million assessment on the city's tax roll.

The enduring economic return to New York City from these towers comes in four bumps over four years, when the four towers should start paying full property taxes after the 20-year abatement burns off: 2021 (Four Times Square), 2022 (Three Times Square), 2023 (Five Times Square), and 2024 (Seven Times Square). What will this new take amount to? My conservative estimate, for 2025, based on Finance Department market values and tax rates as of 2020—made before Covid-19 threw a wrench into the gears of the city's economy, especially its office market—is about three and a half times what the sites paid in base rent and percentage rent payments, as supplied by EDC ($132 million, in contrast to $37 million [before ESAC credits] for tax year 2019–2020). Other sites have already shifted to paying full property taxes: Westin Times Square (2013), E-Walk (2015), and 11 Times Square (June 2012). In the 2019–2020 tax year, these three sites paid $41 million in property taxes.

The big bet city and state officials made to intervene, cleanse the street, and return it to "productive use" has been an economic winner. The revigorated strength of New York City (once the trauma of 9/11 had worn off) and the scores of millions of tourists who do not think of leaving New York without coming to Times Square are part and parcel of what has made this project such an economic success. The pandemic's severe impact on everybody and everything, especially the tourist-and-office-based economy of Times Square, has bounded this robust record of performance with an uncertain future.

The street's property boom has finally been generous to its pioneering tall settler, the 24-story Candler Building. The Candler had been through all the hard times on the Deuce. In 1985, still surrounded by sex shops, cheap theaters, and quick-food places, the tower's fortunes seemed to be rising when it was sold for $14.75 million, just five years after it had traded for $1.3 million; attracting tenants remained a problem, even though it had been recently renovated. In 1993, after a short stint with a lot of debt on the building, its owner lost the building at foreclosure to the lender, Massachusetts Mutual Life Insurance Company. It was "looking slightly scruffier year by year as if in anticipation of reaping a jackpot from the surrounding rehabilitation," the architectural historian Christopher Gray wrote in 1996. It had been listed on the National Register of Historic Places in 1982, but still it remained somnolent. It was roused to new life in 2000, when SFX Entertainment, soon to be the nation's largest provider of live entertainment, decided to lease the entire newly renovated building for 20 years. "A lot of our business is right there in the neighborhood," its president told the press.[40] The jackpot came in 2006. When the fund of the private equity firm that owned the building sold the 228,000-square-foot tower for $208 million, approximately $914 a square foot, its financial fortunes were clearly on the rise. When it changed hands once again in 2012 in what *Commercial Property* called "an epic sale," so did its market value: $261 million, $1,146 a square foot. Asa Griggs Candler did not live to see his vision of 42nd Street as a business address come to fruition, but 100 years later, the public-driven transformation made it a reality. And it opened the door to an expansion of West Midtown all the way to the shores of the Hudson River.

## DIRECTIONAL CONTROL

EDC is New York City's primary engine for economic development, charged with leveraging the city's assets to drive growth, create jobs, and improve the overall quality of life within the five boroughs. In 2012, it took over ownership of all property in the 42nd Street Development Project through a planned transfer from the Empire State Development Corporation in what is referred to as the "reversionary event."

The transfer made EDC, as agent for the city, manager of both operational and financial matters for the properties of the 42nd Street project, and by way of its contract with EDC, the city gained control over how rental revenues from those properties would be used.

The "Apple 42nd Street" project, as it is known, is one among the many assets EDC manages, but it is the most important one in the amount of revenue the agency receives from property rentals, revenues that can be directed to support its own operations as well as city priorities. During the years since EDC gained stewardship, project rentals have become a powerful source of revenue, growing steadily—even after the pandemic hit the tourist economy of Times Square—from $29 million (2011–2012) to $50 million (2018–2019) to $67 million (2020–2021), totaling some $476 million over the past 10 years.[41] To put this in perspective, in the most recent year, Apple 42 property rentals were more than twice those of the city-owned Brooklyn Army Terminal, a huge warehouse complex of four million square feet in Sunset Park, Brooklyn, built for war use 100 years earlier, which EDC operates as a light manufacturing hub and food-manufacturing complex. (When completed, these warehouses, designed by architect Cass Gilbert and now listed on the National Register of Historic Places, were among the world's largest concrete structures.) Apple 42 property rentals exceeded even the city's maritime assets (wharf, waterfront, public markets, and public aviation and intermodal transportation properties, including the city's ferry system), which EDC manages. Unlike the revenues from property taxes, however, when a tenant under a 42nd Street ground lease decides to exercise its option to purchase the underlying land (as the hotel and entertainment/retail center on the northeast corner of 42nd Street and Eighth Avenue [Site 7] and the office tower across the street on the southeast corner [Site 8N] have already chosen to do), EDC's lease rental stream will decline some.

As has been the case for another highly successful large-scale public-private development project, Battery Park City in Lower Manhattan, public ownership of the land under large-scale developments generates long-term benefits for New York City. Proprietary control over land resources also expands the range of discretionary decision making by city officials; by being able to tap into revenues generated from property leases (which typically do not flow directly into the Department of Finance), they are freed from the need to use taxpayer monies allocated to higher priorities (such as policing, firefighting, education, and health and social services) to support strategic initiatives such as the NYC Ferry service.

**4.15** This map of the NYC Ferry system—partially underwritten with rental revenues the Economic Development Corporation collects from the 42nd Street Development Project—shows the five routes and services connecting New York's five boroughs: Manhattan, Brooklyn, Queens, Staten Island, and the Bronx. Pre-pandemic, the ferry system averaged 14,159 riders during the weekdays and 10,992 on the weekends. The newest route, Soundview, inaugurated in January 2022, shortens the commute from the East Side to Wall Street to sixty minutes. NYC Ferry.

Through its annual contract with EDC, the city determines how the agency uses the many sources of funds coming from the 42nd Street project, which can change over time in line with city priorities. Until the 2016–2017 tax year, EDC remitted to the city treasury all payments in lieu of taxes, real estate taxes, and substantially all rental revenues it collected from the Apple 42nd Street leases, except for $1 million per year to cover its administrative services. That changed when the city decided that instead of receiving a remittance, it would direct commercial rents from the 42nd Street project to the NYC Ferry service, partially offsetting the costs to EDC of establishing and operating the system. The monies from the 42nd Street Development Project launched the highly popular ferry system; at the same time it made EDC more dependent upon the city after it used up all of its built-up reserve.[42]

New York City initiated a system of ferry service in summer 2017. Designed to meet the transportation needs of neighborhoods traditionally underserved by public transportation, the routes connect to twenty-one ferry piers in the Bronx, Brooklyn, Manhattan, and Queens. Compared to New York's other public transit modes, ridership on the heavily subsidized ferry system—5.6 million trips in the pre-pandemic 2018–2019 tax year—is low, but the system is very popular. NYC Ferry's initial flat $2.75 fare (the same as for the subway and bus system) is a primary driver of its comparatively high subsidy: $9.34 per trip, which is almost ten times that of the city's transit and buses, according to the Citizens Budget Commission's October 2019 comparative analysis of large public ferry systems in the United States. (In September 2022, the one-way fare was increased to $4.00.)[43] In the five years since the 2017 agreement, EDC has directed approximately $111 million to support the ferry system without drawing upon the city's budget funds.

Forty-second Street's historic jewel, The New Amsterdam Theatre, generates revenue for the city and state as well. Since the Art Nouveau theater reopened to rave reviews of its beautifully renovated interiors, Disney has mounted three long-running productions drawing capacity audiences: *The Lion King* (November 1997–June 2006), *Mary Poppins* (November 2006–March 2013), and *Aladdin* (March 2014 until the pandemic temporarily suspended attendance). The public sector benefits directly from the success of Disney's theatrical productions when the theater's "net gross revenues" (including sales of food, beverage, and audio, musical, or video reproductions of performances at the theater) meet certain targets of commercial success: 2 percent of the first $20 million of all net gross revenues and 3 percent above that. "We did the deal in order that Disney would bring others in," said Vincent Tese, head of UDC at the time. "We knew this would be the *only* sweet deal. And we had a mission." As a loss leader, the deal's largess has produced revenues beyond its base-rent obligation. Before the pandemic shut down performances, the theater's net gross revenues exceeded $77 million, primarily from ticket sales, generating over $2 million in percentage rents shared 50/50 by the city and the state.[44]

The financial benefits to the city from the transformation of 42nd Street flow through multiple and complex channels and remittances from deals that were complex in their making more than 20 years ago. It is extraordinarily difficult to tabulate a complete consolidated picture of the returns to the city from its investment in transforming 42nd Street or to calculate the overall subsidization of the transformative project. The type of precise cost-benefit or return analysis I have done elsewhere is nearly impossible. At one point, EDC was planning to begin a return-to-the-city analysis, but there was no time frame for completion, and the analysis may not happen. From the data available to me, one thing is clear: the 42nd Street Development Project has been a potent cash cow for New York City, channeling funds into EDC and the city treasury. Pre-pandemic, all the revenue flows from the project were increasing, and as the tax abatements burn off and tourism returns to Times Square, the cash flows to the city are likely to continue to increase by large amounts.

## "IT'S IN THE LEASES"

It was gutsy, there's no better word to describe the decision to create a children's theater—the first in New York City—on naughty, bawdy 42nd Street. The irony of the idea was transparent: particularly so in 1992, since pornography still dominated the western end of the block where some twenty or so thriving porn shops had yet to be condemned. The 92-year-old Victory Theatre was decrepit. The 42nd Street Entertainment Corporation, soon to be renamed New 42nd Street, later shortened to New 42, was a shell of an organization. Though the organization was not yet something, it had a lot going for it: peerless leadership in the unusual duo of civic leader and leading philanthropist Marian Sulzberger Heiskell and the talented doer of the near-impossible in the nonprofit performance arena, Cora Cahan; joining them was a distinguished twenty-four-member board of directors drawn from the commercial and nonprofit arts and business communities. It had a 99-year lease with the city on the street's six (soon to be seven) legacy theaters. It had seed money: $18.2 million from the office developers targeted for theater renovations. And it had a mandate to do at least two not-for-profit theaters. The board wanted action, not another plan; it wanted "to prove that something is possible." But whatever it did could not become a failure like Westway; what they did would have to be important enough to succeed because, Cahan recalled, "Marian [Heiskell] could not be embarrassed by something she put her name on."[45]

Cahan was far from naïve about the big implications of going in that direction, even with the board galvanized by the idea of a children's theater. "There had to be low-price tickets. The theater had to be for everyone, of all incomes. It had to be popular theater. There had to be educational programs attached to the theater. Kids could not just pass through the theater. And teachers needed help," she explained in one of several conversations with me. "A children's theater had to be more than just putting on plays." She also believed the New Victory, newly renamed, should be a producing house. "All this would require big subsidies."[46] It was a gamble. Rental revenue from commercial tenants that would underwrite New 42's operations and cross-subsidize the theater agenda was still pretty much wishful thinking at the time.

By undertaking a project that signaled an unprecedented turnaround from porn movie house to legitimate theater for youth entertainment, New 42 launched the transformation of the block. It was the catalyst that set future events in play and became a key factor in getting Disney to commit to a renovation of the New Amsterdam Theatre. "Making a silk purse out of this particular sow's ear seemed an impossibility only a few years ago," the *Times* editorialists noted upon the opening of the New Victory in mid-December 1995. "The paradox," Cahan told me, "is that the lineup of legitimate theaters at the turn of the century made 42nd Street the most famous block in the world, and theater has led to its resurrection."[47]

The irony in New 42's catalytic role was complete. From the start of the 42nd Street project, the theater agenda had struggled for attention. Preservation of the midblock theaters and the low-density character of the corridor running between Seventh and Eighth Avenues had been put forth as the justification for the enormous densities of the office towers on the corners. The policy logic, however, lacked planning substance. Missing were the detailed economics of how the plan to preserve the theaters would work. There were no specially designed incentives to attract prospective bidders for the theater sites, and only in the month before the public hearing on the final environmental impact statement did the state and the city conditionally designate a developer to renovate and operate five of the theaters. But the selected developer,

**4.16** Marian Heiskell (right) and Cora Cahan at New 42's 25th anniversary gala held on April 11, 2016, celebrating the catalytic role the nonprofit played in the return to live theater on 42nd Street. Susan Cook for New 42.

Michael J. Lazar and his Cambridge Investment Group, did not last long: less than twenty months later, the former City Transportation administrator was indicted on charges of racketeering and mail fraud stemming from a major scandal at the city's Parking Violations Bureau, and the city revoked the conditional designation. For four years the theater agenda remained suspended until 1990, when Cahan and Heiskell were appointed to make something important happen.

The project's planners had been under great pressure to find a solution to the theaters following the Lazar scandal. After much deliberation, Weisbrod concluded that a nonprofit, nongovernmental entity was the only way a structure for the theaters would work; start-up funds could come from a special public-purpose fund that had gone unspent since the controversial demolition of the beloved Morosco and Helen Hayes Theatres in 1982. Charged with long-term oversight of the renovation and ongoing operation of the street's historic theaters, the nonprofit would be governed by an independent board of directors and given powers to select entertainment uses that would broaden the audience drawn to the theater street. While the governor and the mayor appointed the initial board, that board became self-perpetuating. "Marian Heiskell set it up that way, insisted on it," Weisbrod told me. "Mayor Koch was okay with it; he did not see it as a problem. Governor Mario Cuomo was not okay with it, but Marian was unassailable."[48]

The nonprofit's legal control over the theaters through a 99-year lease with UDC fortified its political independence and would shield it from budget exigencies and changes in mayoral administrations. Long-term control was essential to the funding strategy for the theater agenda; the $18.2 million contribution required of the office developers could only to be used for renovation of the theaters, not operations. Held forever in public trust, the theaters would revert to New York City in perpetuity when the lease expired. In the long meantime, New 42's lease for the theaters created a real estate endowment for the organization, ensuring a self-sustaining capture of revenue from ground rents and other revenues that would come from repurposing the legacy theater sites.

When Rebecca Robertson took over as head of the project after Weisbrod moved on to a senior position in the Dinkins administration, she invented a flexible structure for how New 42 would work. In a deal with George Klein, she strengthened New 42's financial structure: tenants in the four office towers would pay an annual "theater surcharge," money New 42 could use for operations and programming of its not-for-profit theaters. In time, every deal she made with tenants on other sites of the 42nd Street project included a theater surcharge, in essence a subsidy for the nonprofit organization. The embryonic organization was being set up to benefit from every commercial site on 42nd Street (except for the New Amsterdam Theatre). In concert with the nonprofit's legal structure, these "Street Deals" provided the foundation for the role New 42 played as a catalyst for the return of live theater on 42nd Street: "It has been incredible for any nonprofit to have a sure and growing revenue source without depending on the box office and being free of political interference as well," said Cahan.[49] For Robertson and Weisbrod, it was among their proudest and most creative accomplishments.

The uniqueness of New 42's structure proved to be providently important after the mayoral turnover from David Dinkins to Rudy Giuliani. A hard-charging former US Attorney for the Southern District of New York, Giuliani and his top officials disliked the independence of New 42; they wanted the lease revenues from the street to flow to the city, not to some entity they could not control. The theater group, they argued, should have to go through the Department of Cultural Affairs for its budget funds. Why should it be different from other interests? When they first learned about New 42's special structure, including its nominal $10-a-year base rent to the city (and only many years later some direct revenues once certain benchmarks were hit), they sought a way to undo it, or, as a second-best move, take away its second nonprofit theater. Cahan vowed not to give an inch and neither would

**4.17** The New Victory Theatre, an adult entertainment theater transformed into the first children's theater in New York originally, built by Oscar Hammerstein as the Theatre Republic (1900), converted to a house of burlesque (1933), and later a porn theater (1970s), pictured in 2016. Today, the nonprofit theater hosts international performances of theater, circus, puppetry, opera, and dance for kids of all ages, including each year 40,000 New York City school kids through its award-winning New Victory Arts Education program. Danilo Milhome, CC BY-SA 4.0 0 via Wikimedia Commons.

Heiskell; after a stormy confrontation, city officials backed off from their demands, but not without residual anger.[50]

The leases held promise. Still, the test of success was intimately bound to how New Yorkers and visitors responded to the transformation of 42nd Street, whether they came in droves or stayed away. Whether the Street Deals delivered depended upon attendance at the theaters leased to for-profit operators. Ticket sales at two of the performance theaters with nearly 2,400 seats would have to be sufficiently robust to generate material sums from the half-dollar or so of each going to New 42. The 478-room hotel built primarily above the Liberty Theatre would have to attract consistently high levels of visitors to generate material sums from the $.50 to $1 per occupied room (depending on room rates) going to New 42. And armatures for signage above some premises would also produce revenue for New 42 if they were leased to third parties. The office towers would have to lease up with business tenants to generate the theater surcharge.

Each of these sources of revenue would augment what New 42 collected annually in minimum base rent from each tenant occupying one of its six historic theaters sites. By design, the young organization was launched on a self-sustaining basis. The Street Deals would support its operation and cross-subsidize the two nonprofit theaters required as part of the 42nd Street project (the 499-seat New Victory and 740-seat theater built on the site of the Selwyn), as well as a third (the 199-seat black-box The Duke). That was baseline. If it succeeded with the New Victory—making people pay attention—in time the organization would be able to underwrite educational and professional cultural activities with funds from the street. That's what Cahan wanted to achieve as those revenues grew.

Steadily they did grow. Year after year, beginning in 1997 and ramping up in the early aughts, funds from the street grew to approximately $11 million, covering more than half of New 42's $20 million budget for the 2018–2019 tax year.[51] In its earliest year of operations, revenues from the street amounted to less than $1 million and approximated what New 42 collected from its box office sales and concession revenue. By 2005, they were three times what the box office was bringing in; in 2011, four times. By 2018, the last year for which I was able to get financial data, the Street Deals were generating more than five times what the box office, scaled to affordably priced tickets for kids and their families, brought in. This was all pre-pandemic. The magnitude of financial magic from these Street Deals—the strong underpinning of New 42 leases, the sturdiness of New York's real estate market, and the

**4.18** New 42 Studios. Fourteen studios of varying sizes and support spaces for stage, film, TV, or media rehearsals are a vital component of New 42's building designed by Platt Byard Dovell White Architects. Courtesy of Alexander Severin.

popularity of the entertainment attractions on 42nd Street—proved to be more significant than either Weisbrod or Robertson anticipated. "We underestimated the magnitude of the cash flow," Robertson told me. "It's very significant."[52]

For New 42, the street dollars have been a means to an end, the end being an extensive range of programs to support the legacy of the theater street as a cultural hub and entertainment destination. In 2000, New 42 Studios opened, a seven-story building with a glass façade bathed in colored lights designed to showcase performing artists. As with the children's theater, the award-winning New 42 Studios has been a catalyst supporting performing artists in creation of their works by addressing the city's lack of rehearsal space in fourteen rehearsal studios and offices for nonprofit cultural organizations. Pre-pandemic, two-thirds of the rehearsal space was typically rented to nonprofits, but about three-fourths of the building's revenues came from rentals to for-profits, which subsidized use by nonprofits. The shop downstairs was also an important revenue generator.

**4.19** Cora Cahan with the New 42 Usher Corps at City Hall for the Proclamation Ceremony congratulating the youth group upon receiving the 2014 National Arts and Humanities Youth Program Award in Washington, D.C., March 2015. New York City, City Hall photographer, Courtesy of New 42.

A decade after it began, the work of spearheading the cultural revitalization of 42nd Street was mostly complete, but the mandate to do more than "put on shows for kids" led Cahan and the board to an early decision to create a program to hire and train ushers, the New Victory Usher Corps, young New Yorkers who work the front of the house alongside the professional staff. What began as an idea evolved into a three-year program that offers paid employment, job training, academic support, and mentorship for fifty New Yorkers aged 16 to 22, who also attend life skills workshops. Next came New 42 Street Apprentice Corps for thirty college and graduate students to provide hands-on involvement in the business of running a nonprofit performing arts organization. They too are paid: "There are no volunteers at New 42," Cahan said.[53] Continuing with the idea behind the youth corps, New 42 spearheaded two additional development programs—New 42 Street College Corps (a college success program in collaboration with CUNY Arts to address obstacles that often prevent students from graduating) and New 42 Street Fellow Corps (for usher corps alumni interested in a career in arts administration or production). After 29 years at the helm of this creative organization, Cahan retired in June 2019 and was later named president and CEO of Baryshnikov Arts Center.

New 42 was invented. Although its structure had been modeled after Lincoln Center for the Performing Arts, the specially designed entity had a markedly different task—to restore *use* to 42nd Street's neglected and outmoded theaters and recreate a sense of place consistent with its 100-year-old theater legacy. Having achieved its mission and prospered by its real estate endowment, is the structure that has been so successful for 42nd Street a model for other situations? Yes, with a caveat.

The key to this kind of structure is giving a nonprofit entity real estate; the immobility of real estate means it does not go away. It can deteriorate if not maintained and continually improved, but it stays in place. It can become more profitable as economic activity accelerates, especially when base rents under the ground leases are revalued,[54] yet it can also become less valuable if the economics of place shift, as was true of the theater block in the 1920s. But it is also true that there is nothing like 42nd Street with its concentration of popular entertainment and worldwide recognition. London has the West End; Toronto too has well-known theater credentials, but the theater venues in both cities are dispersed. As was true historically, theater on 42nd Street and in Times Square benefits from its concentrated presence. As cities continue to build entertainment districts, they can learn by looking carefully at the New 42 model. First, preservation of building structure in and of itself is not sufficient. Second, the knack of invention is to create something that does not already exist, to add a theater that does not compete with existing entertainment but reinforces and enhances what's already in place. Third, for a theater district to thrive, it must actively curate entertainment excitement with innovative performances that constantly stimulate interest in attending live theater. Last but far from least, political independence and strong leadership to create the vision and steward a coalition of stakeholders through the process are essential complements to a solid financial structure.

## THE QUID PRO QUO

During the Q&A at the premiere of *Against All Odds*, a tall man with hair graying after decades of activism for affordable housing stood up, introduced himself, and told of what had been accomplished with the little-known and long-forgotten $25 million commitment Mayor Koch reluctantly made to the Clinton community in the wee morning hours of the Board of Estimate public hearing in November 1984 to approve the $1.6 billion plan for rebuilding West 42nd Street. Thirty-four years later, the importance of those dollars ($70.3 million in 2022 dollars)—a lot of money then—remained a vivid reminder to Joe Restuccia, the long-time executive director of the Clinton Housing Development Company, of the means by which community resolve matched with political savvy could pressure government to do what's right. What's right in this case meant funding for "a laundry list of twelve things to attend to, things we wanted," when he and others on a Times Square Redevelopment Project Negotiating Committee first met to talk about the impacts of the 42nd Street project on Clinton.[55]

High on the list for his community: the rehabilitation of several hundred apartments, aid for the retention of small business, and efforts to fight the spread of juvenile prostitution and pornography from Times Square to Clinton. Though divided in their opinions of the massive project seen as "a spear" aimed at their neighborhood, community residents and local merchants were united in wanting protection from being "pushed out" by rising housing costs triggered by gentrification sweeping through the neighborhood and the effects of real estate speculation. "We're not against growth or upgrading, as long as people don't get kicked out so that others can come in," Community Board 4 (CB4) chair Mary Brendle said. But the community was worried about the spillover effect of the 42nd Street project. "A little more spillover, and we'll drown," said one resident who grew up in the neighborhood. The community had already won a $15 million commitment from city and state officials (to come from budget funds spread out over five years) after weeks of negotiation with Herb Sturz (City Planning) and William Stern (UDC); still the Board of Estimate vote approving the project only came after twelve hours of back-room negotiations at 1:20 in the morning. "We had to buy Clinton twice," Koch told me. "It was an outrage; it was wrong, but something had to be done to move the project forward."[56]

New York City's fifty-nine community boards have a formal voice in the review of land use proposals, social service delivery, and budgetary issues impacting their districts, on an advisory basis under authority granted in the 1975 revision of the city's charter. They hold public hearings and make recommendations for consideration to the City Planning Commission or, in the case of special permits or zoning variances of a local nature, to the Board of Standards and Appeals; they also review and comment on environmental assessments or environmental impact statements. Development projects that are as-of-right in which the city has no discretion are not subject to community review. (In a 1990 revision of the charter, they were given the authority to prepare plans for development within their district and submit them to the City Planning Commission and City Council for approval.) Although their opinions are purely advisory, in the case of CB4 and many of its peers, their power is political. Their monthly meetings draw the neighborhood's elected representatives; borough presidents have staffs assigned to work with the boards and send representatives to the monthly meetings, which are open to the public, often intensely spirited, and tend to draw diverse groups, including developers or their representatives with projects under board consideration or soon to be under it. In the fullest sense, community boards serve as mobilizing institutions for community input on specific projects, allowing the community's residents and business interests to express their opposition or approval and/or push for changes to a proposed development. They are a gauge of the attitude of the community, a repository of institutional knowledge, and often include members who have high levels of specific expertise. Through bargaining and negotiation, boards like CB4 have been activists seeking to influence the shape of development in their community and gain direct benefits such as affordable housing.

Clinton, or Hell's Kitchen as it was known until it was rebranded around 1959 by local organizations seeking to improve the neighborhood's image, was no stranger to large public works projects. In the 1930s and '40s huge land takings necessary for the West Side Highway, the New York Central Railroad West Side Improvement Project, and the elaborate entry/exit networks of the Lincoln Tunnel and the Port Authority Bus Terminal radically truncated the neighborhood, leaving in their scarred path speculative landholdings, vacant plots, and a proliferation of parking lots. (When the bus terminal was built in 1950, dozens of buildings were demolished, including thirty-eight houses of prostitution.) Officially smaller now, the neighborhood stretches north from 41st Street to 59th Street and west from Eighth Avenue to the Hudson River (Hell's Kitchen South extends to 34th Street). In 1968, Mayor Lindsay announced plans for a huge West Side Convention and Exhibition Center at the Hudson River and 42nd Street running north to 47th Street. Clinton was already threatened by the expected spread of midtown, but the scale of what was being proposed would make the exhibition center the largest of its kind in the United States—and far more impactful on Clinton in terms of congestion, traffic impacts, and displacement than the customary progression of development. Although alternative west side locations emerged during the years of protracted planning and controversy, any one of these sites, except one at Battery Park City, threatened to further decimate this "transitional" neighborhood.

Clinton was an old-fashioned polyglot neighborhood where residents knew their neighbors, children played on the sidewalks protected by watchful eyes, shopping was local, and small neighborhood restaurants the norm. It was well known for its ethnic food suppliers along Ninth and Tenth Avenues. Economically, warehouses and light manufacturing mixed with residential buildings. Four-story and five-story walk-ups with generally poor sanitary facilities and poor ventilation predominated (built before 1901, these were Old Law Tenements in New York parlance, also called "dumbbell tenements" after the shape of the building footprint), but housing was a bargain, considerations of quality aside. Low average rents in these old structures meant that typical Clinton residents paid a smaller fraction (approximately 17 percent to 18 percent) of their income for rent than the norm (25 percent). This made family life affordable for the many low- and moderate-income residents in the walk-to-work neighborhood close to the Theater District. Population had been on the decline for two decades (approximately 34,000 people recorded in the 1970 federal census); racially, it had remained stable at about 91 percent white. It was a cohesive community with a "tradition of fight and feistiness," a history of gangs and gangsters that goes back a century to when Hell's Kitchen was filled with families of longshoremen who worked the Hudson River piers. It was not just the low-cost rental housing that would be lost to uncontrollable development, but the way of life in this working-class community that in so many ways reflected the historical trajectory of Manhattan's evolution.

The upscale potential of the neighborhood was all too apparent by the time the convention center fight engaged the community. Anticipating redevelopment, speculators and developers had been assembling sites in the neighborhood since the 1950s; by 1974, 35 percent of Clinton's land was already held in assemblages. A map of "soft sites" ripe for development which appeared in a news article showing eighty cleared sites was probably not as revelatory for Clinton residents as it was for the *Times*' readers. Forty-eight of these sites were within three blocks, north, south, and east, of the proposed convention center; four were full-block assemblages. "Clinton's basic problem is not its housing, which is old, nor its population, which is in decline, nor its average income, which is low," the consultants concluded in a 28-page report prepared for the Clinton Steering Committee (overseeing the neighborhood's zoning and urban planning) with the participation of community and city representatives. "The essential problem is its location. . . . Clinton is sitting on what may become, in the relatively new future, some of the most valuable land in New York City."[57]

In a bargain struck with the community, in 1974 the city officials created the Special Clinton District to preserve its low-density residential character and hopefully stabilize it, if not prevent it from becoming another generic upper-middle-income area of high-rise apartments. The special zoning, said the City Planning Commission, would provide for "the balanced development of Clinton."[58] In endorsing the approach, a *Times* editorial observed, "it was not until recently that the relationship between community health and the city's survival was perceived as anything more than a set of real estate transactions." In fashioning this new policy, the city has "finally understood this urban equation."[59] The "good planning and good sense" behind the Special Clinton District would not stop development—"Only a miracle will stop development in Manhattan," quipped one member at a Clinton Steering Committee meeting;[60] rather, it would direct high-density development to the perimeter area of the district, as discussed in chapter 7. The special zoning with its emphasis on preservation bought time. Development projects, some publicly funded, eventually opened the door to gentrification of the neighborhood. The first and most notable was the eventual success of Manhattan Plaza (1977), the twin-tower apartment complex of 1,690 units on 42nd Street (figure 3.11) operated under a federal subsidy program and rented mainly to performing artists, including celebrated artists Larry David, Terrance Howard, Samuel I. Jackson, Angela Keyes, Angela Lansbury, and Estelle Parsons.

Although the threat of development remained, the protections against imminent loss under the regulations of the special district marked an unambiguous victory for the community's activist groups. In particular, this was the first special district in the city to include protections again tenant harassment, which, in essence, requires new development to prove that no harassment ever existed, an almost impossible standard, said one expert, before a building can be demolished or renovated. Owners of properties in which harassment has been documented must provide permanent affordable housing before altering or demolishing those buildings.[61]

The special district "was the quid pro quo for the convention center," Restuccia told me. In Clinton, he explained, groups form quickly around individual issues; individual blocks also have their own associations with their own agendas. Typically, these community groups meet an hour before a major meeting—"there may be blood on the floor, but they are united when they meet with officials." The internal organization of the community, this way of coming to a compromise on a community position, is what made a difference in the Special Clinton District outcome. It became a template for how the community would deal with future threats, as it did ten years later during negotiations over what the city would do to mitigate the impacts on Clinton of the cleanup of 42nd Street. "There is a lot of memory among the groups," Restuccia said; "I was *taught* about the Special District."[62]

When first presented with the plan for the redevelopment of 42nd Street, CB4 passed a resolution in support of the project. Soon, though, other groups in the community pushed, successfully, for a resolution to reverse the original position, which Mary Clark, a community activist and member of the negotiating committee representing the Clinton Planning Council, believed gave them a better bargaining position with UDC. For weeks prior to the Board of Estimate public hearing, the negotiating committee—"a large garrulous committee"—chaired by Father Robert Rappleyea of Holy Cross Church on 42nd Street between Eight and Ninth Avenues, often met in a basement room of the church, which was notable for being the oldest building on the street.[63]

The committee had a lot of ideas for how the community would benefit from the $25 million from the 42nd Street project; "there was a battle royal over these funds," said Restuccia. The McManus Midtown Democratic Association, the oldest Democratic club in the city and the last of the Tammany-era holdouts, had run politics in Hell's Kitchen ever since it had been founded by Thomas McManus, a state representative first elected to the Assembly in 1892. Thomas's great-grandnephew James McManus had been running the club for some 22 years when the negotiations over the 42nd Street project started. Restuccia was getting in the way; he was attacked. The club fought to freeze him out from being reappointed to CB4 and after six months won that battle over the citywide appointment. The story was all over the community newspaper, the *Clinton Chronicle*. But the political world of Hell's Kitchen was changing, and though CB4 came out against the 42nd Street project, the club's power was not what it was in the old days. Being pro-development, it had wanted to make a deal quickly, but the community, Restuccia said, was suspicious of the club.

In 1985, the state and the city established the $25 million Clinton Preservation Fund for a five-year period. Of the $25 million, half came from the city and half from the state. City officials insisted that $1 million would be spent on the Clinton Community Garden (on 48th

Street between Ninth and Tenth Avenues), which would become a public park. Another $500,000 was to go for increased law enforcement, which left only $10.5 million in the city pot; subject to the annual appropriations process, it would take five years to get the funding, but amazingly, Restuccia said, the commitment was fulfilled. The city was funding its commitment from its capital budget, which limited the use of Clinton monies to capital costs in city-owned buildings, in rem holdings which included hundreds of landlord-abandoned tenements; the tenements in Clinton had not been renovated in 50 years, though they were fully occupied. The state money was more flexible; it could be used to acquire and rehabilitate buildings, support physical improvements to community institutions, and fund services like legal aid for tenants facing harassment and eviction and for tenant assistance in the conversion of buildings to low-income cooperatives. For any of these activities, the majority of people served had to be of low and moderate income. The goal was to preserve and improve the residential character of Clinton and its variety of existing stores and activities.[64]

A fifteen-member Clinton Advisory Committee (the "25 million committee") was set up to govern the allocation of funds, with six representatives from the Community Board, six representatives from the Clinton Planning Council (a clearinghouse for the community established in 1959), one from the Clinton Coalition of Concern, one from the Midtown North Precinct Council, and one from the Ninth Avenue Business Association. The McManus club took over the Clinton Planning Council when it realized the pot of money to be had, according to Restuccia. Each year for the five-year payout of the funds, the Advisory Council put out an RFP for use of the funds and held monthly meetings to decide how they would be allocated; after a time, CB4 took over the process, which turned into a 10-year, largely public-process endeavor by a persistent community that "would not let go."[65] The priorities were legal services to staunch the tide of displacement; acquisition of privately owned distressed buildings, especially landlord-harassed buildings; renovation of city-owned buildings to create affordable tenant ownership; and preservation of small businesses, though this last item could not get done.

The acquisition of distressed and harassed privately owned buildings with state funds proved to be difficult and controversial; in the end, the Fund acquired at least thirteen buildings, spending between $400,000 and $2 million for a building. To create permanent housing affordability, nonprofit community groups worked through the New York City Tenant Interim Lease Apartment Purchase Program (TIL) (ultimately allocating 83 percent of the city's $10 million housing commitment from the Clinton Special Fund),[66] which assists organized tenant associations in city-owned buildings to develop economically self-sufficient low-income cooperatives where tenants purchase their apartment for $250; tenant associations enter into a lease with the city to maintain and manage the buildings in which they live. Set up in 1979 (a time when the city "would try anything" to deal with the hundreds of city-owned buildings that had been abandoned by landlords), the TIL program provides training to tenant associations in building management and restructures rents before buildings are sold to the co-op corporation so that buildings remain financially viable after sale.[67] Renovating and modernizing these tenements—railroad flats with tubs in the kitchen and toilets in the hall—bringing them up to code, installing kitchens and private bathrooms with a door, was a challenge. Bathroom renovations were essential. If tenants were poor, they could not qualify for rent subsidies if the unit did not have a bathroom, which was defined as three pieces—sink, toilet, and tub in the same room—and cost between $15,000 and $25,000 for a bathroom. At the end of the day, at least 340 bathrooms (and maybe as many as 450) were renovated or created. Over the seven years it operated, the Advisory Committee spent all but $1 million of its funding.

The Fund had a major impact on the Clinton neighborhood and on Restuccia's CHDC as an organization, as he made clear in his remarks at the premiere of *Against All Odds*. It could not stop the strong pressures of midtown development's westward expansion that had been building for several decades. Inevitably, market-driven economic pressures would rule; it was just a matter of time, as discussed in chapter 7. But the preservation regulations of the Special District sheltered the low-rise buildings of Clinton's residential core while encouraging high-rise development to take place around it. And the quid pro quo monies made a big difference in safeguarding housing tenure of existing tenants and improving their housing conditions, especially the bathrooms. It was a most unusual and little-known outcome of the city's largest redevelopment project.

## TOURIST MECCA

Every one of the changes on West 42nd Street validated the New York City's investment in the biggest and riskiest redevelopment project in its history. At its most telling, the pre-pandemic crowds on 42nd Street spilling over into Times Square are its truest measure of success. They validate the project's goals in restoring the luster to New York's iconic attraction. Kids, families, teens, adults, and couples meld in the mix. Many, especially the New York teens, were coming for the movies showing on multiple screens at the cinema center theaters on both sides of 42nd Street as they did in the past. "That's where the latest James Bond movie always premiered," recalled American novelist Richard Price, who grew up in a Bronx housing project. "You'd get ready at 9 a.m. with your friends, you'd take a backpack, some food—you know. It's like we're going across the desert."[68]

Irony exists in the big draw of movies on 42nd Street. Movies on 42nd Street—60 years spanning from glamorous first runs to popular action flicks to pornographic—had left a controversial legacy as a potent symbol of urban decay. If allowed as part of the redevelopment, the project's planners feared movies would once again bring pornography and accompanying crime back to 42nd Street. That logic led to the elimination of movies from the original plans for the street; movies only became an acceptable use with the reconfiguration of the entire plan, 42nd Street Now!, which permitted them as an option for all of the midblock theaters, though still in a limited way.

In Times Square the crowds were swelling exponentially, so much so that even tourists joined local voices in constant complaints about crushing congestion. More than fifty million tourists visited Times Square in 2019, the last full year before the pandemic. For over 100 years, the district's variety of entertainments (including people watching), bright lights, and energic pace created an excitement few visiting New York chose to miss.

As an economic engine, visitors' spending power generates billions for hotels, Broadway ticket sales, retail purchases, and food-and-drink tabs in the district's restaurants and bars, not to mention the billions the city treasury takes in tax revenues and the hundreds of thousands of direct jobs for New Yorkers. On an average pre-pandemic day, some 350,000 visitors would pile into the Times Square bowtie; on peak days in the summer, the crowd has swelled to nearly 425,000. The mass of people makes for a lot of pedestrian crush, even in the expanded pedestrian plazas, discussed in the next chapter. For years, it has been a point of dissatisfaction for locals and visitors alike. "Crowding in Times Square is a big problem right now," said Tim Tompkins, president of the Times Square Alliance, a nonprofit, self-taxing coalition of property owners organized to foster business improvement in the district, in 2015.[69]

As the crowds increased in unprecedented numbers year after year, tensions between tourists and local residents and area employees, who walk with different purposes—to get to a destination (determinedly) or to sightsee the square (aimlessly)—and at different paces—hurriedly or leisurely—on the same narrow sidewalk strips, became a source of friction. This too was the case in the early twentieth century when tourism stamped an indelible commercial mark on the tenor of development in Times Square; then too, tourists were ambling too slowly, infuriating locals. The fact that tourism was supporting New York's growing economy and Broadway's economic health then as it does today has only sharpened the tension between tourists and local residents. The Pulitzer Prize-winning critic Justin Davidson said it clearly: "New York is not easily overwhelmed," he wrote, "but even so, hating tourists long ago became a marker of snobbish authenticity." That is not the norm, and all New Yorkers are not provincial. Many are "inveterate givers of advice" when visitors look lost or befuddled and need help finding their way around town, or a suggestion for a good place to eat, or special things to see that might not be in the guidebooks. New Yorkers want visitors to enjoy their city and, just as they did when sending those millions of postcards to friends and family, bring the word back home. "The character of a great city is defined as much by the people who pass through as by its fixtures," Davison wrote in conclusion. "The urban spectacle needs a fresh audience every night."[70]

Still, as it has come to feel too touristy, Times Square has become less and less a place for New Yorkers. Its new status as a safe destination and its heavy corporate veneer has made more than a few New Yorkers question whether the city was going soft, losing some of its legendary toughness, its moxie, its grit—something authentic, if not unique. Where was the allure? The new Times Square is not edgy, nor cutting edge, and even visitors want more of that, more of what they perceive New York to be. The pedestrianization of the bowtie, a major initiative of the Bloomberg administration, further exacerbated the tensions, especially for those who live and work there. Where is the balance, the legacy—can Times Square reestablish itself as a place for New Yorkers? Even at the nadir of tawdriness, Times Square was an authentic New York place. It's a place that needs New Yorkers to be a New York place. The fear among many today is that Times Square might be slipping (or has slipped) out of the day-to-day life of New Yorkers. The fear among planners and real estate professionals, who do not always see eye to eye, is that Times Square could turn into a single-focus tourist zone, which would undermine the economic force behind 42nd Street's transformative redevelopment.

# 5 BOWTIE ANXIETIES

Sure, let's tear up Broadway! We can't govern, manage or police our public spaces, so we should just tear them up. That's not a solution. It's a surrender.
Tim Tompkins, August 2015

In the summer of 2015, the city's tabloids poured forth indignation about the topless women wearing body paint hustling for tips in Times Square. For five days running, righteous rage filled the front page of the *Daily News*—"BUST THIS FLESH PIT," "TOO MUCH TO BARE," "TIT FOR BRAINS," "FLESH PIT PIMPS," and "BOUNCE THOSE BOOBS"— conveniently forgetting the fact that hustling for money was a long-time custom in New York, as was sex in Times Square. No matter. The tabloids were having their day. The *desnudas*, complained a *Daily News* editorial, were adding "end-of-the-line tawdriness to the cheap carnival-ity that has taken over the most famous crossroads of the world."[1] After some one hundred bare-chested women and hundreds of supporters marched through midtown on a Sunday in a "Go Topless Parade," the *New York Post* castigated Mayor Bill de Blasio and Police Commissioner Bill Bratton for singling out the *desnudas* in an effort to clean up Times Square. For three weeks as the tabloids churned out a steady stream of news about the goings-on in Times Square, media outlets far and wide chronicled New York's topless tumult. The tabloids found their culprit in the pedestrian plazas created by banishing cars from five blocks of Broadway.

When the work crews were nearly finished constructing a series of pedestrian plazas, costumed characters and *desnudas* began to descend on Times Square in ever-increasing numbers, many panhandling with ever-increasing aggression—pawing tourists and berating them for not handing over enough money for a photo-op. The human crush of Elmos, Cookie Monsters, Spider-Men, and multiples of Micky and Minnie Mouse was smothering pedestrian movement. The chronic predatory panhandling was turning a tourist snare into a quality-of-life nuisance, especially for local workers in Times Square who were not on vacation. In a place legendary for its chaotic spontaneity, the hustling, hawking, and harassing was simply out of control. Times Square had become "a casbah of con artists and fleeced tourists," writer and producer Denis Hamill wrote in an op-ed, and "scamming and hustling tourists is bad for New York."[2]

In response, New York City's progressive mayor said he would give "a fresh look" at whether the Times Square pedestrian plazas, a signature accomplishment of the Bloomberg administration and an inspiration to other cities, should remain. "You could argue that those plazas have had some very positive impact," said de Blasio. "You could also argue that they've come with a lot of problems." The mayor said he discussed the idea of tearing up the plazas with Commissioner Bratton, who bluntly told a local radio station, "I'd prefer to just dig the whole damn thing up and put it back the way it was."[3] The backlash—louder than the normal New York loud—was immediate. Civic groups and urban planners and transportation advocacy groups became alarmed, especially since the plazas, built at a cost of $55 million, were credited with relieving dangerous pedestrian overcrowding and injuries in an area teeming with tourists. Seeking some political space from the immediate controversy, de Blasio quickly announced the creation of a task force of city officials to review the options for dealing with activities deemed to be illegal—aggressive panhandling—or legal but harmful to the area's quality of life—topless women wearing body paint.

Tim Tompkins had reached a point of exasperation. A passionate believer in public space and head of the business-sponsored Times Square Alliance since 2002, he had been hard at work to create a safe, secure, and exciting public space for visitors, workers in the district, and New Yorkers at large. His sarcastic response to city officials' off-the-cuff remarks about how to solve the congestion of costumed characters and *desnudas* marked an unusual departure from his otherwise diplomatic advocacy for improving Times Square as a unique public space. Even though New Yorkers were not pouring into public squares to hear important news as they had in the past, Times Square had witnessed some of the greatest national events (V-Day in 1918, V-E Day in 1945), and it continued to be the iconic place for ushering in every New Year, especially the new millennium.

Tompkins wasn't seeking to cleanse the plazas of the costumed characters or *desnudas*, nor was the Alliance calling for a ban that might run afoul of First Amendment protections. He believed the general chaos of Times Square was authentic. For several years he had been advocating for legal and regulatory tools to manage the aggressive solicitation tactics and predatory behavior of ticket sellers, tour bus hawkers, fraudulent charities, CD sellers, and costumed characters, and he had the data to back up his concerns. On Saturday nights, when the square was especially full of fun-seeking people, the Alliance's monitoring data revealed that as many as 181 ticket sellers, 61 CD sellers, and 139 costumed characters could be soliciting in the pedestrian plazas of Times Square.

Tear up the plazas? The plazas were not the source of Times Square's problems. To many, it seemed preposterous that taking away the plazas would rid the place of misbehaving actors. The problems, Tompkins argued, were rooted in the fact that New York City lacked a clear framework for managing the huge demands on Times Square, with some 47 million annual visitors and upward of 350,000–450,000 pedestrians passing through the area daily at that point, multiple times more pedestrians than cars, taxies, buses, and delivery trucks. The prostitution and three-card monte scams of the old Times Square were gone, but quality-of-life issues remained front and center in the perception of the place. Times Square has always had a perception problem, Tompkins said. The tabloids' obsessive focus on the seminude women was obscuring the central policy issue. "Quirky is fun, creepy is not."[4]

Times Square is a screen for urban anxieties. Its celebrated transformation did not wash away fears that the bad behavior of the past could reappear. Its well-known legacy as a place of vice—porn, drugs, crime, and con games—persisted in the minds of city officials, civic leaders, politicians, and editorialists, perhaps more so for those who had not lived through those dark days. It hung there, a lurking specter no amount of success could expunge. It made the tenor of the place vulnerable, susceptive to overreaction when forces of disorder appeared to be beyond control: the threat of the threatening.

Ironically, Times Square was having a problem with success. The aggressive misconduct and crass panhandling in 2015 did not foretell a regression to the grim and dangerous 1970s and '80s. Not even close. The uncontrolled harassment and crushing congestion of costumed characters did, however, pose a threat to the economic engine that had transformed Times Square. The viability of the commercial

**5.1** "Remember When Times Square Was Full of Menacing Creeps?" © Bill Bramhall/*New York Daily News*/TCA, July 14, 2014.

office market in Times Square—one of New York's proudest and long-sought-after economic-development achievements—was at stake if the bankers, lawyers, accountants, media companies, and other corporate tenants started to leave when their leases expired. Theater owners too worried about the negative publicity and whether incidents of predatory behavior would discourage tourism. For more than a decade, the trend had been ever upward, yet Broadway theater owners worried about the growing imbalance between tourists and New Yorkers in ticket sales and its effect when the high tide of tourism "inevitably begins to ebb." What the anxieties unleashed during that summer of 2015 revealed, Adam Sternbergh wrote in "Times Square: The City's Id, Now and Always," is that "Times Square exists less as a crossroads than as a repository for our collective hopes and fears for the city."[5]

## PEDESTRIAN TAKEOVER

On February 26, 2009, at a press conference at the Marriott Marquis Times Square, Mayor Michael R. Bloomberg announced "Green Light for Midtown"—a six-month experiment beginning over Memorial Day weekend in which Times Square from 42nd to 47th Streets and Herald Square from 33rd to 35th Street would be closed to vehicle traffic, with the cross streets to remain open.

Intended to improve traffic flow, reduce accidents, and enhance safety, the daring closures—likened to "bypass surgery on the heart of

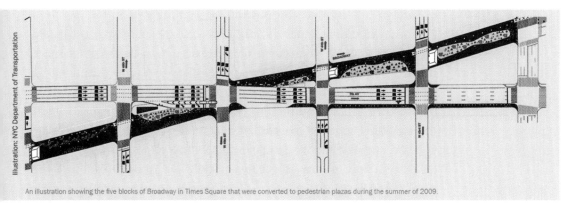

An illustration showing the five blocks of Broadway in Times Square that were converted to pedestrian plazas during the summer of 2009.

**5.2** The dark shadings in this illustration show where Broadway at Times Square was closed and converted to pedestrian plazas during the summer of 2009. Under the determined leadership of Janette Sadik-Khan, the Department of Transportation's experiment became permanent shortly thereafter, in 2010. "Green Light for Midtown," New York City Department of Transportation.

New York"[6]—would create more open space in Times Square—two and a half acres, more than the size of two football fields—for tourists, office workers, and shoppers and would alleviate the crunch of pedestrians on sidewalks so crowded that people frequently found themselves forced onto the roadbed amid cars in order to move forward to wherever they were going. The plazas promised environmental safety and a fresh take on the quality of life in New York City.

Following the transformation of Times Square to an office and commercial hub, the pedestrian crush grew with remarkable speed. Between 1999 and 2008, pedestrian counts conducted by Philip Habib & Associates for the Times Square Alliance showed a 58 percent increase in pedestrian volume in fourteen sidewalk locations throughout the business improvement district from 8:30 A.M. to midnight on a Saturday (a little less on a Wednesday); it was more crushing on the heavily traveled sidewalk between 42nd and 43rd Street and on the southwest corner of 44th Street. In 2001, the Transportation Department had widened the sidewalks with asphalt extensions and separated pedestrians from vehicular traffic by installing planters, pavement markings, and posts throughout the bowtie; successful enough, these temporary measures were made permanent a few years later. In another move in 2006, the Transportation Department closed the crossover between Seventh Avenue and Broadway, providing 50 percent more sidewalk space.

It was not enough. The district's growth trends kept overtaking the department's stopgap measures. The jostling for space against the rush of cars, trucks, and bicycles was the same at night as in the day. In a 24-hour period on a Friday in April 2008, 356,000 pedestrians, 125,000 car passengers, and 15,500 bus passengers vied for move-about space in the bowtie. When the theaters let out, some 60,000 people either hailed taxis, waited for their pickup ride, walked to where they had parked their cars, found their way to the subway, or just walked about the square. The dense pedestrian experience was an authentic New York experience, but the mayhem of sidewalk-slipping-into-the-street congestion was unsafe, especially for children, the disabled, and the elderly. "Pedlock" the Alliance called it, tagging the pedestrian gridlock. With the anticipated additional development of offices, hotels, and stores in the works, the competitive congestion would only get more intense. "Times Square is successful because people wait in huge hordes, in numbers the size of entire towns in North Dakota, for the light to change so they can cross the street," author Robert Sullivan remarked in 2004.[7] By 2015, that insight seemed less witty: walking around Times Square had become a contact sport.

The problem has been "hidden in plain sight for 200 years," said Transportation Commissioner Janette Sadik-Khan. Broadway, the meandering route of the old country byway Bloomingdale Road, creates "pinch points and traffic congestion as it traverses Manhattan crossing busy avenues."[8] Near major intersections in midtown, grueling traffic bottlenecks gave way to blasting horns, irate drivers, and impatient passengers, and engendered feelings of despair in the interminable crawl that accompanied gridlock. Accidents were commonplace: 562 crashes involving pedestrians and motor vehicles in Times Square between 1995 and 2005 made it one of the most dangerous stretches in the city, according to Wiley Norvell of Transportation Alternatives, a nonprofit organization dedicated to advocating for better walking, biking, and public transit for all New Yorkers.

Sadik-Khan's ambitions for taming traffic came across as counterintuitive: closing roads to reduce congestion? The idea cut against the very grain of New York: trading what could be considered the city's signature cacophony of activity for an oasis of pedestrian leisure? It signaled a radical reversal of car-centric policy in one of the most pedestrian-friendly cities in the world, in short, a transfer of power to pedestrians. The bold plan was immediately controversial. New Yorkers were skeptical, naturally, and many enraged at the audacity of taking away something akin to an urban birthright in the nerve center of the city. As with "all proposals to change the fabric of the city," remarked *Times* reporter William Neuman, "this one aroused a range of passionate reactions,

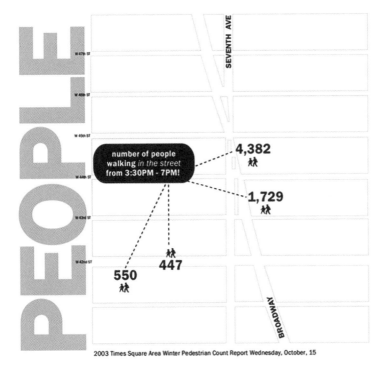

number of people walking *in the street* from 3:30PM - 7PM!

4,382

1,729

447

550

2003 Times Square Area Winter Pedestrian Count Report Wednesday, October, 15

**5.3** The immediate success of Times Square's turnaround triggered crippling congestion, day and night. The pedestrian count shown in this chart alongside a daytime photo indicates the number of people walking in the street during a peak time, late afternoon to early evening, 2003. Courtesy of Times Square Alliance.

**5.4** World-class traffic jam in the Theater District, 2011. Although the reduced amount of roadbed brought almost no change in traffic levels, the numbers of pedestrian, motor vehicle, and bicycle accidents did decline. Joiseyshowaa, Creative Commons CC BY-SA 2.0.

many of them driven, not surprisingly, by self-interest: from cabbies, pedestrians, drivers, tourists, business executives and office workers."[9]

Visitors from nearby voiced concern that the bustle and vitality of the place could be diminished with less congestion. An out-of-town commentator (who perhaps hadn't been in New York anytime in the recent past) believed "limited auto access could turn Broadway itself into a deserted wasteland." Motorists complained that the closures made no sense because they had to traverse Times Square to get where they were going. Cabbies and truck drivers vociferously defended their use of the streets, arguing that they would not be able to pick up fares and that deliveries would be ever more challenging. Hotel doormen worried that arriving guests would no longer be able to get in and out of cars or taxies in front of hotels, forcing them to negotiate a series of detours. Theater executives were not keen on the idea but would go along with the shift as long as their customers, who generally arrived by taxi, limousine, or private car, weren't hurt. Shop owners were not sure: some thought the increased foot traffic would bring in more customers, but those who were used to having tour buses drive up and stop in front of their doors expected fewer customers. Tourists applauded the idea: "Not having to worry about crosswalks and stop lights makes it that much easier."[10]

The idea itself evoked a problematic history. Reflecting the planning ethos of the 1960s, the pedestrian mall was initially hailed as a panacea for troubled American downtowns, but most such malls failed abysmally and mutated into empty spaces; the worst were plagued by crime and loitering. The experience demonstrated that pedestrian malls could not revive failing downtowns. In New York, the idea had been proposed multiple times for different reasons, each a dead end.

In 1969, the Regional Plan Association suggested closing Broadway to vehicular traffic between 59th and 23rd Streets for exclusive pedestrian use as a way to make the city's plazas more successful public places. Broadway, the civic organization said, was "particularly suited to exclusive pedestrian use because its diagonal direction confuses traffic movement and because it is not paired with a northbound avenue." Two years later, Mayor Lindsay's Office of Midtown Planning and Development proposed a permanent Madison Avenue Mall between 42nd and 57th Streets as part of a larger proposal to recapture space in central Manhattan for outdoor life, reduce air pollution, and untangle the city's traffic jams. The group proposed widening the street to create more than double the space for pedestrians, planting large trees, and installing benches; two traffic lanes would be left open for small buses and trucks and emergency vehicles. Fearful that the restrictions on traffic would "be ruinous to their business," local merchants and their associations voiced strong objections, as did the city's taxi industry. The idea died in 1973, after an appeals court ruled that the ability to make "monumental changes in the physical and economic existence of Madison Avenue" was within the power only of the Board of Estimate, not the Transportation Department.[11]

The next year, Mayor Abraham Beame's Office of Midtown Planning and Development proposed a three-block closure of Broadway between 45th and 48th Streets on "a rather seedy stretch of the Great White Way" that was to be reconstructed as a "beautiful oasis in the very heart of the city" and "mark the renaissance of the entertainment district." At the time, Atlanta-based architect John Portman was struggling to find financing to develop a 2,000-room luxury hotel on the west side of Times Square between 45th and 46th Streets; the pedestrian mall would provide a front-door plaza for the hotel. Known as Broadway Plaza, the $7.5 million street project was too contentious to survive the prevailing politics of Times Square, even though all the approvals were in place and $500,000 of pilot financing from the federal government was on hand. Theater and business interests worried that the open space created by the project would become a gathering place for street people,

**5.5** Proposed pedestrian mall for Broadway Plaza that would also serve as a front-door plaza for the proposed hotel of Atlanta-based architect John Portman, 1981. New York City Office of Midtown Planning and Development.

drug traffickers, and peddlers. The editorial board of the *Times*, perhaps worried about its front door, said it would make a "nice pimp and prostitute promenade." Shortly before the plan was scrapped in 1982, the president of the City Council warned that the open space "will only serve as a stronger magnet for the illicit activities we are striving to remove from Times Square."[12]

Even before Broadway Plaza failed to gain traction, transportation planners had repeatedly put forth proposals to tame the traffic chaos around the bowtie at Herald Square, one of the city's busiest and most dangerous intersections where three major streets (Broadway, Sixth Avenue, and 34th Street) converge. In the late 1960s, a proposal to turn the whole bowtie from 32nd to 34th Streets into a pedestrian mall met with ridicule. In 1988, transportation officials had a plan to reroute traffic from Herald Square by narrowing Broadway just north of the square and closing Broadway as a through street just below 34th Street where it intersects with Sixth Avenue. The closed-off streets would have tripled the open space in the area, but opposition from retailers, who feared the new parks would attract more drug dealers already operating openly at nearby Greeley Square, scuttled the plan. In 1993, the Dinkins administration put forth yet another plan to close Broadway from 34th to 32nd Street, but opposition from Macy's and the 34th Street Partnership, a business improvement district representing more than 500 area businesses, doomed that plan.

The situation changed in 1996, when the private 34th Street business group reached a deal with the city's Department of Parks to spend $2 million to transform the two tiny traffic islands into new parks. The new Herald and Greeley Squares would be paved, trees and roses planted, benches added, movable chairs scattered about, and public restrooms added in each park. Three years later, in 1999, after 30 years of go-nowhere plans to tame traffic around the Herald Square bowtie, the city's Department of Transportation and business groups that had opposed earlier traffic plans finally reached an agreement for a more modest reconfiguration of traffic. Sidewalks would be widened, crosswalks added, a lane of traffic eliminated, and the two tiny traffic islands extended to make it safer for the millions of pedestrians who crossed the square each year. It was an experiment that favored pedestrians in a spot that was always near the top in pedestrian accidents, and it became a testing ground for what transportation officials would do at Times Square.

For too long, the Broadway bowties had been "treated as leftover space." The fast-growing city lacked enough public squares, bemoaned the *Real Estate Record and Builders Guide* at the turn of the twentieth century. The cutting diagonal of Broadway, it said, gave "some variety and distinction to the grid system of streets, [but] the opportunities that it offers have not been used to advantage." More than a century later, the quest to tame traffic congestion in Times Square had the effect of refashioning the city's most public of public spaces. "Walking down the cramped, narrow sidewalks, a visitor could never get a feel for the vastness of the place," the *Times*' architectural critic Nicolai Ouroussoff wrote after the five-block stretch of Broadway had been closed to cars on Memorial Day weekend. "Now, standing in the middle of Broadway, you have the sense of being in a big public room, the towering billboards and digital screens pressing in on all sides." The plaza, he added, "can now function as a genuine social space: people can mill around, ogle one another and gaze up at the city around them without the fear of being caught under the wheels of a cab."[13]

New Yorkers were of two minds. A July 2009 Quinnipiac University independent poll found that city residents thought pedestrian plazas in Times Square were a good idea (58 percent) but did not want them where they lived (57 percent). Others were of the opinion that "It's not good to make a difficult city to live in more difficult." Still others were irate: "For real New Yorkers—those of us who live, work and occasionally indulge in a cab ride home after enjoying a few too many—the plan to close off great swaths of this city from vehicular traffic is punishing, costly and downright mean." The plan would force a rerouting of the final stretch of the Macy's famous Thanksgiving day parade off Broadway, where crowds traditionally lined the Great White Way. "It's no longer the Crossroads of the World if there's only one avenue in the crossroads."[14]

David Letterman joked that the city had turned "the greatest street in the world" into a "petting zoo." The *Post*'s columnist Steve Cuozzo said "the 'experimental' scheme will create a broad loitering zone along the Broadway side of the bowie, where we can avail ourselves of such dubious pleasures as noshing alfresco on benches." Others were outraged that the only people benefiting from the plan would be tourists, not those who inhabit Times Square on a daily basis and for whom it was a workplace. Then there was (almost proud) resignation: "New Yorkers . . . they can get used to anything and everything." The mayor too had to be convinced. At first, Bloomberg "thought this was the stupidest idea I'd ever heard" and was skeptical of the simulated impacts of car traffic before and after the changes. Reportedly, the mayor was persuaded when Sadik-Khan told him that the effects of the change on congestion could be tracked using Global Positioning System data from taxicabs.[15]

The reconfiguration of Times Square would become the administration's signature pedestrianization project (among the more than sixty pedestrian plazas in various stages of design, construction, or completion under Sadik-Khan's Department of Transportation), though not before the provocative $1.5 million "Green Light for Midtown" proved itself with data. Although the Bloomberg administration presented the low-cost project as a pilot, this transportation commissioner was unlikely to leave much to chance in pushing through such a high-profile

**5.6** Times Square looking north, before (top) and after (bottom) pedestrianization of the roadway, 2010. Creative Commons Arch_Sam CC BY 2.0 (top); Gary Hack (bottom).

**5.7** Ribbon-cutting for the first phase of the permanent Times Square pedestrian plazas, 42nd and 43rd Streets, 2013. Mayor Michael Bloomberg, Transportation Commissioner Janette Sadik-Khan, flanked by elected officials and stakeholders. Scheduled for completion in 2015, the work was still ongoing between 43rd and 47th Streets. The City of New York.

change. On two (of the four) lanes of Broadway that had been closed to vehicular traffic between Times Square and Herald Square six months before, she had recorded several days' worth of traffic patterns that undergirded her confidence in the pedestrianization scheme.

A transportation policy wonk with both government and private-sector experience who had trained as a lawyer, Sadik-Khan was as data-driven as the mayor she served. She was passionate about transforming city streets for cyclists and pedestrians and had taken the job—brashly telling the mayor during her interview that she did not want to be traffic commissioner, she wanted to be transportation commissioner—because she "wanted to innovate alongside an envelope-pusher" like Bloomberg. With a sure sense of her convictions, a forceful personality, and the instincts of a streetfighter (with a confrontational style that did not sit well with some), she aimed to execute a vision of urbanity that recalibrated city streets toward greater use for bike paths and pedestrian esplanades and open-air seating for civic enjoyment. Soon after her appointment, she started shaping a new strategic plan for the department, emphasizing the benchmarks set out in the mayor's 2007 blueprint for a sustainable and resilient future, PlaNYC. "One of the good legacies of Robert Moses is that, because he paved so much, we're able to reclaim it and reuse it," she told journalist Michael Crowley.

"It's sort of like Jane Jacobs's revenge on Robert Moses." As the builder of some 400 miles of bicycle lanes—using many on a regular basis as she rode her bicycle to meetings—she fashioned herself as "the largest real-estate developer in New York City."[16]

The idea model Sadik-Khan adopted for improving the environment of New York streets came from the pedestrian realm of downtown Copenhagen with its eighteen car-free areas and several pedestrian promenades linked by a network of bicycle and pedestrian paths. Initiated as a trial in 1962, the pedestrianization of the Strøget was made permanent in 1964. Though controversial, the project quickly proved a success. The work of Danish architect and urban designer Jan Gehl, who started studying the new pedestrian area in 1962, formed the basis of Copenhagen's broader policy shift toward pedestrians and bicycles. Aiming to apply Gehl's influential ideas to reimagining New York City streets, Sadik-Khan raised private funds to give the Dane a consulting contract, which resulted in the 29-page 2008 report "World Class Streets: Remaking New York City's Public Realm."

"A lot of the ideas that we put into play . . . weren't new," she admitted. "But [we] did pioneer the idea of changing streets in real time. Going straight to the people with the ideas and showing them [with] temporary materials what can happen was a game changer." She did not want to spend years and years on planning studies and computer modeling only to "show a dry engineering drawing that nobody could really understand." She thrived on fast implementation and believed "you got a very different buy-in when people could see, touch, and feel changes."[17]

What people first saw elicited both derision and wonderment. As overseer of the furniture decisions for the plaza, the Times Square Alliance provisionally populated the empty traffic lanes with some 376 plastic folding lawn chairs and loungers in candy colors of pink, blue, and green of the type "our grandmothers used to bring to the beach on the Jersey Shore," said Tompkins. He bought the chairs and loungers for an average price of $15 apiece from a local hardware store as a temporary fix before sturdier chairs and tables on order arrived later in the summer. Tacky yet endearing and campy, they emerged as embodiments of the new zeitgeist. The idea of Times Square as an "outdoor lounge" was incongruous, if not wacky, but in short order the newest problem became finding a seat. Tourists with aching feet were thankful for someplace to rest and take in the all-around digital commercialization bathing the bowtie. Some local workers found it convenient to work or lunch in open air. To some, the cordoned-off area could even be "strangely peaceful," odd as that seems. To critics, the temporary aesthetics of the pedestrian space—lawn chairs that soon frayed and sagged, orange construction barrels used to mark off the pedestrian area, and white-painted asphalt surfaces—were "a little unworthy of New York." "People seem to be jumping right past the issue of whether there should be this pedestrian space to what it should look like," remarked Tompkins.[18]

Not Steve Cuozzo of the *Post*. His complaints during the summer of 2009 echoed his early animus toward the idea of closing these five blocks of Broadway to vehicular traffic. It was not just that the "squatters' camp" was "ugly," and the "cheaply graveled and paved surfaces, painted with dopey colored circles," an affront to the square's historic legacy and the "glory of its landmarks." All summer, the Crossroads of the World had been "a five-block-long sea of dazed, low-rent tourists glued like chewing-gum wads to the cheapest seats in town." Tourists, he argued, weren't the only ones who used the square. The lawyers, bankers, accountants, news people, and media producers who work, live, and eat in Times Square every day "have a right to feel disenfranchised from what it's become."[19] He was worried about the threats of tourist dominance on the economic viability of office space in Times Square.

Whether Times Square was a place for tourists or New Yorkers was a question as old as its transformation from Longacre Square. "Broadway's new tentative divide between a street for cars and a space for people," wrote journalist Susan Dominus, was "also an apt description for Times Square itself, a space half-defined by the city and half-defined by the tourists who inhabit it."[20]

In January 2010, the department released the results of its pilot program in a 45-page "Green Light for Midtown Evaluation Report."[21] Packed with granular-level detail on travel flow and speed (mixed), bus travel times (fallen slightly), safety (greatly enhanced), pedestrian travel (large increases), and satisfaction with Broadway among New Yorkers and visitors (dramatic improvements), the findings validated the pilot's success. Surveys conducted for the Times Square Alliance reinforced the change in perception of the square. In 2004, overcrowded streets ranked as the number one reason why local employees would wish to work elsewhere; four years later, just before pedestrianization, another survey found that Times Square was a place New Yorkers sought to avoid. Results from a Transportation Department follow-up survey a year later, shown in figure 5.9, revealed that the perception of Times Square had undergone a profound change as a consequence of the pedestrianization. The plazas earned high satisfaction among

**5.8** The provisional "outdoor lounge" in Times Square outfitted with multicolor lawn chairs in the months immediately after Broadway was closed to vehicular traffic (2009), replaced soon after with red collapsible tables and chairs (2010). Frances Roberts/Alamy Stock Photo (top); Gary Hack (bottom).

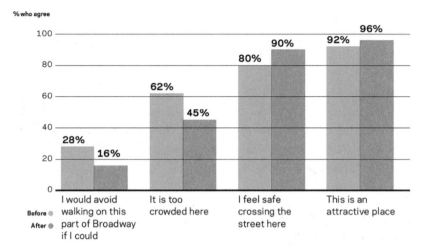

% who agree

Before ● After ●

| | I would avoid walking on this part of Broadway if I could | It is too crowded here | I feel safe crossing the street here | This is an attractive place |

**5.9** Survey results of the changing perceptions of Broadway at Times Square before (May) and after (October) creation of pedestrian plazas, 2009. New York City Department of Transportation, "Green Light for Midtown Evaluation Report" (January 2010).

a majority of tourists, New Yorkers, suburban residents, and workers in Times Square; theatergoers too felt the plazas had a positive effect on their theatergoing experience.[22] The open area was good for retailers. Although the hopes that traffic would actually move faster after removing Broadway from the system did not materialize, decreases in pedestrian, motor vehicle, and bicycle accidents persuaded Bloomberg to announce the following month that the Times Square pedestrian plazas would become permanent.

To lead the job of designing a permanent New York-worthy transformation of the pedestrian space, the city's Department of Transportation and Department of Design and Construction ran a design competition and in 2010 selected Snøhetta, a Norwegian-American architectural collaborative internationally known for its projects that have enhanced civic life: the Oslo Opera House (2008) and the modern replacement for Egypt's legendary Library of Alexandria, which burned in 48 BC, the Bibliotheca Alexandrina (2001). After receiving the commission to design the National September 11 Memorial Museum Pavilion at the World Trade Center in 2004, Snøhetta had opened a New York office, managing the project through ten tortuous years of political and program changes before the pavilion opened in 2011. That and the experience of designing high-profile civic buildings had prepared Craig Dykers, the firm's American-born principal, for what it would take to see the Times Square plaza project through the rough-and-tumble of New York City politics. Articulating the complex psychology of public space through design was a Snøhetta specialty, and the Times Square project promised to further burnish its reputation for using architecture to alter a city's relationship with itself. Snøhetta was "an obvious choice to revise Times Square," said architectural critic Martin Filler.[23]

"Our goal is to improve the quality and atmosphere of this historic site for pedestrians and bicyclists while also allowing for efficient transportation flow for the betterment of the city," said Dykers. The subtext to that goal, as told to *New Yorker* writer David Owen, was "to reconfigure the space in such a way that city residents will stop walking blocks out their way to avoid it." On a walk through Times Square in 2013 with Owen, Dykers remarked, "It's commonly believed that tourists love Times Square and New Yorkers hate it. That's fairly true, but New

**5.10** *Cool Water, Hot Island* (2010) by artist Molly Dilworth, selected by the Department of Transportation as the winning entry in its international design competition to beautify the new pedestrian plazas while awaiting a full redesign and permanent build-out. Dilworth designed the mural with an eye to the urban heat island effect, by which cities tend to experience warmer temperatures than rural settings. The blues and light shades of the design reflect more sunlight and absorb less heat. Courtesy of Molly Dilworth.

**5.11** Street view looking south from the finished pedestrian plaza designed by Snøhetta, the new pavement and benches a foil for surrounding bright lights of the digital billboards, 2015. Michael Grimm, Courtesy of Snøhetta.

Yorkers, no matter how cynical they may be, are always going to be amazed by the lights, even if they're angrily running through it."[24]

By the time Dykers visited Times Square, red café tables and chairs (à la Bryant Park) had replaced the kitschy lawn chairs, and large plastic planters had been installed on the painted asphalt surfaces, mostly tan (like beach sand) and blue (like the ocean). "The paint is fun," he said, "but these kinds of bright colors seem out of place in Times Square. In people's collective memory, Times Square is not about the beach." After Dykers and his colleagues studied historical photographs, they concluded that "a critical element missing from the square's modern iteration was a relative darkness at street level, in contrast to the frenetic light show created by billboards and other signage." Their design would aim to "frame the existing illumination, not to augment or compete with it."[25] There's enough spectacle there already, he said.

## CORPORATE WORKPLACE

Long anticipated, office development in Times Square finally arrived, with zeal, by the mid-1980s. With the incentive of the 1982 special rezoning of midtown that increased allowable density west of Sixth Avenue, developers tore down landmarks on Broadway to erect new office skyscrapers. In 1987, wrecking machinery clawed into the Strand Theatre (1914), Times Square's first movie palace, to clear the site for Solomon Equities' 52-story tower at 1585 Broadway, which Morgan Stanley bought for its headquarters (1989). That same year, Broadway's first $1 million theater, Loew's State (1921), built as part of a 16-story office building for the theater company, succumbed for Ian Bruce Eicher's development of 1540 Broadway (1990), a 42-story tower with a distinctive prow, which became home to the media conglomerate Bertelsmann. Thomas Lamb's Greek Revival Rivoli Theatre (1917) at 1620 Broadway went down that year as well for a 35-story tower, 750 Seventh Avenue (1989), designed by Pritzker Prize-winning architect Kevin Roche for Solomon Equities, initially occupied by Morgan Stanley and later by Lehman Brothers.

With the addition of the six towers developed under the aegis of the 42nd Street Development Project (6.5 million square feet, 1999–2010), by 2011 Times Square had become what determined city policy had sought: a substantial commercial office hub with 29 million square feet of space, accounting for 12 percent of the office space in midtown Manhattan. Put in perspective, this newly developed office hub surpassed the space inventory in the central business districts of Dallas (28.6 million square feet), Denver (26.9 million square feet), and Los Angeles (27.3 million square feet). These Times Square towers housed global media and finance companies with 106,000 daytime workers, whose presence—more than nine times the number of entertainment employees in Times Square—profoundly reshaped the economic dynamic of the entertainment and theater district, and with it the New York City economy.

This tiny land area, just one-tenth of a percent of the city's total, was now generating, directly and indirectly, $1 out of every $9 of the city's economic output and one-tenth of its jobs, according to a 2011 economic-impact report prepared for the Alliance by the New York-based economic development and real estate advisory firm HR&A Advisors. This amounted to $110 billion from a district roughly bounded

**5.12** The economic power of Times Square is concentrated in a very small land area, just one-tenth of a percent of the city's total. Courtesy of Times Square Alliance.

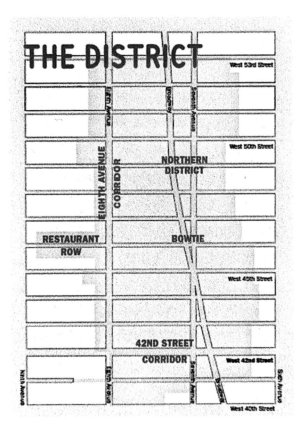

by a block on each side of Broadway between 40th and 53rd Streets. Some 170,000 people worked in the district, and the multiplier impact of money earned and spent on goods and services there supported an additional 215,000 city jobs. Since 2000, brisk demand for space to desk the tens of thousands of lawyers, bankers, accountants, publishing and media professionals, engineers, and employees in other business services had pushed average rents in the district to levels higher than those in midtown as a whole, despite distress during the great recession of 2008–2009.

Similarly, the retail real estate market in this pedestrian-clogged district burned white hot. Jostling for space in Times Square, retailers faced asking rents trending upward faster than rents in Manhattan's most desirable retail corridors: SoHo, Madison Avenue, and Upper Fifth Avenue. In the years ahead, constantly escalating rents for street-level space would continue to amaze real estate observers. In other words, after the plaza program closed Broadway to cars, "Carmageddon didn't happen: business boomed," remarked architectural critic Michael Kimmelman.[26]

Other benchmarks of economic success accompanied the expansion of economic activity in Times Square: residential living (more than

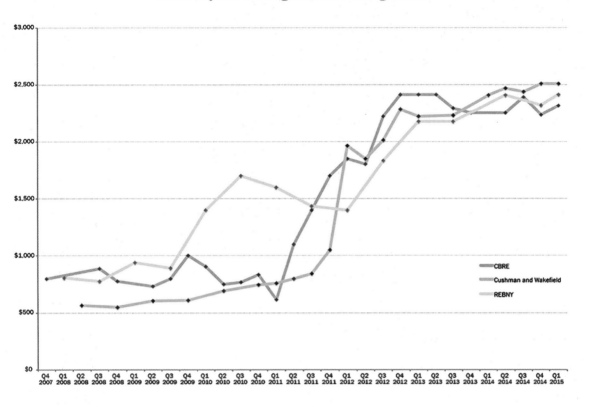

**Times Square Average Retail Asking Rents**

**5.13** Retail asking rents in Times Square spiraled rapidly upward following pedestrianization of the blocks between 43rd and 47th Streets (compare 2009 and 2015 in this graph). Courtesy of HR&A Advisors.

1,100 new units since 2005), hospitality expansion (2,000 additional rooms, in total 17,000 or 21 percent of hotel rooms in the city, sustaining the convention business of the nearby Javits Center), and astonishing growth in the assessed value of real estate in the district between 1996 and 2010 (233 percent), exceeding the growth rate for the city as a whole during this time (92 percent). As fiscal engine, Times Square's economic activity delivered $2.1 billion to the city and $2.5 billion to the state in taxes from personal income, sales, business income, property taxes, and related real estate taxes, according to the HR&A Advisors' report.

By far the most dramatic addition to the public realm in Times Square came in the form of the cascading staircase—dubbed "Ruby-Red Stairs with a View of the Great White Way"—covering the new TKTS discount ticket booth in an expanded Duffy Square at the north end of the bowtie. "The best seats on Broadway are now absolutely free,"

**5.14** The iconic glowing red-glass amphitheater in Father Duffy Square draws tourists and New Yorkers alike to sit and take in the bright-lights panorama of Times Square. A fiberglass orb below houses the Theater Development Fund's popular discounted ticket booth (pictured in 2009). Courtesy of Perkins Eastman.

wrote *Times* veteran reporter David W. Dunlap following the opening ceremony on October 16, 2008.[27] A climb up the twenty-seven steps made of structural glass to the top of the bleachers 16 feet above the sidewalk opened a "kinetic panorama" of Times Square, of passersby and rushing cars during the day and in the evening a blaze of syncopated signage that had been drawing thousands to the square for more than a century. One did not need to buy a discounted theater ticket at one of the Theater Development Fund's twelve ticket windows beneath the stairs' peak to enjoy the spectacle.

The staircase became an instant icon, offering a new way of experiencing Times Square that tourists and New Yorkers alike found mesmerizing. It was a spontaneous theater of the people-watching variety. The $19 million project, born from an international-competition-winning concept by the architects John Choi and Tai Ropiha of Australia, did not easily come into being, but then not much does in a contentious city like New York, especially such a true public amenity. It took all the muscle of local collaborating architects Perkins Eastman, who designed the TKTS booth, to help make the project a reality. Accolades and awards for the city's newest public gathering space were plentiful. The glowing scarlet-hued amphitheater soon became a destination in itself.

"The public realm is what we own and control," urbanist Alexander Garvin said in a walk-through of midtown with *Times* architectural critic Michael Kimmelman in 2011. It is not just common property; "the streets, squares, parks, infrastructure and public buildings make up the fundamental element in any community—the framework around which everything else grows."[28] The public realm, Garvin would argue continuously before he passed away in late 2021, is where people come together, where they come to be in the middle of things, where they congregate for events, or where they head to just look around. In dense cities, the shape and scale of those open spaces dimension the opportunities for people-watching, eating, reading, promenading, or enjoying a work break. In and of itself, the physical structure of a particular space does not ensure a good urban experience or make it a treasured place. The best in Manhattan—Rockefeller Center, Bryant Park, Vanderbilt Plaza, Union Square, and Times Square—are both public spaces and commercial hubs where that mixture of activity energizes the urban experience of place. In Times Square, the landscape of possibilities changed dramatically with the doubling of pedestrian space and the ruby-red staircase in Duffy Square.

As the congestion of costumed characters and aggressive behaviors flooded the plazas, the experience for many turned sharply negative. The dissatisfaction was especially acute among some of the big corporations in the towers that had made Times Square an office market. In the aftermath of the initial lease-up of the 42nd Street project's towers, it made perfect sense to be in Times Square, remarked one well-placed commercial broker, but "the neighborhood deteriorated right after the creation of the pedestrian plazas." It definitely has had an impact on the demand side, said another. Some commercial real estate

**5.15** Individuals costumed as iconic characters flocked to Times Square as a natural habitat—the place with the greatest potential for making money posing for photo-ops with tourists. Gary Hack (2014, top two), Stan Honda/AFP via Getty Images (2013, bottom).

professionals believed that the plazas confirmed Times Square as a tourist center. Was it now too congested for New Yorkers to conduct business there? For more than 100 years, the magic of the location has been the transit hub, but would it be enough to sustain the economic health of the Times Square office market?

## ECONOMIC BATTLEGROUND

Success had triggered unanticipated consequences: the spacious pedestrian plazas presented new opportunities for belligerent as well as benign behavior. Like moths drawn to light, individuals working for themselves costumed as film characters and cartoon icons flocked to Times Square. The costumed multiples of Elmo, Spider-Man, Super Mario, Iron Man, Dora the Explorer, Batman, Aliens, Cookie Monster, Hello Kitty, Miss Statue of Liberty, Minnie Mouse, and Mickey Mouse congregated in Times Square for the obvious reason: it was New York's tourist-rich mecca. The Naked Cowboy—Robert Burck in patriotically painted white briefs and cowboy boots and hat busking on a guitar since 1999—was already a fixture in Times Square. In 2005, the first Naked Cowgirl—Louisa Holmlund in sparkling pasties with red, white, and blue tassels covering her nipples and a patriotic micro-skirt that covered her bottom—busking on a guitar made her debut in Times Square. The first *desnudas* reportedly appeared in the summer of 2013. Soon they had "carved out a conspicuous niche for themselves—a mix of Las Vegas showmanship and New York flair," said a *Times* reporter. "Their success has even eaten into the business of more established and better-known risqué performers."[29] More than at any other tourist destination where their costumed cousins were appearing—the Battery and Bowling Green in Lower Manhattan, Rockefeller Center in midtown, and Coney Island in Brooklyn—Times Square presented the greatest commercial potential for garnering tips for photo-ops with children and adults. It was a natural habitat.

The aggressive panhandling and verbal abuse of more than a few bad actors set off alarm bells, threating as it did the vibrant diversity of the Times Square economy. "First came an anti-Semitic Elmo, ranting outside Toys "R" Us. Super Mario groped a woman. Cookie Monster shoved a 2-year-old. Con artists began pressing CDs on teenagers," wrote Kimmelman in a short essay in which he argued the case for nurturing the plazas in Times Square. That was not all of it: a man dressed as Woody from *Toy Story* was charged with molesting two women. Another dressed as Spider-Man was arrested for punching an NYPD cop in the face in

**5.16** *Desnudas* in Times Square posing for an entertaining photo-op with a tourist, 2014. Gary Hack.

**5.17** Pulitzer Prize-winning political cartoonist Matt Davies on the *desnudas* and cartoon characters of Times Square, *Newsday*, August 23, 2015. © Matt Davies.

front of stunned tourists. An abusive panhandler drew frightened stares with his handwritten sign "F—k you! Pay me!!!!!! I need money 4 Drugs & Hoez & Weaponz Mother F-kerz!" He was later arrested for allegedly breaking camera equipment used by a *Post* photographer who snapped pictures of him. Not to be omitted from the scene were the ubiquitous bogus monks, who "tend to stand out for the attire and for their sense of entitlement." They too might resort to aggression if not satisfied with the donation given for an offered amulet or bracelet; in 2014, the police arrested at least nine, mostly on charges of aggressive begging or unlicensed vending.[30] And there were the CD sellers of dubious materials. Scams aplenty.

Times Square's pedestrian plazas quickly became an economic battleground. There were too many characters out there. The competition was lessening what the characters could earn. On a good day, maybe two hundred dollars for eight hours—maybe, on a good day—but on many days, what a Mickey or Minnie or Elmo might take home was less than a hundred dollars, a reporter explained in a 2014 article in the *New Yorker*. The dozens of characters wearing the same costume affect how much money each can make, varying on the time of year, the day of the week, hours in the evening or day, the weather, and ultimately luck, wrote another journalist chronicling the life of several characters. Besides disputes over turf, it was hard work, subject to all kinds of indignities, sometimes bullying and harassment. "Kids' smiles are the way into parents' wallets," said one costumed Elmo, but not every tourist who takes a photo gives a "tip," or they might hand over only $1, not the $5, $10, or possibly $20 a character expected. Some just walk away.[31]

The competition for tips and donations was getting "very intense, causing friction between the costumed workers themselves, which in turn, leads to aggressive solicitation of the public," the commanding officer of the Midtown South Precinct, Inspector Edward Winski, told the City Council Committee on Consumer Affairs during hearings in 2014 on the proposed licensing of costumed characters in Times Square.[32] Complaints were growing more numerous; so too, arrests.

The arrests would keep growing, as the media were quick to report. Anxieties spiked. Times Square appeared to be spinning out of control. A trade group representing theater owners and operators blamed a drop in ticket sales to suburban folks on the proliferation of costumed characters who harassed potential patrons. "What I hear more than anything else is it's just so intimidating to walk through Times Square," said Charlotte St. Martin, executive director of The Broadway League.

**5.18** Aggressive solicitation from costumed characters for photo-ops with tourists in Times Square evolved into a troublesome issue as complaints of verbal abuse and inappropriate touching grew more numerous. As their numbers increased, competition among the characters intensified the problem on the plazas. The New York City Council would take up the issue in 2014 and again in 2016, when rules for solicitation were put in place. Yann Kebbi, "Times Square," originally produced for the *New Yorker*, July 2, 2012.

Support for regulating the chaos in Times Square was growing, at least among the business-oriented community. Mayor de Blasio said he was open to legislation being considered in the City Council that would require people dressed up as cartoon characters to display identification as they work in Times Square. "I think this has gone too far," he said. "It needs to be regulated."[33] Somewhat ironically, while the chaos was growing, Snøhetta was being showered with accolades from the design field for its reconstruction of those pedestrian plazas.

In "Times Square's Crushing Success Raises Questions About Its Future," *Times* veteran reporter Charles V. Bagli gave voice to the concerns and fears of commercial landlords (and their brokers), all of whom worried about Times Square's future as an office district. "Few landlords were willing to talk about the issue publicly for fear of turning their concerns into reality." Long-term leases kept tenants in place, but once those leases expired, anchor tenants in the towers of the new Times Square—Skadden Arps, Ernst & Young—would leave. The highly competitive office market was offering corporate tenants newer state-of-the-art buildings and trendier locations west and south of the midtown core, at Hudson Yards, and in Lower Manhattan at the World Trade Center, giving landlords of office buildings in Times Square ample reason to be agitated about the disorder of Times Square. Already Condé Nast had announced it was moving to the World Trade Center site, where it had gotten a very favorable deal, "but conditions in Times Square lurked in the background," noted Bagli.[34] Others like Morgan Stanley would explore alternatives.

Disquiet over the increasingly chaotic conditions in Times Square had been building for several years, but it reached a tipping point in the summer of 2015 abetted by the tabloids' indignation over the *desnudas*. The immense popularity of Times Square finally overwhelmed the capacity of the public realm, threatening the district's vulnerable balance between tourist spot and workplace. Those who worked in the square viewed the invasion of costumed characters and the topless painted ladies less benignly than tourists, though both groups were annoyed by aggressive solicitation and harassment by bad actors. Aggressive panhandling is illegal in New York City, but there's a slippery slope between strong solicitation and aggressive panhandling, and a constant conflict with First Amendment rights of free speech. Civility was hard to find. Public rules of engagement were needed, but none were in evidence in this most acclaimed public place.

The situation as many saw it went beyond tolerance for minor episodes of street nuisances that are part of the hustle and bustle of New

York's intense street life. "It had become lawless," remarked a long-time City Council legislative expert who requested anonymity. A free zone that all can enter presented a tempting target of abuse for some. Unlike Duffy Square, a park space where rules set by the Department of Parks and Recreation prevail and where commercial activity could be kept out, the pedestrian plazas in Times Square were streets, legally, under the jurisdiction of the Department of Transportation, whose broad mission covered the movement of people and goods in the city and maintenance and enhancement of transportation infrastructure. During the planning for Broadway's vehicle closure, no thought was given to how the plazas would be used, how the space would be managed, and who would manage it. The Transportation Department had been given a mandate to increase pedestrian space, and it had done that. Some said it could not be held responsible for the behaviors that emerged. However, this was Times Square. And pedestrianization was not an incubator waiting to emerge. City officials should have anticipated these kinds of issues, but they did not.

The disorder in Times Square posed an undeniable threat to the positive image of the city and the transformative economics that had done so much to enhance the urban experience of New York's most iconic public place. As the total number of visitors coming to New York City swelled during the post-transformation decades—to 58.5 million in 2015, up from 35.2 in 2001—tourism assumed new status as a powerful driver of New York's post-9/11 economic boom. "This remarkable surge in tourism has done more than merely clog sidewalks in Times Square," the Center for an Urban Future reported in "Destination New York." "It has sparked hundreds of thousands of new jobs—not just at hotels, but in restaurants, retail shops, museums, airports, tour bus companies, and even travel tech start-ups." Tourism had replaced manufacturing in the city's economy. "It provides diversification and a counterweight to Wall Street," said business writer Greg David. "It generates many middle-class jobs. It employs immigrants and unskilled workers and speeds them up the economic and social ladder far better than factory work. It is especially hospitable to women, it makes few demands for tax breaks and other incentives."[35] Billions of tourist dollars from direct spending on hotels, entertainment, and retail purchases in Times Square, Broadway ticket sales, and taxes on sales and hotel stays were flowing into the city's treasury. Jobs held by workers and residents were adding billions more in personal income tax revenues to the city's fiscal intake. The economic stakes in ensuring civic comity in the pedestrian plazas of Times Square were high—and indisputable.

Some type of regulation was needed to bring order to the mayhem. Workers in the district and other pedestrians needed free flow-through space to get where they were going. Tourists needed space to enjoy the scene and partake in the entertainment. And the characters, costumed or otherwise, needed space for their commercial transactions. Restraining the aggressive panhandling and intimidating behavior of bad actors among the scores of hustlers, hawkers, and unlicensed vendors trawling the pedestrian plazas in Times Square was crucial, city officials and civic leaders agreed. It was a matter of public safety. Quality of life. When in the summer of 2014 the *Wall Street Journal* asked its readers "Should New York City regulate costumed characters in Times Square?," 77 percent of the 274 who responded said "yes." Seventy-nine percent of those responding to a similar poll conducted by *Crain's New York Business* that same month said "yes."[36] But how? A consensus prevailed that regulation should not erase the historical authenticity of place, but what kind of rules would fit a place celebrated for its urban spontaneity and social tolerance, a place where anything goes?

## CHAOS CONTROL

"The fundamental question is what will solve the problem," City Council member Daniel Garodnick said in his preliminary remarks at the opening of the November 19, 2014, hearings on a proposed bill to license costumed individuals who solicit in public spaces in the city. "Is it more aggressive enforcement of existing laws as was done to address squeegee men in the 1980s and early '90s? Is it setting time, place, and manner restrictions for entertainment in Times Square so as to limit obstruction in a very busy area? Is it a self-regulatory scheme with background checks and identification cards coordinated with the NYPD? Or is it as my colleague Council Member King proposes a New York City license?"[37] The challenge for Garodnick and his legislative colleagues was to find a pragmatic pathway through constitutionally protected speech—costumed characters were arguably First Amendment vendors—that set apart commercial transactions and ensured economic justice for the many immigrants (including those undocumented) and others supporting families by their photo-op solicitations (for tips and donations) in Times Square. This was an important consideration tied to New York's historic identity as an immigrant metropolis, one could say a strategic consideration given the role immigration has played in the growth and culture of New York City.

This was a local issue for the 42-year-old Garodnick, serving his second and final term on the Council representing District 4 (including the eastern portion of Times Square), and his first-term colleague, 32-year-old Corey Johnson, representing District 3 (including the western portion of Times Square). "There is nothing easy about this issue and every possible solution has flaws," Garodnick said. "We need to beware of some of the legislative fixes that we could pass quickly while the fundamental questions of enforcement still dominate." He believed licensing created "two problems: One is you need to enforce existing rules against a licensed and now legitimized Elmo, and you still need to enforce against unlicensed Elmos who may or may not be doing any bad acts."[38] Licensing put a stamp of approval on being a costumed character in Times Square, and that was problematic for Johnson as well. In other instances, the city's licensing of the activity conferred value on the activity. Both councilmen went on record skeptical that a license would solve all the problems that had led the City Council to consider the behavior problems in Times Square. This was hardly an auspicious start.

To Andy King, the Bronx first-term councilman (District 12) leading the effort to regulate the costumed characters, the expressed reservations of his colleagues were considerations for discussion. The bill, cosponsored by twenty-two of King's Council colleagues, detailed a new "robust and complex licensing regime" that would require "costumed individuals" who solicit in public places to first secure a license from the Department of Consumer Affairs. It also imposed "significant location and manner restrictions for costumed solicitation" and provided for enforcement and penalties for noncompliance. To apply for a license, an individual had to be at least 18 years of age, provide name and home address and a full-face photograph taken within thirty days of the application, agree to be fingerprinted (with a one-time fee of $75) for the purpose of securing criminal history records, and pay a $175 licensing fee good for two years. No applicant could be asked about immigration or citizenship status as part of the application process.

Among other particulars in the bill, the commissioner of consumer affairs had to be "satisfied" that the applicant was of "good moral character"—meaning a person "not registered as a sex offender with the division of criminal justice services or convicted of another criminal offense with a direct relationship to the activities permitted by a license." The bill explicitly prohibited four forms of aggressive solicitation (generally consistent with the city's existing aggressive solicitation law): "(1) approaching or speaking to a person in a manner that is intended or likely to cause a fear of bodily harm or property damage, or intimidation into giving money or other thing of value, or unreasonable inconvenience, annoyance, or alarm; (2) intentional touching or physical contact with person or occupied vehicle without consent; (3) intentional blocking or interfering with pedestrian or vehicle traffic; or (4) using violent or threatening gestures toward a person being solicited."[39]

The licensing mechanism, which the Police Department would enforce, targeted the problem of anonymity. When a police officer gets a complaint of an Elmo groping, grabbing, or inappropriately touching a person, or hitting on young girls or frightening children, or of an angry Spider-Man demanding money, money, extra money when a tip was deemed insufficient (or given not at all), who can say which Elmo or which Spider-Man of the army of costumed individuals trafficking in the plazas on a daily basis was the aggressor unless a police officer witnessed the incident? Identification was difficult, if not impossible, because a character's face was obscured by a mask or a costume head. Anonymity created a fundamental problem for enforcement, notwithstanding the city's existing law against aggressive panhandling, which requires that a police officer must witness the activity and the victim must be harmed in some way. A pack of costumed characters surrounding an individual or a group of tourists in an intimidating manner until each in the pack got a payment (a not uncommon occurrence) did not seem to meet that standard. Still, it is a form of harassment, a verbal abuse tourists are not hardened to in the way New Yorkers are. Tourists are more vulnerable; they don't expect verbal assault. The intimidation may not be criminal, but it is part of the problem of the Times Square pedestrian plazas.

The police needed an enforcement aid. The proposed legislation would require costumed characters to carry the license and exhibit it on demand to any police officer or other city-authorized person. This seemingly commonsense approach, however, raised constitutional problems. Since 1965, federal constitutional decisions had limited the power of cities to control panhandling and other minor street nuisances, legal scholar Robert C. Ellickson cogently explained in a 1996 influential review article. Ever since, the scope of that control had narrowed. In any bill being drafted to regulate behavior that could arguably conflict with First Amendment rights, the language had to be very carefully chosen. Was solicitation by costumed characters First Amendment-protected as an expressive act, or was it commercial activity? The Constitution protects panhandling and commercial activities differently, and the latter are not fully protected by the First Amendment. The situation in Times Square "is an oddball situation," Chris Dunn of the New York Civil Liberties Union told a reporter for the *New Yorker*. He explained: the characters aren't begging for money, a constitutionally protected form of panhandling, nor are they providing a service for some predefined remuneration, as the tips are only "suggested."[40] In point of fact, that summer the police had started to hand out red leaflets written in five languages to tourists in Times Square, letting them know that tipping is optional.

Senior legislative staff at the Council were concerned about what could be enforced under the licensing bill. This was not like licensing home improvement contractors, home sales brokers, employment agencies, tow truck companies, and other types of vendors. Licensing is designed to regulate and monitor what is being sold to safeguard consumers from fraudulent material or work. How would you enforce problems with First Amendment vendors? They were unsure whether the city could license somebody based on behavior (solely for loitering for the purpose of soliciting tips in exchange for a photo opportunity) because it might restrict speech *before it occurs*. In legal circles, this was "prior restraint," a form of censorship historically viewed as a form of oppression in the United States.

Separately, the Council and the Police Department approached Disney and Marvel Comics, asking them to enforce their trademark and copyright rights over the costumes, their identifiable brands. Both city entities were looking for a way to address the issue that was enforceable. Disney did not want to engage. Whether or not their unwillingness to get involved turned on the question of identification, Disney "strategically tolerates theft," explained Michael Heller and James Saltzman in *Mine!* "For decades, the company was known for defending its copyrights and trademarks. But now Disney often looks away." Why does it tolerate knockoffs? Because, they argue, Disney has learned that fan-made, unlicensed products—whether twenty-five-dollar T-shirts, in their example, or costumes individuals wear to hustle in Times Square—benefit the company by increasing brand loyalty and sales in Disney stores or Disney parks.[41]

The public hearing on the Council's proposed licensing bill, held in a small nondescript room on the sixteenth floor of a downtown office building, brought forth a predictable mix of outright support, support with caveats, recommended changes, and outright opposition. Lining up behind the Police Department's testimony in support of the bill were business, real estate, and theater interests; hoteliers and retailers;

the Municipal Art Society; and the Times Square Alliance, which submitted forty-five pages of hearing testimony, including ten pages of tweets from visitors who had experienced bad interactions with costumed characters, which Tompkins also handed out at the hearing. Manhattan Borough President Gale Brewer lent her support to the bill, citing two key factors that made the behavior in Times Square worthy of attention—that the behavior is targeted toward children (excited to see Elmo or another branded character) and that the characters' masks or heads make identification of bad actors difficult, if not impossible— but she wanted a nominal licensing fee (which could be waived for proof of hardship) as well as "only minimal and necessary locational restrictions in order to ensure easier and more uniform enforcement."[42]

The Department of Consumer Affairs, represented by its first deputy commissioner and general counsel sitting at the panelists' table to answer questions from council members, seemed lukewarm at best to the bill that would add another mandate to the fifty-five different categories of licenses it already managed. "Does DCA have any view . . . why or whether we should be licensing panhandling?" Garodnick asked. "DCA's position," responded General Counsel Marla Tepper, "is that as discussed here there are challenging issues and we want to have a, as you said, a spirited discussion as to how we can advance the goals of this, this bill. There are various options that can and should be explored."[43] Maybe the department's view was cooler than lukewarm.

The emotional tenor of the proceedings intensified when individuals who regularly put on costumes of branded pop-culture icons to work the crowds in Times Square sat down at the panelists' table to give testimony. In one panel, five who had been costuming in Times Square for years spoke in support of the bill. Speaking passionately in English, sometimes in Spanish, they told the Council's Consumer Affairs Committee they were well-meaning people earning a living to support their families and that they brought joy to a lot of young people. People love us, they said. But the work was not easy. "Being a character in Times Square is not all that joyful," said Alberta Gerra, who makes her own costumes and dresses as Hello Kitty, sometimes Minnie Mouse. "We do experience a lot of harassment from tourists and from pedestrians and we experience cold, snow, rain, hot, heat . . . all kinds of, of things," she said in Spanish (translated). "I don't think this license is actually going to educate the individual under the costume."[44]

This panel of individuals who dressed to entertain in Times Square wanted to be protected, and they wanted respect from the authorities and respite from the negative public image caused by bad actors. They also believed that the police were singling them out unfairly. Gerra and more than two hundred others were part of New York Artists United for a Smile, a project of the immigrant labor advocacy group La Fuente. Based on their experiences and what some saw to be a problem in their ranks, the organization was in the process of developing a voluntary self-regulation system; its members were willing to wear photo identification tags. Though the voluntary nature of the system seemed unlikely to attract those who were most disposed to aggressive panhandling, the approach elicited genuine respect and generated a long question-and-answer discussion between council members and those testifying about how such a system would work and would interface with the Police Department.

The mascots in attendance at the hearing had shed their costumes for street clothes (other than the Joker aka Keith Albahae and Batman aka Jose Escalona-Martinez—minus mask when testifying per the chairman's rule). Eight individuals spoke against the bill, making the case that the bill would violate their freedom and rights of free expression, make it harder for them to earn a living, and potentially put some in danger of being deported. The licensing bill was unnecessary, said one; it is "just another classic case of overregulation." There were laws on the

**5.19** Costumed characters aligned with New York Artists United for a Smile, a group proposing self-regulation, holding signs in Times Square prior to a news conference to address their public image, August 19, 2014. Councilman Andy King from the Bronx was sponsoring a bill that would require those who solicit in public places to first secure a license from the Department of Consumer Affairs. AP Photo/Vanessa A. Alvarez.

books to handle "inappropriate behavior" and "the bad apples will still be rotten. The only difference is they will now have a city-issued license to continue with the behavior."[45]

The crime-fighting superhero Batman and his archenemy the Joker in white makeup, garish red lipstick, and a bright red coat covered with black bats, ramped up the oratory, adding some amusement to the circus-like hearings. The Joker likened the bill to "fascism" in testimony that mixed emotion, humor, and self-promotion. "I might look like a clown but I'm speaking from the heart," he said as council members suppressed laughs. At the start of his testimony against the regulations, Phillip Williams, better known as Spider-Man and/or Darth Vader, said "I saw big smiles on everybody's face when Batman sat here. That's the energy in Times Square. That's what we bring. We bring smiles to people."[46]

Fingerprinting was the third rail of the proposal; it was the single aspect that made Committee Chair Espinal "most uncomfortable on

**5.20** Keith Albahae aka the Joker speaks to the City Council's Consumer Affairs Committee during public hearings on the licensing proposal, while Batman aka Jose Escalona-Martinez waits his turn to speak, November 19, 2014. William Alatriste for the New York City Council.

the bill." "Is it possible to do a comprehensive background check without having fingerprints on the record?" he asked. Where would the records be stored? Would the fingerprints be used to check the costumed individuals' legal status in this country? Would the fingerprint information be secure from any overreach from the state or federal government? And was any other personal information that would be contained in the licensing application subject to requests under the Freedom of Information Law, and if so, how would the Department of Consumer Affairs respond? The questions into these and other details of how this bill would work in practice opened a Pandora's box of uncertainties. The venerable civil rights organization the New York Civil Liberties Union opposed the licensing scheme as set out in the bill "as both a deterrent to activity protected by the First Amendment and a policy that would have a disproportionate impact on undocumented New Yorkers." It wanted the city to "explore other, less disruptive avenues to promote safety and performance in public areas."[47]

Social disorder was not new in a place as open and socially tolerant as New York City. The 1996 law against aggressive panhandling passed during the Giuliani administration grew out of the backlash against the socially marginal in New York, which began with the social disorders of the 1970s. Crime, prostitution, and graffiti increased, as did homelessness. "Squeegee men, panhandlers, and people sleeping in public spaces came to be the most visible symptoms of an urban environment that many people felt was out of control," sociologist Alex S. Vitale wrote in *City of Disorder: How the Quality of Life Campaign Transformed New York Politics*. The Police Department then under Commissioner Bill Bratton famously singled out "squeegee men"—panhandlers who would approach stopped motorists, "clean" their windows, and demand donations for these "services." The approach synched with George L. Kelling and James Q. Wilson's influential theory of broken windows—with its emphasis on law enforcement to address quality-of-life violations like public urinating, public drunkenness, and panhandling.[48]

The problem in Times Square in 2014 was of a wholly different order; it was a problem of success, but a problem nonetheless. As a quality-of-life issue, aggressive panhandling in Times Square was not quite the same as the in-your-face panhandling of the 1970s and '80s. The costumed characters, vendors, and *desnudas* were not the destitute street people of that era, though like them they were heavy users of public spaces. They were not being characterized as destitute beggars and stigmatized as such, but rather presented by the media, council members, and their own testimony as hard-working people trying to earn a living and support a family in a hard and expensive city. A *Times* editorial called them "fee-for-service entrepreneurs, with—you have to admit—a pretty good product: They deliver smiles for cheap." The bad actors accused of aggressive panhandling were casting a shadow on most of the others in the pedestrian plazas who were not being obstructive or threatening in their pursuit of photos for tips. Most were there to earn a living by entertaining tourists. The *Times* was advocating caution: "They should be careful, though, in a city that values eccentric expression and an entrepreneurial street life, to avoid cures that are worse than the disease. Free speech and association are bedrock rights, even for furry monsters."[49]

Panhandling was not illegal, so was it different if an individual put on a mask or costume? Garodnick was unsure. The fundamental behavioral problem, aggressive panhandling, he said, is not permitted whether you are loitering for the purpose of begging or loitering for the purpose of taking a photograph and asking for a tip.[50] Licensing was problematic for more than a few council members on the committee, yet legally there was no way of making misbehaving costumed individuals identifiable without a licensing regime—that was the policy conundrum, whether or not fingerprinting was a piece of the bill. The city's ingrained liberal sympathies, a history of treading very lightly on First Amendment rights, and a strongly held equalitarian belief in the right of illegal immigrants to earn a living, all these cultural attributes shaped policy in New York City, and landed the licensing proposal in shaky territory. Hustling has long been a part of the city's psyche, part of the tapestry of its social and cultural history. After this hearing, there seemed to be no clear path forward to voting the licensing bill out of committee. No vote was taken, and the bill lapsed in a committee layover. It would be brought up again in 2016, amended in ways that sought to satisfy the objections to fingerprinting and fees and penalties, and a second set of hearings held—but once again the bill would lapse in a layover in committee.

## AN INCONVENIENT ISSUE

On October 1, 2015, the Mayor's Task Force on Times Square—inevitably labeled Topless Task Force by the media—issued recommendations to "improve traffic, pedestrian plazas, the solicitation of tips, and a number of other issues in and around the Times Square area."[51] After years of advocacy, Tim Tompkins and the business and theater stakeholders of the area were hopeful that when implemented the recommendations would go a distance toward reining in the daily fray of costumed characters, painted topless women, CD sellers, ticket sellers, and unlicensed vendors trawling the plazas for commercial ends and whose increasingly aggressive tactics had spurred the mayor's intervention. The Times Square Alliance could also take pride of ownership in the fact that "the administration has endorsed and supported the key elements of the community's plan" put forward in its briefing book prepared for the task force, "Roadmap for a 21st Century Times Square."

The announcement of the task force's recommendations—a laundry list of seventeen "action items"—was, however, close to a nonevent.[52] No press conference. Only the mayor giving an interview on a morning radio show the next day: "We are clearly going to move toward this segmentation of Times Square where certain activities are not allowed in some areas, others in other areas," he said. Among the city's three dailies, only the *Daily News*, having set off the tabloid bruhaha over the topless women, offered editorial comment, its seventh addressing the issue since mid-August, calling the recommendations "an official blueprint to hem in the swarms of prancing selfie-hustlers and touts—furry, near-naked and otherwise—who have had the run of Times Square for too long." The *Times* had earlier published an editorial about the task force after the mayor announced its formation in mid-August. "Shirtless Bodies in Pointless Times Square War" was as much a dig at the "righteous fury" set off by the *Daily News* as it was criticism of the mayor's apparent willingness to eliminate some of Times Square's pedestrian plazas or other officials' suggestion to create "a pen for the women and costumed characters—sort of a panhandling zoo—or turning this great bustling commercial zone into, of all things, a park. Such proposals, and Mr. de Blasio's sudden willingness to roll back years of ambitious streetscape redesign," the editorial board said, "are a monumental overreaction." Times Square was not "going to hell, or anywhere near hell's vicinity."[53] What did this relatively quiet response to the recommendations in such a boisterous city reveal about the seriousness with which the administration viewed the panhandling situation in Times Square?

The fifty-member multiagency task force cochaired by Police Commissioner Bill Bratton and City Planning Commissioner Carl Weisbrod had been given a short six-week window in which to address what from any number of angles was unquestionably a complex, genuinely hard task. Yet it met only two or three times, and the first meeting happened just two weeks prior to when the task force was scheduled to report its findings.[54] The process for getting to a set of recommendations was of a type not uncommon in city government—catch as catch can, quick negotiations among agencies, and proposals that come about behind the scenes. Members of the task force, the press announcement said, "regularly spoke and met with Times Square business owners, advocates, elected officials, and others to create a series of comprehensive recommendations."[55]

The *Post* wasn't buying it. "OK, it was an obvious gimmick from the start—de Blasio's bid to seem to be doing something in the face of daily headlines about the topless women and aggressive Elmos plaguing the Crossroads of the World," its editorial board said the day before the task force's first meeting. "Times Square's festering problems will need some inventive solutions. But whatever gets done will be despite Bill de Blasio—not because of him."[56]

The mayor had been pushed into convening the task force by media pressure and by those few in government who really did care about Times Square. As the time clock for a "solution" ticked away, the pattern of minimal-at-best attention to the task force appeared to reflect a view that City Hall considered the issues in Times Square "an annoyance." As advocates for their communities, elected officials did care about the situation; they wanted a better Times Square, though they would not want their reputations endangered by being labeled as anti-First Amendment. Weisbrod was in a different position from the others. Because of his decades-long involvement with the cleanup and transformation of Times Square, he had more of a vested interest in finding some solution to the problem. The place was part of his legacy of professional achievement in New York. Although he was never a fan of the plazas because they changed the dynamic of the area and no thought had been given to how they were to be managed, he told me, "Times Square was not getting the attention it deserved. It was starting to unravel."[57]

In early September, Bratton walked back his tear-'em-all-up position on the Times Square plazas in the form of an op-ed in the *Wall Street Journal*. Deploying an expression in police work—"awful but lawful"—he forewarned of the limits to police intervention. "The heart of the current problem," he said, "is that we have established, in the form of the Times Square pedestrian mall, a public space without public-space rules," as would prevail in "designated public spaces" subject to "stricter rules of conduct" than streets. "People are offended and distressed by the spectacle," he said, "but in many cases the spectacle qualifies as free speech under the law." Police officers would "of course intervene whenever aggressive begging occurs or public safety is threatened. But getting the law right in these circumstances is a challenge even for lawyers." That is why, he said, the Police Department was establishing a new unit to patrol Times Square and address quality-of-life issues, a role distinct from the counterterrorism duties of other officers there. Following the neighborhood policing model, officers on foot patrol in Time Square would "get to know the players and, most of all, the law." Taking on tabloid alarmists who foresaw a return of the squalid and sordid days of old, he said, "To equate current conditions to the square of 25 years ago is preposterous."[58]

The following week the *Daily News* published a related op-ed, this one penned by the elected officials most immediately tied to the issues in Times Square, all of whom were members of the task force: Manhattan Borough President Gale Brewer and Councilmen Daniel Garodnick and Corey Johnson. It briefly laid out a new regulatory framework that would become a central element of the task force's recommendations. Based on six months of extensive discussions with the Times Square Alliance and the stakeholders it represented (from hotels and theaters to the many New Yorkers and businesses in the district), the political trio pressed for a new legal structure designed to accommodate "protesting, civic discourse and artistic activity, but with a layout that both tourists and working New Yorkers can pass through comfortably."[59]

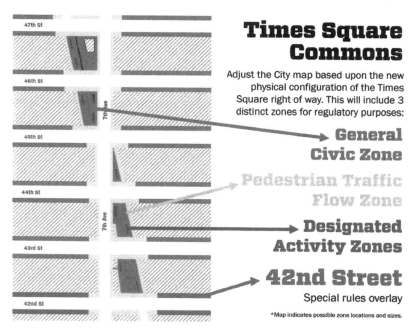

**5.21** Schematic of the 2015 proposal for a Times Square Commons put forth by elected officials representing Times Square and the Times Square Alliance and its stakeholders to create three distinct zones for regulatory purposes: a general civic zone, a pedestrian traffic flow zone, and designated activity zones, where solicitation for photo-ops for tips and other commercial purposes could transact. Courtesy of Alliance for Times Square.

Under the proposal, the city would change zoning rules to redefine the pedestrian plazas no longer as part of a street but as a "public place" called the Times Square Commons; within the commons, activity would be segmented into three distinct zones governed by different rules: "civic zones" for arts programming and occasional events, "flow zones" dedicated exclusively to pedestrians to move freely within the area, and "designated activity zones" for solicited commercial activity by costumed characters, painted topless ladies, and others involved in the immediate exchange of money for goods, services, or entertainment.[60] It was an approach consistent with First Amendment protections allowing for what is known as "time, place and manner regulations." Implicitly, the scheme assumed the plazas would remain in place, which aligned with an emergent consensus. It was important, Garodnick later said, that the task force resolve that question first. After its first meeting, Weisbrod told the press that the task force wanted to see construction of the plazas completed and assess how they were working, maybe tweak some details "to make sure they're up and operating and function as best as they possibly can and enhance the Times Square community."[61] Although Bratton and Weisbrod did not rule out the possibility of just tearing them up, that rash notion was essentially dead on arrival.

Hours before the task force's first meeting on September 17, the Times Square Alliance issued "Roadmap for a 21st Century Times Square." Endorsed by a coalition of fifty including elected officials, property owners, theater interests, and business leaders, the report provided data on the core problems in Times Square and presented detailed solutions, describing legal and regulatory tools to manage the pedestrian plazas, address congestion issues, and sustain and support the Police Department's new Times Square Unit. Packed with data, legal research, citizen testimonials documenting aggressive and predatory behavior, media coverage of the issues, letter endorsements from elected officials and civic groups, and additional materials supporting its vision for Time Square, the 296-page document represented the culmination of the Alliance's ongoing efforts since 2003 to reimagine the pedestrian environment of the place. It was formally presented to the mayor's task force under the joint authorship of Brewer, Garodnick, Johnson, Community Board Five, and the Alliance. An editorial in the *Daily News* called it "the best blueprint on the table to date," adding "The Commons plan—or something a lot like it—needs to be passed by the Council."[62]

The extent to which the city should regulate the costumed characters and *desnudas* was the most contentious issue discussed by the task

**5.22** Tim Tompkins, president of the Times Square Alliance, speaking during the celebration of the 10th anniversary of the pedestrian plazas in Times Square, 2019. Courtesy of Danny Perez for the Times Square Alliance.

force. By the end of September, its leaders had endorsed key elements of the proposal to create restricted zones where the costumed characters and topless women could transact business. The corridor solution seemed reasonable and minimal under the notion that there should be very little regulation. Enough of the chaos had to be tamped down to make Times Square safe without making it unappealing to tourists. The express or fast lanes for pedestrians, as some took to calling the flow zones, would warm the hearts of New Yorkers often frustrated by how difficult it was to walk through the area, not just in 2015 but for as long as crowds had thronged Times Square. "Complaining about gawking tourists and pedestrians who saunter down the street is practically a rite of passage for New Yorkers," remarked a *Times* reporter.[63]

Under Tompkins's professional leadership and personal style, the Alliance had become an effective advocate for the interests of Times Square at home, and a passionate booster of this iconic destination during his frequent invitations from outside the city to talk about the transformation of Times Square. His perspective on city issues had been honed during his undergraduate days at Yale where he studied history and was a member of Dwight Hall, a student-run organization concerned with issues of social justice and public service. Melding those views with the practical business skills of an MBA acquired at Wharton, he founded and directed the Partnerships for Parks, a public-private partnership to support New York City's neighborhood parks, which won an Innovations in Government Award from the Kennedy School of Government at Harvard for its work to restore the Bronx River. By the time Tompkins became president of the Alliance in 2002, the organization faced post-9/11 security challenges and quality-of-life issues captured in one word: congestion.

During its first decade of service in the 1990s, when crime and seediness still prevailed in the district, the clutch point for the business-based not-for-profit had been providing clean, safe, and friendly service to its constituents: local businesses and property owners, tourists, and New Yorkers traversing the 123 street faces of its territory. Looking ahead to its second decade, Tompkins aspired to create an attractive public realm alive with civic events, creative energy with its own special edge, and less congested sidewalks and streets, all the while maintaining the essential focus on safety and sanitation. He wanted to reinvent the experience of Times Square through design initiatives, distinctive programming, and public art, making the square a center for culture and entertainment for New Yorkers as well as tourists. He wanted to introduce an attitude toward public space he believed was missing in the city.

Toward that end he had tirelessly expanded the agenda of the Alliance, curating a program of events in the newly created pedestrian plazas that functioned as a theater set. Any number stand out: the "Taste of Times Square" food fair showcasing local eateries and entertainment, "Solstice in Times Square: Mind over Madness Yoga," "Broadway on Broadway" with free concerts and sneak previews of some upcoming Broadway shows, and "Met Opera Opening Night: Verdi's Otello" broadcast on a giant screen viewed by thousands. In 2015 alone, the Alliance held forty-one events that drew nearly fifteen million attendees to its public events. Not the least of those was the celebratory Times Square ball drop on New Year's Eve, a tradition since 1907, which brought more than a million people to the square while a worldwide audience of more than a billion watched it live. Nevertheless, the media-obsessed kerfuffle over the costumed characters and painted topless ladies quickly overshadowed the organization's success in changing the experience of the place, and it pushed Tompkins into overdrive to find a solution for managing conditions in the square—and assuring a future for all the Alliance had achieved.

**5.23** The Times Square Alliance has programmed a diversity of events to appeal to wide audiences: "Met Opera Opening Night: Verdi's Otello" broadcast on a giant screen (2015) and "Solstice in Times Square: Mind over Madness Yoga" (2014) are marquee events, two of many each year. Courtesy of Lovis Dengler Ostenrik (top) and Amy Hart for the Times Square Alliance (bottom).

That record of achievement made the Alliance an influential voice when it came to the city task force's recommendations. It knew the district better than City Hall. It owned the analytics that documented the problematic conditions. It had consulted legal experts to back up its arguments for a Times Square Commons with "time, place, and manner" restrictions consistent with prevailing First Amendment protections. Its board of directors and member roster included leaders in the city's business, real estate, theater, media, and arts communities. It had deep experience marketing and communicating a clear message. Moreover, with the largest annual revenue stream among the city's seventy-two business improvement districts, it had the kind of financial clout that made City Hall pay attention because that clout mirrored the commercial geography of the tourist businesses, propertied interests, and Broadway enterprises so central to the city's economy.

The score on the task force recommendations: the Police Department did deploy a dedicated police force to Times Square, and its substation in Times Square was remodeled. The Department of Consumer Affairs did produce "Welcome to New York City" information in multiple languages warning tourists about being pressured by street performers or overcharged for pedicab rides, urging wariness of false advertising, and giving advice on tour prices, among other consumer tips to help them avoid being hustled or scammed. More place-making programming was brought to the square. However, most of the task force recommendations did not get implemented. Remapping Times Square as a public place did not go anywhere—how likely was it that the Transportation Department would give up control over the street? And even had it gone through, the pedestrian plazas would still not have become a public "park." Getting control over busking, street fairs, and vendors—tour bus ticket sellers, comedy club hawkers, food vendors, and First Amendment vendors, among others—was a genuinely hard issue to deal with. New York's long-standing, unresolved problems with its licensed vending system, an issue beyond the scope here, compounded the complexity of the situation in Times Square. Moreover, the most compelling case for regulating vendors was on West 42nd Street. After rules permitting late-night vending went into effect, the crush of vendors lining the sidewalks forced pedestrians onto the street amid traffic. The task force could not possibly handle the complexity of the issues in Times Square it was charged with "solving" in four to six weeks. It would have taken years and the mayor's backing to do it right.

## NEW RULES

Six months after the task force issued its recommendations, the City Council Committee on Transportation took up a bill introduced by Garodnick and Johnson that would give the Department of Transportation the authority to establish "reasonable time, place and manner regulations governing pedestrian plazas in order to manage the competing uses of finite public space." The Police Department would be responsible for enforcement. Although the task force recommendation formed the basis for the authorization bill, the two councilmen had voiced their preference for this approach earlier during the 2014 hearing on the licensing bill. By creating a clear legal framework for limiting the areas where the costumed characters could operate (without a permit)—the "designated activity zones"—they believed the regulations would be more enforceable than a licensing scheme. "Designated activities" in these zones would mean "commercial activities, entertainment or performances by individuals or groups, posing for or taking photographs or video, and vending expressive matter, where any form of compensation, donation, or gratuity is requested or accepted." No person was to use the "pedestrian flow zone" "for any purpose other than the safe and continuous movement of pedestrian traffic." That would not be the Law Department's interpretation of the statute, but that gets a bit ahead of the story.[64]

The Transportation Department would be empowered to develop general rules covering conduct, litter, and quality-of-life issues on a citywide basis, and in "meaningful consultation" with plaza sponsors in individual neighborhoods, tailoring specific rules to the individual pedestrian plazas and the communities they serve. It was not a one-size-fits-all solution, Garodnick emphasized: each plaza was unique and would require its own set of rules to account for site-specific conditions. Politically, the new rulemaking authority had to work for each individual plaza in the city, not just solve the challenges of Times Square, as neighborhood-based representative after representative testified during the bill's hearing on March 30, 2016. Although the Council was debating how to regulate fifty-plus pedestrian plazas throughout the five boroughs, "the headline tomorrow," said Committee Chairperson Ydanis A. Rodriguez, "is going to be Times Square."[65] And it was.

From its start, the pedestrian plaza program was one of New York's most influential success stories. Almost immediately, the newly created open spaces became an "indelible part of the streetscape in neighborhoods throughout the five boroughs," a valued amenity in urban neighborhoods where a lack of public space was all too common. Some believed, as did the president of the Garment District Alliance, that the plazas had "lifted the image of the city" by softening the harshness of city streets and glass, steel, and concrete environments.[66] By 2015, fifty-three plazas were open to the public, with an additional twenty in development or under construction. Under the de Blasio administration's One New York Plaza Equity Program, $7 million was allocated to lower-capacity plaza partners to help maintain plaza spaces as well as provide technical assistance and management expertise, enabling many more communities in the city to have successful public space. As their numbers grew rapidly, it became imperative that the city formulate workable rules of the road and a process for accommodating the new reality of commerce in these new public spaces.

Spillover was a concern. On 42nd Street vendors crowded the narrow sidewalks overflowing with pedestrians, and Johnson asked Transportation Commissioner Polly Trottenberg what steps her department would be taking to make sure that those involved in commercial activity in Times Square did not get pushed to 42nd Street by the proposed regulations. "We're going to have a very strong partnership with NYPD," said Trottenberg; "the men and women on the ground there . . . know immediately what's happening, what the state of the characters are, the sellers, who's migrating where." It was an answer, but the question exceeded the scope of the territory—the five blocks of Broadway from 42nd to 47th Streets shown on an enlarged map in the hearing room—covered by the bill's authorization. The process of getting right where the flow zones and designated activity zones were placed would be one of trial and error, Trottenberg said; she did not want to predict where the characters might go and what might happen next. Times Square was "full of surprises," constantly changing. The bill would be "a good start for us," she added, and "there'll be some adjustments we'll have to make as we see potentially where it's working well, where we need to—to take a fresh look."[67]

The size of the "designated activity zones" was another issue of concern. As proposed, each would be approximately eight to ten feet by 50 feet, bus-size lanes able to accommodate fifty to fifty-five people, in total a maximum of 400 people. Might there be cramping up of individuals in one location, maybe causing some trouble, some rifts and altercations that might be posed by competition? asked council member Antonio Reynoso, who represented several Brooklyn neighborhoods. "These zones are not locked in hard and fast to the specific locations, their sizes," said NYPD Captain O'Hare. It was going to be "a

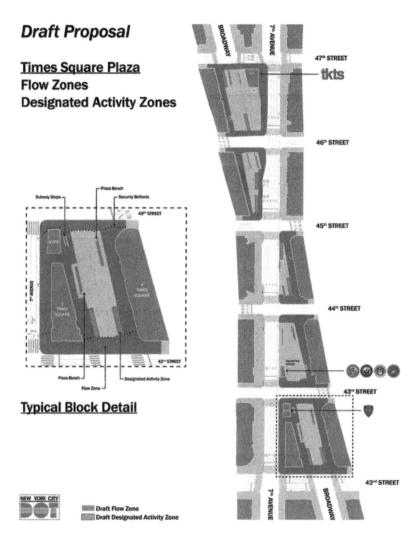

Purple signifies place to walk behind slow-moving tourists; blue signifies sea of Elmos. Photo: NYC DOT

**5.24** Rendering of the proposed flow zones and activity zones that would section off Times Square's pedestrian plazas, 2016. New York City Department of Transportation.

developing process," something on which they would "have an open dialogue" and "continually evaluate is it working, not working?"[68]

As in few other symbolic spaces in the city, the on-the-ground issues in Times Square, galvanized by the summer 2015 bruhaha over the *desnudas*, bought forth a cacophony of New York voices and competing interests with opinions on the political drama intensifying in Times Square. Fifty-five people submitted statements; more than eighty testified in person, including the Joker, Batman, and Superhero in costume, once again making for a modest amount of political theater attracting media focus. As might be expected, city officials, civic organizations, business and theater interests, and business improvement districts spoke in favor of the bill; ticket sellers and agents, costumed performers, and union representatives spoke in opposition.

The hearings had an impact. Maybe the legislation could have done away with the Elmos, but a regulated environment, not a ban of costumed characters, was its intent. The legislation was another imperfect solution, but everyone got a little of what they wanted in it. The Elmos got a place to do their commercial activity, the Police Department got a better arrangement for managing the aggressive behavior of costumed characters, the Times Square Alliance got regulation of its district, and the Transportation Department got rulemaking authority over its pedestrian plazas. In terms of legislation, maybe it wasn't going to get much better. "It wasn't perfect," said a council staffer, "but then no piece of legislation is perfect."

The fifty-one-member Council passed the bill on April 7, 2016, with forty-two yea votes, one nay, and five abstentions (three others were absent), and the mayor signed the bill into law on April 21. The new regulations went into effect on June 21, 2016. Garodnick was satisfied. "We needed to do something, try something. We didn't know what would work, what would not work. We had to put contours on the situation," he told me.[69] The "topless painted women in Times Square were never the problem," Johnson said. The "problem was that there was no order at all, and that it was just a free zone that was causing many problems with some bad actors."[70] In fact, although they were the lightning rod for the mayor's task force intervention, the "painted performers" were rarely mentioned throughout the legislative hearings.[71] However much of a moral panic they may have aroused in the tabloids, the body-painted seminude women had law on their side: being topless in New York is not illegal after a 1992 ruling by the state's highest court clarified that women had the same right as men to be bare-chested in public.

**5.25** Gaggle of costumed characters in a designated zone taking photo-ops with tourists, 2017. The standing sign says "If you take a picture with an entertainer, please note that they expect a tip." Gary Hack.

Whether or not the regulatory scheme would create order out of chaos remained an open question; only time would tell once the regulations went into effect. At first, the designated activity zones—teal-painted boxes—brought widespread compliance; "from the look of things, [the rules] are working," Garodnick and Johnson wrote in a *Crain's* op-ed shortly after the regulations went into effect. "For the first time in recent history, Times Square felt like it was for everyone—especially New Yorkers who spend time there and who have rightfully demanded the incessant harassment be addressed—and we hope this feeling is here to stay."[72] It was not to be.

The law had been carefully crafted because ample room had to be left for people to engage in commercial activity. The Law Department's interpretation of the statute, however, ended up parsing the designated activity, because people could not be told where they can speak; when an exchange of money takes place, it's a different matter. So, asking tourists and others if they wanted a picture taken could take place anywhere, but taking the picture or taking tips or donations in exchange was only permitted in the designated activity zones. As more and more characters crowded into the plazas, once again some became super-aggressive, grabbing people and dragging them into the designated activity zones for picture taking and exchange of money. In high season, they were blocking people and touching people—déjà vu. The law had failed. The Elmos just adapted, Garodnick admitted in 2019.

This was not the intention of the legislation. Yet among those familiar with First Amendment issues, it was not unexpected that the law might work this way in practice, because the performers could not be prohibited from walking in the flow zone. The law could only limit where the commercial activity could take place, and out of concern for running into the law of prior restraint, the Council could not prevent the solicitation of tips-for-photos until the solicitation was seen. Nevertheless, the interpretation became a point of contention. The Alliance believed the Law Department, gun-shy when it came to First Amendment issues because of past litigation experience, was being overly conservative. Still, allowing commercial panhandlers to engage passersby in all parts of the square undermined the effectiveness of the law. The special police force would be in Times Square, but it was an open question of how vigorously enforcement of the new regulations would be pursued.

To clarify and strengthen the rules governing commercial activities in pedestrian plazas, as well as the spread of unregulated commercial activity to 42nd Street between Seventh and Eighth Avenues, new legislation was introduced in 2019 by Councilman Keith Powers, whose Manhattan district includes Times Square. Then Covid-19 hit. Discussion of the bill resumed in 2021. Hearings were held in May, the Council passed the bill in August, and in December, after the required public hearings, the law went into effect, without the signature of Mayor de Blasio.

The new law had been a long time coming. It established a Theater District Zone—which included the 42nd Street Development Project area—and mandated that the entirety of a street performer's designated (commercial) transaction occur within the designated activity zone; as with previous legislation, pedestrian flow zones were established on the sidewalks on Broadway, Seventh Avenue, and all blocks with three or more theaters of 500 or more seats. During the ups and downs of the pandemic, the costumed characters still hustled in the square, but they were a small presence, often outnumbering the actual tourists. The rules still prevailed, but enforcement was relaxed. The test of whether these new rules make a difference will be clearer post-pandemic, once tourism returns in full.

## PUBLIC AWARENESS

The political controversy over the costumed characters and the cultural tug-of-war over painted topless ladies in Times Square were newsworthy across the globe. They illuminated the role and importance of the public realm, not just in New York, not just in the United States, but in cities around the world where tourists in large numbers are drawn to iconic places. For the media, the New York controversy was irresistible. Photographers repeatedly captured the scene. Editorial cartoonists took up this local issue because it held broad significance for the tenor of urban life in general. Public space, especially in Times Square, served as a metaphor for bigger urban issues that capture the spotlight. What happens in high-profile spaces symbolizes the values and culture of commerce in big cities. For example, in London's Trafalgar Square (pre-pandemic), which plays a similar role in the life of the city as Times Square in New York, the costumed characters are not as aggressive as some are in Times Square; they do not assault passersby. There the government appears to exercise greater power, either through legal means or cultural norms, to control the public space. The pandemic changed the way residents used public space. Tompkins does not believe the issues of Times Square as a public space were resolved. "Outdoor dining will change the impacts in and awareness of public spaces going forward; it has opened people's eyes."[73]

In this legendary place where nothing shocks, the controversies over hustling, panhandling, vending, and seminudity in the summer of 2015 became a testing ground for what is acceptable and unacceptable public behavior. The context was radically different from the challenges of public disorder that besieged city officials in the 1970s and '80s. These new but old controversies of civic life revealed that being in public requires norms and acceptable rules—even in Times Square. "Anything goes" has limits.

The pandemic brought a dramatic halt to this and so much else in New York and around the world. Absent the normal throngs of tourists, especially those from abroad, and the indefinite shuttering of Broadway theaters, images of a vacant Times Square captured the pandemic's painful economic impact. The lights still flashed on digital billboards, but in the absence of an audience, rather than project blankness, some were filled with public service messages. The photojournalist story needed no words; the ubiquitous images of Times Square symbolized the wounds being inflicted on urban life derivative of catastrophe inflicted on individual lives everywhere. Doom-and-gloom articles about Times Square became a stand-in for the uncertainty prevailing among urbanists, especially city officials questioning when (and whether) tourism would return to New York City. Some things—the Naked Cowboy and cartoon characters outnumbering tourists in the square, for example—seemed too painfully ironic.

The pandemic had created another twenty-first-century natural experiment for the city. What remains to be seen is how this unique public place adjusts to the expected "new normal" of an era when unpredictable virus attacks are likely to reshape the future. During the summer of 2021, the activity in Times Square was beginning to return to normal, albeit less tourist-congested given the restraints of international travel, but then Covid's highly contagious Omicron variant hit. The coda picks up where this storyline lets off. But first, a look at what animates the enduring attraction of Times Square: the blazing billboards and their messages.

# 6  ICONIC SPECTACLE

It's going to be funny to see so much financial information in Times Square, instead of a Coke bottle or a can of Planters peanuts. Someone who hasn't been here in many years is going to think they're in the wrong place.
George N. Stonbely, August 1998

They have reigned as the star attraction, always—the flashing, pulsating, sometimes disorienting messages radiating in all directions from the supersized signs in Times Square. As this illuminated theater of American commerce evolved over time, it shaped an imagistic personality for the district, one that thoroughly embodied the theatricality of the place. It was not a place of subtlety. The outside space was a fantastical show—a visual maelstrom free to all who came, ever changing moment by moment. Constantly heightened by the ambition of successive innovators abetted by advances in display technology, the robust energy and dynamism of the commercial culture of Times Square brought into being a singular place where advertising spectacle became entertainment, where private interests transformed an open space into an arena for visual pleasure of enduring appeal to tourists and locals alike. "In collapsing onlookers, business interests, a new electric technology, and the new urban setting into a single dazzling space," architectural historian Sandy Isenstadt wrote in *Electric Light: An Architectural History*, "Times Square became a landmark of modernity, a permanent fixture of New York life built on frothy evanescence. . . . It was a new urban destination, founded on flickering electric light, forged in the canyons of Manhattan and subsequently spun off to cities around the world like sparks from a flame."[1]

WHAT MAKES THE "GREAT WHITE WAY" WHITE: SO MANY ELECTRIC SIGNS THEY ARE IN EACH OTHER'S WAY.

**6.1** Postcard of Times Square as a portrait of the competitive practices of American business, 1921. Brown Brothers Photography.

This dazzling theater of outdoor advertising, initially set upon great metal frames atop the square's low-rise buildings, became the architecture of the place. The signs physically overtook the modest structures (Hotel Astor, sans sign, being an exception), and their ubiquitous presence defined the iconic face of Times Square. The early twentieth century was the era of emerging corporate giants seeking mass audiences for their products, and being visible in Times Square was key. The square's bright signs were held up as a portrait of the competitive practices of American business; the caption of a 1920s postcard of Times Square aptly proclaimed, "So many electric signs on the 'Great White Way,' they are in each other's way." For most of the century, the lights emblazoned the brand names and slogans of mass-market consumer products: household appliances, underwear, chewing gum, coffee, spaghetti, toothpaste, ginger ale, beer, whiskey, cigarettes, first-run movies. With its dense profusion of visually competing signs, the streetscape could be said to be a form of public art.

In the late 1990s, the emergence of big, bold, captivating signs employing the latest technologies signaled competition for the newest consumer product: financial information. "There's going to be shootout in Times Square between Nasdaq, Reuters, Morgan Stanley and Dow Jones," said George Stonbely, pioneer of the first full-color, computer-programmed message billboard, Spectacolor. "Bullish on Times Square Neon: Wall Street Muscles into Mecca of Commercial Glitter," chronicled the *Times*.[2] The competitors clustered near one another. At the corner of 43rd Street (Four Times Square) stood the largest and most expensive video screen in the world—a $37 million seven-story turret spectacular for Nasdaq. Across the way, the electronic stock market sign faced one for Reuters on its headquarters tower (Three Times Square) and the Dow Jones electronic "zipper" on the former Times Tower, known as One Times Square. All three clustered five blocks south of two others flashing real-time financial information—Morgan Stanley's three tiers of traveling financial tickers and the electronic bulletin boards for Dow Jones and Bloomberg.

The newest iconography of Times Square reflected the fact that more and more households were consuming financial products. Between 1989 and 2001, the share of middle-aged households in America with some exposure to the stock market, either through direct ownership of shares or through some form of investment or retirement plan, rose to 61 percent from 40 percent, according to studies by the St. Louis Federal Reserve Board. Wall Street had come to Main Street. Not so suddenly, the stock market had invaded popular culture—stocks were news way beyond cocktail party chatter—and nowhere did this become more evident than on the biggest advertising stage in the nation's biggest city, also a reference point for global culture. What other single place could capture as many "eyeballs," in the vernacular of the signage business?

The new signs simultaneously announced the transformation of business conducted in the new office towers of Times Square: financial services, information, and media. Between 1992 and 1995, three high-profile acquisitions signaled a new economic era in the entertainment district: Bertelsmann's purchase of 1540 Broadway, a 42-story tower on the corner of 45th Street, and Morgan Stanley's purchase of the 42-story tower at 1585 Broadway between 47th and 48th Streets, followed by its purchase of a second building, the 38-story tower two blocks away at 750 Seventh Avenue. A series of big leasing deals brought other big-name tenants to the area: Deloitte & Touche (1633 Broadway), Viacom (1515 Broadway and 1633 Broadway), Macmillan Publishing (1633 Broadway), Mayer, Brown & Platt (1675 Broadway), American Management Association (1601 Broadway), Virgin Megastore and Sony Theaters (1540 Broadway), and Condé Nast Publications, Inc. and Skadden, Arps, Slate, Meagher & Flom (Four Times Square).

As had been true throughout the twentieth century, the new signs—distinguished by their individuality, size, brightness, and animation—commanded attention. Impossible to ignore, they premiered a new performance in a district of historic performances. In the mid-1990s, advances in LED technology—based on computer-controlled semiconductor diodes that give off light when charged with electricity—vastly increased the spectrum of brilliant colors possible in outdoor advertising. The development of blue-light LEDs revolutionized the power of the light-emitting medium to grab the attention of the hundreds of thousands of tourists and office workers passing through the square every day. Daytime or nighttime, the signs surrounding the square have been a magnet, a primary reason why throngs of people have flocked to the place year after year, decade after decade. The congestion of signs is "colorful, exciting, vibrant"; they make the place "energetic" and add to the appeal of Times Square, said 83 percent of respondents to a 2017 survey conducted by the Times Square Alliance and the Times Square Advertising Coalition.[3] Theater made Times Square a renowned place of entertainment—spectacular signs made it iconic.

## ADVERTISING PARK

Times Square owes much of its storied history to a physical anomaly: the bowtie configuration of streets created by Broadway's diagonal intersection with Seventh Avenue. The geometry of this space with its twin goalposts of visibility at either end formed a natural stage for the theatricality of bright lights. The long sight lines along Broadway and Seventh Avenue are exceptional. Walled by theaters, restaurants, retail shops, and small business buildings, the open space was "especially well-suited for squinting at signs." Before they were replaced by office towers, the rooftops of two- and three-story buildings were easily transformed into sky-hugging metal frameworks for mounting supersized billboards and flashing signs that drew pedestrians to the square. From the center of the bowtie at 45th Street, "looking either north or south, the space opens up like the field of vision itself. With signs situated on façades or rooftop scaffolds, views were encircling and unimpeded," Isenstadt explained. It "resembled an arena, though inverted, with the audience at the center and the performance along the periphery."[4]

The Times Square bowtie offered advertisers a perfect showcase—a generous physical space tailor-made for product ads—and it would not take long for the nation's commercial purveyors to understand its potential, especially after electricity supplanted gaslit signs. Broadway was New York's first electrified street (1890), and soon the dark, off-putting urban nighttime was being transformed into a sparkling environment of incandescent lights. But it took the entrepreneurial actions of Oscar J. Gude to make Times Square the most dramatic gathering place of all. Gude invented the "spectacular," an enormous electric sign consisting of hundreds of light bulbs wired to elaborate circuits which dictated animation patterns and different lighting effects. The goal was to stop people in their tracks, to sell through entertainment. Electric advertising, he said, "literally forces its announcement on the vision of the uninterested as well as the interested passerby . . . everybody must read them, and absorb them, and absorb the advertiser's lesson willingly or unwillingly."[5] By 1913, Times Square dazzled with hundreds of thousands of bright lights, emitting an intense glow that gave the district its nickname, "The Great White Way." (The slogan, attributed to Gude, conveniently omits the fact that the blazing canyon of lights included many signs with colored as well as white lights.)

Drawing huge crowds of lingering, gaping consumers, Gude's spectaculars were legendary. His first—the Trimble Whiskey sign (1904), placed at the central triangular block at 47th Street for maximum display—was visible for many blocks. The combination of Gude's marketing brilliance and his creative designers produced a "constantly changing roster of enormous moving light displays in the sky about the square. Within a few years," Darcy Tell wrote in *Times Square Spectacular: Lighting up Broadway*, "Gude almost single-handedly transformed Times Square into America's most important outdoor advertising market."[6] Between 1904 and 1917, his company put up approximately twenty large spectaculars in Times Square, each more elaborate and dazzling than its predecessor.

A charismatic promotional genius, Gude was the son of immigrant parents from Germany who started as a sign hanger and bill poster, before opening his own outdoor advertising business in 1889 to design marketing campaigns for corporate clients selling branded commodities. His success built on aggressive salesmanship combined with high-quality visual images. In a strategic maneuver, he bypassed local business and went directly to national companies when looking for clients, convincing them that a properly placed sign would reach a huge audience of entertainment seekers coming to Times Square on foot or by the new subway at 42nd Street. He gained control of a network of the most visible rooftops around the square, and with his designers applied technological breakthroughs of the day that allowed groups of connected bulbs to be turned on and off in sequence and lights to be dimmed or raised. The result was cinemalike actions in lights: A girl

**6.2** This view of Times Square looking north illustrates the long sightlines of the bow-tie and O. J. Gude's positioning of his Trimble Whiskey spectacular at 47th Street for maximum display (pictured in 1904). The sign was quickly replaced by a sign for a rival whiskey brand, Sanderson's. By the early 1910s, the owners of the Studebaker building realized it was more profitable to lease their roof for spectaculars and replaced their discrete sign with a huge scaffold for mounting higher signs at this strategic site.

performed stunts on an electric tightrope. A polo player galloped on a horse and wacked a ball in an arc above Broadway. Boys boxed in their underwear. The signs promoted almost every product imaginable: safety razors, dental cream, cars, tires, bran flakes, coffee, whiskey, gin, cigarettes, chewing gum, movies and shows, gloves, and underwear, among many others.

Gude's truly memorable and remarkable (and expensive) spectaculars came to dominate the growing nightscape of the square: the "coyly erotic" Miss Heatherbloom (1905), the 50-foot Petticoat Girl, who struggles under an umbrella in an electric rainstorm as her dress whips up to reveal her petticoat and shapely legs; the frolicking Corticelli Kitten

**6.3** The father of sign spectaculars, O. J. Gude, brought visual life to a troupe of corporate brands during the first decades of the twentieth century displayed in this advertisement, 1913. O. J. Gude Co.

(1912) tangling with a spool of thread in different locations; the flowing fountains of sparkling White Rock Table Water (1915) glittering in changing pastels; and one of the square's longest-running spectaculars, the block-long Wrigley's Spearmint Chewing Gum sign (1917–1923) atop the Putnam Building, a six-story office building on the west side of Broadway between 43rd and 44th Streets built by the Astor Estate in

**6.4** Top: Gude's elaborate block-long Wrigley's Spearmint sign was one of his most memorable spectaculars, boasting more than 17,000 white and multicolored bulbs (pictured in 1917). Lasting seven years, it was then one of Times Square's longest-running spectaculars. William D. Hassler Photographic Collection, nyhs_PR83_U01538 © New-York Historical Society. Bottom: postcard view of a second full-block Wrigley's spectacular on the east side of Broadway from 44th to 45th Street above the International Casino. This sign lasted even longer, from 1936 to 1960, with a brief hiatus during World War II (pictured in 1936). Collection of the author.

1909. This was Gude's most elaborate animation: 70 feet (eight stories) high and 250 feet long, boasting more than 17,000 white and multi-colored lamps with flowing fountains, peacocks with 60-foot-long tails, flora and foliate motifs, and six prancing Spearmen, each measuring 15 feet high, who went through twelve calisthenics, which the public promptly dubbed the "Daily Dozen." More than the flavor of gum, the brand itself was being advertised. "The largest electric sign in the world advertises WRIGLEY'S. . . . The sign is seen nightly," its 1920 adver-tisement boasted, "by approximately 500,000 people, from all over the world" passing through Times Square.[7]

The mystique behind outdoor advertisements aimed to evoke some-thing beyond the prosaic commodity. For White Rock Ginger Ale, "the water for all time" (1910), Gude designed a large clock that changed color every few seconds bracketed by flowing fountains of light. "The flowing fountains and colorful lights of the White Rock sign suggested that Times Square was an exotic and magical paradise existing outside the constraints of everyday life," wrote the curator for the wall panel in the New-York Historical Society's 1997 exhibition *Signs and Wonders*. The use of color, light, and exotic motifs was a popular device in stores, restaurants, and nightclubs. "Using these devices in advertisements imbued products with a mystique . . . and suggested that consumers could obtain that exoticism by purchasing the product."[8]

Never subtle, the commercial bottom-line aesthetic that came to define Times Square was not appreciated by the city's elite or by civic organizations promoting the "City Beautiful." They railed against "sign evil"—a growing aesthetic problem of large-scale billboards prolifer-ating indiscriminately all over the city since the turn of the century. Sufficiently powerful, the public outcry convinced Mayor William J. Gaynor (1910–1913) to appoint a Billboard Advertising Commission (1913) to investigate the problem and issue recommendations, which it did, though none were adopted. "The ubiquity of these advertisements is an aggravating phase of the situation," the commission's report com-plained. "They are no respecters of place. They are not confined to the unimproved tracts and rubbish yards on the outskirts of the City. On the contrary, they are thrust into the finest vistas which our public places present."[9] Of course, that would be where the most eyeballs would see them.

Fast forward to the 1920s. However much the businessmen and mer-chants of Broadway were benefiting from the economic power of the effusion of color and light that brought thousands upon thousands to Times Square, the same anti-billboard forces pressed on. "Throughout

**6.5** Gude's White Rock Water spectacular at the north end of the Times Square bowtie, as presented in a *Theatre Magazine* advertisement, 1912. Wallach Division Picture Collection, The New York Public Library.

**6.6** An illustration of "sign evil" adjacent to the residence of Andrew Carnegie, Fifth Avenue between 89th and 90th Streets, circa 1913. "Nearly every important street is infested with outdoor advertisements, huge, crude, tasteless and disfiguring." The Mayor's Billboards Commission of the City of New York.

the twenties," historian William Leach explained, "a battle was waged in Manhattan between rival trade associations over signage restrictions. On one side was the Broadway Association, which wanted no controls whatsoever placed on signage; on the other side was the grandiose and aggressive Fifth Avenue Association." Fearing that the electric signs would spill out of Times Square, where they had been allowed under the city's new zoning ordinance of 1916, the Fifth Avenue Association fought for control from 1916 onward, insisting that all projecting and illuminated signs be banned on Fifth Avenue from Washington Square to 110th Street. The merchants of Fifth Avenue "*wanted* the patronage of the tourists who were attracted to New York by the lights of Times Square; and they certainly had nothing against commercial light and color." What they did not want was a "'carnival spectacle' that might bring an influx of the 'wrong kind of people' into the Avenue on a daily basis, an influx that might jeopardize real estate values and undermine the control these merchants had over *their* property." In 1922, the Fifth Avenue merchants succeeded in convincing the Board of Alderman to pass an ordinance that put strict controls on signage everywhere around Times Square, which had the effect of intensifying the glitter and concentrating it in that one sanctioned area, where it would have a "carnival field day."[10]

## HOLDING PEOPLE RAPT

He was "a spiritual pioneer of today's Times Square, where giant neon displays are required on new buildings," Douglas Martin wrote of Douglas Leigh in his obituary for "the dazzling impresario of electrical splendor," who passed away in 1999 at 92. Called the Sign King, Leigh was a southerner who arrived in New York in 1930 with $9 in his pocket and a soft-spoken sales ability, and not long after was on his way to making a fortune. His "antic, innovative style summed up all the excitement of the Times Square tradition."[11] Using theatrical special effects, Leigh's numerous sign spectaculars delivered a distinctive look to Times Square. His most memorable spectacular—the celebrated Camel sign with its ring-blowing smoker, which became an international celebrity duplicated in twenty-two other cities—made Broadway's sign wizard of the era more than the equal of Gude. By all historical accounts, his imaginative dramatizations made the Great White Way greater, certainly glitzier.

Leigh advanced Times Square's ever-evolving advertising dynamic by adding animated motion: smoke rings in the case of the Camel man (1941–1966); steam from a gargantuan cup of A&P Coffee in his first Times Square spectacular (1933); fountains in the part-sign, part-movie show of the Wilson spectacular (1940), his biggest showstopper, a 35-foot-tall metal whiskey bottle surrounded by eight 20-foot-tall fountains enclosed in clear plastic tubes; a 27-foot-high waterfall flanked by larger-than-life nudes over the Bond Clothes store (1948–1954) at the "Crossroads of the Crossroads" across from the Hotel Astor; thousands of "floating" soap bubbles for his Super Suds detergent sign (1944–1946); Mr. Clown's ring tosses for Ballantine's Beer (1936), which when finished completed the Ballantine logo. Leigh's light productions injected a new personality into Times Square, based on his particular vision of crowd pleasers that would "hold people rapt," draw spectators in such large numbers that they stopped traffic—the ultimate success for a Times Square sign. "A good sign," he said, "has two aspects, and only two. It must attract attention, and it must have memory value." Scale and brightness drew viewers, he explained, "like moths to a flame." But motion was the essential force. "Anything that moves captures attention. The more animation in the display, the more memory value it contains."[12]

Leigh's imagination went beyond the gigantic letters and large-than-life figures that characterized the advertising milieu of Times Square. "No room in our business for men who can't dream," he told Meyer Berger, a Pulitzer-winning reporter for the *Times*, for a profile in the

**6.7** This cartoon "Above the Crowd" by Stookie Allen profiles the ambitious ideas of Douglas Leigh as a "reg'ler Horatio Alger hero from Alabama," circa 1935. Douglas Leigh Papers, Archives of American Art, Smithsonian Institution.

*Times Magazine.* Spectaculars display "multiple amounts of electric light and neon," he said, but it was the "special effects" that add a "dimension beyond the normal." Leigh envisioned Times Square "as an open-air theater or a sprawling world's fair environment rather than as the outdoor picture gallery, however monumental, that other sign designers before and after saw." Tell, who explored in depth Leigh's papers at the Archives of American Art at the Smithsonian Institution, writes that he captured this idea best in the Wilson spectacular, which "burst out of the usual flat, rectangular billboard format and demonstrated Leigh's lifelong love of sculpture and special effects, scaled to project for blocks." The design for this sign moved him beyond "the simpler local forms he had mastered in fewer than ten years and progressed from single-idea dramatizations toward a fantastic Times Square baroque."

**6.8** One of Douglas Leigh's most famous spectaculars: the animated smoke of the Camel Man mounted on the façade of the Claridge Hotel on Broadway and 44th Street, 1941–1966. Fabricated by Artkraft Strauss, the sign anticipated the onset of World War II and imposition of blackouts by attracting attention without using neon. Manuscripts and Archives Division, The New York Public Library.

For the opening of his spectacular Wilson production, the master of promotion employed "the kind of ballyhoo that was pure Broadway. He issued tickets, put tables on the sidewalk across from the sign, and lined up Joan Crawford to throw the switch on opening night." Other marquee actors and actresses celebrated in the "luxurious" control room behind the sign, and "the dancer Vera Zorina gave an impromptu live performance seen in moving silhouette from across the square."[13]

With consistent showmanship, between 1937 and 1941 on Broadway sites he controlled, Leigh produced one memorable sign after another: Gillette Blades (1937), Four Roses Whiskey (1938), Bromo-Seltzer (1939), Silex Coffee (1940), Camel smokes (1941). Even during the lights-out blackout of World War II in Times Square, he created ways for his signs to be seen with other methods. Where Gude saw art and advertising joined by electricity, Leigh made Times Square "a giant performance event in the service of advertising."[14]

By the 1950s, however, fashion in Times Square advertising became less imaginative and decline set in; it was all about the big movie. By the early 1960s, the era of great Times Square signs was over. Instead of putting the new first-run films in blazing lights, movie marquees of the Rialto and Globe Theatres, which specialized in sex, promoted adults-only movies on their neon-lit marquees: "The Filthiest Show in Town," "No Morals," "Too Young, Too Immoral," "Take It Off," "The Rape—It Gores All the Way," "Uncut-Uncensored Shame Dame," "Land of 1001 Nudes."[15]

As portrayed by the media, Times Square had become the epitome of urban despair. The area's decline was vividly apparent in John Schlesinger's 1969 Oscar-winning film *Midnight Cowboy*. As Tell described it, "the remaining spectacular signs, partially visible and seldom seen straight on or in long shots, are joyless and tawdry. At the center of attention are the peeling arcades, second-run movie houses, all-night restaurants, with their casts of hustlers, marks, and crazies."[16] American companies did not want to advertise in an area considered destitute and dangerous, frequented by pimps and prostitutes.

In a superficial effort to improve conditions, owners removed billboards and marquees. "They were taking the position that marquees

**6.9** This 1960 view of signs on the east side of Broadway at 43rd and 44th Streets—the old-style Kleenex "pops-up" spectacular (1955–1965) juxtaposed with the marquee of the Globe Theatre's adults-only films—illustrates the advertising transition in process amid everyday merchandising in Times Square. CBS Photo via Getty Images.

cause crime because they allow criminals to get out of the rain," said Tama Starr, third-generation president of the family business Artkraft Strauss Sign Corporation, which had dominated the production of Times Square spectaculars for so many decades that it was rightfully called "Neon's Royal Family." "Everybody knows the primary function of light is to make streets safer." The city's mid-1970s fiscal crisis further exacerbated the area's downward trajectory. In 1977, the owner of One Times Square halted the operation of the famous Motograph News Bulletin, or "zipper" as it was known, with its 12,400 light bulbs that had been flashing news and other messages around the icon's fourth floor since 1928; it had gone dark before, between 1961 and 1965, after the *Times* stopped operating the zipper. In 1986, *Newsday* turned it on once again with the words: "New York Newsday Lights Up New York," though in 1994 the newspaper decided not to renew its lease, saying "Frankly, there's not that much bang for the buck."[17]

Times Square's spectaculars were firmly associated with their environment, and when sex became the square's major industry (even though only a small percentage of the area's businesses were sex-related) in the 1970s, "signs for rent" began to appear. A domestic tunnel vision obscured the latent power of Times Square as an advertising venue, despite the decrepitude that prevailed. Disenchanted by what they perceived to be the quality of the audience, long-time advertisers pulled out of Times Square leaving the billboards blank. Kent, Beefeater, Accutron by Bulova, Gordon's Gin, Canadian Club, and Woolmark, all there in 1972, were gone 10 years later.

Coca-Cola was the exception; the world's largest soft-drink marketer had been advertising on the north end of the bowtie since 1932, and its dominant sign remained throughout the 1970s and '80s, only to be replaced in 1992, by a multimillion-dollar animated spectacular with its own phone number: a 42-foot-high bottle of Coke with a giant straw that popped up and down to simulate the level of liquid inside the bottle's Coca-Cola-green color. When the fourteen billboards controlled by Douglas Leigh were sold in 1979 to Van Wagner Communications, thirteen were blank. Jason Perline, Van Wagner's chairman, recalled a salesman for Philip Morris saying, "We don't want a sign seen only by pimps and prostitutes," to which Perline responded, "Who smokes more than pimps and prostitutes?" Seemingly sound, the logic nevertheless failed to make the case: "It wasn't a good sales pitch." Not long thereafter, however, Perline succeeded in marketing his billboards to Japanese advertisers and could honestly say, "The area is booming."[18]

**6.10** Blank billboards grew increasingly noticeable in Times Square during the late 1960s and 1970s. Manuscripts and Archives Division, The New York Public Library.

Manufacturers of Japanese consumer products knew the tourist appeal of the place, and they flocked to the area because they saw Times Square as the ultimate symbol of America. They also understood better than any other group of brand merchandisers the transportability of the icon's branded location. Sony pioneered, in 1972, followed by Canon, JVC, Midori, Panasonic, and Suntory, breaking the darkness of Times Square with large, bright neon supersigns full of animation. By the early 1980s, the ranks of Japanese advertisers included Aiwa, Brother, Casio, Fuji, Maxell, Minolta, Seiko, TDK, Toshiba, VCX, and Yashica, and for much of the 1970s and '80s, most of the district's signs advertised Japanese products.

The proliferation of Japanese advertisers during that period reflected more than just prescient advertising logic. The men behind these decisions, like the president of the American subsidiary of Minolta Corporation, Sama Kusumoto, first came to the United States in the 1950s with

**6.11** This southward view of the bowtie in 1985 shows the dominant presence of Japanese-brand advertising in Times Square, after American brands had withdrawn from billboard advertising there. They would not return until the early 1990s. Collection of Charles M. Weiss.

a mandate to expand Japanese sales "in the world's richest customer market." They shared similar career paths and, as Kusumoto discovered, a nostalgic attachment to Manhattan. Short on money but long on time, they had whiled away many an evening in Times Square, which he called the "neon heart" of the city. "We struck a gentleman's agreement to relight Times Square," he wrote years later. "We considered giant neon signs a good advertising medium and believed Times Square to be perhaps the best location in the United States. Our companies were doing well, thanks to the openness of the American market and the buying power of American consumers; what better way to symbolize our achievements in that market than to revive one of its vernacular art forms."[19] That the square was physically in decline did not weaken their motive: when the signs were lit at night, the images the Japanese companies projected looked fine. American firms, on the other hand, viewed signs as a corporate-image vehicle, and they could not get beyond the grim grimy reality of the place.

During the 1970s the most memorable skyward visions of Times Square chronicled by the area's photographers singled out images of vacant spaces adjacent to the Coca-Cola sign, the demolished Budweiser and Camel signs, and "for rent" signs on what had been since the 1920s a jungle of billboards along Broadway. Gone were most of the gorgeous gigantic neon spectaculars, the huge electronic billboards that formerly promoted restaurants and nightclubs as tourist attractions, and the movie marquees, which in an earlier time producers regularly festooned with thousands of lights to promote new films. "For rent" notices on the former Times Tower heralded decline. The national energy crisis of 1973 with its threatened stoppage of Middle East oil dampened the commercial logic of exuberant advertising spectaculars by making them appear wasteful of electricity. The lights went out as advertisers canceled their displays. This in contrast to times past when even the 1929 stock market crash and the Depression did not dim the lights of the spectaculars in Times Square.

In keeping with pornography's dominance in Times Square in the 1970s, the only new spectacular in the district was a neon fancy with swagged "curtains" nearly 60 feet across and 600 feet of red neon that Artkraft Strauss designed for the Pussycat Lounge and Cinema. Between the curtains traveled a message board and a half medallion with 810 feet of neon flashing the figure of a masked woman with a cat's tail. Set against 1,216 feet of blue and gold neon in letters almost six feet tall, the word "Pussycat" reigned until 1986, when the sign was torn down to make way for the 44-story Holiday Inn Crowne Plaza Hotel being developed by the Zeckendorf Company. The 89-year-old Artkraft Strauss Sign Company had fashioned many a spectacular, but the Pussycat remained a favorite of Tama Starr "because it embodies the Bauhaus ideal of form follows function."[20]

The heyday of Times Square spectaculars had passed, and Artkraft Strauss was passing into history as well. After the family-owned business contracted and sold off its billboard business and production plant, Tama Starr sold off the drawings, models, and tubing "that once made magic in the air" in a live public auction at Freeman's, the Philadelphia auction house, in 2006. Nostalgia reigned among the many bidders—collectors, museum people (including Tod Swormstedt, founder of the American Sign Museum in Cincinnati), and others like me—sitting in neat rows in the gallery waiting to raise their paddles in hope of capturing some reminder of the "Signs and Wonders" that once spectacularly lit up Broadway. "The days of the handcrafted neon spectacular are pretty much gone with the 20th century," Starr said. "We built all these one-of-a-kind, fantastic displays throughout the century, but now, in the 21st century, the medium is electronic: computer-controlled screens; the big video screens; the big pictorials printed by giant drum printers on vinyl. The art—or craft or trade—of painting is gone."[21]

**6.12** During the bleak 1970s, this neon fancy was the single new spectacular in Times Square, circa 1978. The vibrant ever-memorable sign would be replaced by signs for the Crowne Plaza hotel in 1998. © JackFalat.com (top); Scott Lotokis for author (bottom).

Leigh too moved on—to lighting up another New York icon: its skyline, designing dramatic exterior architectural lighting schemes for more than a dozen of the city's more important icons, among them the Empire State Building (bathing the building's crown in red-white-and-blue lights), Citicorp Tower (installing three lighting systems to illuminate the crown), the Crown Building (lighting a regilded cupola like an ornate jewel), and the New York Central Building (Helmsley Building, flooding the top with gold-colored lights). His two-and-a-half-story snowflake with 3,000 lights installed above Fifth Avenue at 57th Street became an instant icon of the city. Upon his death, Leigh willed Stonbely the famous snowflake, which has been suspended above the Manhattan intersection where it first debuted every holiday season since 1984. In 2001, Stonbely dedicated the snowflake to UNICEF, which has used the enormous crystal ornament (rebuilt and updated) as a fundraising vehicle for its lifesaving programs for children.

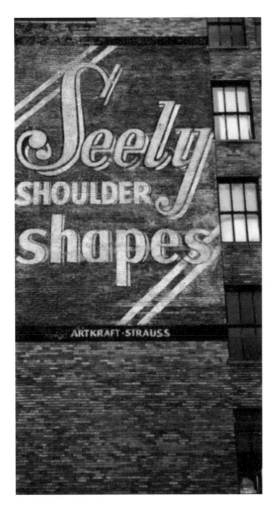

**6.13** This vintage color photograph of the mural advertisement for Seely Shoulder Shapes, a garment business, was painted by Artkraft Strauss in the mid-1930s on the 16-story wall of 265 West 40th Street, now part of the site of the *New York Times* headquarters. It was taken in 1997 by Frank H. Jump as part of his longtime project, the Fading Ad Campaign, which documents mural advertisements throughout New York City. Collection of the author.

**6.14** With this 1945 image drawn by Hugh Ferriss of three-dimensional signs lining Broadway, Douglas Leigh promoted a conception of postwar Broadway as a "Greater" White Way. He believed that a great symphony of light would continue to play a part in the commercial triumph of Times Square. Douglas Leigh Papers, Archives of American Art, Smithsonian Institution.

Ever the booster for Times Square, Leigh worked hard to promote the place, as president of the Broadway Association and local property owner (the Crossroads Building with Irving Maidman and the Times Tower). In his archive of papers at the Smithsonian Institution in Washington, D.C., Leigh "emerges as visionary of commercial pageantry and light spectacle whose scope was much broader than his commercial practice would ever suggest or allow."[22] His conception for a postwar Broadway, for example, appearing in the 1944 *Times Magazine* profile shows the avenue completely reimagined in a world's-fair style of commercial promotion, with three-dimensional advertising signs lining skyscrapers along Broadway. In using a building to demonstrate a product, a seemingly radical idea at the time, Leigh envisioned what the mandated signage regulations, designed to protect the visual character of Time Square, would later bring forward: the building as sign.

## MESSAGES TO THE PUBLIC

In the dark days of Times Square in the early 1980s, a time when no American company wanted a sign in the square, something strikingly new appeared on the billboards in the sky: art messages encoded in brightly colored animated dots looking like electronic needlepoint on the giant Spectacolor computerized light board mounted four stories up on the prow of One Times Square. *Messages to the Public* originated with artist Jane Dickson, who was working for Spectacolor as an ad designer and computer programmer, and it was sponsored by the Public Art Fund, an organization dedicated to taking art out of the galleries and placing it in the city's streets and parks. "I picked that title," said Dickson, "because I thought the propaganda potential from this project was terrific." The Spectacolor board, she noted, was regularly used for "commercial propaganda."[23]

The exhibition series was pioneering. Not only did it provide artists with a new means of transmitting their ideas to millions of viewers each day, but the project "paved the path for a long history of transforming the city's ubiquitous advertising spaces into exhibitions." Every month a different artist presented a thirty-second spot, repeated more than fifty times a day for two weeks, wedged into a twenty-minute loop of commercials on the 40-by-20-foot digital screen. From 1982 to 1990, over ninety artists including Keith Haring, Nam June Paik, Crash, Alfredo Jaar, and Jenny Holzer had a chance to interpret the idea of "message." Holzer, who uses the simplest bold statements as her medium to push the public into reflection, placed several provocative selections from her series *Truisms* on the eye-catching Spectacolor board: "YOUR OLDEST FEARS ARE THE WORST ONES," "FATHERS OFTEN USE TOO MUCH FORCE," "ABUSE OF POWER COMES AS NO SURPRISE." The signboard was a "wonderful way to present art clearly," she said. "It's not that I'm trying to thumb my nose at advertising; it's simply that I want to use means of communication that work." She had "learned to choose interesting subjects and presentations," she said in an interview, because "I started in the streets where I had only a few seconds to catch people's attention."[24]

After it debuted in 1976, the eye-catching Spectacolor screen soon became another icon of New York (a profitable one), featured on news broadcasts around the world and used for the opening credits of *Saturday Night Live*. "Animated-light billboards are not new to Times Square, of course," remarked the *New Yorker* in 1977 in its "Talk of the Town" coverage of Stonbely's electronic screen. "But these new lights, marching across a panel labelled 'Spectacolor,' were of a much greater order of magnitude and design, and were in changing colors, too." The screen "appeared to be a revolutionary advance in the technology of American advertising." Content is what really set it apart, Stonbely told the *Times'*

**6.15** One of Jenny Holzer's *Truisms* (1977–1979) on the Spectacolor light board on One Times Square flashed for two weeks in 1982 as part of the exhibition *Messages to the Public* (1982–1990). Known for her provocative phrases of incisive social observation, Holzer's use of the computer screen in Times Square gave her direct access to a larger public audience than an exhibition in an art gallery. Gary Hack.

advertising columnist: the screen would flash editorial matter as well as advertising, making it a true communications medium.[25]

With its moving images and text, Spectacolor ushered in a new era of spectaculars in Times Square, and Stonbely joined the rare ranks of innovative billboard entrepreneurs who made their mark in the one place that mattered above all others: "sign heaven." He was a successor in a remarkable commercial tradition: after the passing of Douglas Leigh, Stonbely, said Christopher Gray, "is now the grand younger man of Times Square spectaculars." Billboard technology had not been updated in decades, Stonbely explained as we talked over lunch surrounded by caricatures of theatrical and political figures on walls of Sardi's, a Times Square institution. He ventured forth in the business because he was convinced that the advertising environment of Times Square was ripe for something new. People were spending more time outside the home, which meant more opportunity for outdoor advertising. "We had the idea of creating a broadcast medium on a sign," he said; Spectacolor "would be selling *time* on billboards rather than the customary practice of selling *space*."[26] It would be easier said than done.

The idea gestated while he was working in Kuwait for the Ministry of Tourism and saw a simple four-color sign flashing image after image. Told the machine manipulating the images was made in Hungary, Stonbely went directly there from Kuwait to speak with the manufacturer, but unlike what he saw in Kuwait (archaic equipment and technology), the sign he wanted to make would plug into the computer age and have more powerful light-emitting bulbs. To put together what became the Spectacolor system, he needed software to produce at least eight frames per second of animation, hardware for the electronic innards, and powerful display bulbs for the electronic billboard that would last several years and beam out messages night and day. "Most bulbs don't shine very brightly outside in the sun—and that was an absolutely critical element for us."[27] In 1975, he formed a company to incorporate the new technology of outdoor advertising, but he first had to find companies to make the software, hardware, and bulbs to match his vision of what could be. He had no expertise in the outdoor advertising business, just the kind of vision and energy that drives entrepreneurs.

Stonbely was 30 when Spectacolor flashed its first supersized messages in 1976 on the north end of the namesake former Times Tower. Brooklyn-born and a graduate of New York University, he had worked as a legislative researcher for Robert F. Kennedy, then following Kennedy's assassination briefly in sales promotion and advertising for the *New York Times* before starting his ad company serving small clients. He wanted to make Spectacolor equalitarian, accessible to individuals as well as to advertisers who could buy a 30-second spot for $25. Gustavo Alfredo Noguera made news when he proposed to Magda Stella Ossa on August 8, 1977, via the Spectacolor screen: "Magda Stella Will You Marry Me?" It was the first of many a "plight troth," solemn promise of marriage. The direct message that Stonbely promoted was new to the outdoor-advertising business model. People paying to ask questions on Spectacolor became very popular; it was the immediacy of the response to direct promotional questions, he said, especially among radio and show people.

As one of only two exceptions to the void of new advertising spectaculars in Times Square during the 1970s, the inspiration for Spectacolor was almost too ironic for words: "Believe it or not," the *Times* advertising columnist exclaimed, it was inspired by "similar installations in Moscow, Kuwait, and Tijuana, Mexico. Talk about carrying coals to Newcastle." The inspiration came full circle when the person in Kuwait who had the Hungarian-made display heard about Stonbely's Times Square spectacular, "flew to New York, took one look at the Spectacolor display, walked into my office and wrote out a check."[28] It was the start of Stonbely's worldwide licensing of Spectacolor screens in more than fifty places. In Times Square, Spectacolor remained in place until 1990, when, in the typical course of technological advances in outdoor advertising, Sony approached Stonbely with a proposal to replace Spectacolor with its large-scale video board Jumbotron, the first of its kind.

**6.16** The JVC billboard and giant globe at Broadway and 43rd Street (pictured in 2011), the newest sign by George Stonbely, known for introducing the first computer-programmable electronic message board, Spectacolor, in 1976. Gary Hack.

Stonbely continued with the making of spectaculars in Times Square: a tipping can of peanuts for Planters ("Party with a Real Nut"), a huge $20 bill coming out of a slot in an enormous replica of a Fleet Bank ATM, Maxwell House ("Good to the Last Drop"), and the JVC globe at the northeast corner of 43rd Street and Broadway, among others. The JVC globe sitting across from competitors—the cylindrical Nasdaq electronic billboard on the south and the ABC display to the north—harks back to Leigh's third-dimension spectaculars. "We decided we couldn't compete with the electronics of Nasdaq and ABC, so we went for something three-dimensional, elemental," he said. But the outdoor advertising business is a different business from that of the 1920s and '30s. "Then, the revenue was pin money—maybe a few thousand a month. But now it's in the millions, and it's a measured value you can predict. Developers are basing their financing on sign income."[29] It wasn't always that way.

## CODIFYING VISUAL CHARACTER

When George Klein put forward his transforming vision for 42nd Street—a uniform quartet of mansard-roofed office towers designed by Philip Johnson and John Burgee (figure 3.14)—the disapproval was immediate and vociferous. Their vision of a corporate park at the iconic crossroads threatened to expunge what was unique about Times Square—its visual character—and replace it with yet another midtown "office canyon" replicating Sixth Avenue a block to the east, what Tom Wolfe called "Rue de Regret." The glitzy in-your-face gestalt of Times Square cried out for a different aesthetic, one respectful of the district's legacy. The architects, however, saw things differently. They believed they were giving Times Square an identity it did not have. That was the problem. "Times Square is an advertising park; it's not Rockefeller Center," remarked Starr.[30]

Kent Barwick of the Municipal Art Society led the opposition, joined by the city's civic groups and performing-arts community. The intense reaction to Johnson and Burgee's sanitizing corporate vision set in motion a vigorous and noisy conversation about the value of the city's irreplaceable Theater District. The goal: raise public consciousness about Times Square. To convince an unknowing and skeptical public that the lights, glitter, and tawdry character were worth preserving, Barwick staged PR events, developed effective pamphlet literature worthy of a political campaign (which it was), and deployed organizational tactics designed to make the square's "character" issue a cause célèbre.

To dramatize what would be lost in a corporate-dominated redevelopment plan and to attract a big audience likely to be sympathetic to the cause, the MAS teamed up with other concerned civic groups and at the invitation of Van Wagner Communications and Artkraft Strauss, which together owned and operated 99 percent of the Times Square signs, sponsored a half-hour blackout of all signs in the district at 7:30 P.M. on March 24, 1984. The idea was to surprise and stun the thousands of theatergoers bustling through Times Square on the way to their 8:00 P.M. curtains. For maximum effect, they turned off all the signs, one by one, at two-second intervals, so the television cameras could pan the spreading darkness from south to north. The one sign deliberately left lit on the giant Spectacolor display flashed the message: "HEY, MR. MAYOR! IT'S DARK OUT HERE! HELP KEEP THE BRIGHT LIGHTS IN TIMES SQUARE!" The hugely effective attention-getting event—nothing like it had happened since World War II—was repeated in November, on the eve of the Board of Estimate's final deliberation on the 42nd Street Development Project.

City officials and the MAS eventually worked out a compromise in which the City Planning Commission agreed to reopen the planning for Times Square as a whole. The process gave birth to special signage "razzle-dazzle regulations" mandated for new buildings developed in the bowtie area from 43rd to 50th Streets with frontage on Broadway and Seventh Avenue. This was a real turn of events. Investors and developers initially

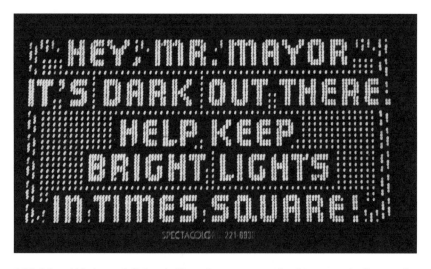

**6.17** A timed blackout of all signs in Times Square—except for this one on the Spectacolor board—was staged in 1984 to dramatize what would be lost in the sanitizing corporate vision of the Johnson/Burgee designs for the proposed office towers on the crossroads corners at 42nd Street. Dorothy Alexander, Courtesy of the Municipal Art Society.

saw such a mandate as disastrous. They argued that if the lawyers and investment bankers were in Times Square by day, it would still revert to an undesirable area at night. The signs, unexpectedly, nullified that assumption: they gave the new towers a twenty-four-hour presence in Times Square. As a result, policymakers and investors realized that the place was most profitable when it was utilized round the clock.

The all-out controversy over the Johnson/Burgee designs for the 42nd Street project played an inadvertent role in reshaping the ultimate vision for the historic street, and by extension, for the entire Times Square district. "The miserable quality of [their] design awakened people to the project's deeper flaw: New York City was about to sacrifice its precious entertainment district and replace it with a dreary new world of office buildings," Gregory Gilmartin wrote in his history of the Municipal Art Society. "The designs," the civic-minded influential architect Hugh Hardy told me in an interview for *Times Square Roulette*, "were, in retrospect, a great asset to the cause [of renewing the entertainment district]. It was, in fact, a wake-up call to the people that something wrong was about to happen."[31] The increased density allowances of the 1982 Midtown Zoning Resolution were compounding pressure on the Theater District, which theater owners and preservationists alike agreed was irreplaceable. By setting in motion an alternative vision for what Times Square should be, critical reaction and public opinion forced the issue of entertainment onto the redevelopment agenda, compelling city and state officials to respond, on the defensive, if, at first, in no other way.

The MAS was an unlikely advocate for the glitz and popular entertainment gestalt of Times Square. Founded in 1893 to advise the city fathers on aesthetic matters, the nonprofit organization spoke in the name of the "public interest," entering countless debates over the great plan of the city; the design of its municipal buildings, parks, and monuments; the preservation of its landmarks and historic districts; and the public responsibilities of private developers. It was an advocacy group sustained by the elites of the city, one that still exists, notwithstanding the greater diversity and broader base of its current membership.

As an elite organization, the MAS was historically at odds with the values of popular culture. In one of its many struggling campaigns to make New York "an attractive city," the MAS had "won a reputation as the city's leading foe of outdoor advertisement." Billboards were considered visual pollution, a terrible blight on the public environment, and during the first decades of the twentieth century the MAS's dedication to an anti-billboard campaign—the first in the nation, beginning in 1902—led the Society to try to ban sky signs, also known as rooftop billboards (unconstitutional); to control their height (willfully violated, unenforced by the city, overturned by state courts, which declared signage to be an aesthetic concern); to tax them (politically dead-ended); and to shame advertisers (who proved to be virtually shameless). When the "gaudy electric signs" in Times Square, which the MAS pictured as "the deepest circle of billboard hell," were briefly switched off to save coal during World War I, the society found "some grim satisfaction." Even when Times Square was at the height of its glory before the Depression, the elites of the Society, Gilmartin reported, never appreciated the place: "Times Square stood for popular culture, bright lights, billboards, and the messy vitality of commercial culture—for everything the Beaux Arts aesthetes deplored."[32]

The Society's new-found aesthetic mission centered on the whole Theater District identified with Times Square. Persuaded and guided by Hardy, the MAS board sought to preserve the character of the district and secure landmark status for the forty-four "listed theaters," for cultural preservation more than architectural preservation. Its characterization of Times Square as an "entertainment district" swayed the City Planning Commission, which subsequently put in place the 1987 far-reaching design guidelines for the district. The organization succeeded in no small part because of its ability to accommodate conflicting interests and strike a philosophical balance in preserving as much as possible of the past without precluding development in the future. Once leading individuals within its ranks became galvanized by a new understanding of the diverse vibrancy of the district, the MAS sought to assure its constituents that Times Square's symbolic role and visual character would continue despite the impending development projects, and that entertainment activities would not be crowded out in the face of the inevitable westward expansion of the midtown office district. Even if development proceeded slowly at first, it was obviously on the way, as judged by the organization's identification of twenty-seven "soft" sites, large parcels ripe for development.

The 1987 "razzle-dazzle" regulations for Times Square crafted by the Department of City Planning articulated and codified Times Square's unique historical sense of place. They did not aim to recreate the era of neon spectaculars, but rather to recall its idealistic past and prevent the new office towers from turning the entertainment district into a deadened business quarter: "To preserve, protect and enhance the sale and character of Times Square," developers were required to incorporate three categories of signs on new buildings: small-scale signs within retail establishments, signs located on a building's street wall (normally considered "business signs"), and "supersigns" located on and above the building's street wall.[33] The requirements were specific and complex in application.

The signs of the first buildings constructed under the new regulations—1540 Broadway (Bertelsmann Building), 1601 Broadway (Holiday Inn Crowne Plaza), 1568 Broadway (Embassy Suites Times Square/ DoubleTree Guest Suites), 750 Broadway (Morgan Stanley Building), 1585 Broadway (Morgan Stanley Building), and Two Times Square (Ramada Renaissance Hotel)—were not spectaculars in the historic sense. However, the mandated "razzle-dazzle" did transform developers' intentions beyond squeezing their bottom line: they changed the architecture of buildings as architects worked to accommodate the visual power of signage and its booming economic value. "Signage is built *into* the buildings," said Robert Fox, one the architects of Four Times Square. "It's not applied," he told *Times* reporter David W. Dunlap. "If you took it off, the building would look very funny. It wouldn't look right."[34] The sign had become the building, a layer of its architecture.

Because it was mandated as aesthetic policy, the resurgence in riotous commercial signage in Times Square evident by the mid-1990s caught real estate interests by surprise, except for Jeffrey Katz, president of Sherwood Equities and developer of Two Times Square, the narrow signpost housing the Ramada Renaissance Hotel and retail behind it at the north end of the bowtie. Katz maintained that without public policy, there would not have been signs except for One Times Square and Two Times Square: "They're a financial burden," he said in 1994. "They're a net plus to the city but they're not a plus for each individual project."[35] Apart from aesthetics, businesswise the issue was how a sign gets integrated into a building in terms of light and air. Once designers solved that problem with a combination of new technology and thinking that a sign need not be a billboard, the new see-through fin-like signs became compatible with office usage.

Compatibility with corporate image remained another matter, however. The biggest question at the time was how Morgan Stanley, as the new owner of 1585 Broadway, would comply with the special zoning rules for Times Square. The 1987 rules required the blue-chip investment bank to install minimum amounts of signage at three different heights: illuminated retail signs at the ground level, illuminated signs at the mid-level, and supersigns at specific building heights. No decisions about the new signage were made for months as executives debated internally how to resolve the seeming conflict between the requirements for big and kinetic signs and the elite firm's preference for understatement.

**6.18** Top: the prototypical block of Broadway between 46th and 47th Streets (pictured in 2001) used to craft the "razzle-dazzle" regulations for Times Square. Gary Hack. Bottom: signs on the Embassy Suites Times Square/DoubleTree Guest Suites (1998) constructed after the mandated regulations went into effect. Scott Lotokis for the author.

The surprising, but not shocking, result was half an acre of glittering light-emitting diodes (LEDs) formed into a continuously moving high-tech display of real-time financial information fabricated by Artkraft Strauss. Not just riveting and kinetic, it was a stunning personification of the new character, technology, and imagery of the emergent Times Square. Zipping at irregular speeds in three strips along the building front, each 160 feet long and 10 to 12 feet high, was real-time data in bright amber letters and numbers. On the side walls of the building, a pair of 30-by-60-foot, 256-color LED video-data boards showed charts, symbols, and other graphics. Anchoring the corners of the building were intensely blue 44-foot cylindrical world maps indicating the time across Morgan Stanley's global network of offices. Ten decorative fins along the Broadway façade, clad with mirrors and blue-neon edges, spelled out "1 5 8 5 B'W A Y." The name of the firm was in discrete pale letters only eight inches high on the global clock. No more identification was needed. "The information is the building, and the building is Morgan Stanley," said Bob Jackowitz, Artkraft Strauss's project manager. Architects Gwathmey Siegel & Associates designed this stunner. "The idea is that for the information to appear integral to Morgan Stanley, it had to emerge smoothly as if from the heart of the building, travel, and reenter the building smoothly, as if for reprocessing."[36] Brilliantly adapted, Wall Street culture danced in Broadway lights—a new icon for the era of the marketplace, a blue-chip supersign on a once gritty corner. (In 2015, as part of Morgan Stanley's socially minded ad campaign called "Capital Creates Change," another stunner replaced the 25-year-old sign.)

There was no clearer message about the success of public policy than the market's delivery of pulsating signs in overabundant quantity: on average 25 percent and as high as 61 percent beyond the minimums mandated for the six towers built between 1987 and 1991. What Morgan Stanley ended up doing takes the prize for irony: in putting more signage than the regulations called for on both its towers, the pinstriped investment-banking firm "outclassed" every other new building. Given its initial objection to signage on a new headquarters building, placing odds on that outcome would have been dicey. By early 1993—before the big announcements heralding the coming of Morgan Stanley, Disney, Madame Tussauds, and the Virgin Megastore later that year—it was clear that the quantity and quality of new signs put in place was being driven by a commercial mandate newly unshackled from the district's negative investment psychology. Sign revenue had become bankable.

**6.19** Supersigns on the façade of Morgan Stanley's 42-story world headquarters at 1585 Broadway in Times Square. Interpreting the regulatory mandate for large-scale, illuminated, kinetic signs, the bank presented a giant display of financial information that would change over the years: 1998 (top), 2022 (bottom). Gary Hack.

## BILLBOARD BOOM

For American brands, Times Square once again became a place to promote with pride. "Times Square is a place where you can make a dramatic statement;" said the president of the Anheuser-Busch's media planning and buying unit about the company's return to the district where prominent Budweiser signs had promoted the brand from the 1930s through the '50s. After nearly a 40-year absence, Wrigley's was returning too, with a billboard that would include nearly every element of historic Times Square signage: neon, a video screen, a backlit lightbox, and a zipper-style message board. The new sign would be one block south of the site Wrigley's earlier sign had occupied from 1936 to 1960 (with only a brief hiatus during World War II), which followed the chewing gum company's first Times Square spectacular mounted in 1917. Stating the obvious of what had attracted brands to Times Square, a senior director for consumer marketing at the Chicago-based company said it is a place "a phenomenal amount of people move through."[37] In 2001, the Alliance reported that advertisers benefited from an audience of 1.5 million people moving through Times Square each day, as well as the "immeasurable bonus of collateral images" appearing in other media: broadcasts from news studios in Times Square, and over two billion television viewers worldwide who watched the ball fall on New Year's Eve. Branding through social media was then just around the corner and would further magnify the impact of having a position on a billboard in Times Square.

As the transformation took hold, landlords rushed to cash in on the frenzy for billboard space. By 2001, the number of signs in Times Square had grown fivefold in the short span of six years, to an estimated 250, according to Katz, who controlled the two premier locations in the square: One Times Square, where the drop drops each New Year's Eve, and Two Times Square, the tower at the north end of the bowtie. As many as fifty were considered supersigns that could cost millions of dollars to build, light, and lease. Advertisers' increasing demand for visibility in the premier outdoor emporium of commercial display showed up immediately in rapidly escalating prices for billboard spaces and supersigns in Times Square. In 1995, leasing costs for big billboards ranged from $180,000 to $1.2 million a year, depending upon the display space and visibility of a location; this was up from $150,000 to $500,000 annually just four years earlier. At these rates, Times Square ranked as the highest-priced place to advertise outdoors in America. Two years later, the *Wall Street Journal* reported that asking rents for advertising spaces on Four Times Square had reached a stratospheric level—between $500,000 and $2.1 million annually, ranging from $139 a square foot to an eye-popping $536 a square foot. "Viewed on a square foot basis, the signs are probably the most expensive real estate in the world," said the president of sign broker Van Wagner Communications.[38]

Billboard prices kept rising. "Outside Walls Fetching More Than Offices," a *Crain's* headline emphasized later that year, in reference to the fact that billboards had almost become "the tail wagging the dog."[39] In 1998, the income the Durst Organization expected to take in from signs on Four Times Square, estimated by the firm at more than $10 million, had become comparable to that expected from the building's 120,000 square feet of retail space. And prices were still going up. All of this also benefited the city treasury: signs in Times Square signs were reported to bring in $140 million a year to the city, including their rental, production, maintenance, and operation; in property taxes alone, signage in Times Square added over $76 million to taxable values, as reported by the Alliance. While the *Crain's* article went on to note that both brokers and landlords thought these prices "verge on the nutty," the unexpected financial windfall from a surge in signage induced by regulatory policy that developers bitterly opposed during the travails of implementation was rich with irony. But then, the sign business is not real estate.

The boom in the economic value of billboard signs reached over Eighth Avenue to the mammoth Port Authority Bus Terminal. The attraction for the terminal's owner was cash—to help staunch the flow of red ink at the busy terminal—from what was expected to become the largest and flashiest billboard in New York wrapped around the upper levels of the building. Based on the bistate authority's records, the exterior ads were reported to have some 600,000 potential viewers a day, including people in passing vehicles and the 185,000 people who arrive at the terminal on 7,500 buses each weekday. The Port Authority hired outdoor advertising company TDI, a Manhattan company also under contract to provide signs for E-Walk, the planned entertainment complex across the street, and told it to design massive signs—"with no holds barred on size, animation, and illumination," according to TDI's senior vice president for marketing. The planned 40-foot-tall billboard, to hang from the terminal's twenty-seven giant X-shaped girders, would stretch across the two-block bus terminal at the once-raffish location on the southwest corner of 42nd Street and Eighth Avenue. Writing for *New York* magazine about the proposed exterior "improvement," critic Karrie Jacobs spared no words: "logic dictates there is no way to ruin a building as unfortunate in every respect at the Port Authority Bus Terminal. But the vinyl billboard that wraps Christo-style, around the building has done the illogical, the impossible, the inconceivable: It has made the bus terminal uglier still."[40]

The investment bottleneck broken, old advertising patterns reasserted themselves: brand visibility, competitive rivalries, costly spectacular constructions. Fuji's green-and-white spectacular (40 feet high by 90 feet long, covered with neon tubes) on 43rd and Broadway flashed not far from Kodak's giant promotion (30 feet high by 50 feet wide) on the façade of the Marriott Marquis Hotel. Squaring off against MCI, AT&T erected a giant technological masterpiece of a fiber-optic sign containing a 35-foot-diameter globe simulating AT&T data tracking across oceans and continents on the front face of the Marriott. Across the street from a steaming 35-foot-high by 22-foot-wide mug of Eight O'Clock Bean Coffee, General Foods planted a Maxwell House "Good to the Last Drop" spectacular (40 feet high by 60 feet wide)—a return to Times Square after a 55-year absence.

The new competitor in the cola wars, Virgin Cola, strategically placed a 40-foot billboard to butt heads with the famous three-dimensional Coca-Cola sign (65 feet high by 41 feet wide) across the way and the Pepsi sign (40 feet high by 40 feet wide) on the northern face of One Times Square, forming something of a "cola triangle." Playfully sporting a giant spoon and the theme "Smile More," Kraft Foods's Jell-O billboard (55 feet high by 105 feet long) joined other food purveyors, Nabisco's 40-foot-high by 102-foot-wide Oreo promotion and Nissin Food Products' 60-foot-high red neon steaming cup of noodles. Levi

**6.20** The façade of the Port Authority Bus Terminal in 2011 debuted the world's largest transparent media façade—a 6,000-square-foot digital billboard made of stainless-steel fabric with integrated LED profiles. The up-to-date billboard technology covers the big corner of X-shaped steel girders of a building that in 2008 had earned a spot on VirtualTourist's list of the "World's Top 10 Ugliest Buildings and Monuments." David Joseph, courtesy of GKD Metal Fabrics.

Strauss challenged Calvin Klein Jeans on billboard turf. Joe Boxer squared with Jockey International and Calvin Klein, prompting the company's chief executive to remark in reference to his rivals, "What's an underwear company without a Times Square presence?" The Boxer billboard added a technological twist: email broadcasting through an electric-light strip on the bottom for displaying email messages from around the world, many of them personal. The "high-tech cast" of this and other vibrant new signs in Times Square was more evidence "that the place was regaining a breadth and vitality not seen since the golden age of signage in the 1950s and early 1960s."[41] Covid would throw a temporary kink into the resurgence, but that threat was not yet known.

## HOT-BUTTON BATTLEGROUND

The messaging market in Times Square is as unique as its visual character. Seen by 1.5 million daily, it is a go-to place for branding messages and all kinds of advocacy seeking a mass audience. If a sponsor wants to be provocative, Times Square is the place to be. The district's legacy of anything goes practically courts testing the limits, welcomes controversy. Shock value with business value. Yet is there a point at which pushing the envelope to stop traffic is too much—even in Times Square? Is it still a place where nothing shocks—a place where almost anything goes to sell a product or advocate a position? Or are the nation's cultural, ideological, and political schisms testing its historical limits of tolerance—at least when it comes to what private owners will accept as messages on their billboards?

Stuart Elliot, the advertising columnist for the *Times*, reported on the emergence of social-issue signs in 1994. In that year, "visitors to Times Square gaped at a blocklong spectacular imploring them to 'Cut fat intake and live longer!'" The spectacular, paid for by a wealthy industrialist known for "crusading again fat and cholesterol, advertised a supermarket sweepstakes he created to generate interest in the new nutritional labels on food packages." As a social-issue sign, it had company. A "death clock" on Broadway counted the mounting fatalities caused by handguns; the handgun clock, as it had come to be called, was controversial during its two-year run. Tama Starr recalled those opposed to the sign telling her, "Don't you dare put that up"; they "tried to put me out of business," believing the sign "would be bad for Times Square."[42] By way of contrast, the giant dollar-bill-green national-debt clock at 43rd Street and Sixth Avenue sponsored by Seymour Durst, mounted high up on a nondescript building on 42nd Street and Sixth

Avenue in 1989, aroused no such controversy. If anything, controversial signs have nurtured the legacy of the place.

In 1982, when Calvin Klein debuted an erotic ad for men's underwear, a product thereto not known for being billboard-sexy, the impact was revolutionary: men can titillate. The eye-popping sign advertised a pair of white briefs modeled by a well-muscled tan man (Brazilian Olympic athlete Tom Hintnaus) leaning back like Adonis against a whitewashed wall. The perspective in the photograph, taken by Bruce Weber on the Greek island of Santorini, focused on the "obvious bulge in the briefs." It caused much controversy, but did not cause the company to blink. Two years earlier, a spot featuring a 15-year-old Brooke Shields—"Nothing comes between me and my Calvins"—established the company's reputation for risqué advertisements. "Provocative images of women in lingerie have long been a staple of both erotic art and advertising," fashion historian Valerie Steele wrote, "but the puritanism of American society has made it seem shocking to emphasize male sexual beauty." The ad was an opening salvo for sexualizing various CK product lines over the coming decades. Other even more provocative ads—for jeans and perfume—would follow. "The models in Klein's advertisements," Steele said, "with their young faces and hard bodies, look as though they don't just have sex. They are sex." "Quaint morality is banished," remarked *Adweek Markets and Marketing Special Report* trade magazine.[43] Pornography would soon be gone from Times Square, but sex not likely ever. Banishing the image of sex in Times Square would seem sacrilegious.

Anguished critics of a 1995 "hot-blooded" CK jeans campaign—featuring sexualized images of youthful models in "striking suggestive poses in little more than underwear"—likened the ads to child pornography (at least bordering on it); the company dropped the campaign after running it less than two months. Still, the Justice Department began an investigation. Federal law prohibits "lascivious exhibitions of the genitals or pubic area of a minor," said a former head of the Justice Department's child pornography and exploitation division (who went on to work for the conservative American Family Association). Klein said his new ads for kids' underwear were designed simply to "show children smiling, laughing, and just being themselves." The New York Civil Liberties Union did not think the ad was something to worry about: "The government is bowing to political pressure and misusing the child pornography laws," said its veteran executive director, Norman Siegel. "There is no evidence that the models were sexually abused and the ads, whatever you think of them, don't descend to obscene."[44]

**6.21** The eye-popping advertisement for Calvin Klein Underwear featuring Olympic-aspirant pole vaulter Tom Hintnaus appearing on the 40-by-50-foot billboard in Times Square in his white bikini brief, 1982. Bettmann via Getty Images.

Though Klein was known for pushing the bounds of sexuality and good taste in advertising, the backlash was the first time he had terminated a campaign before its scheduled end. "Calvin Klein has made a career of stepping over the line, shocking consumers to create word of mouth," said Bob Garfield, the ad critic for the trade publication *Advertising Age*. "Maybe this will put an end to some intentionally outrageous and provocative advertising, and make people think twice about shocking a million people to impress nine."[45] What was to follow—ads so hot that they had to be toned down, if not pulled—offered contrary evidence.

In 2005, for example, an ad for Plugg Jeans showed a "himbo holding a sultry babe—who in turn, clutches his uppermost, innermost thigh in an extremely cordial way," as the *New York Post* put it. In that case, pushing the envelope to stop traffic, literally (as the media company reportedly had been asked to do), proved to be too much, even in Times Square where porn had once had an unrestricted run. Boston Properties, the owner of the building with the billboard in question, and its ad agency rejected the raunchy advertisement. "They welcome innovation, but they don't welcome a return to pornography," a firm representative remarked. "When a lady appears to be grabbing a young man's crotch, that's a little out there."[46] In 2014, one of the world's largest online adult-entertainment platforms, Pornhub, was forced to take down its massive billboard, "All You Need Is Hand" (a play off the Beatles song, "All You Need Is Love"). The picture of a person's hands coming together to form a heart shape had been mounted on a building occupied by the DoubleTree Hotel; the billboard was taken down just forty-eight hours after it was put up after complaints by the hotel's general manager. The same thing happened in Los Angeles just days after the sign was put up above a popular family hot-dog-and-hamburger restaurant.

Hot-button messages of a different sort soon materialized on billboards in the legendary crossroads fast becoming a prime spot for advocacy on social and political issues. In 2004, a group of antiwar advocates sought to display an image critical of the war in Iraq in Times Square on a billboard site on the Marriott Marquis Hotel at Broadway and 45th Street in early August, in time for the gathering of the Republican National Convention in New York City to nominate President George W. Bush for a second term. Seeing the image—a red, white, and blue bomb with the words "Democracy Is Best Taught by Example"—Clear Channel Communications, then one of the nation's largest media companies, reportedly with close ties to national Republicans, went back on its leasing agreement with the group, Project Billboard, citing the bomb imagery as inappropriate; it also objected to revised imagery of a blue dove in place of a bomb. So did the management of the Marriott Marquis under its lease agreement with Clear Channel that allowed the private hotel firm to reject any advertisement with "political content." After several weeks, the dispute was settled when Clear Channel agreed to post the dove image (instead of the bomb with a burning fuse) on two other billboards, one on the billboard that wraps around a prime location on the Condé Nast building at 42nd Street and Broadway and another on the side of the W Hotel at Broadway and 47th Street, which would read "Total Cost of Iraq War."

When the owner of a building objected to a digital ad placed by the pro-Trump Committee to Defend the President that attacked "The Fake News . . ." and alleged fundraising abuses by Hillary Clinton, it yanked the ad after receiving multiple "complaints or negative feedback," as per its agreement with the giant media firm that controlled the billboard on 1515 Broadway, Viacom's headquarters (2018).[47] The year before, Tom Steyer took his campaign to impeach President Trump to Times Square: "Sign the Petition: Impeach! Join 2,595,430 Americans" (2017). More political-message billboards followed, including one showing Trump hogtied (2019); another by the Lincoln Project, an anti-trump PAC, with Ivanka Trump and Jared Kushner that stirred controversy (2020); "Trump Lost, No More 'Audits'" (2021); and a billboard altered to falsely claim Trump won the 2020 election (2021).

Next up: provocative social-advocacy ads. In 2013, "To all our atheist friends, 'Thank God You're Wrong,'" messaged the evangelical organization Answers in Genesis on the digital billboard on the corner of 42nd Street and Eighth Avenue. Freedom From Religion Foundation followed with a rejoinder: "OMG, there is no god!" In 2014, a provocative ad for an over-the-counter oral spray called SnoreStop—"keeping you together"—depicted a US soldier embracing a Muslim woman dressed in a niqab. When the company launched their #betogether campaign, they knew the billboard would command at least as much attention as the product, whose slogan is "If we can keep this couple together, we can keep anyone together." Finding a company to accept the "creative" had been difficult, the company spokesperson said. One major company flat-out rejected it, citing "its 'sensitive nature' and 'uncomfortable imagery.'" Although New York is the toughest market to place a billboard, the company did not experience an outpouring of rage. "It hasn't been burned down or anything."[48] And so it goes. The post-transformation market in Times Square signage attracts a gamut

**6.22** This blank billboard on 47th Street and Broadway is where the provocative advertisement for the adult-entertainment platform PornHub could be seen for forty-eight hours before it was removed after the hotel manager found it objectionable, 2014. Gary Hack.

**6.23** The "Fake News" electronic billboard ad at the corner of Broadway and 45th Street paid for by the Committee to Defend the President (formerly Stop Hillary PAC) chastises the media for not covering the investigation of Hillary Clinton's alleged campaign finance money-laundering scheme, 2017. The ad was yanked by the building's owner. Richard Levine/Alamy Stock Photo.

of advocates for and against the hot-bottom issues of the day: 9/11 truthers, same-sex marriage, animal rights, body image topics, ending an epidemic like AIDS, church membership, climate change, copyright infringement, Black Lives Matter, Covid-19 jab injuries. They keep coming and going, including advertisements for porn star Riley Reid.

Commercial purpose factors into a private owner's decision to accept a sign or reject it, as the cases above illustrate. In a 2010 profile interview for the *Times*, when asked if he ever rejected sign content, Jeffrey Katz of Sherwood Equities, owner of two signpost buildings in Times Square, responded: "The companies that advertise there are pretty much big companies and they're image-conscious, so it's pretty much self-policed. Every once and a while, you hear a crackpot idea and you've got to reel it back, but it doesn't happen very often." When people wanted to do political statements on the signs, his firm shied away from that. Those ads, he said, were usually for 30, 60, or 90 days. His big electronic LED ads had 10-year leases. When I spoke with him in 2021, advances in technology had so altered the signage business model that the duration of targeted images on the new billboards—nearly all digital, blinking away with thousands of colors—had become shorter and shorter: one or two minutes in a cycle of an hour or two. They come

**6.24** The company selling its over-the-counter oral spray SnoreStop sponsored this provocative billboard advertisement on Broadway at 52nd Street, 2014. Courtesy of SnoreStop.

and go so quickly—"flash in the pan"—that owners are less concerned with content; hot content is not likely to impact the building per se as in the past.[49] Yet, as in the cases above where content was pulled, owners of billboard property are not indifferent to negative reactions from clients or consumers.

Deliberately stoking controversy with hot-button ads is not just a Times Square phenomenon. Billboards have for many years been a go-to medium for expressing advocacy. The critically acclaimed film *Three Billboards Outside Ebbing, Missouri* exemplifies the power of the medium, in that case to increase awareness of an important issue in a rural community. It's hard to stand out in the visual chaos of Times Square, but shock advertisements get a lot of reaction on social media, and sponsors know that. A lot of billboards end up on social media, twitter selfies with a billboard in Times Square in the background. A provocative approach juices the clicks, helping to push the product or the cause. Not exactly a tried-and-true formula, wrote *Times* reporter Anthony Ramirez, it can work "for the occasional advertiser to try and stretch scant advertising dollars by submitting an advertisement so outrageous that the newspaper or magazine has no choice but to reject it."[50]

Clashes over social-issue content are not uncommon. For example, the owner of one screen rejected a commercial with gay content meant to promote tolerance. The spots, called "Why Not Love?/Get Used To It," showed two men fighting, then kissing. The Gay and Lesbian Alliance Against Defamation remained angry at the rejection. "Times Square is a very symbolic place," said its New York public affairs director. "Visibility is the way the lesbian and gay community can combat prejudice." That dispute, advertising columnist Elliot wrote, "raises a question crucial to social-issue signs: the role of the gatekeeper, almost always a private, for-profit company, in deciding whether a paid point of view should be promulgated." She would approve "anything controversial where there's a legitimate division of opinion," Tama Starr told Elliot in 1994. "But she would draw the line . . . at 'something that's so far out there, a really negative, hostile and destructive message that's not a moral use of the medium.' . . . 'Kill yourself' would not be acceptable,' [she] said. 'Go naked' would be."[51]

Today, most billboard ads are placed through big outdoor advertising agencies. Outfront Media, for example, has teams of people who review general ads and a different team for political ad approval. There is no absolute definition, chairman and CEO Jeremy Male told me when we spoke in early 2022. "With political ads, we want an attribution with a point of contact back to the sponsor; we ask approval from the building landlord, whether political or advocacy ads." "And you have to take geography into account," he said. "What may be okay in New York may not be okay in another part of the country." Male previously ran advertising for the London Underground. "What's changed over time," he said, "is that it is so much easier to run PR; for small amounts of money, you can get a huge audience. For advocates with a small budget, it's an easy way to spread their views." Outfront Media, he said, "will reject an ad proposal if it is overly misleading, inflammatory, anti-religious, outside the bounds of decency, or contains misinformation on Covid."[52]

"A private owner of property, in general, has a First Amendment right to refuse any content that the owner does not agree with," said David Cole, National Legal Director for the American Civil Liberties Union in an email response to a question I asked about a case he argued before the US Supreme Court for an artist who was refused a two-month rental of a sign in Penn Station for political art attacking the Coors Brewing Company on its financing of conservative causes. Public owners like the Metropolitan Transportation Authority or Amtrak, for example, cannot act as freely because government is bound by the First Amendment guarantee of free speech. "If government creates a 'public forum' by opening up a particular space to all comers on a first-come, first-served basis, then they can't turn someone away based on the content of what they say." In response to the brouhaha over the Calvin Klein underwear depicting models who appeared to be teenagers in sexually suggestive poses, in 1997 the MTA adopted new rules allowing transit officials to reject advertising for the subways, buses, or trains that are "disturbingly violent, demean racial or religious groups or show people who appear to be minors in sexually suggestive poses." Then in 2015, the authority's board voted to ban political advertising on the city's subways and buses to avoid the legal challenges it had faced after rejecting some ads with political messages.[53]

The advocacy arena has also always been an arena for public service announcements—to promote the sale of war bonds during World War II, for example, to educate the public about AIDS, to present charitable messages and patriotic phrases after the 9/11 terrorist attacks on New York, and during the Covid-19 pandemic to honor essential workers or inspire hope. The tones can change, sometimes overnight in times of stress and civic need. During the pandemic, Poster House, a museum dedicated exclusively to posters, and Times Square Arts collaborated on a project to fill Times Square's billboards (and other donated digital spaces in all five boroughs through LinkNYC kiosks on the city's streets and Silvercast billboards above the Lincoln Tunnel) with messages such

**6.25** This collage presents a sampling of the messages of love, gratitude, and solidarity with New York City's health care and essential workers that appeared on donated digital billboard spaces in Times Square and throughout all five boroughs of New York City, as well as in Boston and Chicago. The citywide initiative sponsored by Times Square Arts was launched by the collaborative efforts of Times Square Arts, Poster House, *Print* magazine, and For Freedoms, and involved more than thirty artists and designers. The artists, from top to bottom: Maria Kalman, Carrie Mae Weems, and Duke Riley, 2020. Courtesy of Ian Davis (top), Courtesy of Maria Baranova (middle and bottom).

as: "Thank You Essential Workers," "Stay Strong New York," "6 feet is 6 feet is 6 feet is 6 feet," among others. Rather than let signs go dark, some billboard owners filled their spaces with inspirational public service ads: "Staying home means saving lives," "Tough times don't last, tough people do," "We are in this together. We are stronger together," "To those fighting for our lives, THANK YOU."

## DIGITAL AGOG

On November 18, 2014, an executive of Vornado Realty Trust threw the switch on its gargantuan electronic video screen in Times Square. Mounted on the front of the Marriott Marquis hotel, the high-density digital display standing six stories tall wrapped around the entire block from 45th Street to 46th Street on Broadway—the center of the bowtie. The launch of the world's largest LED advertising display, also the largest billboard in Times Square's history, promised to "transform the media landscape with its interplay of art, commerce and technology that pushes the boundaries of scale and interactivity," the company said. With twenty-three million pixels, each containing tiny red, blue, and green lights, the attention-grabbing technology with its sharp images bright as day and fast-changing displays stopped pedestrians in their tracks. "Size matters in Times Square," said Harry Coghlan, president of Clear Channel Outdoor New York, which was selling the ad space. "Sometimes it just comes down to wanting to stand out, and it comes down to ego," he said.[54] Watching test images of skiers and fashion models illuminate the giant screen, he said tourists turned their heads to look at the sign, all agog. The sign display was holding people rapt—in the enduring tradition of Gude and Leigh.

Vornado, a New York-based publicly traded company, built this most expensive digital screen—the going rate for four weeks reportedly $2.5 million—as part of a $170 million redevelopment of the hotel's retail spaces. As visually sharp and vibrant as the content was, Vornado's president and chief executive, Steven Roth, told a *Times* reporter the technological advantage would not last long as other companies adopt similar bells and whistles. The two lasting advantages that would prevail, he said, are the new display's sheer size and its location.[55] Together with its ownership of the former Bertelsmann building at 1540 Broadway across the way, Vornado controls both sides of the Times Square bowtie knot.

LED technology ushered in a new era of outdoor advertising. The transformation was made possible by physicists' quest for the vital blue part of the semiconductor spectrum. After three decades of research and

**6.26** Giant LED billboard advertisements in the Times Square bowtie bright as day, legible and spectacular around the clock, 2019. Gary Hack.

experimentation, the invention of the elusive blue-light-emitting diode, for which Japanese scientists Isamu Akasaki, Hiroshi Amano, and Shuji Nakamura were awarded the 2014 Nobel Prize for physics, made it possible to create white light in a new way. Red and green LEDs had existed for nearly half a century, but the absence of blue made it impossible to create white light sources, and it is the very wide spectrum of white light that makes possible many more discernable colors. The laureates' inventions revolutionized LED technology, opening up new opportunities for a myriad of uses in everyday life. LED light is far more efficient than the cathode ray tube and fluorescent discharge tube of the Jumbotron large-screen video display. LED lights work longer and use less power than older light sources, and they allow designers to use light in ways they never have before. They are flexible light sources that allow the colors and intensity to vary, to blink, to change colors and patterns, all controlled by computers—all of which has made the signs of Times Square more colorful and flashier than ever before. "Incandescent lightbulbs lit the 20th century; the 21st century will be lit by LED lamps," said the Royal Swedish Academy of Sciences said in its Nobel award statement.

Interactive advertising on these LED screens came to Times Square in a way that would have pleased Gude and Leigh. It harnessed the power of social media, of mobile or web-based interactive media, to communicate with consumers and to promote products, brands, services, and public service announcements for corporate or political groups. The goal of interactive advertising was not only to entertain but to engage viewers, as Stonbely had done with direct promotional messages on his Spectacolor billboard. Now, the easily changeable displays of clear content using LED digital technology made possible new capabilities of joining social media and branded event advertising. And the creation of Times Square's pedestrian plazas has likely driven interactive ads. *Cosmopolitan* magazine, a popular publication for young women, for example, used Facebook Connect to allow viewers of its video on a Times Square billboard to share the video with friends and spread the message. In advance of the 2012 presidential election, Facebook users could share their political views on digital billboards in Times Square using a specially created app—2012 Matters: What Matters Most. Another push forward in interactive digital display is under construction: a massive LED spectacular display system at TSX Broadway that will bring more bright lights and theatrics to Times Square. The 46-story hotel and retail tower lit up by colorful LEDs will feature a nine-story screen that will wrap around the skyscraper at the southeast corner of Seventh Avenue and 47th Street. A 4,000-square-foot stage suspended 30 feet over 47th Street will allow entertainers to perform from "within" the video wall. This "immersive experience" is bound to hold people rapt.

Perhaps the most interesting expansion of LED illuminating technology to appear in Times Square was the unveiling of *Waterfall-NYC* (2021), a digital art installation sponsored by Samsung Electronics and d'strict, another South Korean company. This was truly a new spectacular: a digital ocean with hyperrealistic waves and a cascading waterfall descending the north end of One Times Square. The towering 350-foot display stacked with four vertical screens was nearly three times larger than the previous waterfall installation Olafur Eliasson brought to New York City in 2008. It played every two to four minutes in sixty-second increments during July and August 2021. In a break from the "traditional never-ending advertising landscape," the goal was to create surreal serenity: "a moment of complete calm in the heart of a city famous for its energy, noise and non-stop action."[56] Even surrounded by rapidly changing colorful billboard ads, it was the one digital display that held people rapt.

The blazing commercial iconography of the square dramatically projected in the supersized billboards lighting up the surrounding sky—the reason spectaculars were called "sky signs" when first mounted on those low-rise buildings—equally lit up the vast open arena of the square. In one-upmanship fashion, the digital spectaculars kept getting bigger and bigger. The vast electronic displays offering full-motion color video enabled by LED technology are larger and more numerous than ever; they mobilize "all the visual power of modern entertainment and consumer desire into a single, intense, almost overwhelming environment. 'You don't wander through it,' one critic observed of the New Times Square. 'It wanders through you.'"[57] The intense illumination of Times Square speaks to the magical energy of the city, the serendipitous encounters among strangers mesmerized by the scope and vitality of New York. It is a strand of the city's DNA, the embodiment of its distinctive commercial energy—rooted in an ability to innovate beyond what proved successful before.

The electronic wizardry in Times Square carries meaning beyond its brilliance and animation. Over the course of one-hundred-plus years of outrageous illumination, in each era the signs have spoken to the psyche of our national culture: the expansiveness of a going-out-on-the-town entertainment culture, the exciting technology that gave birth to the motion picture, the diminished illumination of wartime and promotion of Liberty Bonds, the pull of suburban living and deteriorating urban conditions reflected on blank billboards, the sexual revolution and accelerated corporate branding manifest in outdoor ads, and the emergence of financial-information mass marketing.

During multiple waves of the Covid pandemic, when we missed all the things we might have complained about before, everyday annoyances that made living in this city maddeningly difficult but wonderful nonetheless, Times Square was eerily quiet. The empty spaces of the place personified the loss of energy that had always been so vividly on display. The visual emptiness was unsettling. The scores of telltale photographs of a ghostly, empty Times Square recalled dystopian scenes that many of us of a certain age might have seen in Rod Sterling's 1959 TV series *Twilight Zone*.

The coronavirus shutdown of normal activity confirmed the iconic role of Times Square as the city's singular dramatis persona. Not just for New Yorkers. In newspapers across the globe, images of a deserted Times Square symbolized the question of how dense cities would recover, in an age when we might be living indefinitely with one variant or another of the virus. Once again people were packing up and leaving cities. Would they return? The uncertainty of the answer was unsettling.

# 7 BEYOND TIMES SQUARE

Cities change. It is their nature. Those which stop changing stop being cities.
Cities that change entirely, though, cease to be themselves.
Adam Gopnik, September 2015

It was always about to happen: development. Either high-rise office towers or more likely luxury residential towers. For Times Square's neighbor
to the west, that was the expectation, ever since the early 1970s when
the velocity of speculative acquisitions during the 1950s and '60s accelerated. By 1974, 35 percent of Clinton's land area—the blocks between
41st and 59th Streets west of Eighth Avenue to the Hudson River—had
been amassed in assemblages and held ready for development when
the time was ripe. The industrial lands to the west of Tenth Avenue
had been assembled to an even greater extent (41 percent) than the
more residential areas to the east (29 percent). The area was spotted
with vacant lots, parking lots, empty buildings, vacant storefronts,
and violation-ridden buildings—prime for redevelopment on a massive scale. In 1973, when the city approved a plan for construction of
a convention center along the Hudson River between 45th and 47th
Streets that was to be the largest exhibition center of its kind, community leaders foresaw the destruction of their neighborhood, and they
organized as activists for an alternative vision. In "Clinton: A Plan for
Preservation," prepared with community and city representatives, consultants Weiner/Gran Associates detailed what made Clinton a logical
area for the future expansion of the midtown business district. Actual

**7.1** The "absolutely unacceptable neighborhood" for new middle-class apartments reveals itself in this nighttime scene of Eighth Avenue in Hell's Kitchen, 1985. Matt Weber.

development might be two or more decades in the future, the consultants told the community, but it was just a matter of time.[1]

The certainty of development in this section of midtown, however many decades in the future, was rooted in a single unalterable fact: location. Clinton was threatened, not by housing abandonment so typical of other older areas in New York during the 1970s, but by redevelopment on a scale that "would effectively destroy it as a cohesive neighborhood." Located almost anywhere else in the city, the community's cohesiveness and its residents' tenacious loyalty to their turf despite old housing, declining population, and low average income "would be a model for low income communities," remarked the consultants. "As it happens, Clinton is sitting on what may become, in the relatively new future, some of the most valuable land in New York City."[2] That was the sixth-sense opportunity assemblage experts, practiced in a cunning task of patience, sought out, and its ripening was what long-term investors patiently waited for, waiting for a time when the demographics of residential change turned in their favor.

Over the decades, editors penned a steady stream of phrases to describe Eighth Avenue's unfulfilled potential and shifting personality on the western edge of the Deuce: "white elephant of the midtown real estate world" (1956), "finally making progress, gaining stature" (1966), "heading for better times" (1979), "present to future: dowdy to jaunty"

(1986), "grit to glitter" (1989), "seedy strip slowly gives ways to assaults of the squeaky clean" (1997), "dreary street of architectural leftovers, a motley avenue" (1999). Handicapped by a checkered reputation, Eighth Avenue's "identity crisis is growing acute," wrote David W. Dunlap in a *Times* lede in 1986. "Its name conjures images of doorways where drug dealers and prostitutes seek business, where drunks and addicts seek shelter. . . . It usually does not conjure images of big developers and luxury projects. But they are there, too."[3]

The real estate gold rush in Hell's Kitchen in anticipation of the spill-over effects of the 42nd Street project began in the mid-1980s, though only the boldest of developers actually put shovel into ground for construction in this neighborhood perpetually in transition. Fast forward a decade, a new skyline was rising in Clinton amid a helter-skelter profusion of construction cranes. The dramatic turnaround of 42nd Street and Times Square pushed forward by government actions had finally eliminated the choke point that had frustrated westward growth; now it was happening, and at a scale that could only be described as full-throttle gentrification. Developers were riding a "Times Square wave" of demand for apartments among singles and young professionals in this walk-to-work location fast becoming trendy. On that once-scorned stretch of far west 42nd Street—where Irving Maidman had once held such high hopes for new theater venues—residential tower after residential tower sprouted amid the upscaling of Theatre Row. From every direction, this socially distinct historic neighborhood was being dramatically remodeled by the trajectory of urban land use change.

## RIPE

Beginning in the mid-1980s, skyline-shaping luxury towers rose in a succession of waves that set in motion the transformation of the working-class neighborhood of Hell's Kitchen, aka Clinton, into a trendy upscale area for young professionals working in nearby office buildings. The first developers to break ground for new privately financed market-rate apartment towers leapfrogged over the gritty corridor of Eighth Avenue—through the 1970s and much of the '80s, one of the seediest strips in the city, home to adult movie houses, pross hotels, and a dense concentration of single-room-occupancy lodgings and populated with drug sellers and users, prostitutes, and down-and-out transients—to the industrial spheres of Tenth and Eleventh Avenues. The nascent residential development was just outside the Clinton preservation area in which buildings of more than seven stories or 66 feet were prohibited, among other restrictions designed to preserve the older urban fabric and keep the neighborhood's housing supply affordable.

Harry Macklowe was one of half a dozen real estate men acquiring property in that remote sector occupied by parking lots, gas stations, auto repair shops, warehouses, and other low-slung servicing facilities, including horse stalls for the Central Park carriage trade and, at one time, the Police Department's Mounted Unit. He built the first rental tower in the area, the 42-story Riverbank West (1987), on an Eleventh Avenue parking lot he bought from Fred Papert's 42nd Street Development Corporation, and he made sure to include amenities like a health club and retail space because there were few shops nearby.

Twenty years earlier, the opening of Manhattan Plaza established a residential beachhead on West 42nd Street, but as a subsidized project in the rapidly declining environment primarily filled with residents working in the performing arts, it did not test the market for residential living west of the Deuce. The first privately financed project came online in 1983, a reconstruction of the former Army Reserve Training Center (originally built as administrative offices by the Western Electric Corporation) far west on 42nd Street near Eleventh Avenue, converted by Lewis Futterman into 159 cooperative apartments after adding three stories to the two existing six-story buildings. It was a harbinger of future development activity, but conversion of a modest-size building footprint in an area of warehouses, storage facilities, and gas stations, all west of a notable railroad easement, did not set off alarm bells in Clinton.

On the other hand, the opening of Macklowe's market-rate Riverbank West became "a symbol for community residents of the towering potential of gentrification surrounding the preservation area." "We don't want to become a walled-in community," said the then-current chairwoman of Community Board 4.[4] Not long after Riverbank West, on a Tenth Avenue site of six run-down two- and four-story buildings serving as warehouses, Arun Bhatia opened a 41-story condominium, The Strand (1988). Next up, on the midblock portion of the full-block site of the former Madison Square Garden on Eighth Avenue between 49th and 50th Streets, William Zeckendorf Jr. placed the 38-story residential condominium tower of his huge mixed-use project and a block-face of five- and six-story condominiums facing Ninth Avenue; he named the complex, which includes a 50-story office tower, Worldwide Plaza (1989). Then construction activity abruptly stopped as developers and bankers confronted a collapsed market and the distress of a deep real estate recession. The evidence of irreversible change, however, loomed large: the natural forces that drive New York City real estate

**7.2** In this aerial view of West Midtown, Worldwide Plaza is distinguished by its pyramid top; the image shows the three components of the pathbreaking project developed by Zeckendorf Development on a full city block between 49th and 50th Streets, Eighth and Ninth Avenues: office tower on Eighth Avenue, midblock condominium tower, and low-rise condominium units facing Ninth Avenue and lining 50th Street. Courtesy of Max Touhey.

development were going to redevelop Eighth Avenue in Hell's Kitchen; it was just a matter of time.

The construction cranes reappeared after a seven-year lull, in a different context. Decisive progress on the 42nd Street Development Project had wiped away the decade-long uncertainty surrounding the goal of transforming the Deuce. State and local officials had amended their early policy missteps and were winning case after case of seemingly endless litigation over the project. They had banished the porn and the threatening clouds that hung over that legacy with a sequence of announcements, as surefire as any might be, of confidence-building investment commitments: the Disney Company's commitment to revitalize the legendary New Amsterdam Theatre (1994) (followed three years later with the Hercules Electric Parade of lighted floats along a 1.8-mile route of 42nd Street/Times Square to mark the theater's opening); the gala opening of the New Victory, New York's first full-time performing arts center for children (1995); and the Durst Organization's announcement that it was purchasing the development rights to build an office tower on the northeast corner of 42nd Street, followed shortly thereafter with its announcement that the global media company Condé Nast would anchor the proposed tower (1996). Having acquired title to the last of the blighted parcels on the block in 1995, the New York State Urban Development Corporation cleared the Deuce of its last porn tenant less than a year later. Other announcements in 1995 heralded the coming of Madame Tussauds and a multicinema complex on the south side of the block, a hotel and entertainment complex on the north side, and a Canadian theater company with plans to combine the Apollo and Lyric Theatres to form an 1,850-seat Broadway musical theater.

The biggest pieces of the project were falling into place, finally. Lusty accounts of momentum building in Times Square were plentiful. Sidewalk traffic jams in the square made news. The business press put out upbeat articles about the district's renaissance spilling over to "blighted" Eighth Avenue. Only a few years earlier, a realty executive commenting on a client's purchase of Eighth Avenue property said, "It was like buying on the futures market, betting on a perception of the way 42d Street is going."[5]

Developers read the tea leaves of 42nd Street's transformation in terms of expansive development opportunities adjacent to Times Square. "You can see it already," said Bill Rudin, president of the family-run Rudin Management Company, which was developing the new Reuters Building on Seventh Avenue between 42nd and 43rd Streets. "The garment district is in transformation. New neighborhoods are being created. What's happening on 42d Street is already beginning to spread to the south, to the west and up Eighth Avenue."[6] In the early 1990s, though, the general sense among the real estate community was that the anticipated change was not likely to happen immediately. Despite a flurry of land-buying activity, residential developers were finding it hard to make the numbers pencil out, based on their views of rents that would have to be charged to support the costs of construction. Also, many were still wary of the area's past problems: pornography shops, antidevelopment sentiment in the Hell's Kitchen neighborhood, and a reluctance of corporations to consider Eighth Avenue as an office location.

From a real estate perspective, Eighth Avenue had a split personality. It was both the back door to the commercially active theater district of Times Square and the front door to the activist residential Clinton neighborhood of long-time renters and numerous social, civic, small business, and religious organizations. The southern portion anchored by the Port Authority Bus Terminal was dense with the tourist, visitor, and commercial activities of Times Square, including adult-entertainment businesses and transient accommodations; the northern portion, from 49th to 53rd Streets, in contrast, had no adult uses, and retail businesses along this section of the avenue catered directly to the needs of residents and local office workers.

The revival of New York's economy in the mid-1990s did much to unfetter developers' ambitions for building in Clinton, increasingly referenced by its revived historic name preferred by its older residents, Hell's Kitchen. The time was ripe. The rental market in Manhattan was hot, and especially so in Hell's Kitchen. "Hell's Kitchen Is Burning," headlined the *Village Voice*, bringing awareness of the anguish long-term residents felt about the squeeze facing the community, surrounded by development pressures from all sides save its west edge where the Hudson River reigns. "This is the moment that I think people have feared the most since the 1960s, when the City condemned land and wanted to bulldoze the entire neighborhood," local historian and long-time resident Mary Brendle told reporter J. A. Lobbia. "Now, on 42nd Street beyond Tenth Avenue, there's luxury towers. Trump [from Riverside South] is moving down. Eighth Avenue is getting much bigger, and we'll be left stuck inside this little box." The robust market, Lobbia explained, "is bolstered by an unprecedentedly clear shift in city policy that backs developers and landlords."[7]

For developers, Hell's Kitchen was a location whose time had come. The first wave of towers tested the market; success encouraged others to follow. The boom in office construction in Times Square was fueling a robust demand for housing. Some of the projects put on hold during the previous decade now went forward, including two on Eighth Avenue at 50th Street proximate to Worldwide Plaza: the 26-story Longacre (1997) and the 40-story Gershwin (1998). Developers started many more based on a firm belief that the market was capable of attracting what brokers called "a decidedly upmarket clientele." Still, Eighth Avenue was an out-there location, "something of a castaway among Manhattan's north-south thoroughfares." Longtime *Times* reporter Iver Peterson called it "a real estate no-man's-land between midtown's high-rise office boom to the east, the garment district's manufacturing zone to the south and the low-rise, aging Clinton neighborhood to the west." A decade earlier, Rose Associates, a generational New York real estate family firm, had ventured forth with the 29-story Ellington (1987) after building the Sheffield Apartments (1978) just off Eighth Avenue on West 57th Street. "When we did the Sheffield, everyone thought we were crazy,"

**7.3** Before developers began to build residential towers on Eighth Avenue in the Times Square district, it was full of everyday restaurants, liquor stores, hotels, and parking lots—and pornographer publisher Al Goldstein's Screw Cinema, at 46th Street (pictured in 1976), where admission was 99 cents. © JackFalat.com.

said Adam R. Rose. "They said that Eighth Avenue was an absolutely unacceptable neighborhood and no one would live there."[8] The Sheffield reportedly rented up quickly.

By 2007, the incoming tide was obvious. The "reinvention of Eighth Avenue isn't only happening on the street level, but across the skyline as well, with the addition of distinctive towers along what is quickly becoming the Avenue of Architecture," stated a task force on Eighth Avenue organized by the Times Square Alliance. In "Sign of the Times: Eighth Avenue on the Rise," the group of community members, real estate brokers, architects, landscape architects, residents, and area constituents participating in the planning exercise put together a boosterish eight-step action plan for the continued development of the Eighth Avenue corridor, "a roadmap to accelerate the changes that have already begun to take place." The coordinated effort to address "complicated issues" that affected the avenue included a thirty-six-month timeline for implementation.[9] Market momentum was strong.

Twenty-four privately developed new residential towers sprouted in Hell's Kitchen during a robust second wave of construction (1996 to 2009), more than three times the number completed during the short first wave (1986 to 1989). Construction could start quickly on sites

**7.4** Gary Barnett of Extell Development plans (as of 2022) to build a 1,350-key tower hotel on most of this Eighth Avenue blockfront between 45th and 46th Streets, the same block where Al Goldstein's Screw Cinema once offered hard-core porn to its patrons, as did the Venus and Eros Theaters shown in this 1985 photo of the avenue. Around 1996, the Venus and Eros were shuttered and renovated into trendy theater-crowd eateries. Matt Weber.

assembled decades earlier, ready-to-build sites cleared of buildings and kept in a holding pattern as parking lots—a condition that makes land more negotiable, especially in an area of fragmented landholdings. The area's "relatively fringe location preserved many large development sites, particularly along 42nd Street," said Vitali Ogorodnikov, real estate editor, reporter, and compiler of a data base of residential towers over 30 stories built in Mid-Manhattan (defined as 14th to 59th Streets, river to river). Yet the jumbled landholdings and resistant hold-out owners meant some development sites would take years to assemble. Gary Barnett of Extell Development, an ambitious developer of high-rise towers in Manhattan, for example, began piecing together lots on a valuable theater district block on Eighth Avenue (where Al Goldstein had his Screw Cinema) in 2014; by fall 2021, he controlled eleven of the fourteen lots (three holdouts "wouldn't sell for a reasonable price,"[10] but he had nearly a full block face for development of a hotel tower).

Nowhere was the real estate impact of the transformation of the Deuce more apparent than on the far reaches of 42nd Street. It was "virgin territory" in the eyes of the development community. "There's really no negative infrastructure," said one developer, "since it was formerly industrial." The character of the area, he forecast, would be remade over

**7.5** A view of New York's frenzied development corridor along the far reaches of 42nd Street, dense with new residential towers, 2022. Gary Hack.

the next decades with towers, shops, restaurants, and bars geared to the needs of the new residents. "We're filling in the blocks," an executive of the family-run Gotham Organization told *Times* reporter Charles V. Bagli, speaking about far West 42nd Street.[11] In 1996, the company had opened The New Gotham, a 33-story luxury apartment house on a vacant midblock site on 43rd Street between Tenth and Eleventh Avenues, once the location of a piano factory; later it would develop a second rental building, the 18-story Nicole (2003) on West 55th, and then a third, the 31-story Gotham West (2013) on 45th Street close to

Eleventh Avenue. Hell's Kitchen was becoming more mainstream, no longer out on the edge. Gentrification had taken hold. Eighth Avenue turned into "the city's most frenzied development corridor."[12] By 2008, developers had filled the eight far west blocks of 42nd and 43rd Streets with no fewer than eleven residential towers, the shortest of which rose 23 stories, the tallest 60. By 2021, standing at Eighth Avenue and 42nd Street looking westward you saw a high-rise phalanx of glass, steel, and concrete, sixteen towers strong, in march formation all the way to the Hudson River.

The developers' construction crusade was striking to some, fearsome to others. The physical heart of Hell's Kitchen may have been sheltered from skyscraper development by the zoning regulations of the Special Clinton District, but it could not forestall the economically driven trajectory of land use change on its perimeter. The complex zoning arrangement negotiated for the special district actually shaped the form of future development. By permitting towering residential projects to surround a low-density core, it mapped the neighborhood's physical trajectory. "The zoning is fluked, and it's very easy to build high," said Peter Schleissner, a 10-year Clinton resident and chairman of Community Board 4, when he was asked about the area's first towers in 1987. "The development along West 42nd Street is putting a wall in the middle of a community, because Clinton goes from 34th to 59th Streets."[13] The section below 42nd Street known as Hell's Kitchen South was slower to transition, but what Schleissner foresaw in 1987 would unfailingly come to pass.

Beginning in 1989, in a series of actions, the city rezoned specific blocks of Clinton between Tenth and Eleventh Avenues from a manufacturing zone to high-density commercial, which triggered construction of thousands of residential units, including hundreds of affordable units, in new developments. A decade later, more development opportunity. In 1998, a zoning change expanded the boundaries of the Special Theater District and opened a slice of the west face of Eighth Avenue between 42nd and 45th Streets to high-rise development by permitting the transfer of development rights from designated Broadway theaters on side streets to receiving zones anywhere within the Theater Subdistrict, allowing for much larger buildings along the avenue. In 2011, citing "increased development trends" in the Clinton neighborhood demonstrating that the western portion of Clinton (generally the area west of Tenth Avenue) "is a desirable place to live," the Department of City Planning and Community Board 4 successfully proposed a rezoning of an eighteen-block area of the West Clinton neighborhood to

**7.6** This map of the Special Clinton District clearly delimits the perimeter area (B) where high-density development is permitted, as well as the preservation, excluded, and other areas of the special district. Within the perimeter area, theater bonus incentives apply in the cross-hatched area (subarea 2) where Theatre Row is located. New York City Department of City Planning.

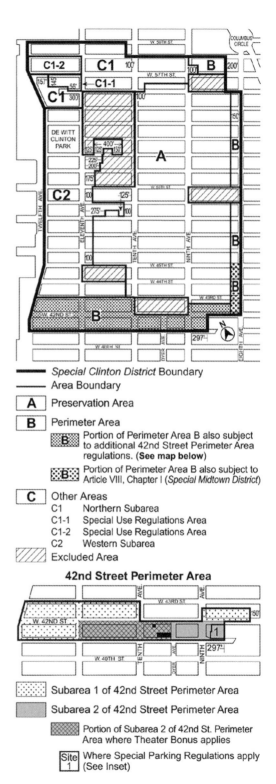

Special Clinton District Boundary
Area Boundary

| A | Preservation Area |
| B | Perimeter Area |

Portion of Perimeter Area B also subject to additional 42nd Street Perimeter Area regulations. (**See map below**)

Portion of Perimeter Area B also subject to Article VIII, Chapter I (*Special Midtown District*)

| C | Other Areas |

C1    Northern Subarea
C1-1  Special Use Regulations Area
C1-2  Special Use Regulations Area
C2    Western Subarea

Excluded Area

**42nd Street Perimeter Area**

Subarea 1 of 42nd Street Perimeter Area

Subarea 2 of 42nd Street Perimeter Area

Portion of Subarea 2 of 42nd St. Perimeter Area where Theater Bonus applies

Site 1  Where Special Parking Regulations apply (See Inset)

provide for residential development, including affordable housing, and to encourage new manufacturing-compatible uses between Eleventh and Twelfth Avenues. The city's unambiguous messages were empowering more development in Hell's Kitchen.

If developers had proceeded cautiously in the 1980s and '90s, testing out the market, in the first decade of the new millennium they were on a tear to capture profits, building at the hot edge of a real estate market following an amazing recovery from the catastrophe of 9/11. After the severe recession of 2008–2009 (this one triggered by the collapse of Lehman Brothers), developers once again picked up where they left off, producing sixteen more residential towers. During this third wave (2011–2021), they built massive structures, amenity-filled, with hundreds of mostly studio and one-bedroom units designed to appeal to a young, mobile crowd drawn to the diverse and dynamic scene in Hell's Kitchen (and feeling priced out of the West Village or Chelsea)—young professionals on a stop along the way in their lives.

Over the course of three waves of development, by my tally developers had built some forty-eight residential towers (16 stories or taller) in Hell's Kitchen with approximately 19,000 new units, including some 2,800 affordable units. Although height restrictions prevailed in the Preservation Area, at least fourteen buildings with some 1,700 units (154 affordable) were newly constructed there. As a result of all this activity, the neighborhood's population surged nearly 47 percent, from 40,595 (2000) to 45,884 (2010) to 59,524 (2020). Growth during the last decade was especially dramatic: Hell's Kitchen was one of three Manhattan neighborhoods gaining more than 13,000 residents (with Chelsea-Hudson Yards and the Financial District-Battery Park as the other two). The increase in housing units in Community Board 4 (Clinton/Chelsea) certified for occupancy during the first two decades of the twenty-first century, 28,242 (or 25 percent of all Manhattan units), exceeded every other district in the city; only Greenpoint/Williamsburg came close with 26,280 units certified for occupancy.

It had taken decades. In 1984, when he boldly ventured "so very far west" and purchased the full block of West 42nd at the Hudson River, Larry Silverstein called those industrial lands "barren"; now his twin 60-story Silver Towers (2001, 2009) and 40-story River Place (1999) offered tenants stunning views of the sunset over the Hudson River. "How does a developer measure time when time just seems to stretch on and on?" a reporter asked Silverstein as his "monumental" twin-tower project was finally starting to rise in 1999 after 15 years of

**7.7** The completion of Larry Silverstein's efforts to develop the westernmost block of West 42nd Street between Eleventh and Twelfth Avenues, a "barren" industrial area, which he had purchased in 1984: *Silver Towers October Sunset*, 2009. Creative Commons CMMooney, CC BY-ND 2.0.

rezoning issues, litigation, and the ups and downs of the real estate market. "Well, I have six grandchildren I did not have when I bought the property," he said.[14]

One transformation had followed another. The market-driven transformation of far west 42nd Street, emblematic of the changes across Hell's Kitchen, followed the public sector's transformation of the Deuce. It was the latest industrial district of the city to reinvent itself, and it was as dramatic a transformation as Manhattan had witnessed in its history of changing land uses.

The neighborhood was now dense with high-rise rentals, condos and co-ops, trendy restaurants and artisan food shops, and the amenities of the newcomers' upscale lifestyles (pre-pandemic). "Call it Hell's Renovated Kitchen," wrote *Times* reporter Joseph Berger.[15] High-rise development had rewoven the fabric of the working-class neighborhood once closely tied to an industrial waterfront and that later served as a "backstage" community for the theater industry initially attracted by the cheap rents. It was a chill foil to Times Square. "Ruled by folklore,"

**7.8** An "identifiably New York" block in Hell's Kitchen in the Special Clinton District; in the far rear loom the W Hotel and other towers in Times Square, 2022. Gary Hack.

remarked a long-time community activist.[16] Many old landmarks were gone, though not all. On the side streets, the core of Hell's Kitchen still feels like an old-school neighborhood, chockablock with four- and five-story tenements, many now renovated, some converted to condominiums. Though it is not the same neighborhood long-time residents fondly recall, in character it remains diverse—in streetscapes, building types, local institutions, and people. It still houses a mix of young and old who value the convenience of its walk-to-work location. Over the decades of growth, the demographic profile of the neighborhood has grown more diverse. Eighth Avenue has not lost all its grit, yet. The adult DVD store The Playpen and Gotham City Video still ply their goods at 43rd Street. Change is still a part of the urban equation there.

## "TO STRIKE A BALANCE"

The manifest impacts from the explosion of commercial and residential development in Hell's Kitchen were twofold. On the one hand, the development boom intensified pressure on properties that were affordable. On the other hand, it created opportunities to accelerate the pace of redevelopment in the Clinton Urban Renewal Area. Real tension existed between the two. Hell's Kitchen might be one of the most development-pressured neighborhoods in the city, but the six-block urban renewal area from 50th to 56th Streets between Tenth and

Eleventh Avenues—perhaps the largest parcel of developable, mostly city-owned land in Manhattan south of 96th Street—was the best prospective resource for increasing the community's stock of affordable housing.

Established in 1969, at the tail end of the city's urban renewal program, the CURA area, as it was known, was originally earmarked for 3,000 units of subsidized housing, 1,000 low-income units, and 2,000 moderate- and middle-income units. (When the Special Clinton District was created, these blocks were "excluded" from the 1974 regulations.) The city took title to some properties through its powers under the urban renewal program and razed dozens of homes; when the Nixon administration ended the program in 1974, federal money to redevelop the properties dried up, and none was available locally as New York City struggled with a bruising fiscal crisis. Many buildings sat empty. Some former building owners managed to hang on, continuing to rent space in structures now owned by the city, which had become a reluctant landlord. Between 1979 and 1981, with what was left of the federal funds before the money ran out, the city built four major assisted housing developments (including a public housing complex) with a total of 1,498 units for low- and moderate-income families and seniors. The Koch administration (1978–1989) then turned to encouraging luxury residential development in Clinton (and other increasingly desirable neighborhoods), though it was blocked by organized community opposition for years.

There was no question that the forces driving real estate development in New York would seize the opportunity awaiting in the tenement-filled neighborhood in a prime midtown location. The inevitability of change, even in a neighborhood that had successfully advocated for special preservation zoning, was obvious—developers had started to arrive in force in the mid-1980s. "There are big economic pressures on the area now, and history shows that economic pressures rule," said Stephen Wolf, owner of the 116-year-old Wolf Paint Company on Ninth Avenue at 56th Street.[17] Wolf had twice chaired Community Board 4, and he had been instrumental in setting up the special district in 1974.

Already, two residential towers on West 43rd Street were under construction. Zeckendorf was clearing a site he owned on Eighth Avenue between 57th and 58th Streets (which had taken six years to assemble) and, as discussed in earlier chapters, he had purchased the full-block site once home to Madison Square Garden—what he called "the city's largest open-air parking lot"—on Eighth between 49th and 50th Streets. Other large, blockfront properties on Eighth Avenue, either vacant or parking lots, were obvious development sites in waiting. Land prices were rising rapidly; almost any piece of property, whatever its outward appearance, was valuable. "You have to buy around here in tomorrow's dollars," remarked one broker, who believed the major projects would trigger further development on a smaller scale.[18] The activity was all of a type—and it stoked the fears of community leaders and longtime residents who had a very different vision for their neighborhood.

Their vision became strikingly clear in a four-year protracted battle over the Koch administration's plan to sell two sites on 52nd Street at Tenth Avenue in the stalled 17-year-old urban-renewal area to private developers for market-rate housing. Selected under a request for proposals from his Housing Preservation and Development Department, the developers planned to replace the existing buildings—"a row of turn-of-the-century tenements, a few modest storefronts, a gas station, and around the corners, empty lots, half-empty buildings, auto repair shops and," reporter Martin Gottlieb added, "for the last few days an unforgiving wind spinning off the Hudson River two blocks away"—with a pair of towers "with rents that, for the most part, would be higher than anything offered in the neighborhood until recently."[19] They planned a total of 780 apartments, 20 percent of which would be subsidized for below-market rents. The McManus group, which was "a big pusher for the CURA establishment," told the city not to worry; they would get the community behind the project, according to Joe Restuccia's recounting of the episode.[20] This did not happen.

When it came up for review in a public hearing before the City Planning Commission in early 1986, the two-block private housing plan was greeted with hostility and skepticism by organized community interests, including longtime residents, businessmen, and performing artists who felt the city had turned its back on the original intention of the special district to save the heart of the Clinton neighborhood by preserving its older physical fabric. If the project was approved, many feared it would change the neighborhood forever with two "in-your-face towers" facing the special district. Outside the preservation core, development forces were pressing, and, as Paul Goldberger wrote at the time, "many residents of the Clinton area, community activists and planners have begun to question whether even the industrial blocs west of 10th Avenue ought not be saved."[21]

The community countered with pressure. Carrying a big red-and-black banner that read "Love and Defend Clinton," CURA residents converged on City Hall for the Board of Estimate hearing on the project. Under intense pressure from charges of political favoritism and lacking the votes on the Board of Estimate, Mayor Koch abruptly canceled the two-block private housing plan and said the site would be auctioned instead. An auction was going to cut out the local community, which had drafted its own plan for the site, and would also "cut out anyone who wants to do low-income housing," Margot Lewitin, a community leader, told David Dunlap. Local interests defeated this plan—"a victory with a bitter taste. But still, it was a victory," remarked one activist. Following the defeat, Koch, wouldn't do anything for the neighborhood, and the buildings "just hung around forever," recalled Restuccia, the longtime influential executive director of the not-for-profit housing developer Clinton Housing Development Company.[22] Years later, CHDC would develop most of this western end of the CURA block, a story told further on.

Much more was at stake than just the two sites in CURA, as Goldberger emphasized in his reporting on the official review of the administration's plan for the two apartment towers before the City Planning Commission. The real subject ran much deeper. "It was the very future of Clinton itself, and the question of to what extent this complex and ramshackle neighborhood on the west side of Manhattan ought to be rebuilt at all." Not a few urban observers thought it might be better to clear away the abandoned buildings because such buildings poison neighborhoods. Renovating seriously deteriorated tenements was not viewed as a viable option; considered at the scale of city-owned buildings seized for nonpayment of taxes, the costs were prohibitive, "far above what the city can afford," said Joseph Shuldiner, who was in charge of city-owned residential properties. The underlying thread of the debate, Goldberger said, "eerily recalls the arguments over urban renewal that were common a generation ago, when tearing down old buildings and replacing them with tall towers was standard operating procedure."[23]

In response to the city's plan for sweeping demolition and displacement of the renewal area, a group called the Clinton Preservation Local Development Corporation (empowered with some of the "quid pro quo" funds from the 42nd Street Development Project)—what *Times* reporter Gottlieb called a "novel coalition" of residents, local entrepreneurs, and performing arts organizations supported by Community Board 4—had commissioned an alternative plan. Prepared by Peterson Littenberg Architects, the plan was considered "highly sophisticated" by architectural reviewers for its commitment to preserving all of the site's existing tenement stock through renovation while maintaining the area's historic commercial and light-industrial character. "It was the

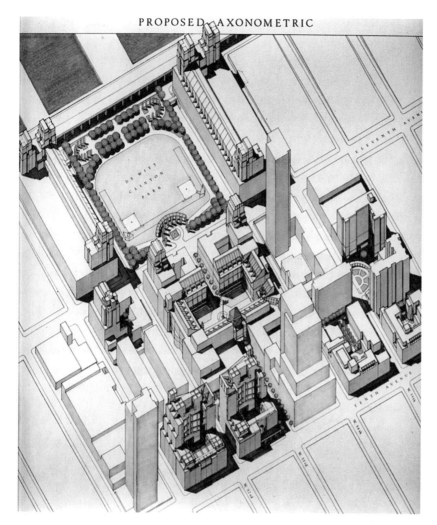

**7.9** The award-winning plan for the urban renewal area of Clinton prepared by Peterson Littenberg Architects in 1988 was commissioned by a local community group in response to the city's plan for sweeping demolition and displacement of six blocks of Clinton. The alternative plan was sensitive to the community's vision and neighborhood context, but the city could not see beyond the prevailing clearance model of urban renewal. Courtesy of Peterson Littenberg Architects.

right direction for Clinton," said Goldberger, who praised the plan and the character of Hell's Kitchen as being "the closest thing left in Manhattan to a true mixed-use neighborhood . . . and a true ethnic mix in its population."[24]

The community's alternative plan did not shy away from providing a significant amount of new housing in two apartment buildings, but "reversing the developers' formula, would provide only 20 percent of the units at market rate while the remainder would serve low- and moderate-income tenants." The goal was to keep small businesses as well as the many artists living in Clinton. The large-scale plan—praised as "a landmark for New York . . . decisive in its rejection of proposals for a generation or more in favor of an urbanism of streets and squares"—won the coveted Urban Design Award from *Progressive Architecture* magazine in 1990—but nothing happened.[25] The Department of Housing Preservation and Development, the city's administrative unit for the renewal area, said the proposal was too impractical and too costly; it also did not believe the community group could execute the plan. Several years would pass before department officials saw the wisdom of preservation. It would come in 1993, when officials told the community board that it would consider the board's proposals for the renewal area and then agreed to the rehabilitation of buildings in the urban renewal area, including the parcels on the contested block at 52nd Street and Tenth Avenue.

This change in policy came about because the city needed something from the community: space to temporarily house sixty sanitation trucks in an old bus depot at 30th Street and Twelfth Avenue. Most neighborhoods had strongly opposed housing the buses in their areas.

**7.10** This lovely, keyed community garden on West 51st Street (pictured in 2022) was created in the mid-1990s as part of the rehabilitation of five tenement buildings and a vacant lot in Clinton (frequented by drug addicts) and later was expanded to serve as an entrance to the new Irish Arts Center on Eleventh Avenue. It is dedicated to the memory of Juan Alonso, a long-time resident and devoted community gardener. Gary Hack.

Facing a loss of $95 million in federal funds for reconstructing the Williamsburg Bridge if it did not find a site, the city "acceded" to the community demands that it rehabilitate six buildings in the renewal area and to three other requests. The tradeoff got the community forty-four units of affordable housing (554 West 52nd Street) in renovated buildings and the Juan Alonso Community Garden (565 West 51st Street), both developed by CHDC.[26]

Hell's Kitchen was squeezed between two realities: the first wave of market-driven private development and the city's out-of-date approach to the neighborhood's existing housing. "What we've always been interested in is controlled growth and encouraging housing for a mix of incomes, ages and professions, which Clinton has always had," said a community board chair. It was a neighborhood—"not just land." That's what the community board and many other dedicated local organizations wanted to preserve and sustain with affordable housing for low- and moderate-income families and individuals. They wanted to provide for the residents who were there, to work with the existing housing stock, rehabilitating as much as possible and retaining as many existing residential, commercial, and cultural tenants as feasible. And they wanted flexibility from the city government and the private sector to develop and preserve affordable housing. "The city is about change," said Joe Restuccia. "It doesn't mean that change gets to wipe out the people and the places that were there. I don't subscribe to wholesale change; that's when you have lots of problems. That's a really old idea for cities."[27]

Restuccia and the Clinton Housing Development Company would come to play an outsized role in the preservation and creation of affordable housing in Clinton/Hell's Kitchen and Chelsea. The activism that became Restuccia's life and work at CHDC stood in sharp contrast to what he had in mind when he moved to New York in 1979 to pursue a career in theater production. Trained as a stage director, he was working at Theatre Row in a tenement building on Ninth Avenue (where he was burglarized twice), producing a workshop series; at times, he would cut out during the day and usher at Playwrights Horizons for "great money," $7. He was living by going from "couch to couch." Then as so often happens in New York, an "apartment" changed his life—although the space he moved into hardly qualified as such: the fifth-floor walk-up unit was totally burned out, entirely black from soot; all the windows were sealed with tin; there was no front door, no electricity, and no gas; the bathroom was nothing, and the kitchen was a pipe in the wall, as he recalled in a podcast interview. The six-room "apartment"

**7.11** Joe Restuccia (standing) at a Community Board 4 meeting discussing the first steps of a plan to battle architects and owners who illegally harass tenants out of their rent-regulated homes, 2015. Courtesy of Winnie McCroy.

was in a building on West 35th Street abandoned by the owner and taken over by the city in 1978; it was available for $225 a month, and he could apply for it, "But it required a little bit of work," he was told.

Besides fixing up the place, the other condition of a move-in was that he join the building's tenant association, which needed a vice president, a position for which he had no experience. A month into his residency, in the middle of a tenant association meeting, the group was served with legal papers saying the former owner (through the owner's bank lender) was taking the building back. "And that was very curious," he said, "because he was dead at the time." Restuccia and his tenant association eventually won the fight to keep the building. Not long after that, he was offered a job as a tenant organizer at the nonprofit organization Housing Conservation Coordinators (established in 1972) working on housing issues in other buildings around the neighborhood. In 1983, he joined CHDC and three years later became the organization's executive director. On the front lines of community activism, he would face the full force of gentrification.

In 1984, vacant buildings began to appear in Hell's Kitchen en masse; arson and harassment of tenants were commonplace—there was a real sense that development was happening, he told me in an interview for this book. There was a lot of fear. The neighborhood had not yet begun to gentrify, but the plan for the cleanup and redevelopment of West 42nd Street was in motion. It seemed certain to drive up real estate values, increase tenant harassment, and potentially force out residents of low, moderate, and middle incomes. Community Board 4 had come out against it. In his position as chair of several Community Board 4 task forces, including the one dealing with Times Square's redevelopment, Restuccia would lead community negotiations and settlements with the city for affordable housing renovation and acquisitions, as described in chapter 4.

Managing growth on the cusp of neighborhood change would become very difficult. It would test community leaders' ability to counter the transactional nature of real estate in a rapidly gentrifying neighborhood. "You can't stop change ever," Restuccia said; "our goal in the neighborhood is to manage it, protect the people who are there, get something for them." That was what would drive his negotiations with developers and the city. "In every step of the way, what I've learned is that you can pick from two choices: one is, you say, 'This is horrible on principle; we are against it; we're going to speak out against it, testify.' Or, you can say, 'This is horrible, but we have to sit down and figure out a way to make it work somehow in order to get something for our neighborhood.' This is an older political tradition, frustrating, but extremely successful with mega-projects."[28]

Zeckendorf's Worldwide Plaza presented one such case. The site was "excluded" from the Special Clinton District, and so exempt from its regulatory restrictions, which meant it could be built much larger and at much greater density than the rest of the special district. "There was no question that this complex was going to change the neighborhood dramatically," Zeckendorf wrote in an autobiography of his life as a developer, published posthumously. "The housing stock in Clinton was in terrible shape. Whatever tenements and brownstones on the blocks around our site hadn't been boarded up or taken over as flophouses were occupied largely by rent-controlled tenants, mostly the elderly and the working poor." He knew the local residents had a vested interest in what happened in their neighborhood, and, he said, "they were very vocal with their objections to our plans: the project was too big; development would force out existing residents and drive-up prices in the area; the design was ugly. And I, as the developer, was the Bad Guy."[29]

The scale of the project "is not exactly modest," remarked Goldberger; "1.5 million square feet of office space rising 45 stories, plus a residential tower going up 38 stories, is hardly ever going to slip quietly into the cityscape." The proposed $500 million complex would unquestionably make a powerful impact on its location and the wider Clinton community, and its transformative character was a signal of what was likely to come in the not so distant future. "Worldwide Plaza was one issue that no one was indifferent to," said Ruth Kahn, chair of Community Board 4 at the time Zeckendorf and his investment partnership were trying to gain board approval.[30] When Zeckendorf announced his proposal for the site, CB4 had quickly passed a resolution opposing it.

Not everyone agreed with a small group of opponents, the Clinton Coalition of Concern, ideologically against development, recalled Mary Brendle, a former chair of CB4. The resolution against the project was "ludicrous because everybody waited 15 years for the development of that site." The neighborhood needed affordable housing, and others were willing to try to accommodate development as long as they got something for the community in return. "For me," said Mary Clark, "the current conditions were worse than the proposed development. On the north side of 49th Street," she explained, "the homeless set up camp every evening, with cardboard and newspaper shelters, clothing hanging out in the air, and blankets attached [to] the fence. That was benign compared to the sex and drug bazaar that blossomed on the south side of the street." There, she continued, "Men in hot pants courted well-dressed couples, drugs were sold and taken on the stoops, and prostitutes, male and female, young and old, black and white, straight and gay, bargained with people in Lincoln town cars and white stretch limousines with baby blue running lights." Was this right, the best, she wrote in her journal, for "the good people" living on this block?[31]

The community wanted low- and moderate-income housing as part of the new construction, the equivalent of 20 percent of the apartments in the project to be handed over to them, and the Ninth Avenue portion of the project to reflect the low-rise character of Clinton. Its leverage with the developer would come from zoning changes Zeckendorf was seeking for the project, which would have to go through the city's Uniform Land Use Review Procedure. The Clinton Steering Committee of the board first asked for $30 million and the six tenements in the vicinity that Gulf and Western Industries sold with the site to be handed over to them. But members of a newly formed negotiating committee, an ad hoc committee of CB4, rejected that approach based on what had happened with the Clinton Advisory Committee (the "25 million committee" managing the allocation of the quid-pro-quo funds of the 42nd Street Development Project described in chapter 4), "which set community groups fighting with one another, and the city and state governments playing games with us," said Clark.[32] Also, the cost of renovating those six badly deteriorated buildings would be beyond what the community could raise.

The ad hoc committee worked for nearly three months with Edith Fisher, a vice president of the Zeckendorf company—described as "a tough, energetic businessman who lives and breathes New York"—and at times directly with the developer on plans for the site. Zeckendorf agreed to fully renovate the six dismal tenements, but he was not willing to put any subsidized units in the new development, only off-site in buildings on nearby streets. To meet the community's quota of 20 percent, he would have to buy additional buildings. In May, the community board announced its support for the project at a City Planning Commission public hearing in City Hall, with the exact number of affordable units yet to be worked out between the community board and the developer. It would take another of those late night/early morning marathon sessions in which approval of the project was held up for hours as city officials and local leaders negotiated with the developer on final terms of an agreement before the all-powerful Board of Estimate approved it—along with a controversial provision required by Mayor Koch for *citywide* allocation of the new apartments—at 4 A.M. on July 18, 1986. The Zeckendorf partnership would provide 132 permanently affordable units (reportedly up from 60), one for every five of the 661 luxury apartments in the project, fully renovated and delivered to a nonprofit group for ownership. The community would also get some theater space and a neighborhood daycare center, among other things. "It was not perfect," said Restuccia; "we didn't get all we wanted, but we got a package."[33]

Community leaders in the forefront of trying to manage growth in Hell's Kitchen were dealing with a decidedly difficult set of housing issues complicated on several dimensions: legal, physical, and social. Between 1974 and 1980, the city had acquired a remarkable amount of residential property. Not only in Clinton but across the five boroughs, the city's inventory of multifamily buildings (occupied and vacant) seized for nonpayment of taxes during the distressed 1970s totaled more than 11,000, home to about 35,000 households. "Abandonment hit New York City's neighborhoods like a firestorm," explained David Reiss in his analysis of New York City's response to housing abandonments in the 1970s. In Restuccia's podcast on the history of Hell's Kitchen, he summarized the scenario of abandonment and decline impacting his neighborhood: individual speculators had bought property in expectation of the convention center being built nearby with "grandiose ideas that never materialized; their solution was to walk away." Buildings with low rents and low values, a situation that lent itself to exploitation. "Landlords began to milk them. They put on insurance. After a while, they would torch the top floor, collect insurance, then walk away. The city took possession of the buildings. But they were not abandoned; they were 'owner emptied'—tenant occupied."[34]

Single-room-occupancy structures presented a related concern. In the 1980s, the area between Times Square and Columbus Circle had one of the city's densest remaining concentrations of SROs. A legacy of urban low-cost housing, SROs—small rooms lacking or sharing complete bathroom and/or kitchen facilities—provided shelter to large numbers of low-income people who would be homeless without them. Over the course of time and with the subdivision of tenements into single-room living units in the 1960s, SRO housing came to be predominantly occupied not by families but by low-income single adults living alone. The units had acquired an unsavory reputation as substandard housing, the home of last resort for drug addicts, ex-offenders, and deinstitutionalized mental patients without sufficient community support services. In an era of city housing policy geared to upgrading neighborhoods, single-room-occupancy housing became expendable.

"What happened in New York was a great irony," a former director of the low-income housing group Community Housing Improvement Program told Malcolm Gladwell in 1993. "We had literally hundreds of thousands of SRO units that provided housing to large segments of the population. Then the city decided that it was inadequate and unsuitable and beginning around 1955 and continuing through the 1970s developed zoning provisions and incentives to put them out of business. The result is the enormous homeless mess we have now."[35] One incentive created by the Koch administration was a tax abatement for upgrading an SRO unit to a full-size apartment with its own kitchen and bathroom, an implicit invitation to owners to convert those units to higher-rent apartments. With unsurprising effectiveness, the measures "drastically shrank" the SRO housing stock. One study by the New York State Assembly found that between 1976 and 1981, the city's tax program caused the elimination of nearly two-thirds of all remaining SRO units—and "irreversibly altered" patterns of SRO occupancy such that they were increasingly occupied by "the poorest of people."[36]

This chapter of New York City's housing policy is a long sad story, deserving fuller treatment beyond the scope here. The consequences of New York's anti-SRO crusade—harassment, homelessness, and misery— took their toll at a personal level on individuals and families whose means blocked them from renting better-quality housing. At an economic level, buildings less desirable for conversion and seen as poor investments by their owners suffered from disinvestment and were left to deteriorate. Tenants who could afford to leave moved out; buildings were left to rot.

In a belated attempt to reverse the consequences of its prior anti-SRO campaign, in 1985 the city passed a law protecting SROs from "conversion, alteration, or demolition." But what was gone could not readily be reconstituted. In a 1996 report prepared for the city's Department of Housing Preservation and Development, officials acknowledged that the city had "abjectly failed to plan for a post-SRO New York," and in "a remarkable about-face," wrote the report's author, "shifted from a policy of SRO elimination to one of SRO preservation." Nevertheless, the scale of the disaster was "staggering." Legal-aid lawyers Brian J. Sullivan and Jonathan Burke found that "by 1985, the City government had engineered the elimination of more than 100,000 units of affordable housing—and replaced them with nothing." In July 1989, the New York Court of Appeals struck down the moratorium on SRO demolition. *Newsday* reported that "landlords were jubilant, calling the decision a great victory for property owners and for those who want to develop midtown Manhattan. Tenant groups were dismayed and predicted the ruling would force thousands of mentally ill, disabled and elderly tenants onto the streets." *Crain's New York Business* said the decision, in effect, "declared open season on the city's seedier hotels, most of which are classified as single-room occupancy, or SRO, dwellings."[37]

Hell's Kitchen was packed with the legacy of single-room-occupancy housing—reportedly, some 4,300 units between 42nd and 57th Streets, far less than what had been there before the city's anti-SRO campaign. On Eighth Avenue, the demolition prohibition had stymied redevelopment as many potential development sites on the avenue shared the blockfronts with SROs. The demolition law was not protecting tenants so much as buildings, and before it was declared unconstitutional, even an empty SRO—even part of one—was shielded from demolition. Speaking in 1989, months before the law was struck down, Restuccia told *Times* reporter Iver Peterson, "Everyone wants to see Eighth Avenue redeveloped. The only question is how. On the City's map of developable sites, half of them are S.R.O.'s. Some of them are pretty crummy, but they also house a lot of people who would be homeless without them. I mean, they're not pretty, but they're needed."[38] By the end of 1989, after US Supreme Court let stand the lower court's ruling that found unconstitutional New York City's moratorium preventing the conversion or demolition of single-occupancy buildings, the last barrier to SRO "open season" was gone. Less constrained, the market would now drive Eighth Avenue redevelopment—and intensify pressure on affordable housing in the neighborhood.

After years of inactivity during which the buildings in the Clinton Urban Renewal Area "just hung around forever," in 1999 a coalition of nine not-for-profit community organizations called the CURA Coordinating Committee—including Clinton Housing Association, Clinton Association for a Renewed Environment, Clinton Housing Development Company, Encore Community Services, and Housing Conservation Coordinators—joined forces to develop an updated plan for the remaining CURA sites. The plan continued to advance the key planning vision animating the community leaders' advocacy "to strike a balance" between housing preservation and new construction. Beyond the plan, the members of the group would become active in developing and sponsoring affordable housing projects in the renewal area.

The notion of "balance" did not mediate the concerns of every activist group in the community, known for its feisty internal differences: "Fifty-story skyscrapers are out of character, out of line," said John Fisher, president of the Clinton Special District Coalition, another local civic group. "They are not good, just not good." Speaking of the dedicated efforts to preserve the neighborhood's character, Chuck Spence, president of one of Clinton's many block associations, said: "The good news is we succeeded . . . the bad news is we made it so desirable that real estate values popped up, which is really the driving factor behind our losing some of the Old World charm." "The neighborhood character is up in the air right now, and we're trying to get control," said Bob Kalin, a resident and tenant organizer for Housing Conservation Coordinators.[39]

Community Board 4, one of the city's most sophisticated community boards, had long been a staunch advocate for affordable housing serving a range of incomes; marshaling its intimate knowledge of the neighborhood, it had sustained a steadfast focus on the six-block Clinton Urban Renewal Area for decades. Progress in moving forward with affordable housing in the renewal area had been slow and halting, subject to the usual shifts in development plans under different mayoral administrations and the unpredictable vicissitudes of the real estate market. For over a decade, construction in CURA was stalled until 1993, when the Department of Housing Preservation and Development offered for development a site with a parking lot and taxi garage, where the Gotham Organization developed The Foundry (2001, now

Archstone West), a two-building apartment complex of 280 units; built under the city's 80/20 housing program with tax-exempt bond financing, forty-five units would be rented to tenants with low incomes. "The neighborhood has the potential to be the next TriBeCa," said the company president David L. Picket.[40] Just what the community feared.

"We are trying to keep it as a low-density community," said Simone Sindin, chair of the community board's land use committee at the time. "This is one of the last moderate-to-low-income areas that is ready for development, and the developers are salivating to build, build, build." Several residential projects were in the offing in the West 50s (mainly on or off Eighth and Ninth Avenues), where the majority of units would be market-rate. Rents were increasing, steadily. Activity in CURA, however, proceeded at a snail's pace. In 1996, the Clinton Association for a Renewed Environmental finally secured control of the city-owned site at 52nd Street and Eleventh Avenue directly across from DeWitt Clinton Park and developed the 11-story Clinton Parkview Apartments (2005), with ninety-six affordable units for low- and middle-income households, who, the group's president said, "are being priced out of the neighborhood."[41]

Ironically, the development boom was fast becoming an economic tool for realizing the original affordable housing goals established for the Clinton Urban Renewal Area in 1969. In the rapidly gentrifying neighborhood, the still-lingering urban renewal sites presented a prime opportunity for increasing the neighborhood's stock of affordable housing. Developers were looking carefully at the last of the "dwindling number" of city-owned sites awaiting development—undeveloped lots used as parking lots or occupied by low-slung warehouses and vacant one- and two-story buildings—where they could build new market-rate residential towers under incentive programs that would deliver affordable units for the community. Not-for-profit developers were considering ways the Old Law Tenements and former commercial buildings could be renovated within the preservation tradition and limits of the Special Clinton District for affordable units for families, seniors, and individuals, accommodate existing commercial uses and cultural and nonprofit institutions, and add community gardens. It "is pleased," Community Board 4 said in its 2002 annual statement of district needs submitted as part of New York City's annual budget process, "to note [that CURA] has been part of the development boom."[42]

As market-driven development loomed, two CURA sites aroused deep controversy—from neighborhood-based competition. They were a hangover from the past on the same block where the Koch administration

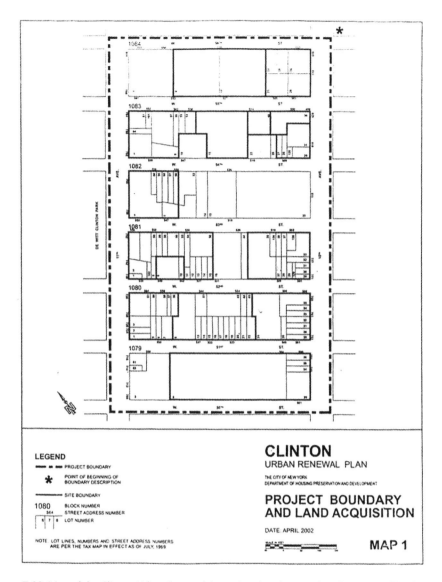

**7.12** Map of the Clinton Urban Renewal Area, showing the parcels to be acquired by the city and redeveloped, as of 2002. New York City Department of Housing Preservation and Development.

had unsuccessfully sought private housing development in the early 1980s. One site was home to a turn-of-the-century seven-story partially boarded-up tenement called The Flats on Eleventh Avenue between 52nd and 53rd Streets, which had opened in 1915 (as The Emerson, named after its owner and architect, William Emerson), as part of the model tenement movement. Under the city's original renewal plan, it would have been demolished and its tenants displaced. Two local preservation-oriented groups vied to develop The Flats but were never able to win

**7.13** Renovated by Clinton Housing Development Company, The Flats/Old School structure on the corner of West 53rd Street and Eleventh Avenue was originally completed as
two separate structures in 1894 and 1915, respectively. Completed in 2006, the revitalization project provides affordable housing and social services for families and formerly
homeless individuals. Courtesy of Clinton Housing Development Company.

approval from the Department of Housing Preservation and Development. Years passed before CHDC was selected to complete a thorough
modernization and reconfiguration with the adjacent five-story former
trades-school building, which also had originally been slated for demolition. When it reopened in 2006, The Flats/Old School had been sen-
sitively restored to its original social purpose with eighty-six units for
low-, moderate-, and middle-income families and formerly homeless
individuals. "The restored Emerson," the Community Board wrote to
the Preservation League of New York State in its recommendation for
the League's 2009 Excellence in Preservation award, "is close to the last
and surely the finest building block of the community thus recreated."[43]

The 10-story deteriorated loft building on West 52nd Street housing
the Women's Interart Center was the focus of an intense and public
controversy, this one newsworthy. Surrounded by new projects that all
included some portion of below-market housing, this city-owned building was the last undeveloped lot on the western half of the same block
as The Flats/Old School. After a prolonged litigation between the arts

organization and the city over the fate of the property, CHDC gained site control in April of 2007, and is currently renovating the building for permanently affordable artist studios, rehearsal and performance spaces, offices for not-for-profit theater companies, music studios, and two galleries.

This particular block, block 1081 on the city tax map, tells the full story of the Clinton Urban Renewal Area, at the same time as it reveals the range of approaches to producing affordable housing in New York City. When the project area was mapped in 1969, all but two of the block's thirty-four tax lots, mostly small 25-by-100-foot lots of the type laid out for development to fit the typical grid block of Manhattan, were to be acquired via condemnation, cleared of existing "blighted" structures, then reconfigured into three large sites for redevelopment. Decades later, a sequence of confounding events—in-rem foreclosures of abandoned buildings, the city's fiscal crisis, a new climate in City Hall and changes in housing policy, community activism for preservation not clearance, specific site controversies and litigation, stalled progress, and continual pressure for permanently affordable housing—all contributed to a 180-degree reversal of the intended approach to redevelopment. On these city-owned sites, nine housing projects—some new construction and others extensive rehabilitation, a community garden, and an arts center—physically revitalized the social fabric of the block; some projects were market rentals, others affordable condominiums, another a cooperative for seniors. Two were built by private companies, the other seven by nonprofits; the city's Department of Parks and Recreation sponsored the community garden. Of the 1,200 units of housing on the block, 617, or 51 percent, were affordable. CHDC was directly engaged in development of four of the nine housing projects.

"The big struggle was to prove that tenements could be renovated instead of demolished," said Restuccia. "This was the '70s, when the idea was to knock it all down and start all over again." Renovating these tenements—walk-ups known as railroad flats because the rooms were organized in a line like cars on a train—was not for the faint of heart. Tubs were in the kitchen and toilets in the hall. "The challenge is to take a building like that and modernize it, installing kitchens, private bedrooms, a toilet with a door," he said. "This was like a major achievement—a toilet with a door!"[44] Beyond making physical improvements, the challenge was marshaling the financing from diverse and complex sources and working with city agencies and activist groups of tenants focused on staying in the homes they had long occupied, often despite deteriorated conditions. Connection to the place ran deep.

Restuccia has had an enormous positive impact in Clinton. In his decades of commitment to the mission, his knowledge of what it would take to deliver permanently affordable housing and that the details matter matched up with his skillful understanding of how to work the complex system of securing funds and negotiate with developers and city officials. Add to that persistence and a clear vision of the end goal. Since its founding in 1973, CHDC has directly developed 1,031 units of permanently affordable housing and 55 commercial spaces in 79 buildings in the Clinton/Hell's Kitchen and Chelsea communities, with public and private investments totaling more than $200 million; in addition, it has assisted in the development of another 300 units of cooperative housing and 300 units of rental housing (as listed on its website). For Restuccia, the mission has been about balancing development and the creation of affordable housing with preservation of the existing community fabric.

Fifty years is what it took to redevelop those six blocks in the Clinton Urban Renewal Area. The holding-pattern parking lots are gone. Many existing low-rise buildings have been fully renovated without permanently displacing former tenants. On some blocks, luxury residential towers sit cheek by jowl with low-income publicly subsidized residential towers. Vibrant cultural institutions like the Irish Arts Center have gained expanded space in new buildings. Sprinkled within the area are new community gardens. Through a combination of public and private forces, new construction and rehabilitation of existing buildings, approximately 2,676 affordable housing units—not quite the 1969 goal of 3,000 units—have been created in the former urban renewal area: 1,498 affordable units between 1979 and 1981, and at least 1,178 affordable units during the aughts' development boom, by my accounting. In a city with a chronic shortage of affordable housing, it would not be enough, only an achieved record of production. Yet, if the city had not taken the properties in the early days of the urban renewal project, most certainly many more high-density market-rate luxury towers would now be looming over the neighborhood.

Hell's Kitchen has experienced it all. Writ large over its roughly ninety blocks, government and private actions over seven decades embody the trajectory of urban change—its problems, planning solutions, government actions, and market-driven responses to opportunity in post-World War II Manhattan. First, the decline of waterfront industrial uses and loss of manufacturing jobs that had clustered near the piers. Years after the job losses, population losses and physical deterioration of the environment accompanied by speculative property acquisitions in the

**7.14** The new Irish Arts Center on Eleventh Avenue in the former Clinton Urban Renewal Area designed by Davis Brody Bond, 2022. Gary Hack.

"transitional" neighborhood. The fallacy of urban-renewal clearance as a revitalization strategy, leaving abandoned buildings and empty lots in its wake when the money for redevelopment dried up. Encroachment of crime, drugs, and prostitution. Arson after owners "milked" their buildings. Threats of displacement and fear of gentrification triggered by government proposals for a convention center and a transformative plan to clean up the Deuce. As prospects for property upgrading appeared, harassment and evictions as landlords worked to clear out tenants from tenements in a well-situated historic neighborhood of appealing ethnic character. Local opposition among dedicated community activists to preserve affordable housing and sense of place. Successive waves of market-driven development spurred by demographically driven demand for urban living and the growth of professional jobs in financial services in midtown. What distinguishes this neighborhood's experience in holding on to some of its physical and social character while gentrifying? Well-organized local activism, persistence, political savvy, and not-for-profit entities with development capacity preserved much more of the community fabric than would otherwise have been the case. What also mattered: the consequences of time.

# 8  THE CONTRADICTIONS OF TIME

To a New Yorker the city is both changeless and changing.
E. B. White, 1949

Impermanence is a part of New York's commercial and social psyche. However long in realization, midtown's westward migration followed a pattern of restless movement in line with the city's growth following consolidation into the five boroughs of New York City in 1898. Historically, the march was northward, up the island in pursuit of larger development sites and more daylight than were available in the high-rise canyons of Manhattan's historic business district downtown. In 1893, there were just four office buildings 10 stories or taller north of Canal Street; by 1900, there were more than four times as many, 18, but still a small number. Until that time, the trajectory of growth was up Broadway (which angles west from 23rd Street), before the subway opened up Times Square, and before the new Grand Central Terminal opened in 1913. Beginning in the 1920s and accelerating after World War II, real estate developers displaced existing lower-density residential uses along the avenues around Grand Central Terminal to build a concentration of office towers that made East Midtown the predominant business center in the city, and the nation. At the beginning of the twenty-first century, the transformational movement shifted markedly westward, to a large 59-block district known as Far West Midtown (generally 42nd Street south to 24th Street west of Eighth Avenue to the Hudson River) that the Department of City Planning had targeted for growth and juiced with zoning incentives. The emergence of this newest commercial area

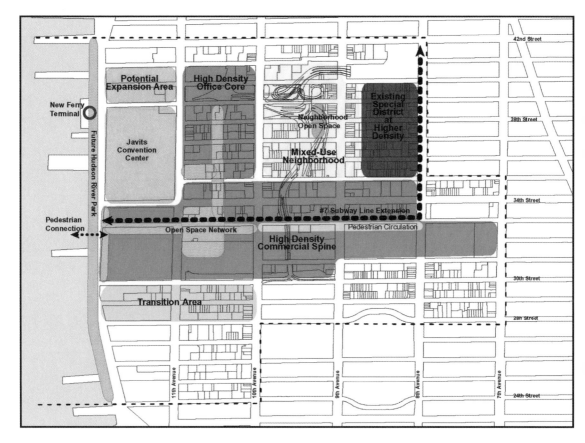

**8.1** In 2001, the Department of City Planning made public its conceptual framework for the development of Far West Midtown with this map outlining three high-density growth areas. New York City Department of City Planning.

in a cluster of buildings known as Hudson Yards, followed by the reset of development parameters for ever-higher density in East Midtown in 2017, inevitably intensified the competitive office market of midtown—and straight-on challenged the office towers in Times Square that had undergirded the district's revitalization success.

In a fashion, the trajectory of change in Times Square set off by the transformation of 42nd Street evoked prophetic voices from the past. In 1920, the auctioneers of the Henry Astor Trust Estate lands envisioned great increases in the value of Henry's Times Square properties with their "appearance of bye-gone [sic] usefulness and an absence of modern improvements." Select corner parcels, reported the *New-York Tribune*, "indicated to the real estate fraternity what rapid strides that part of Eighth Avenue has made toward becoming a real factor in the amusement life of New York." Of all those nondescript buildings lining

**8.2** Callahan's General Dry Goods store as it appeared in the Henry Astor Trust Estate auction catalogue in 1920, one of the five buildings Clinton Housing Development Company transformed into seventy units of permanent supportive housing with on-site social services (pictured in 2022). Collection of the author (top); courtesy of Clinton Housing Development Company (bottom).

the side streets, "there was not one in the whole offering that has any merit. Tenements and small houses cover all the lots, structures erected twenty to forty years ago, and now entirely out of place."[1]

Times Square was booming then. What realty men could not have imagined is the 80 years it took before many of those buildings were fitted out with "modern improvements." Today, on the southwest corner of Eighth Avenue and 46th Street—the gateway to Restaurant Row—is a five-building complex that speaks to the passage of time. At the Astor auction, the buildings were sold in five separate lots to three different speculators. Originally built as housing for the middle class, the large apartments in the three French Flats on Eighth Avenue and the two private-dwelling brownstones on the side street were converted to rooming houses sometime in the 1920s, after their Astor-tenant leases expired. A photograph in the auction brochure shows the ground floor of the desirable corner location occupied by Eugene Callahan's General Dry Goods store. Cut up in the 1920s, the spaces in these four-story buildings mutated into eighty-one extremely small rooms, shared bathrooms, and a few kitchens. "Affordable accommodations for working people of modest means," as described on the Clinton Housing Development Company website recounting the case history of the buildings.[2] By 1999, CHDC had managed to purchase the buildings, reconfiguring them into seventy units of permanent supportive housing with on-site social services. The arduous task of doing so followed the script we have seen in the district. The saga follows a trajectory common to so many buildings, citywide, during that difficult era which only those of a certain age have experienced, except through stories of the past.

With the decline of Times Square, the buildings were sold to real estate speculators, who leased them to a series of disreputable operators who sought to maximize income by renting to tenants involved in illegal activities; these operators, not the speculators, were responsible for property taxes and any other building maintenance expense. By the mid-1980s, the buildings had become the center of drug dealing, prostitution, and crime, while long-term tenants remained in place. Extremely rundown, the buildings were very poorly maintained and dangerous. The courts were kept busy as multiple legal actions were filed against the owner and lessee of the buildings. Eventually, the State Supreme Court appointed a temporary receiver for harassment to administer and restore the property, and in 1986 the Clinton Housing Development Company took over as managing agent for the receiver in its efforts to stabilize the buildings. Beyond efforts to make repairs and improve living conditions, CHDC managed the removal of criminal activity, which included 23 drug evictions coordinated with Manhattan South Narcotics, Midtown North Precinct, Manhattan Community Board 4, and the Restaurant Row Association. After a legal settlement of the receivership in 1995, CHDC was able to purchase the buildings from the owner. Drawing upon public and private financing sources, construction of the renovation project was completed in December 1999.

In another part of Hell's Kitchen, the trajectory of change supercharged a dramatic transformation of Theatre Row. In November 2002, a newly constituted collection of Off-Broadway theaters emerged from the construction din and debris that had consumed the block for two years; the *Times* headlined the change "Upscale March of Theater Row." The gritty old theaters built within the shells of derelict buildings had survived through tough times, "stickups, recessions, and aborted development projects . . . to see a renewed Midtown rise around them." They possessed "simple charms" and a "dogged let's-put-on-a-show (we hope) ethos" built on a sense of purpose "on this bizarre block of Manhattan." But the theaters were tired, getting shabby, recalled Papert, whose 42nd Street Development Corporation had overseen the development of Theatre Row since 1976. (In the 1970s, Papert's organization had acquired fourteen or more buildings between Ninth and Tenth Avenues, six of which became Theatre Row.) Now, 25 years after what *Times* theater critic Ralph Blumenthal had called "its first uncertain beginnings," Theatre Row had become a centerpiece of the district's redevelopment.[3]

Five small theater companies considered incubators for developing new work were moving into new state-of-the-art facilities, all under one roof. It was "an unheard-of theatrical real estate phenomenon," given that the city's other Off-Broadway theaters had all been converted to their current purpose from other uses. At the other end of the 400 block of 42nd Street that meets the Dyer Avenue cut (where traffic spills out of the Lincoln Tunnel), another premier: the 499-seat Little Shubert (Stage 42)—the first commercial Off-Broadway theater built from the ground up in the city—constructed within the Brodsky Organization's 41-story residential tower but owned and fitted out by the Shubert Organization. And in the works was a new five-story home designed to house two theaters, rehearsal space, and offices for artistic, production, and administrative staff for Playwrights Horizons—the pioneering not-for-profit that prefigured the far larger revival of 42nd Street and Times Square. (The theater's sale of its air rights for an apartment tower helped fund its new home.) All together, seven new theaters—the biggest

**8.3** Theatre Row newly renovated; to the right is Chez Josephine, a long-time French restaurant in a building that once housed French Palace, a massage parlor, 2022. Gary Hack.

Off-Broadway theater redevelopment project in New York City history. What helped to make this cultural feat financially feasible: demand for residential living in Hell's Kitchen sprung from the rejuvenation of Times Square. Still, the developer of the residential tower Daniel Brodsky would call his $90 million project "a risky little building."[4]

"In all, from pornographic past to high-rise future, the resurgence became, quite literally," Blumenthal wrote, "a groundbreaking story of urban renewal through the arts."[5] By the early aughts, culture as a driver of economic transformation was a well-established strategy, though it had not been in the mid-1970s. Circumstance, not strategy or logic, pushed the "uncertain beginning" of what became a largely unscripted urban drama on the west spur of the Deuce. It was desperation that forced Robert Moss, the founder of the four-year-old Playwrights Horizons, to venture onto 42nd Street to look at a possible temporary space for his theatrical production company. He had recently lost what was to have been a resident home for Playwrights—known as a "writers'

**8.4** Playwrights Horizons' new home on Theatre Row, funded in part from the sale of its air rights for the apartment tower in the background of this image, 2022. Gary Hack.

theater" for its dedication to cultivating new American playwrights—and for four months had been searching unsuccessfully for a new space. Facing the potential loss of a grant from the New York Council of the Arts, he had little choice but to check out what he had been avoiding: the 400 block of 42nd Street—Irving Maidman's block. Maidman had once had a real estate vision of reconstituting the historic legacy of the famous street with small, Off-Broadway theaters, but worsening conditions and the difficulties of making small theaters pay conspired against him, and after five years he had shuttered his theaters.

**8.5** The beginnings of Theatre Row. In addition to Playwrights Horizons, the first theaters included Black Theatre Alliance, Harlem Children's Theatre, Actors and Directors Lab, INTAR (International Arts Relations, a Hispanic cultural organization), Lion Theatre, Nat Horne Musical Theatre, and South Street Theatre, as shown in this late 1970s photograph. Courtesy of Building for the Arts NY, Inc.

By the time Moss inspected the vacant space, a former porno theater, at 422 West 42nd—what Anthony Bianco in *Ghosts of 42nd Street* called "the moldering two-story pile of lumber and concrete" that had been Maidman's 150-seat Midway Theatre—the block was a physical disaster zone. "The sidewalks were strewn with rubble, and many of the buildings were vacant. Clustered near the Dyer Avenue cut were four sex venues . . . [that] formed a phalanx of sleaze broken only by 422, which was vacant." Moss looked around and decided, he later told Blumenthal, "Sometimes you have to do things that don't make any sense and this is one of them." He had no intention to stay more than the six-month term of his initial lease for 422. Yet not long after (and after short runs of two not very successful plays), an epiphany hit: "Wait a minute, we're on 42nd Street! This is the middle of the world! This is a good place to be. We're going to stay." It was a daring conviction that made others incredulous, but he would pull it off within two

**8.6** Playwrights Horizons honors Bob Moss in 2014 for his path-breaking achievement in creating the writer's playhouse, for which he served as artistic director for ten years. After founding Playwrights in 1971, Moss joined with Fred Papert (left) and his 42nd Street Development Corporation to establish 42nd Street's Theatre Row. Jennifer Broski.

years after joining forces with Papert, who packaged "a not-for-profit real estate project in the aura of financial credibility."[6] And there in that dire place, cleaned out and fixed up with the help of volunteers, Playwrights would go on to produce hits like *Vanities* (Jack Heifner), *Driving Miss Daisy* (Alfred Uhry), *The Heidi Chronicles* (Wendy Wasserstein), and *Sunday in the Park with George* (James Lapine and Stephen Sondheim).

It was 1975, and the street that made Times Square famous was stuck in a time warp of seemingly irreversible decline, beyond redemption. Moss, 42 and indefatigable, believed that "The way to clean up this area is not to harass the prostitutes, but to open up the theaters. The rest will follow." And it did, with time. Opening in 1977, Manhattan Plaza, that apparent red elephant of a gigantic project, also helped turn around the neighborhood. Its initial failure to draw sufficient tenants to what was a harsh, dangerous environment produced an unexpected opportunity when 70 percent of its units were earmarked for low-earning people in the performing arts. "Suddenly, we didn't feel as desolate," recalled André Bishop, the award-winning American theatrical producer and second artistic director of Playwrights.[7]

Ironically, Theatre Row's pioneering impact on the renewal of Maidman's tawdry block was built on the profoundly depressed conditions of the times—on the contradiction of fostering a turnaround from the depths of distress. Many forces contributed to the cultural renewal on a block that had been all but written off: distressed owners who walked away from property taken over by bank lenders, who handed over or sold the parcels for little to Papert's organization; cheap performance space, which has long been an essential ingredient for innovative upstart cultural experiments; an alliance with the Port Authority of New York and New Jersey, which had a direct stake in the neighborhood and sold a vital piece of property to the development corporation to advance the transformation; transaction assistance from the state's Urban Development Corporation; city help on property taxes; and a real sense that when things are as bad as they were on the 400 block, they could not get any worse—so why not try something bold? Theatre Row had yet another ironic advantage: access to a mainstream audience, people from New Jersey and Long Island, who find it easier to come to midtown than downtown, where many smaller stages were located. Theatre Row's remarkable role as a catalyst for renewal underscores the power that passionately committed individuals can have on the shape of a city, even one as large as New York. In a post-pandemic world, the staying power of all that had transformed Times Square and 42nd Street would lie in the city's recovery from the patterns of life and work it brought about.

## RIVER-TO-RIVER

When the run of luxury residential towers lining the western reaches of 42nd and its adjacent streets supplanted the vacant lots, storage garages, lumber yards, and abandoned warehouses, even the shadow of the area's industrial past vanished into history. Nineteenth-century businesses had populated those blocks near the riverbank in the region of Eleventh and Twelfth Avenues with factories that turned out carpets, pianos, twine, and carriages, among other goods. The swampy area had offered desirable sites convenient to water transportation on the Hudson River piers. Land was cheap and the undeveloped area tolerant of nuisances—slaughterhouses, gas tanks, truck terminals, breweries, and repair shops—that would be intolerable in residential parts of the city. As industry and shipping declined, obsolescence set in; the old structures were either taken down to wait for future development or fell down from decay. That section of the waterfront was a forgotten edge. Only the latest chapter distinguishes this nearly universal evolution in urban land use. The new glass-and-steel residential towers of the twenty-first century are the exclamation mark on a century-long modernization of

**8.7** River-to-river view of 42nd Street as seen from New Jersey, 1946. Andreas Feininger, Getty Images.

New York's most famous crosstown street: 42nd Street was now built-out river-to-river, anchored on both ends by residential living.

On the east end of 42nd Street, industry nuisances had passed into history half a century earlier. In 1925, the ambitious Bronx-born developer Fred Filmore French, a noted real estate success, began secretly assembling approximately five acres in a seemingly undesirable area between 40th and 44th Streets and First and Second Avenues, several blocks east of Grand Central Terminal, an area known as Prospect Hill cluttered with tenements, breweries, and slaughterhouses. (First Avenue was reportedly popularly known as Blood Alley because of the stench of freshly killed animals.) On those four blocks rose Tudor City, his "city within a city," the largest single residential project New York had ever seen: nine large apartment houses for middle-class households, a hotel, and two gardens, which his publicity material compared to Gramercy Park, exclusive and private. He had concluded on the basis of a business survey of midtown that the center of gravity in Manhattan was shifting from downtown to midtown as the district developed around

**8.8** View of Tudor City high-rise apartment complex between 40th and 44th Streets, First to Second Avenues, towering above the low-rise buildings of midtown and shielded from the industrial area on the waterfront, 1930. Milstein Division, The New York Public Library.

CHAPTER 8

Grand Central Terminal, and he fashioned a dense neighborhood of Tudor Revival architecture for white-collar workers who wanted to live near their jobs rather than commute to the city from the suburbs. By arranging the buildings in a way that was open to the west (with almost no east-facing windows), the pioneering complex turned its back on the industrial area and its noxious meat-packing houses, gasworks, and glue factory to the east. On a cohesive site plan that connected over 42nd Street via a bridge, he built an in-town environment above the roar of traffic and the commercial life of the street, a place designed for easy living. French's bellwether project "extended the sphere of respectability eastward and other developers followed."[8] In 1988, Tudor City was designated a New York City Historic District.

Several decades later those noxious uses along the East River that French took to be a permanent presence finally disappeared. In 1945, envisaging the real estate potential of what could be on the enormous property quadrangle without the reeking presence of those slaughterhouses, the enterprising developer of majestic dreams, William Zeckendorf Sr., began assembling 17 acres of shoreline between 42nd and 49th Streets, just north of Tudor City. Again, the land was relatively inexpensive because of noxious abattoirs. The owners of those outmoded facilities, Swift and Wilson meatpackers, were ready to close them, and then the land would be far more valuable. On these lands, Zeckendorf intended to develop X City, a vast complex of office and apartment towers, his vision of "a megaproject that would make Tudor City look like a sand castle," remarked architectural critic Justin Davidson. It never materialized, but rather, in an oft-told story, the site became the permanent home of the United Nations when Zeckendorf sold his assemblage to John D. Rockefeller Jr., who donated the land to the newly created international organization. When the UN Secretariat designed by Brazilian architect Oscar Niemeyer and the Swiss-French architect Le Corbusier opened in 1950, it became the East River anchor of what would evolve as an extraordinary lineup of "Manhattan's most visionary places and institutions."[9]

Forty-second Street is like no other cross street of the Manhattan grid. The other thirteen—14th, 23rd, 34th, 57th, 72nd, 79th, 86th, 96th, 106th, 125th, 135th, 145th, 155th—do not compete; 42nd is preeminent. It is a street acting like a boulevard because of the many proud architectural assets—landmarks when they were built—that parade the length of its roughly two-mile traverse of the island. Starting at the East River and the United Nations, Tudor City (1927), the refined headquarters of the Ford Foundation (1967), and a lineup of world-famous

**8.9** The 42nd Street Property Owners and Merchants Association map of 42nd Street, river to river, revealing the more built-up west end around Times Square, 1919. J. Clarence Davies Street Views Scrapbook, J. Clarence Davies Street Scrapbook Collection. Museum of the City of New York. X2012.61.34.53.

**8.10** Blue-hour view of 42nd Street, river to river, as seen from New Jersey, 2016. Courtesy of Andrew Weiss.

skyscrapers that includes the Daily News (1930), Socony Mobile (1954), Chrysler (1930), Chanin (1929), Bowery Savings Bank (1923), Pershing Square (1923), Lincoln (1930), and Manufacturers Trust Company (1954) buildings, plus Salmon Tower II (1931)—all but one New York City landmarks—and its newest enrichment, One Vanderbilt (2020).

Strategically centered on East 42nd Street sits Grand Central Terminal (1913), the noble gateway to the city generally considered one of the greatest monuments to twentieth-century mass transportation. When the terminal opened, it was "anything but central," wrote *Times* veteran Sam Roberts; "midtown Manhattan was largely undeveloped," and the conventional wisdom at the time assumed "the tenements, shanties, slaughterhouses, and other industrial buildings and vacant lots" stretching to the river "would develop only gradually."[10]

Anchoring the street at Fifth Avenue, where the Croton Reservoir once served the growing city, stands the New York Public Library (1911), one of the world's greatest cultural institutions, flanked by the renowned pair of marble lions "Patience and Fortitude." Behind the public library on a site that once housed the magnificent cast-iron New York Crystal Palace exhibition center (1853) is a rare public park in a commercial district, the 9.6-acre Bryant Park (1895), named for abolitionist and journalist William Cullen Bryant. A destination in itself, the park leads the way to Times Square.

The early years of the twentieth century, when the action in midtown commercial development was all on the west side, endowed 42nd Street with architectural distinction. Five early twentieth-century buildings set the pace: Hammerstein's Victoria (1900) and Republic (1900) Theatres, Klaw and Erlanger's Art Nouveau New Amsterdam Theatre (1903), the *New York Times'* eponymous tower (1904), and John Jacob Astor's Knickerbocker Hotel (1906), most of them now designated New York City landmarks. Other theaters followed in rapid succession (Lew M. Fields, Liberty, Eltinge, Cohan & Harris, Selwyn, Apollo, and Times Square), fashioning a legendary theater block between Seventh and Eighth Avenues. Prominent office towers too spouted beyond Fifth Avenue: Candler (1914), Bush (1917), Aeolian (1925), and McGraw Hill (1931), the latter three also city-designated landmarks. In the post-World War II era, they were joined by the Grace Plaza Building (1972), the six towers of the 42nd Street Development Project (1999, 2001, 2002, 2004, 2010), including a new headquarters for the *New York Times* (2007), and the Bank of America Tower (2009). Further west at Eighth Avenue, the Port Authority Bus Terminal (an exception to architectural distinction) links Manhattan to New Jersey and the region beyond. At Ninth Avenue, Manhattan Plaza and Theatre Row give way to the march of new residential skyscrapers all the way to the Hudson River, completing the fourteen river-to-river blocks of 42nd Street.

In 1979, when 42nd Street was "a stalemated mix of squalor and splendor," what architectural critic Ada Louise Huxtable wrote in review of a small, unpublicized exhibition called *Inside 42d Street* remains ever so true in 2022: "The quality and variety, the range of styles, the beauty of the spaces, materials, details and execution to be found on this one street, are a genuine revelation." River to river, the street is "consummately New York."[11] That a single street has long served as a metaphor for the city as a whole makes a powerful statement about the promise and possibility of the built environment to embody the dreams, ambitions, and inventions of urban change that have continually intrigued writers, artists, critics, planners, and builders of New York City.

# PANDEMIC MICROCOSM: A CODA

It was eerie. The emptiness. The silence. The stillness. Times Square was not itself, day or night. Empty of traffic. Empty of tourists. Empty of activity. Empty of energy. The emptiness of absence. The digital billboards insistently flashing only to be seen through media messages sent around the world. The crowds had disappeared from the city's most public of public spaces—could it still be said to be a public space when there was no public activity and interaction? Broadway theater indefinitely suspended. The district existed as an architectural shell of creative activity. Hotels emptied out; an extraordinary number closed. Restaurants closed, by the scores. Retailers registered no sales of souvenirs; most closed their empty stores, at least temporarily. Subway platforms nearly empty in the Times Square station, the city's busiest. The iconography of emptiness, so unnatural, was unsettling. Times Square when the city was largely shut down, said Alice Ripley, the Broadway star and songwriter/musician, "was a cardboard cutout, a piece of scenery."[1] New York City was the epicenter of the Covid-19 outbreak in the United States during spring 2020, but as it spread throughout the world, the emptiness of Times Square became a metaphor for the social and economic pain of the global pandemic, images more compelling than words for what everyone was going through.

The emptiness of the pandemic differed from other types of emptiness in the city's history: manufacturing districts hollowed out by departing industries and jobs during the 1960s, neighborhoods closed up at night from fear of crime during the 1970s, and the closure of access to parts of Lower Manhattan for weeks after 9/11. The forced social distancing of

**9.1** Times Square—eerily empty as New Year's Eve 2020 approaches, with only a lone police car and the anonymity of computer-driven digital billboards keeping the place lit up. For the first time since anyone could remember, Times Square would be closed to the public on New Year's Eve; the ball drop would be a private affair, honoring frontline workers who continued to provide essential services for the city during the pandemic. Courtesy of Max Touhey.

Covid-19 made the emptiness feel different, acutely so. Of course, the city was not empty for the essential workers who could not work at home and still had to travel the subways and buses to their jobs, and for the delivery people who made life a little easier for all staying at home. Although Broadway did not close down during the 1918 influenza pandemic, it had closed its doors at other times in the past prompted by labor strikes, natural disasters, and tragedies like 9/11; but those earlier shutdowns lasted mere days, the longest, of 25 days, coming during a 1975 strike by musicians. The coronavirus would shut down Broadway's theaters for seventeen months, an existentially crippling financial event for the industry, a shocking darkness silencing another symbol of New York.

On 42nd Street, soon after the theaters and movie screens went dark, businesses aligned to entertainment and retailers shut down, some permanently, others temporarily: McDonald's, gone, permanently. Hilton Times Square, gone, permanently—the keys handed back to its lender. Ripley's Believe It or Not, closed, temporarily. Madame Tussauds, closed, temporarily. By the end of 2020, roughly 80 percent of the street's businesses had shuttered, turning the previously vibrant anchor for the district into "a shadow of its pre-pandemic self."[2] At night, the street had the bleak look of a tired, semi-abandoned place. Landlords of the office towers emptied out of workers held to their financial commitments to the city, as did Disney paying its rent on the New Amsterdam with no concessions to the pandemic. As office occupancy plummeted and leasing activity dried up, the financial impact of the pandemic on the crossroads towers of the 42nd Street project became strikingly evident. When the city's Department of Finance determined estimated market values for the 2021–2022 tax year, its assessed valuation of the quartet of towers dropped $545 million, or 20 percent, to $2.24 billion from $2.78 billion for the pre-pandemic tax year (2019–2020). The Candler Building, which had experienced distress several times during its 100-plus years of history, once again hit hard times. Against the backdrop of a likely foreclosure on its $150 million mortgage, in March 2022, the modest tower acquired a new owner with the deed changing hands at the cost of the mortgage assumption. It was a 43 percent comedown from the "epic" 2012 sale transaction at $261 million.

Citywide, the downward trajectory of office building values telegraphed a worrisome message. New York City houses the largest office real estate market in the world, with 464 million square feet of inventory as of midyear 2021. That inventory accounts for an outsized portion of the city's economic activity, contributing $705 billion, or 66.2 percent of the city's gross product in pre-pandemic 2019. Property taxes on office properties raise more in taxes than any other type of property, and office-sector employment makes up about one-third of all city jobs. The pandemic's impact on the office market was immediate: asking rents dropped and vacancy rates hit over 18 percent—a level not seen in over 30 years. The low percentage of office workers returning to their desks quickly raised questions about the future viability of in-office work, causing property values to plummet and citywide tax assessments with them. According to a report issued by the State Comptroller's Office in October 2021, the decline in office demand triggered a drop in the market value of all office property in the city of $28.6 billion, or 16.6 percent, for the 2021–2022 tax year—the first decline in more than 20 years—accounting for more than half of that year's $1.7 billion decline in property taxes.[3] It was an ominous fiscal reference point. As the pandemic altered how and where people worked, the city's Department of Finance, in anticipation of declining rental income for commercial properties and residential apartment buildings, had sharply reduced its assessments (which are based on estimates of income and expenses). The immediate budget-gap implication from the decline in property tax revenues would be modest, the city's Independent Budget Office said, but "the economic and fiscal risks New York City faces are not."[4]

That the city's economic recovery would be slow and the climb back steep was hardly a surprise. The economic fallout for New York was brutal because its economy relies heavily on activities that had been largely shuttered to limit the contagion: office work, tourism and entertainment, restaurants and retail, and transportation. The challenges of rebuilding from that damage—severe job losses, especially hard for those at the lower end of the economic ladder, decimation of entire industries (tourism, arts, hotels, and restaurants), cessation of business travel to the city, and pummeling of the office market—were formidable. There was no snapback switch, no simple return to a pre-pandemic "normal." Business leaders and analysts were asking how long the recovery would take—not whether the city would retain its premier global position.

The pandemic devastation of the economy of Times Square revealed the fragile reality of the district's ecology. The Covid-19 shutdown cost hundreds of thousands of jobs. The tourism industry alone lost 89,000 jobs, nearly one-quarter of its pre-pandemic employees—a vulnerable workforce of minorities, immigrants, and those without a bachelor's degree—and its economic impact dropped by 75 percent to $20.2 billion in 2020 from $80.3 billion in 2019, according to the Office of the State Comptroller. The pandemic's scar on the tourist industry accounted for 59 percent of the city's $2 billion decline in tax collections, or about $1.2 billion for the 2020–2021 tax year. The grim statistics affirmed why the past 10 years of tourism growth had made it a vital industry for New York City. Times Square's reliance on tourists and theatergoers appeared as its biggest weakness, yet in time, as the availability of a vaccine made people more comfortable going out and as travel restrictions were lifted, entertainment and tourism would reemerge as a source of strength in the city's recovery.

It wasn't just that the crowds had disappeared from Times Square. When the normal activity of a place is sharply and suddenly disrupted, as during the pandemic, things begin to happen. Vacancy and the fears of vagrancy spiked as the number of homeless individuals living on the streets of Times Square, previously often disguised by the crowds, increased. In Hell's Kitchen, residents began feeling the impacts of a city not in control of life, with a worrisome reversion to panhandling, crime, and a culture of drugs, ushered in, some said, by the transition of hotels catering to tourists to shelters for the homeless. Conditions were difficult. Fear settled into the district. Restaurateurs and business owners were apprehensive that the past crime-ridden Times Square was creeping back. That era is hard to forget for those who remember it.

**9.2** West 42nd Street at midday two years after the Covid shutdown, awaiting crowds of tourists to reignite activity, April 2022. With the reopening of Broadway theaters in fall 2021, followed by the return of international visitors, two key elements for the recovery of the Times Square economy were in place. Neighborhood businesses were still troubled, but optimism prevailed that the entertainment economy of the place would lead to a faster comeback than in other parts of midtown more dependent on office workers. Gary Hack.

As renters moved out of their high-priced apartments, affluent New Yorkers left their homes in the city for their weekend retreats, and office workers moved to wherever it would be most convenient to "work from home," the 1970s' specter of an empty city seemed to take hold. It was a powerful antecedent. To some artists, the empty city of the 1970s held a sense of play, a promise of something that could happen, an encounter, the possibility of a return, of people coming back, remarked *New Yorker* writer Vinson Cunningham during a fall 2020 webinar panel discussion on "The Empty City" sponsored by the Museum of the City of New York. The New York-based Belgium-born author Luc Sante spoke of the mystery of the empty buildings of that era in the city's history. These remembrances, however, are remote from the pandemic's personal tragedies evoked in the emptiness of public spaces that made this empty experience so different from those of the past. New York in 2020 was nothing like what it was in the 1970s; moreover, the fiscal distress of the mid-1970s was in no small part of the city's own making.

"There's simply no similarity at all," Richard Ravitch, developer of middle-income housing and former chairman of the state's Urban Development Corporation (1975–1977) and the Metropolitan Transportation Authority (1979–1983), told Nicole Gelinas in a 2021 interview for *City Journal*, a publication of the Manhattan Institute, a conservative think tank. "What happened in the seventies was simply that the City of New York borrowed money to cover its operating expenses," he said. That mounting liability—$7 billion ($35 billion in 2021 dollars) or more than half of the city's 1975 budget—was so troubling that the banks cut off the city's borrowing, and the city was forced to cut back services and lay off hundreds of thousands of workers and find a creative way to repay the debt. "The major problem was all this overhanging, inappropriately incurred debt. That's not the problem now."[5]

The twenty-first-century pandemic jolted New York's economy and way of life, throwing into confusion the reasons why so many had chosen to live in this maddeningly expensive and vibrant city. With the shutdown of cultural venues and sporting attractions, restaurants and bars, and neighborhood socialization, the city was hanging "in a state of suspended animation."[6] It was a precarious time in the life of the city. At the height of the pandemic safe-at-home order, photographers walked the desolate streets, plazas, and transit hubs to capture views of parts of the city New Yorkers might otherwise avoid or rush through.

How would New York respond to this latest rupture in the life of the city? How would its historic resiliency manifest itself this time, under conditions strikingly different from what residents and elected officials had ever experienced? "The question is," former Deputy Mayor Dan Doctoroff told a reporter for the *Economist*, "Is it going to be like 9/11, or is it going to be like the 1970s?"[7] No one had a crystal ball in 2020, and a year later, the view was only somewhat less cloudy. During much of 2021, doom-and-gloom commentary prevailed. The dystopian social context of an empty city, the early belief that density must have been to blame for the rapid spread of the virus and New York's tragic death toll, and the ominous fiscal implications of the pandemic created the basis for much of the negative narrative, but so too did the long tradition of anti-urbanism in America that sees the demise of cities just around the corner.

As successive waves of the virus swept across the city, emptying midtown of its intense daily activity, even the most astute observers of New York's urban dynamic found the future return to business "normal" unknowable, a "new normal unpredictable." Early opinions were rendered moot by the repeated recalibration of back-to-the-office dates and uncertain future demand for office space arising from the pandemic experience of how readily businesses and hundreds of thousands of office workers had adapted to remote work. Real estate professionals were anxiously uncertain and atypically confused about future rents in New York, a key barometer of the city's economic health. They wondered what type of improvements would be required to make office buildings attractive enough for workers to come back to their desks, and what kind of new thinking would be required to cope with the current challenge of vacant office space. Would health and wellness centers be an amenity or a necessity? They were deeply concerned about where property values were headed.

For owners of the towers in Times Square impacted by the overcrowded and chaotic conditions of the pedestrian plazas, the retreat from office work compounded future prospects for strong tenant leasing. Even before the pandemic-enforced retrenchments, the development of up-the-minute, technologically advanced office towers in Hudson Yards packed with luxury amenities had posed a threat to the competitive attraction of those in Times Square. Would the young workers for whom the city offered so much economic and social opportunity return to the city? If so, when? Without the legions of young professionals returning to the office, how would all those luxury residential towers with walk-to-work proximity to midtown that developers built with such ambition along the western spine of 42nd Street perform?

Analysts were watching those rental buildings, looking for signs of a rebound or further pain, and what they saw in spring 2020 was indicative of how the real estate market typically responds to a downturn in demand: vacancies shot up, rents declined, and "deal-sweetening freebies" (months of free rent, waived broker fees, and complimentary services at the owner's expense) became plentiful. But the coronavirus-driven change was sudden. Buildings packed with smaller apartment sizes, studios and one-bedroom apartments attractive to singles or childless couples, registered price declines almost immediately. Two months after the shutdown, the median monthly rent for apartments in the submarket of West Midtown as reported in "The Corcoran Report" had dropped an amazing 49 percent to $2,343, from a January median of $4,570, and average vacancy rates had risen to 2.07 percent from 1.34 percent. By the end of the year, rents in West Midtown had recovered some but vacancy nearly doubled again, reaching 3.9 percent. Sweet as they were, the Covid discounts did not last long. A large proportion of the one-year leases started to expire in the first half of 2022; encouraged by returning renters, landlords started cutting back on concessions and raising rents. The comeback was almost as swift as the downward spiral. It had been a roller-coaster year in rental trends, perhaps unprecedented in Manhattan. By September 2021, average monthly rents in West Midtown (Corcoran no longer reporting median rent by neighborhood) reached $4,242, a 30 percent increase from the year before at $3,268; average vacancy rates had come down as well to 2.61 percent from 4.15 percent. In other Manhattan neighborhoods in high demand, average rent escalations were even greater: SoHo/TriBeCa, 38 percent, and Chelsea/Flatiron, 33 percent. Less than a year later, by July 2022, average monthly rents in West Midtown set a new record, $5,608. Quite a bellwether. Judged by these residential benchmarks, the recovery appeared to be well on its way, evidence of the local adage: Don't bet against New York.

Just beyond Times Square, the quest to build on the commercial prowess of Times Square was continuing, with a couple of patient realty interests making big bets on Eighth Avenue. Over the years, Extell Development and Trans World Equities, both Manhattan-based real estate firms, had been buying low-density parcels or parking lots for assemblage into development sites for new high-density towers. Gary Barnett of Extell now controlled most of the east side of Eighth Avenue between 45th and 46th Streets (and development rights from the Imperial Theatre), where he plans to build a 51-story hotel (see figure 7.4), and Trans World Equities controlled half of the west side of Eighth Avenue between 43rd and 44th Street, intended plan not yet revealed. To realty interests, this still undeveloped stretch of the avenue in the 40s—"a sort of bridge between the past and the present"—was a good place to gauge the prospects of a recovery for Times Square, and what they saw showed promise.[8]

Times Square was functioning as the barometer of recovery, and tourism was rebounding much more strongly than expected. The reopening of Broadway theaters in September 2021, followed by the reopening of US borders to vaccinated travelers, reinstated two fundamentals of the district's economy. Visitors from across the United States, especially those from the New York-New Jersey-Connecticut region, streamed back to the city throughout 2021, accounting for 30.2 million of the 33 million visitors to the city that year (half of the 2019 record of 66.6 million). Pedestrian counts in Times Square averaged 174,000 a day in 2021, up nearly 40 percent from 2020, though still much below the 2019 mark of 356,000 a day. As prospective as those numbers on domestic tourism were, the economic crutch of tourism depended most heavily on a robust return of foreign tourists and business travelers, because they tend to stay longer and spend more money. Before the pandemic, tourists to New York spent $47 billion annually; about half of that spending came from international tourists, according to official estimates, although they accounted for just 20 percent of all visitors. Travel from abroad bounced back in 2022; more than eight million were expected to visit the city, 14.6 percent of the 56.7 million visitors forecast by the city's tourism agency, NYC & Company.[9] By summertime, Times Square tourism appeared poised for a strong recovery, as reported out by the Times Square Alliance. In July, the daily count of pedestrian traffic averaged 367,947 people; this was the closest monthly average to pre-pandemic levels, only 8.9 percent below July 2019; hotel occupancy, at 85.6 percent, was at its highest rate since the start of the pandemic and close to the highest of any major market in the country, according to Smith Travel Research, which tracks travel and tourism. Broadway attendance and gross sales were moving closer to their pre-pandemic levels.

The tourists were coming back, but Times Square still needed something more, something new in the way of reinvention to reset the stage of experience in a post-pandemic era. Reinvention has been integral to the legacy of the place. So too the installation of the newest technological gismo, whether for enhancing the dazzling digital lights of the advertising mecca or presenting a unique entertainment experience. For several years, construction workers have been busy on two massive reinvention projects that boosters for the district could point to as signs of future strength: TSX Broadway, a $2.5 billion, 46-story entertainment venue and luxury hotel scheduled for completion in 2023, and a $500 million redevelopment of the globally recognized 26-story iconic tower, One Times Square, site of the New Year's Eve ball drop since 1907, scheduled for completion in 2024. The developers of both projects are set on reinventing the experience of Times Square.

TSX Broadway promises to provide "a new palace of possibility" through the unprecedented engineering feat of lifting the 14-million-pound famed Palace Theatre (1913) 30 feet above ground level to make way for "experiential retail space" on a corner with possibly the highest foot traffic in the district, West 47th Street and Seventh Avenue. The development team of L&L Holding Company, Maefield Development, and Fortress Investment Group conceived their project as an "entertainment ecosystem," the first entire-building immersive experience, equipped with three floors of retail galleries; an entertainment stage and 150-seat venue for launches, concerts, events and brand experiences; a food and beverage hospitality lounge featuring the largest terrace in Times Square; and a hotel with 660-plus rooms (Tempo, a Hilton flag returning to Times Square), all packed into a 46-story tower with 550,000 square feet of space. David Levinson, cofounder of the development firm, described the new building as a "vertical Disneyland" that would be like "the metaverse intersecting with Times Square and Las Vegas" without the gambling (though various interests are lobbying to bring a casino to the city, possibly to Times Square).[10] Fifty million dollars was being spent to overhaul the Palace Theatre—the district's most famous playhouse and a national symbol of vaudeville that became the premier variety house in the world, as the New York City Landmarks Commission wrote in its 1987 designation report for the theater's first-floor baroque Beaux-Arts interior. Founded by West Coast showman and entrepreneur Martin Beck, it is currently owned by the Nederlander Organization, which converted it to legitimate theater in 1965. Except for its current interior space, most of the original theater was demolished in 1988 to make way for the DoubleTree Suites hotel, which in turn was demolished to make way for the start of TSX Broadway. The showstopping element of the site's newest inhabitant—which could be expected to attract New Yorkers as well as tourists—is a 4,000-square-foot indoor-outdoor performance stage elevated above Seventh Avenue; when closed, the doors to Times Square's only permanent outdoor stage will meld into a 18,000-square-foot digital sign that wraps the building—the newest Times Square spectacular historically evocative of Douglas Leigh's showmanship.

The redo of One Times Square similarly follows the district's tradition of hosting bigger-and-better visual spectaculars replete with branding opportunities. For decades, the wedge-shaped building originally built to house the headquarters of the *New York Times* was something of a white elephant, mostly vacant since the 1970s because its small unconventionally shaped floors did not fit the modern-day needs of office tenants. The investment bank Lehman Brothers purchased the building at a bankruptcy auction in 1975, exploiting the building's position anchoring the southern edge of Times Square to generate millions in sign revenue. Now in 2022, in another shift of architectural gears under the ownership of Jamestown Properties, which acquired the advertising tower from Lehman Brothers in 1997, twelve floors of its interior space are being transformed into "a next generation brand experience offering brands the added ability to connect with their customers in Times Square through immersive technology-enabled activations." Inside and outside, the entire tower will be a giant billboard. In addition to the essential ground-floor retail, six floors of the building will be devoted to a museum that "will tell the story of the building, New Year's Eve celebrations, and its place in the history of Times Square"—"kind of an ad for Times Square itself," remarked reporter Kim Velsey. The completely new façade will host massive LED displays and an outdoor viewing platform—"the go-to for any new tourist attractions these days."[11] The projected opening is summer 2024.

Even McDonald's has upped its game, "modernizing the customer experience through the intersection of technology and hospitality" in a new location (with table service, mobile order and pay, and digital kiosks) on a high-visibility corner location at 45th and Broadway; corporate executives expect the 11,199-square-foot 173-seat eatery, which opened in 2019, to be one of the busiest McDonald's in the United States. Coupled with a 9,280-square-foot LED billboard (said to be the third largest in the district), the new flagship restaurant offers a "Big Mac with a view" of Times Square and the billboard circus through three levels of floor-to-ceiling glass—"as entertaining a McDonald's as you can get," one customer wrote in a TripAdvisor review.[12] And in an expansive move to capitalize on the return of robust foot traffic to 42nd Street, in July 2022, the golden-arches corporation signed a 20-year, $40 million lease for space at 661 Eighth Avenue right across the street from the Port Authority Bus Terminal.

The new high-tech projects represent big bets on the future of Times Square, and by extension on the economic health of the city. Still, vulnerabilities remain ever present in the minds of many landlords, corporations, and civic leaders. Retail rents in the area, once the highest in the city, had been dropping for years, but the pandemic exacerbated the decline. The office market in Times Square, where the vacancy rate in the second quarter of 2022, as reported by the global commercial real estate firm Newmark, reached an astounding 24.5 percent, is far more challenged than for midtown as a whole, where vacancy reached 18.3 percent, also extraordinarily high. Notwithstanding its excellent transportation nexus, Times Square is a harder sell as a location because office workers do not want to walk through the constant crush of tourists and congestion of costumed characters. In place of blue-chip corporate tenants, a new mix of tenants (digital media firm Roku, video-sharing app TikTok, and Touro College, for example) has been taking advantage of pandemic discounts.

Discounts are opportunities, especially in high-demand locations. Lower rents can attract the vitality of new retailers who otherwise could not afford the location. So too brand-name restaurants have been taking advantage of retail rents that have fallen below $1,200 per square foot for the first time in a decade to open or expand venues in Times Square. In the hotel realm, the 1,780-room Sheraton Times Square traded hands for $356 million, nearly $400 million less than its 2006 purchase price; the buyer was a hospitality group acquiring other Manhattan hotel properties. Another opportunistic sale: investors agreed to purchase the closed 460-room Hilton Times Square on 42nd Street for roughly $85 million, barely one-third of its $242.5 million sale price in 2006. Underlying the investment optimism is the belief that any spike in crime will be controlled, safety on the streets will assured, and quality-of-life issues in Times Square will be addressed—all vulnerabilities to the district's economy.

In June 2022, a US Supreme Court ruling striking down New York State's tough concealed-carry handgun law, which for a century had effectively banned firearms in public areas across the city, made gun control an immediate issue for the city. Within a week of the ruling, in an emergency session called by Governor Kathy Hochul, state legislators rushed to pass and the governor signed, the Concealed Carry Improvement Act, creating rules that would prohibit people from carrying firearms in public places deemed to be "sensitive places." The law identified an expansive list of twenty places where guns would be banned, including: health care facilities; houses of worship; colleges and universities; places where children gather (schools, libraries, day care centers, public playgrounds, parks and zoos); public transportation; places where alcohol or cannabis is consumed; theaters, concerts, casinos, and other entertainment venues—and one specific place, Times Square, a last-minute addition in the late-night negotiations, reported the *Times*. The city was left to define precise boundaries of Times Square, "provided such area would be clearly and conspicuously identified with signage." As proposed by city officials, the district's formal boundaries are rather generous, roughly covering three dozen blocks from Ninth to Sixth Avenues and from West 40th to 53rd Street, which will include eight blocks of Hell's Kitchen. On September 1, the signs went up: "TIMES SQUARE: GUN FREE ZONE." The law was passed in a rush, but how its enforcement is to be managed will be key to its effectiveness. The law was "a forceful retort to the Supreme Court decision," and, with litigation likely, "may be an early test of how far a state can go to limit the spread of handguns without violating the Supreme Court's ruling."[13]

Times Square is a high-profile target of opportunity for violent attacks. Since 2008, there have been at least three terrorist bomb attacks, two of which detonated; how many others may have been foiled by the police is unknown. A bomb threat from an armed gunman tipped off by an anonymous phone call led the authorities to evacuate the Times Square Disney Store in fall 2021. In a high-profile unprovoked assault the next month, a 58-year-old New Jersey cancer nurse walking through the square died after being slammed into at high speed by a 26-year-old man "running on foot after having just robbed one woman in her apartment and another on the street." Reporting on the crime and a list of others, Nicole Gelinas wrote, "Times Square has been a mess for months." Also in 2021, three shootings. In August 2022, an unprovoked attack on a 59-year-old Asian woman pulling a shopping cart near Seventh Avenue and 42nd Street was deemed a hate crime. A constant drumbeat by the media and the uptick in gun violence reportedly have made residents from the region concerned about their safety. Hard not to be; crime has increased in the Midtown South precinct, yet despite the tabloid headlines, New York is still one of the nation's safest big cities. Crime is much lower than it was at its peak in 1980s and 1990s.[14]

New York's recovery came to life in 2022: tourism and entertainment are back. On the other hand, the contours of the "new normal" in office work that drives the activity of the city's business centers remain uncertain. As I write, it is still evolving, to-be-determined, as corporations, investment banks, legal and finance firms, and related entities consider what level of in-office personnel is needed to sustain and grow their businesses. The data reveal few clear conclusions. Decade after decade, though, proximity to professionals in aligned fields of endeavor and the benefits of agglomeration of economies have fostered the growth and prosperity of urban centers. There is little reason to believe that

Zoom interactions can substitute in the long term for what is commonly labeled the "water-cooler" effect of person-to-person interaction in pushing forward professional careers as well as business opportunities. The urban scene also fosters a social life for those fresh out of college as well as unattached professionals gathering in midtown's bars and restaurants after work. For service-sector jobs in venues other than high-rise office towers, in hospitals and health centers, schools and universities, retail, restaurants, and hospitality, among others, work at home is not an option.

New York City is well practiced in the mission of renewal. Although the city faces a daunting recovery, the pandemic did not obliterate the essential elements that made for its robust pre-pandemic economy, and this makes the prospects for a continued recovery entirely different from the experience of the 1970s. Today, the city's economy is not singularly dependent upon Wall Street and financial services as in the past, but rather is more diversified than at any time in the past 60 years. The resident population still sees itself as resilient and rooted in the city's tradition of grit and determination to cope with whatever, go out, eat out, and socialize. New York City is a gravitational center for talent, the type of talent businesses of all types are seeking today. It is the city young people still yearn to be in, to make their mark, find a new occupation, a love life. It is a city historically welcoming of immigrants, who have contributed in diverse ways to its economic and entrepreneurial power. And it is a city of neighborhoods offering diverse lifestyles, attractive to retirees who have more leisure time than others to avail themselves of the city's cultural resources. The pandemic did nothing to change the fact that New York is still one of the few truly global cities, a magnet for business and culture, where investment-grade real estate is in high demand and lower prices are likely to enhance buying opportunities.

# ACKNOWLEDGMENTS

Writing a book is a solitary experience. It is relieved by conversations with colleagues and friends who share a passion for the topic, and I have been most fortunate to have many of both who graciously shared their insights and enthusiasms for this sequel to the story of Times Square. Although I was well versed in the history and current events of the place, there was still much to unravel from historical newspapers and trade journals, primary documents, secondary sources, and, most importantly, interviews with public officials, professionals in public agencies, developers, lawyers, consultants, civic players, and community activists, all of whom gave liberally of their time to share stories, as well as opinions, of the changes in Times Square over the past 20 years.

I am deeply grateful to all, but several stand out for their extended efforts on behalf of this book: Cora Cahan, Joe Restuccia, and Carl Weisbrod spent many hours talking with me so I might understand as much of the inside stories of change as possible, without ever asking how I would record events in which they figured so prominently. As leaders of the Times Square Alliance, Tim Tompkins and Tom Harris shared their up-front experiences of the place, as well as providing data and images for the book. New York University's Furman Center and the New York City Economic Development Corporation also provided critical data for analyzing the impacts of the transformation. Thanks go to James Patchett and Rachel Loeb, both former presidents and chief executive officers of EDC, for their cooperation in supporting my requests for data to analyze the impacts of the 42nd Street project. I want to single out Patrick Conway, EDC's vice president for asset management, who spent many hours fielding my many requests for data, documents, and clarifications so that I could accurately write about the economic impact of the 42nd Street Development Project, as well as the insights gained from Matthew Kwatinetz, former EDC executive vice president for asset management. My friend Susan Fine kept peppering me with questions that were helpfully provocative and offered suggestions while reading the manuscript. Carol Willis, founder and director of the Skyscraper Museum and general enthusiast of urban density, drew upon her deep fount of knowledge about skyscrapers to instantly reply to whatever question I had about the early development of Manhattan's office towers. I am especially grateful for the many extended conversations about city policy and for my long friendship with Alicia Glen; her insights about city politics as Deputy Mayor for Housing and Economic Development in the de Blasio administration provided a critical source for understanding this period in the life of the city.

Finding images that would best illustrate the themes and stories of this book consumed more hours that I can now recall; the quest and what those images revealed were an illuminating (often undervalued) form of research. For historical images, Alexis Greene, Darcy Tell, and Sandy Isenstadt shortened the work by sharing image files from their research on Times Square. The equally time-consuming process of securing permissions for publication was made easier and more enjoyable by the many courtesies extended to me by architects, nonprofits, authors, and particularly photographers, who found Times Square and 42nd Street a constant calling for their professional skills. My appreciation goes to Columbia Business School for funding support of photographic permissions. As in my other books about New York City, the numerous credits for my in-house photographer and husband, Gary Hack, exceed those of my name as author. For the many ways in which his critical intelligence, our life together, and a shared love of cities have uniquely shaped all my writings, this detail is fitting.

To my colleague Betsy Blackmar and Carl Weisbrod, both long-time friends of standing who read every page of the manuscript twice and offered remarkably cogent comments and revision suggestions immeasurably helpful in fine-tuning the manuscript: I cannot thank each of you enough. David Dunlap reviewed parts of the manuscript that followed his own long-time interest in Times Square, making sure I was correct on the important facts. The comments of two anonymous peer reviewers were also helpful in raising questions of importance.

At the MIT Press, I have had the good fortune to work with a team of talented and dedicated professionals, whose enthusiasm for *Times*

*Square Remade* started with a ringing endorsement of my proposal. Appreciation goes to Beth Clevenger and Anthony Zannino, Matthew Abbate for his superb copy editing, and Yasuyo Iguchi who once again designed the layout for my book with sophistication and an understanding of my intent.

Over the three years it has taken to research and write this book, I have been sustained by the love and support of my family. The marker of time here is the joy of welcoming into this world my daughter's daughter, Susannah Grace Brown, whose smile can brighten the day of any soul.

# NOTES

The following abbreviations have been used to shorten the citation of recurrent sources:

DN      [New York] *Daily News*
NYT     *New York Times*
NYP     *New York Post*
RERBG   *Real Estate Record and Builders Guide*
WSJ     *Wall Street Journal*

## INTRODUCTION

1   "Romance of Real Estate Told by Noyes after Leasing the Casino Theater Property," *RERBG*, February 1, 1930, 14.

## CHAPTER 1

1   "Owners of New York: Twenty Individuals and Estates Hold $352,000,000 Worth of Land," *Louisville Courier Journal* (report from the *New York Herald*), April 24, 1897, 9. The *Herald* took pains to explain its methodology for the calculation of landed-wealth valuations that had hitherto been opaque at best. The figures, it said, "have been compiled with infinite care from tax receipts and other reliable sources of information," and then submitted for revision to real estate experts "having intimate knowledge of the great estates." If there are any faults in these estimates, the paper believed that they "are too low—by 25 percent."

2   "Astor Property at Public Auction," *NYT*, February 15, 1920, W20; "Sale of Henry Astor Estate Property Is Epoch Making," *RERBG*, February 21, 1920, 254; "Great Disposal Sale of Properties in 'Heart of New York,'" *RERBG*, March 6, 1920, 306.

3   "Astor Sale Feature of the Week," *NYT*, March 7, 1920, W1; "Sale of Henry Astor Estate."

4   "Astor Was Keen Realty Investor," *NYT*, February 22, 1920, W20.

5   "New York Being Made Over by Shift of Trade Centers," *NYT*, July 7, 1912, SM10.

6   "Times Square Growth Adds Millions to Realty Values," *NYT*, January 1, 1915, 13.

7   "Times Square Growth Adds Millions to Realty Values."

8   Joseph Berger, "Faded Memories: Painted Signs, Relics of a Bygone New York, Become Even More Rare," *NYT*, November 5, 2005, B1.

9   "Last of an Old Favorite: Musical People Especially Will Miss This Landmark," *NYT*, March 15, 1908, SM2; "New Theatre Soon in Times Square," *NYT*, September 22, 1909, 9; "A Glimpse of Times Square in the Year 1911," *NYT*, February 27, 1910, SM1.

10   "Changes in Long Acre Square," *RERBG*, November 16, 1907, 799.

11   "The Real Estate Field: Significance of Some Recent Purchases," *NYT*, January 13, 1895, 11.

12   David W. Dunlap, *On Broadway: A Journey Uptown over Time* (New York: Rizzoli, 1990), 166.

13   Adolph S. Tomars, *The First Oscar Hammerstein and New York's Golden Age of Theater and Music* (Jefferson, NC: McFarland, 2020), a book the author began in the 1950s and that was posthumously completed by his son based on Tomars's notes on repository at the New York Public Library.

14   David W. Dunlap, "Exploring Vestiges of Harlem's Jewish Past," *NYT*, June 7, 2002, E33.

15   "The Real Estate Market," *RERBG*, February 18, 1893, 251.

16   Two months after his initial purchase, Hammerstein bought two standard-size adjoining lots (20 feet by 100 feet) for a total site cost of $940,000. On Al Hayman's purchase, "Al Hayman's Pluck," *San Francisco Chronicle*, December 28, 1891, 2; on Hammerstein's electric light, Robert A. M. Stern, Gregory Gilmartin, and John Massengale, *New York 1900: Metropolitan Architecture and Urbanism 1890–1915* (New York: Rizzoli, 1983, paperback 1995), 208.

17   Sam Roberts, *A History of New York in 27 Buildings* (New York: Bloomsbury, 2019), 154.

18   Mike Wallace, *Greater Gotham: A History of New York City from 1898 to 1919* (New York: Oxford University Press, 2017), 394.

19   Mary C. Henderson, *The City and the Theatre: New York Playhouses from Bowling Green to Times Square* (Clifton, NJ: James T. White, 1973), 196.

20   Mary C. Henderson and Alexis Green, *The Story of 42nd Street: The Theaters, Shows, Characters, and Scandals of the World's Most Notorious Street* (New York: Back Stage Books, 2008), 143.

21   "Long Acre Square Up-to-Date," *RERBG*, October 11, 1902, 516.

22   "The Real Estate Situation," *RERBG*, January 18, 1902, 100; "Real Estate Situation," *RERBG*, November 29, 1902, 802.

23   Wallace, *Greater Gotham*, 395. See 397–403 for a discussion of the Theatrical Syndicate.

24   Wallace, *Greater Gotham*, 397, 398.

25   "Two Active Sections," *RERBG*, October 21, 1911, 590.

26   "New Traffic Plan in Theater Zone," *NYT*, November 23, 1924, E3.

27 "Times Square Growth Adds Millions to Realty Values"; "Times Square the Theatre Center," *NYT*, January 1, 1915, 13; "Theatre Building," *RERBG*, August 17, 1912, 310; "The Multiplication of Theatres," *RERBG*, December 21, 1912, 1163.

28 "Theatre Building"; "The Multiplication of Theatres."

29 David Hammack, "Developing for Commercial Culture," in *Inventing Times Square: Commerce and Culture at the Crossroads of the World*, ed. William R. Taylor (New York: Russell Sage Foundation, 1991), 36–80; Ric Burns and James Sanders with Lisa Ades, *New York: An Illustrated History* (New York: Alfred A. Knopf, 1999), 294.

30 From George J. Lankevich, *Postcards from Times Square: Sights and Sentiments from the Last Century* (Garden City Park, NY: Square One Publishers, 2001).

31 Fred Bassett, "Postcard Collection—Appendix C, Wish You Were Here! The Story of the Golden Age of Picture Postcards in the United States," New York State Library, http://www.nysl.nysed.gov/msscfa/qc16510ess.htm

32 Neil Harris, "Urban Tourism and the Commercial City," in Taylor, *Inventing Times Square*, 78–79.

33 Paul Morand, *New York* (New York: Henry Holt, 1930), 192, cited in Dunlap, *On Broadway*, 170; Darcy Tell, *Times Square Spectacular: Lighting Up Broadway* (New York: Smithsonian Books with HarperCollins, 2007), 15–16.

34 Edward W. Townsend, "New York—The Greatest Summer Resort," *Harper's Weekly* 44 (September 1, 1900): 821–822.

35 Justin Kaplan, *When the Astors Owned New York: Blue Bloods and Grand Hotels in a Gilded Age* (New York: Viking, 2006), 141.

36 "In the Real Estate Field: Important Business Operations Enliven the Week's Business," *NYT*, July 22, 1900, 10.

37 "Longacre Square—North and South," *RERBG*, December 22, 1900, 856.

38 Henry Collins Brown, ed., *Valentine's Manual of Old New York*, new series (New York: Valentine's Manual, 1923), 118, cited in Dunlap, *On Broadway*, 166.

39 "Investment Properties in Upper Broadway, Sale of the St. Cloud Hotel [communicated]," *RERBG*, October 22, 1891, 504.

40 "The Real Estate Market: Two Important Sales," *RERBG*, October 22, 1892, 505.

41 "In the Real Estate Field," *NYT*, October 6, 1901, 20.

42 "Seven Millions Built This Huge Hotel Pile," *NYT*, July 10, 1904, 12. The *Times* may have overstated the cost; according to the Daytonian in Manhattan's online history of "The Lost 1907 Hotel Astor," the hotel cost $5 million: http://daytonin manhattan.blogspot.com/2016/01/the-lost-1907-hotel-astor-1511-broadway.html; see also Stern, Gilmartin, and Massengale, *New York 1900*, 269.

43 John Tauranac, *Elegant New York: The Builders and the Buildings, 1885–1915* (New York: Abbeville Press, 1985), 112.

44 "Knickerbocker Hotel Opens to Guests Today," *NYT*, October 24, 1906, 9.

45 *RERBG*, October 27, 1906, 675.

46 "Young Astor's Lands Worth $150,000,000," *NYT*, May 8, 1912, 2; "Realty Over $63,000,000," *NYT*, June 14, 1913, 3.

47 Christopher Gray, "Streetscapes: Beaux-Arts Façade and 'Old King Cole' in the Bar," *NYT*, February 16, 1997, R7; David W. Dunlap, "After More Than Four Years of Reconstruction, a Landmark Is Unwrapped on Times Square," *NYT*, August 22, 2003, B2.

48 Elizabeth Blackmar, "Uptown Real Estate and the Creation of Times Square," in Taylor, *Inventing Times Square*, 53, 65.

49 Kirkley Greenwell, "History of Hell's Kitchen Neighborhood," https://web. archive.org/web/20101221013615/hknanyc.org/aboutus/history.php; also see John Strausbaugh, "Turf of Gangs and Gangsters," *NYT*, August 17, 2007.

50 Otho G. Cartwright, "The Middle West Side," in *West Side Studies*, carried out under the direction of Pauline Goldmark (New York: Russell Sage Foundation, 1914), 3, 5.

51 Data on density from Walter Laidlaw, *Statistical Sources for Demographic Studies of Greater New York, 1920* (New York: New York City 1920 Census Committee, 1922).

52 "Great Disposal Sale of Properties."

53 "Real Estate Department," *RERBG*, March 1, 1890, 295.

54 Robert M. Coates, "Profiles: King of the Bronx," *New Yorker*, December 7, 1929, 34.

55 Advertisement, *RERBG*, February 28, 1920, 281; advertisement, *RERBG*, March 6, 1920, 313; "Sale of Henry Astor Estate Property Is Epoch Making."

56 "First Astor Realty Sold at Auction Brings $5,159,075," *NYT*, March 10, 1920, 1.

57 "141 Astor Lots Auctioned for $5,159,075," *New-York Tribune*, March 10, 1920, 7.

58 "141 Astor Lots Auctioned for $5,159,075."

59 "First Astor Realty Sold at Auction."

60 "Auction of Henry Astor Property Brings Record Prices"; "Review of Real Estate Market for the Current Week," *RERBG*, March 13, 1920, 341.


## CHAPTER 2


1 Anthony Bianco, *Ghosts of 42nd Street: A History of America's Most Infamous Block* (New York: William Morrow, 2004), 172; Carter B. Horsley, "At 78, Irving Maidman Wants Out," *NYT*, January 26, 1975, 314.

2 Jane Dickson, remarks at "Capturing the Deuce: Times Square in the 1970s & 80s," a public program at the Museum of the City of New York, January 29, 2019.

3 Alhena Katsof, "Collaborative Projects, Inc. (Colab), Times Square Show, 1980," in *The Artist as Curator: An Anthology*, ed. Elena Filipovic (Cologne: Walther König, 2017), 139.

4 "The Rivoli, Newest Film Palace, Opens," *NYT*, December 29, 1917, 8.

5 Will Irwin, *Highlights of Manhattan* (New York: Century, 1927), 329; "The Roxy—New York's Newest and Biggest Movie House," *Decorative Furnisher*, 84–85, as quoted in Robert A. M. Stern, Gregory Gilmartin, and Thomas Mellins, *New York 1930: Architecture and Urbanism between the Two World Wars* (New York: Rizzoli, 1987, paperback 1994), 258.

6 Martin Clary, *Mid-Manhattan* (New York: Forty-second Street Property Owners and Merchants Association, 1929), 199.

7 "Woods for Closing 40 Theaters Here," *NYT*, September 10, 1929, 37.

8 Frank W. Crane, "Manhattan Land Values Rise with Skyscrapers," *NYT*, August 4, 1929, XX6; Robert M. Coates, "New York's Twenty-Four-Hour Corner: Around Times Square There Is a Cycle of Life That Is Ever Changing," *NYT*, June 23, 1929, SM5; "Every Hour Busy in Times Square," *NYT*, December 29, 1929, RE1.

9    Irving Maidman, "A Survey of Theatres in the Times Square Area," *RERBG*, June 22, 1935, 6.

10   "Speakeasies Ruining Midtown Property Values, Hewen Declares," *RERBG*, May 2, 1931, 10.

11   David Nasaw, *Going Out: The Rise and Fall of Public Amusements* (New York: Basic Books, 1993).

12   "Rialto Value Rose 15-fold since 1900," *NYT*, February 4, 1933, 10. Campagna was to build luxury apartment houses, become a philanthropist, and become known to preservationists as the developer responsible for the demolition of the House of Genius, a cultural and artistic landmark for Greenwich Village residents, and the Fifth-Avenue Brokaw Mansion, which sparked an active movement to preserve these mansions.

13   "New Sign for Times Sq.," *NYT*, February 28, 1936, 23; "Rialto Value Rose 15-fold since 1900"; Christopher Gray, "Streetscapes: The Rialto Theater; a Times Sq. Cinema Nurtured by the 'Merchant of Menace,'" *NYT*, July 19, 1987, 8:14; "New Rialto Theater Retains Mementos of Its Predecessor," *New York Herald Tribune*, December 22, 1935, E3; "Rialto Will Open for Yule Season," *NYT*, December 20, 1935, 29.

14   Brooks McNamara, "The Entertainment District at the End of the 1930s," in *Inventing Times Square: Commerce and Culture at the Crossroads of the World*, ed. William R. Taylor (New York: Russell Sage Foundation, 1990), 182.

15   "Times Sq. Is Enjoying Its 'Greatest Boom' as Civilian and Military Visitors Fill the Area," *NYT*, October 28, 1943, 25.

16   Editorial, "Times Square," *NYT*, December 15, 1952, 24.

17   Bianco, *Ghosts of 42nd Street*, 134.

18   Paul Goldberger, "Architecture View: Will Times Square Become a Grand Canyon," *NYT*, October 6, 1985, 2:31.

19   "Midtown 8th Ave. Shows New Vigor," *NYT*, December 30, 1956, R1; see also Stephen G. Thompson, "Real Estate: West Side to Gain Major Improvements," *New York Herald Tribune*, July 18, 1951, 31.

20   By 1963 Maidman owned at least thirty-two properties on the West Side. He had succeeded in building his West Side Airlines Terminal and two of five planned motor inns. In 1965 he opened an eight-story office building—the first to rise on Eighth Avenue in 25 years—on a site that became the headquarters site of the *New York Times*—but he would lose it in a foreclosure in 1976 during the city's fiscal crisis; John P. Callahan, "Realty Men Map a New West Side," *NYT*, September 16, 1956, R1.

21   Callahan, "Realty Men Map a New West Side."

22   David Munk, "Gloria Swanson Standing in the Rubble," http://stargayzing.com/gloria-swansons-connection-to-stephen-sondheims-follies/, June 10, 2013.

23   "Vigor Noted in West Side Realty Field," *New York Herald Tribune*, December 25, 1960, 11C.

24   "Old Stage, New Stars," *Business Week*, October 24, 1964, 132–133; Bianco, *Ghosts of 42nd Street*, 146–147; Ada Louise Huxtable, "Re-Inventing Times Square: 1900," in Taylor, *Inventing Times Square*, 358.

25   William Robbins, "News of Realty Sale in Times Sq.," *NYT*, February 20, 1968, 76; "Broadway Joins City Office Boom," *NYT*, March 19, 1967, R1.

26  Joseph P. Fried, "The Astor, a Lady to the End, Resists the Wrecker's Advances," *NYT*, August 3, 1967, 35; Robert A. M. Stern, Thomas Mellins, and David Fishman, *New York 1960: Architecture and Urbanism between the Second World War and the Bicentennial* (New York: Monacelli Press, 1995), 443.

27  Stern, Mellins, and Fishman, *New York 1960*, 444. For a good history of theater zoning, see Michael Kruse, "Constructing the Special Theater Subdistrict," *Urban Lawyer* 40, no. 1 (Winter 2008): 95–145.

28  Norman Marcus, Esq., "New York City Zoning—1961–1991: Turning Back the Clock—but with an Up-to-the-Minute Social Agenda," *Fordham Urban Law Journal* 19, no. 3 (1991): 713.

29  Stern, Mellins, and Fishman, *New York 1960*, 445, 446.

30  Tony Hiss, "Experiencing Places—II," *New Yorker*, June 29, 1987, 78; Alan S. Oser, "About Real Estate: Times Square Site Undergoes a Gradual Conversion," *NYT*, September 10, 1975, 73.

31  As quoted in Stern, Mellins, and Fishman, *New York 1960*, 467.

32  "Realtor Irving Maidman Offering Movie Theaters for Legit Rental," *Variety*, November 30, 1972, as quoted in Bianco, *Ghosts of 42nd Street*, 185; Ralph Blumenthal, "Maidman Discovers Sex Shows Still Operating at His Properties," *NYT*, November 29, 1972, 35; Gail Sheehy, "The Landlords of Hell's Bedroom," *New York*, November 20, 1972, 72.

33  Quoted in Bianco, *Ghosts of 42nd Street*, 145.

34  Robert Moss, "Letters to the Editor: A Bouquet or Two for Times Square," *NYT*, February 9, 1975, 252.

35  Bianco, *Ghosts of 42nd Street*, 185.

36  Carter B. Horsley, "Irving Maidman, 82, a Major Real Estate Developer," *NYT*, October 8, 1979, B13.

37  Milton Bracker, "Life on W. 42d St. a Study in Decay," *NYT*, March 14, 1960, 1.

38  New York State Urban Development Corporation, "The 42nd Street Development Project: Draft Environmental Impact Statement" (DEIS), prepared by Parsons Brinckerhoff Quade & Douglass, Inc. and AKRF, Inc. in association with Urbitran Associates, Inc., February 1984, 2–102.

39  Laurence Senelick, "Private Parts in Public Places," in Taylor, *Inventing Times Square*, 329.

40  Alexander Connock, "The End of the 42nd Street Strip," master's project, Columbia University, 1988, 11; Sam Howe Verhovek, "Times Sq. by Night: Lurid Drama Beckons," *NYT*, June 20, 1988, B1; Ralph Blumenthal, "A Times Square Revival?," *NYT*, December 27, 1981, 6:36; David J. Blum, "Slice of Life: A Day and a Night on a 42nd Street Block Is Crash Course in Vice," *WSJ*, September 4, 1981, 1; John J. Goldman and Doyle McManus, "Area of Violent Contrasts: Times Square: Best of Theater, Worst of Life," *Los Angeles Times*, August 17, 1981, B1; Carter B. Horsley, "The 'Porn' Thorn in Midtown's Side Gets Less Painful," *NYT*, November 18, 1979, R1; Josh Barbanel, "A Nether World: A Block of 42d Street," *NYT*, July 6, 1981, B1.

41  George Chauncey Jr., "The Policed: Gay Men's Strategies of Everyday Resistance," in Taylor, *Inventing Times Square*, 322.

42  Chauncey, "The Policed," 322.

43  Jill Stone, *Times Square: A Pictorial History* (New York: Collier Books, 1982), 134.

44  William Kornblum et al., "West 42nd Street: The Bright Light Zone," Graduate School and University Center of the City University of New York, unpublished
study, 1978; Mark Jacobson, "Times Square: The Meanest Street in America," *Rolling
Stone*, August 6, 1981, 18.

45  Sheehy, "The Landlords of Hell's Bedroom," 68. See also "Cleaning Up Hell's
Bedroom," *New York*, November 13, 1972, 50–66.

46  Alan S. Oser, "Times Square Finds Erotica Has Impact," *NYT*, August 23, 1970,
8:1, 8.

47  Oser, "Times Square Finds Erotica Has Impact."

48  Jodi Doff, "What 'The Deuce' Got Wrong, from Someone Who Lived It," https://
bust.com/tv/193748-the-deuce-reality.html; "Close to the Edge: Jane Dickson in
Conversation with Carlo McCormick," in Mark Iosifescu and Johan Kugelberg, *Jane
Dickson in Times Square* (New York: Anthology Editions, 2018), 259, 260; Jane Dick-
son, wall text for her five art works shown at the Whitney Museum of American Art,
Biennial 2022, April 6–September 5, 2022.

49  Marshall Berman, "Signs of the Times: The Lure of Times Square," *Dissent* 44
(Fall 1997): 78; Ada Louise Huxtable, "Architecture View: More Bad News about
Times Square," *NYT*, February 9, 1975, 132.

50  Quote of John Williams, Operations Coordinator, Midtown Community Court,
quoted in Linda Ricci, "Hawking Neighborhood Justice: Unlicensed Vending in the
Midtown Community Court," *Yale Law and Policy Review* 12, no. 1 (1994): 231–279,
fn. 12; William Kornblum and Vernon Boggs, "Redevelopment and the Night Frontier," *City Almanac* 18 (Summer 1985): 16; Verhovek, "Times Sq. by Night," B1.

51  "Politicians and Porn," *Economist*, April 2, 1977, 59.

52  William H. Daly, "Law Enforcement in Times Square 1970s–1990s," in Robert P.
McNamara, *Sex, Scams, and Street Life: The Sociology of New York City's Times Square*
(New York: Praeger Publishers, 1995), 97–106, at 99.

53  City of New York, "Times Square Action Plan," August 1978, 27.

54  New York State Urban Development Corporation, "The 42nd Street Development Project: Draft Environmental Impact Statement," 2–113.

55  Daly, "Law Enforcement in Times Square," 102; Todd S. Purdum, "Persistent
'Squeaky Wheel' Finally Heard by City Hall," *NYT*, June 15, 1988, B4.

56  Carl Weisbrod, author interview, August 15, 2000.

57  James Sanders, *Celluloid Skyline: New York and the Movies* (New York: Alfred A.
Knopf, 2003), 371.

## CHAPTER 3

1   Thomas J. Lueck, "Miscalculations in Times Square; Project Shows That Renewal
Needs More Than Bulldozers," *NYT*, August 10, 1992, B3.

2   Ronald Sullivan, "Planner with Tenacity: Herbert Jay Sturz," *NYT*, March 18,
1982, B3.

3   Dennis Duggan, "Visions of a City Red-Light Area Dim," *Newsday*, February 26,
1978, 17Q; Sullivan, "Planner with Tenacity."

4   Ric Burns and James Sanders with Lisa Ades, *New York: An Illustrated History*
(New York: Alfred A. Knopf, 2021), 610; Sam Roberts, *A Kind of Genius: Herb Sturz
and Society's Toughest Problems* (New York: Public Affairs, 2009), 236.

5   Richard Levine, "State Acquires Most of Times Square Project Site," *NYT*, April 19, 1990, 1.

6   Barry Newman, "New York Gets Set for Another Bunch of Conventioneers," *WSJ*, July 9, 1976, 1.

7   New York City Department of City Planning, Urban Design Group, "42nd Street Study," January 1978, NYC DCP 78-04; Herbert Sturz, author interview, December 5, 1991.

8   Sturz, author interview.

9   Jewel Bellush, "Clusters of Power: Interest Groups," in *Urban Politics New York Style*, ed. Jewel Bellush and Dick Netzer (Armonk, NY: M. E. Sharpe, 1990), 318.

10  Edward W. Wood Jr., Sidney N. Brower, and Margaret W. Latimer, "Planners' People," *Journal of the American Institute of Planners* 32, no. 4 (July 1966): 228–234.

11  See Lynne B. Sagalyn, *Times Square Roulette: Remaking the City Icon* (Cambridge, MA: MIT Press, 2001), 61–67, for a detailed discussion of the plan and politics of The City at 42nd Street.

12  Paul Travis, author interview, January 27, 1992.

13  Robert McG. Thomas Jr., "Plans for W. 42d St. Area Back on the Drawing Boards," *NYT*, June 28, 1980, 2:23.

14  The Board of Estimate ceased to exist after its last meeting on August 27, 1990, after the US Supreme Court (*Board of Estimate of NYC v. Morris*, 489 U.S. 688 (1989)) unanimously declared the executive body unconstitutional in its representation and powers: https://supreme.justia.com/cases/federal/us/489/688/

15  Carl Weisbrod, author interview, July 17, 1991.

16  Sturz, author interview.

17  Richard Kahn, author interview, October 16, 1991.

18  Paul Goldberger, "The Legal Hands That Shaped Crowded Manhattan Skyline," *NYT*, July 17, 1980, B1.

19  New York City Department of City Planning, *Midtown Zoning*, 1982, 5.

20  Jonathan Barnett, author interview, January 21, 1997.

21  Jeffrey Katz, author interview, April 11, 1997.

22  Carter B. Horsley, "Eighth Ave. Heading for Better Times," *NYT*, April 15, 1979, R1.

23  Robert E. Tomasson, "Developers Turning to West Midtown," *NYT*, February 18, 1973, 415, 422 at 422.

24  Ada Louise Huxtable, "Architecture View: Old Magic and New Dreams on 42d Street," *NYT*, November 6, 1977, D31.

25  Robert A. M. Stern, Thomas Mellins, and David Fishman, *New York 1960: Architecture and Urbanism between the Second World War and the Bicentennial* (New York: Monacelli Press, 1995), 472.

26  Stern, Mellins, and Fishman, *New York 1960*, 472.

27  Jill Gerston, "Royal Manhattan Hotel, Once Big-Band Center, Closes Its Doors," *NYT*, December 8, 1974, 68.

28  Ronald Smothers, "Tax Break Is Voted for Hotel Renewal," *NYT*, October 4, 1979, A27.

29 William Zeckendorf Jr., *Developing: My Life* (New York: Andrea Monfried Editions, 2016), 143–144; Richard D. Lyons, "Developers Zero In on Columbus Circle," *NYT*, September 22, 1985, R1.

30 Lisa Foderaro, "Real Estate: A Rental Tower for West Side," *NYT*, December 12, 1986, D15.

31 Arun Bhatia, author interview, November 6, 2019.

32 Andree Brooks, "About Real Estate: Luxury Tower at 10th Ave. and 42d St.," *NYT*, June 3, 1988, A20.

33 Gill quoted in Harry Berkowitz, "Times Sq. Project Gains Ground; High Court Rejects Key Lawsuit," *Newsday*, February 28, 1989, 45.

34 Richard J. Meislin, "Long-Delayed Times Square Plan Is Taking More New Twists," *NYT*, April 3, 1987, B1.

35 Ada Louise Huxtable, "Times Square Renewal (Act II), A Farce," *NYT*, October 10, 1989, 10.

36 Richard Kahan, author interview, October 16, 1991.

37 Robertson quoted in Anthony Bianco, "A Star Is Reborn: Investors Hustle to Land Parts in Time Square's Transformation," *Business Week*, July 8, 1996, 104; and in Thomas Dyja, *New York, New York, New York: Four Decades of Success, Excess, and Transformation* (New York: Simon & Schuster, 2021), 236.

38 Rebecca Robertson, author interview, October 21, 1994.

39 David W. Dunlap, "Signs Signal Both Profit and Controversy," *NYT*, February 6, 1994, 10:1; "Hold the Neon: One More Battle on 42d Street," *NYT*, May 1, 1994, CY6.

40 Editorial, "Whither 42nd St.: Better Rethink Those Office Towers," *Newsday*, October 13, 1993, 50; press release from State Senator Franz S. Leichter, "Senator Leichter Blasts Times Square Office Tower Deal," August 2, 1994.

41 As quoted in David W. Dunlap, "Long Delay Likely in Rebuilding Plan for Times Square," August 3, 1992, B2.

42 For a detailed discussion of the Disney episode, see Sagalyn, *Times Square Roulette*, 339–354.

## CHAPTER 4

1 John Taylor, "Fantasy Island," *New York*, April 30, 1990, 69, available at https://books.google.com/books?id=c9Qgcdv7l5oC&pg=PA69&lpg=PA69&dq=Show+Worl d++%22Saks+of+Sleaze%22&source=bl&ots=U0r7MGRiY2&sig=ACfU3U2IWARS3w qfBkZwq2qCPgDoXiMe-A&hl=en&sa=X&ved=2ahUKEwihsqmvqcPpAhVZknIEHe3 LBb8Q6AEwAHoECAQQAQ#v=onepage&q=Show%20World%20%20%22Saks%20 of%20Sleaze%22&f=false; Walter Fee, "Neighborhood Porn Wars," *Newsday*, April 18, 1993, 7. As it affected the Eros zone around Times Square, the mayor's anti-porn zoning policy supplied only the finishing touch on the profound changes to the trade that left the area with but a few quaint relics of its vibrant past, except for Eighth Avenue, which until the late 1990s witnessed little change. In due course, development pressures changed that too.

2 Marshall Berman, "Guys, Dolls, and Deals: Old and New Times Square," in *The Suburbanization of New York: Is the World's Greatest City Becoming Just Another*

*Suburban Tower?*, ed. Jerilou Hammett and Kingsley Hammett (Princeton: Princeton Architectural Press, 2007), 148.

3   Charles V. Bagli, "And Now, for the Next Act . . : Will Times Square Stay Vibrant? Or Will Theaters and Offices Continue Their Relentless March Onward?," *NYT*, June 13, 2004, CY8.

4   Ric Burns and James Sanders with Lisa Ades, *New York: An Illustrated History* (New York: Alfred A. Knopf, 1999), 552–553.

5   Other policy strategies and public actions—licensing laws and anti-sleaze legislation, police raids, code enforcement based on use of heavy fines, zoning amendments, and nuisance abatement laws, among other actions—all aiming at closing down porn establishments in order to return the area's real estate to "good commercial uses" had failed to eliminate the prostitution or undermine the profitability of adult entertainment that kept operators in the business. For a detailed description of the transformation strategy, see Lynne B. Sagalyn, *Times Square Roulette: Remaking the City Icon* (Cambridge, MA: MIT Press, 2001), chapters 3 and 4.

6   1995: New Victory Theatre; 1997: New Amsterdam Theatre; 1999: 4 Times Square Tower; 2000: AMC Theatres, Madame Tussauds, Ripley's Believe It Or Not! Museum, plus eateries and retail; E-Walk Entertainment and Retail Center, Hilton Hotel Times Square, and New 42 Studios; 2001: 3 Times Square Tower; 2002: 5 Times Square Tower, American Airlines Theatre; 2004: 7 Times Square Tower; 2007: *New York Times*' new headquarters on the project's southern block facing Eighth Avenue; 2010: 11 Times Square, the last new commercial tower. Only the small Times Square Theatre, in process of being redeveloped, has yet to open.

7   James Sanders, "Ideas and Trends: Thinking Big; In New York, Seeking a Grand Vision of Public Works," *NYT*, September 1, 2002, 4:5.

8   See Lynne B. Sagalyn, "Explaining the Improbable: Local Redevelopment in the Wake of Federal Cutbacks," *Journal of the American Planning Association* 56 (Autumn 1990): 429–441.

9   Robert D. McFadden, "Edward I. Koch, a Mayor as Brash, Shrewd and Colorful as the City He Led, Dies at 88," *NYT*, February 1, 2013; Steve Cuozzo, "Ed Koch 1924–2013: Obituary Even His Failures Led to Later Triumphs," *NYP*, February 2, 2013; Edward I. Koch, author interview, October 3, 2000.

10  See Sagalyn, *Times Square Roulette*, 388–402 (and related endnotes) for a detailed discussion of the subway improvements.

11  In May 2022, the MTA celebrated the unveiling of a new accessible entrance at the 42nd Street–Times Square Station and completion of the three-year renovation project, which included a rebuilt 42nd Street Shuttle platform, on time and on budget. The new entrance allows customers—approximately 640,000 passing through the Times Square subway station each weekday—to directly enter and exit Broadway Plaza between 42nd and 43rd Streets. The 5,000-square-foot mezzanine space features two new mosaic murals, *Each One* and *Equal All* by Nick Cave, commissioned by the MTA public arts program.

12  Ric Burns and James Sanders with Lisa Ades, *New York: An Illustrated History*, 3rd ed. (New York: Alfred A. Knopf, 2021), 538.

13  Kristine Miller, "Condemning the Public: Design and New York's New 42nd Street," *GeoJournal* 58, no. 2/3 (2002): 139–148; Benjamin Chesluk, *Money Jungle: Imagining the New Times Square* (New Brunswick: Rutgers University Press, 2007), 188–189.

14  Anna Klingmann, *Brandscapes* (Cambridge: MIT Press, 2007), 84.

15  Susan S. Fainstein and Robert Stokes, "Spaces for Plan: The Impacts of Entertainment Development on New York City," Center for Urban Policy Research, Rutgers, The State University of New Jersey, Working Paper no. 123, 1997, 17.

16  Eric Grode, "The Birth of 'Rent,' It's Creator's Death and the 25 Years Since," *NYT*, February 25, 2021.

17  Elizabeth L. Wollman, "The Economic Development of the 'New' Times Square and Its Impact on the Broadway Musical," *American Music* 20, no. 4 (Winter 2002): 446, 454–455. Disney's emergence on 42nd Street also tapped into theater critics' deeper concern about theater's long-term future and a growing tilt away from local productions of dramatic plays and toward mass-market musical productions catering to a tourist audience (whereas metropolitan-area residents, critics believed, preferred plays over musicals). Still, theatergoers who wanted drama could find it, as usual, in Off-Broadway theaters, which offered playwrights and actors greater range.

18  Berman, "Guys, Dolls, and Deals," 154, 152.

19  James Traub, *The Devil's Playground: A Century of Pleasure and Profit in Times Square* (New York: Random House, 2004), 190.

20  Adam Gopnik, "Times Regained," *New Yorker*, March 22, 2004. In the review, Gopnik recognizes that Traub's account "is lit from behind by another, still longer and larger one . . . 'masterly *Times Square Roulette*,'" which had just been issued in paperback. Indeed, while Traub was doing his research, I supplied him with materials.

21  Gopnik, "Times Regained."

22  Kim Velsey, "Urban Legend: Why Times Square (Still) Matters," https://observer.com/2016/02/times-square-at-a-crossroads/

23  Mike Wallace, "Babylon on the Subway," *New York Review of Books*, June 24, 2004, https://www.nybooks.com/articles/2004/06/24/babylon-on-the-subway/

24  "Gotham Theaters Face Demolition," *Washington Post*, July 28, 1929, R3; "Landmarks Pass in Times Square," *NYT*, May 5, 1929, 172.

25  "Great Building Operations on 42d Street Reveal Its Future Commercial Importance," *NYT*, March 31, 1912, XX1.

26  "Realty Values High in Times Square," *NYT*, September 21, 1930, N20.

27  New York State Urban Development Corporation, "42nd Street Development Project, Draft Environmental Impact Statement," February 1984, 2–194.

28  The city's funding strategy, including ESAC, is described in Sagalyn, *Times Square Roulette*, chapter 3; see 161–168 and accompanying notes for a detailed discussion of the subsidy issue.

29  Carl Weisbrod in New York State Urban Development Corporation, "Comments on the Piker Subcommittee Report," February 9, 1989; Carl Weisbrod, author interview, August 15, 2000. In 1994, after the program for the street had been recalibrated to focus on entertainment, a final supplement to the Final Environment Impact Statement offered a preliminary estimate of what the city would gain in full-value real estate taxes from the 42DP: $92.6 million.

30  Charles V. Bagli, "Fierce Bidding Expected on 2 Sites in Times Square," *NYT*, March 8, 1998, 1:37; No. 5 Times Square Development, LLC and AVR Crossroads LLC, "ESAC Receivable Sale Agreement," November 17, 2006, cdn.carrot.com/uploads/sites/12170/2016/11/5-Times-Square-Trophy-Office-Building.pdf; George Klein, author interview, December 7, 1997.

31  Klein, author interview. See Sagalyn, *Times Square Roulette*, 509n25.

32 Jonathan Miller, "For Commuters, It's Not Love at First Sight," *NYT*, December 12, 2004, NJ 1.

33 Mary Ann Tighe, Gregory Tosko, and Timothy Dempsey [Insignia/ESG], "Times Inks Novel Deal for Eighth Avenue," December 14, 2001, cited in Jeffrey Barclay and Yasmine Uzmez, "Development of the New York Times Building: Common Ground before Breaking Ground," Columbia CaseWorks #091702, January 25, 2011.

34 Charles V. Bagli, "Deal Reached to Acquire Land for The Times's Headquarters," *NYT*, February 28, 2001, B:2.

35 Paul Moses, "The Paper of Wreckage," *Village Voice*, June 18, 2002, https://www.villagevoice.com/2002/06/18/the-paper-of-wreckage/; Paul Moses, "The Times' Sweetheart Deal," *Village Voice*, November 16, 2004, https://www.villagevoice.com/2004/11/16/the-times-sweetheart-deal/; Paul Moses, "Times to Commoners: Go Elsewhere," *Village Voice*, August 9, 2005, https://www.villagevoice.com/2005/08/09/times-to-commoners-go-elsewhere/

36 David W. Dunlap, "Blight to Some Is Home to Others," *NYT*, October 25, 2001, D1; Martin E. Gold and Lynne B. Sagalyn, "The Use and Abuse of Blight in Eminent Domain," *Fordham Urban Law Journal* 38 (May 2011): 1120; William Stern, "The Unexpected Lessons of Times Square's Comeback," *City Journal*, August 1999.

37 Stern, "The Unexpected Lessons of Times Square's Comeback."

38 Boston Properties, 2007 Annual Report, 3.

39 The percentage change would be the same for the department's "market valuation," since assessed values for commercial property are fixed at 45 percent of market value.

40 Christopher Gray, "Streetscapes: The Candler Building; Amid 42d Street Renewal, a Façade in Disrepair," *NYT*, March 31, 1996, 9:7; David W. Dunlap, "Commercial Real Estate: An Entertainment Titan Finds a Home Where the Action Is," *NYT*, April 5, 2000, B7.

41 The dollars directly harvested from the 42DP follow complicated paths into different pots of use. Each site pays some form of annual ground rent in lieu of property taxes, and these funds flow into city coffers at the Department of Finance (after accounting for the 50 percent taken as a credit against the amount of ESAC outstanding). In addition to the ground rents, EDC collects "participation rents" linked to the leasing power of office space or gross sales at retail stores. When an office building owner refinances a mortgage, a transaction payment flows to EDC, as was the case when Boston Properties refinanced the Seven Times Square tower in 2014 and EDC received $9.5 million. EDC benefits from still another source of project revenue when a ground tenant exercises the option to purchase its leased site. Net revenues from the 42DP between October 31, 1999, and December 31, 2009, when the properties were managed by ESDC totaled $147.7 million, including amounts credited against ESAC. NYSESDC, "42DP Reconciliation Summary," undated. EDC, supplied to the author.

42 EDC's activities were supported for 20 years with the monies from the 42nd Street Development Project. With the depletion of that financial base, I was told that the de Blasio administration had to give EDC an injection of capital that it did not have to do before then.

43 In June 2022, the New York City Office of the Comptroller issued an audit report on EDC's Administration of the NYC Ferry Operation. The subsidy calculation was among the several points in the 35-page report; in particular, the report

concluded that the subsidy per rider was higher than projected or reported. For detail on the difference, see https://comptroller.nyc.gov/reports/audit-report-on-the-new-york-city-economic-development-corporations-administration-of-the-nyc-ferry-operation/#:~:text=Audit%20Findings%20and%20Conclusion,2020%2C%20and%202021%2C%20respectively

44 Vincent Tese, author interview, December 9, 1996. On the Disney deal, see Sagalyn, *Times Square Roulette*, 349–355. The outstanding balance on the $26 million loan made to Disney for renovation of the theater was $25.56 million as of 2020; as with the percentage rents, the city and state spilt 50/50 the annual interest payments Disney makes on the loan, the principal of which is due January 2027.

45 Cora Cahan, author interview, May 23, 2019.

46 Cora Cahan, author interview, December 13, 1996.

47 Editorial, "Victory on 42d Street," *NYT*, December 9, 1995; Cahan, author interviews, December 13, 1996, May 23, 2019.

48 Carl Weisbrod, author interview, April 3, 2019.

49 Cora Cahan, author interview, January 2, 2019.

50 Cahan did not win all her battles with the city. She had wanted the Disney lease for the New Amsterdam Theatre to come under New 42's master lease with the city. City and state officials took a firm position: they were not prepared to give that prospective gem of a lease to the nonprofit entity, as there would be no rents forthcoming to the city and the state, except to repay the loans made by these government entities. "It was a PR struggle," remarked Robertson. "Finally, New 42 backed off and stayed out of the negotiation altogether." Robertson, Harvard University, Graduate School of Design, teaching notes, February 29, 1999.

51 This sum includes a small amount of other project income (from family workshops, professional development programs for teachers, and school partnerships) that cannot be separated out in New 42's audited financial statements.

52 Rebecca Robertson, author interview, December 17, 2018.

53 Cahan, author interview, May 23, 2019.

54 The reset of the lease for the entertainment complex on the south side of 42nd Street (home to Madame Tussauds Wax Museum and AMC Theatres, land formerly of the Liberty and Empire Theatres) was a multiyear process of negotiation, arbitration, and litigation, which was finally resolved on August 31, 2020. The new base rent to be split by the city and New 42 was reset to $3.8 million for the first two years of the reset period, $4.5 million in years three to seven of the reset period, with 3 percent annual increases for years eight to fifteen. Under the initial 1996 lease agreement between the 42DP and FC 42nd Street Associates, L.P., the base rent for the initial term of 20 years was $1.7 million.

55 Joe Restuccia, author interview, May 22, 2019, including additional quotes in this chapter, unless otherwise cited.

56 Mary Clark, *Community: Journal of Power Politics and Democracy in Hell's Kitchen* (Middletown, DE: independently published, 2022), 41; Martin Gottlieb, "Times Sq. Plan Is Dividing People in Adjacent Clinton," *NYT*, May 5, 1984, 27; Edward I. Koch, author interview, October 3, 2000. The city also made peace with the International Ladies' Garment Workers' Union, which had expressed fear that the project would threaten the stability of the Garment District. In its agreement with the union, the city committed to undertake a six-month study of the effect of the plan on the Garment District and recommend safeguards to protect its manufacturers. Years later,

Sturz told me that this deal was as important to the city as that for Clinton. The report, "New York City Garment Center Study: Program and Zoning Recommendations," New York City Office of Economic Development, Department of City Planning, Public Development Corporation, was finished in October 1986.

57  Robert E. Tomasson, "Developers Turning to West Midtown," *NYT*, February 18, 1973, 415; Weiner/Gran Associates for the Clinton Steering Committee, "Clinton: A Plan for Preservation," n.d. [1974], ninth of unnumbered pages (https://cbmanhattan .cityofnewyork.us/cb4/wp-content/uploads/sites/10/2020/06/clinton_preserva tion_plan_gran_sultan.pdf). The ideas, information, and recommendations of the report were reflected in the special zoning district.

58  It was "a reasonable compromise," said then-City Planning Commission Chairman John E. Zuccotti. The Special District covered an area between 43rd and 56th Streets, Eighth and Twelfth Avenues, and created four zoning categories: Preservation Area, Perimeter Area, Mixed Use Area, and Other Areas. The Preservation Area protected a 13-block-long, two-block-wide area from 43rd Street to 56th Street between Eighth and Tenth Avenues; this was the core of the working-class residential neighborhood where demolition of "sound housing" would be virtually forbidden. A transfer of development rights would permit large-scale development nearby. Grace Lichtenstein, "New Clinton Zoning Plan Hailed by Leader in Area," *NYT*, August 23, 1974, 33; "Transcript of the City Planning Commission meeting on establishment of the Special Clinton District, October 21, 1974, Calendar #1 CP-22758," https:// cbmanhattan.cityofnewyork.us/cb4/transcript-of-the-city-planning-commission-meeting-on-establishment-of-the-special-clinton-district-city-planning-commission-october-21-1974-calendar-1-cp-22758/

59  Editorial, "The Clinton Community," *NYT*, September 2, 1974, 40.

60  Clark, *Community*, 82.

61  While other communities have called for the same provision, the city has held fast against it, I was told by a knowledgeable source.

62  Joe Restuccia, author interview, May 22, 2019.

63  Clark, *Community*, 48.

64  New York State Division of Housing and Community Renewal, "Clinton Preservation Fund Annual Report 1991," author collection of documents.

65  Restuccia, author interview, February 11, 2022.

66  "Clinton Special Fund—$10 Million City Housing Commitment," February 10, 1990, author collection of documents.

67  Restuccia, author interview, May 22, 2019. The process was full of challenges. As of February 1990, there were over 300 buildings with approximately 7,000 units in the city's TIL program and funding could only cover only a portion of the program's workload in any given year. Priority was given to repairs for buildings in the sale pipeline and for emergencies. Many buildings allocated Clinton Fund monies were not regarded as current priorities for TIL funding "either because the nature of the work needed makes it advisable to delay it until completion of 3-piece bathrooms, or because the 3-piece bathrooms themselves will delay sale." "Status—February 1990: Notes," author collection of documents.

68  Sam Anderson, "In Conversation: Richard Price and Junot Diaz: New York Novelists on the Death of Times Square, the Afterbirth of the Lower East Side, and the Importance of Ghosts," *New York*, October 6, 2008.

69  Charles V. Bagli, "Times Square's Crushing Success Raises Questions about Its Future," *NYT*, January 27, 2015, A16.

70  Justin Davidson, "I [love emoji] Tourism: Why the City Is Better When It's Full of Annoying Visitors," *New York*, July 8, 2019.

## CHAPTER 5

1  Editorial, "Reclassify Times Sq. & End the Grift," *DN*, August 17, 2015, 4.

2  Denis Hamill, "'Times' Up, Blaz, Scuzzy Square Needs Do-Over," *DN*, August 23, 2015, 15.

3  Michael M. Grynbaum and Matt Flegenheimer, "De Blasio Suggests Removing Pedestrian Plazas," *NYT*, August 21, 2015, A25; Jennifer Fermino, Rocco Parascandola, and Corky Siemaszko, "Start from Square One, Blaz's Radical B'way Idea, Cars May Drive Scum Out," *DN*, August 21, 2015, 4.

4  Tim Tompkins, author interview, May 22, 2018.

5  Charles V. Bagli, "Times Square's Crushing Success Raises Questions about Its Future; Businesses Feeling Squeeze of Crowds," *NYT*, January 27, 2015, A16; Adam Sternbergh, "Times Square: The City's Id, Now and Always," *New York*, October 5–8, 2015, 28.

6  Michael Crowley, "Honk, Honk, Aaah," *New York*, May 15, 2009.

7  Robert Sullivan, "Razzle-Dazzle Me," *NYT*, June 13, 2004, CY1.

8  Aaron Naparstek, "Bloomberg Puts Forward a Bold, Transformative New Vision for Broadway," *Streetsblog NYC*, February 26, 2009, https://nyc.streetsblog.org/2009/02/26/a-bold-and-transformative-new-vision-for-broadway/

9  William Neuman, "Mayor's Plan for Broadway as a Walkway," *NYT*, February 27, 2009, A1.

10  Randal O'Toole in "The Opinion Pages: Pedestrian Malls: Back to the Future," *NYT Blog*, February 27, 2009, https://roomfordebate.blogs.nytimes.com/2009/02/27/pedestrian-malls-back-to-the-future/; Oren Yaniv, "It's Crosswalk of the World. Quite a Feet, Times Square Turns Pedestrian Mall," *DN*, May 24, 2009, 4.

11  Regional Plan Association, *Urban Design Manhattan, A Report of the Second Regional Plan* (New York: Viking, 1969), 108; Joseph P. Fried, "Madison Mall Barred by Court," *NYT*, May 16, 1973, 98.

12  Charles Kaiser, "Pedestrian Mall on Times Square Will Be Tested with U.S. Funds," *NYT*, January 28, 1977, 42; City of New York, Office of the Mayor, Office of Midtown Planning and Development, "Broadway Plaza," December 1974; Editorial, "When Does a Mall Pall?," *NYT*, February 5, 1977, 18; quoted in David W. Dunlap, "Chasing a Cure for Broadway Crunch," *NYT*, March 2, 2009, A20.

13  Hilary Ballon, ed., *The Greatest Grid: The Master Plan of Manhattan 1811–2011* (New York: Museum of the City of New York and Columbia University Press, 2012), 155; "The Public Squares of New York," *RERBG*, August 3, 1902, 141; Nicolai Ouroussoff, "Architectural Review: Lose the Traffic. Keep That Times Square Grit," *NYT*, May 25, 2009, A1.

14  "New York City Voters Like Car-Free Times Square, Quinnipiac University Poll Funds; Bloomberg Gets Almost 2-1 Backing to Run Schools," July 29, 2009, poll. qu.edu/Poll-Release-Legacy?releaseidd=1355; Amber Suterland, Reuven Fenton, and Alex Ginsberg, "Amazing 'Feet' on Broadway—Walkers Rule as Car Ban Begins," *NYP*, May 25, 2009, 4; Andrea Peyser, "Mad Mike Loves Tourists—But Hates NYers," *NYP*, February 27, 2009, 7; Adam Lisberg, "It's Foot-Traffic Only on Great White Way," *DN*, May 20, 2009.

15  Steve Cuozzo, "Killing Times Square," *NYP*, August 24, 2009, 23; Steve Cuozzo, "Dead End Streets—Times Square Plan a Boulevard of Broken Dreams," *NYP*, March 1, 2009, 22; Samantha Stong and Carrie Melago, "Truckload of Woe, Drivers Fuming over Broadway Mall, Say Deliveries a Disaster," *DN*, May 27, 2009; Bloomberg quote, John Gertner, "Dynamic Duos: Michael Bloomberg and Janette Sadik-Khan on the Future of Walking, Biking, and Driving," *Fast Company*, September 11, 2013, quoted in David Luberoff, "Reimagining and Reconfiguring New York City's Streets," draft, published as part of a sponsored conference, "Transforming Urban Transport—The Role of Leadership," 2016, 14, https://research.gsd.harvard.edu/tut/files/2020/07/NYCCase2016.pdf; Matt Flegenheimer, "Turning the City's Wheels in a New Direction," *NYT*, December 30, 2013, A13.

16  Robin Finn, "Public Lives: A New Commissioner Enters the Fray against Gridlock," *NYT*, June 22, 2007, B2; Crowley, "Honk, Honk, Aaah."

17  Quoted in Luberoff, "Reimagining and Reconfiguring New York City's Streets," 12.

18  Michael M. Grynbaum, "Tourists and New Yorkers Take a Rubber Seat in Times Square," *NYT*, June 11, 2009, A23; Susan Dominus, "A Times Square for Our Time, Pedestrian in More Ways Than One: Big City," *NYT*, July 1, 2009, A25. A stopgap measure, "the well-worn lawn chairs were repurposed twice. First invited artists constructed a 9-foot-tall temporary sculpture by piling on the chairs one on top of the other. Those chairs that survived in tact [sic] were then auctioned off as Times Square souvenirs." Alexis Taylor, "Lawn Chairs in Times Square: An Analysis of the Pilot Streets Program and the Provisional Project Approach for New York City's Green Light in Midtown Project," MIT Master in City Planning thesis, September 2011, 33.

19  Steve Cuozzo, "Times Square Yawn Chairs—Revamp Doesn't Save This Broadway Flop!," *NYP*, August 18, 2009, 5.

20  Dominus, "A Times Square for Our Time."

21  After vehicles were shunted off those five blocks of Broadway, changes to roadways, traffic signal timings, crosswalks, and parking regulations followed. Once these accompanying adjustments had been completed, the transportation department immersed itself in elaborate and detailed data collection: video monitoring, business surveys, hourly and daily traffic counts, pedestrian surveys, bicycle classification surveys, and refinements to its detailed traffic microsimulation model; they also reached out to consult with a broad spectrum of individuals, community, civic, and business organizations, and elected officials at all levels of government.

22  Times Square Alliance and Design Trust for Public Space, "Times Square: The Next 100 Years, Problems and Possibilities," 2004, 6; New York City Department of Transportation, "Green Light for Midtown Evaluation Report," January 2010, 34–35, 36; satisfaction with Times Square experience drawn from Times Square Alliance/Strategy One, "Times Square Pedestrian Plaza Audit," summary slide 11, November 2009.

23  Martin Filler, "Times Square Reborn," *New York Review of Books*, June 7, 2017, http://nybooks.com/daily/2017/06/07/times-square-reborn

24  David Owen, "Annals of Architecture: The Psychology of Space: Can a Norwegian Firm Solve the Problems of Times Square?," *New Yorker*, January 21, 2013.

25  Owen, "Annals of Architecture: The Psychology of Space."

26  Michael Kimmelman, "A Streetcorner Serenade for the Public Plaza," *NYT*, June 2, 2013, AR1.

27  David W. Dunlap, "Ruby-Red Stairs with a View of the Great White Way," *NYT*, October 16, 2008, A29.

28  Michael Kimmelman, "Treasuring Urban Oases," *NYT*, December 4, 2011, AR1.

29  Colleen Wright, "The Painted Ladies of Times Square, Topless but for the Paint," *NYT*, August 16, 2015, MB8.

30  Michael Kimmelman, "A Case for Nurturing Plazas in Times Square," *NYT*, August 22, 2015, C1; J. David Goodman, "Times Sq. Spider-Man Arrested after a Scuffle with a Police Officer," *NYT*, July 27, 2014, A12; Joseph Goldstein and Jeffrey E. Singer, "If He Walks and Talks Like a Monk, but Has His Hand Out," *NYT*, July 6, 2014, A1.

31  Jonathan Blitzer, "Being a Times Square Elmo," *New Yorker*, June 26, 2014; also see Kirk Semple, "Spider-Man Unmasked! Elmo and Minnie, Too," *NYT*, August 2, 2014; Michael Wilson, "Under a Ranting Elmo's Mask, a Man with a Disturbing Past," *NYT*, June 28, 2012, A20; and Sumathi Reddy and Amber Benham, "Behind the Mickey Masks," *WSJ*, September 27, 2011.

32  City Council, City of New York, Transcript of the Minutes of the Committee on Consumer Affairs, Int. No. 467-A, November 19, 2014, 18, https://legistar.council. nyc.gov/LegislationDetail.aspx?ID=1903343&GUID=5A45C651-7373-4589-86B4-F77DD0FD5CFC (hereafter, Int. No.467-A Hearing Transcript).

33  Yoni Bashan, "Costumed Panhandlers Blamed for Broadway Ticket Sales Slump," *WSJ*, July 9, 2014; Mara Gay, "De Blasio: Regulate Elmo in Times Square," *WSJ*, July 29, 2014.

34  Bagli, "Times Square's Crushing Success Raises Questions about Its Future."

35  Christine González-Rivera, "Destination New York," Center for an Urban Future, May 7, 2018, 3; quoted in Ric Burns and James Sanders with Lisa Ades, *New York: An Illustrated History*, 3rd ed. (New York: Alfred A. Knopf), 751.

36  "Poll: Should New York City Regulate Costumed Characters in Times Square?," *WSJ*, July 29, 2014; "Poll: Should Elmo, SpongeBob and Other Costumed Characters in Times Square Be Regulated?," *Crain's New York Business*, July 9, 2014, https:// mycrains.crainsnewyork.com/blogs/polls/2014/07/should-elmo-spongebob-and-other-costumed-characters-in-times-square-be-regulated/

37  Int. No. 467-A Hearing Transcript, 11.

38  Int. No. 467-A Hearing Transcript, 12; Jonathan Blitzer, "Desperate Characters," *New Yorker*, August 19, 2014.

39  City Council, City of New York City, Committee on Consumer Affairs, "Committee Report of the Governmental Affairs Division, Int. No. 467," November 19, 2014, 11.

40  Robert C. Ellickson, "Controlling Chronic Misconduct in City Spaces: Of Panhandlers, Skid Rows, and Public-Space Zoning," *Yale Law Journal* 105, no. 5 (March 1996): 1165–1248; Blitzer, "Desperate Characters."

41 Aaron Smith, "NYPD to Disney and Marvel: Get Minnie Mouse and Spider Man out of Times Square," August 28, 2015, https://money.cnn.com/2015/08/28/news/companies/nypd-disney-marvel/index.html; Michael Heller and James Saltzman, *Mine! How the Hidden Rules of Ownership Control Our Lives* (New York: Doubleday, 2021), 109–110.

42 Int. No. 467-A Hearing Transcript, 80.

43 Int. No. 467-A Hearing Transcript, 41.

44 Int. No. 467-A Hearing Transcript, 90.

45 Int. No. 467-A Hearing Transcript, 99.

46 Int. No. 467-A Hearing Transcript, 84–85, 194.

47 Int. No. 467-A Hearing Transcript, 56, 53.

48 George L. Kelling and James Q. Wilson, "Broken Windows: The Police and Neighborhood Safety," *Atlantic* (March 1982); see Steven J. Ballew, "Note: Panhandling and the First Amendment: How Spider-Man Is Reducing the Quality of Life in New York City," *Brooklyn Law Review* 81 (Spring 2016): 1167–1202; Alex S. Vitale, *City of Disorder: How the Quality of Life Campaign Transformed New York Politics* (New York: New York University Press, 2008), 70, 121.

49 Editorial, "Elmos' World," *NYT*, August 15, 2014, A22.

50 Int. No. 467-A Hearing Transcript, 76.

51 "City Task Force on Times Square Announces Recommendations," press release, October 1, 2015, https://www1.nyc.gov/office-of-the-mayor/news/668-15/city-task-force-times-square-recommendations

52 "City Task Force on Times Square Announced Recommendations." Notably, the Department of Transportation would be empowered with rulemaking authority to develop commonsense "time, place, and manner regulations" in public plazas including but not limited to Times Square. To "codify the significance and uniqueness of Times Square," the task force recommended that the Department of City Planning initiate a zoning change that would create a distinct category of space—property mapped as a "public place" covering areas within a bed of a roadway designated for pedestrian circulation and enjoyment. Other action items included the deployment of a dedicated Police Department detail, limitations on street-permitted activity, an area-wide transportation study following completion of plaza construction, measures designed to ease the congestion in the square and improve traffic flow until completed construction of the plazas, and a recommendation to regulate uncontrolled vending along 42nd Street (between Seventh and Eighth Avenues) that overwhelmed the capacity of sidewalks and forced pedestrians into street traffic.

53 Jennifer Fermino, "Square Deal Soon—Blaz," *DN*, October 2, 2015, 8; editorial, "The Not-So-Naked City as Times Square Gets Its Coverup," *DN*, October 3, 2015, 22; editorial, "Shirtless Bodies in Pointless Times Square War," *NYT*, August 22, 2015, A16.

54 Members of the Mayor's Times Square Task Force: William Bratton (Police Commissioner); Carl Weisbrod (City Planning Commissioner); Gale A. Brewer (Manhattan Borough President); Melissa Mark-Viverito (Speaker, City Council); Letitia James (Public Advocate); Scott Stringer (Comptroller); Cyrus Vance Jr. (Manhattan District Attorney); Corey Johnson (City Council member); Daniel Garodnick (City Council member); Ydanis Rodriguez (City Council member); Richard Gottfried (State Assembly member); Brad Hoylman (State Senator); Carolyn Maloney (US House of Representatives); Alicia Glen (Deputy Mayor for Housing and Economic Development);

representatives of the Departments of Transportation, Law, Consumer Affairs, Planning, Police, Mayor's Office of Criminal Justice, and NYC & Company; Vicki Barbero (Community Board 5); Paul Steely White (Transportation Alternatives); Tim Tompkins (Times Square Alliance); Jeffrey Gural (Newmark); Cora Cahan (The New 42nd Street); Marc Ricks (Vornado Realty Trust); Eric Rudin (Rudin Management); Seth Stuhl (Disney Theatrical); James Nederlander (Nederlander Organization); Charlotte St. Martin (The Broadway League); Michael Simas (Partnership for the City of New York); Mary Ann Tighe (CBRE); Ellen Albert (Viacom); Jessica Taylor (Morgan Stanley); Laura Hansen (Neighborhood Plaza Partnership); Vin Cipolla (Municipal Art Society); Michael Lambert (NYC BID Association); Ethan Kent (Project for Public Spaces); Susan Chin (Design Trust for Public Space); Adam Friedman (Pratt Institute for Community Development); Thomas Wright (Regional Plan Association); Sean Basinski (Street Vendor Project); Andrew Schwartz (NYC Small Business Services); Joseph Spinnato (Hotel Association of NYC); Peter Ward (NY Hotel and Motel Trades Council); Helen Schaub (1199SEIU United Healthcare Workers East); Scott Nadeau (Marriott Marquis New York); and Sean Verney (Westin New York at Times Square).

55  "City Task Force on Times Square Announces Recommendations."

56  Editorial, "Team de Blasio Botches Its Own 'Fix Times Square' Gimmick," *NYP*, September 16, 2015.

57  Weisbrod, author telephone interview, August 13, 2021.

58  William J. Bratton, "Opinion/Commentary/Cross Country: Policing 'Awful but Lawful' Times Square Panhandling," *WSJ*, September 4, 2015.

59  Gale Brewer, Daniel Garodnick, and Corey Johnson, "A Times Square Solution, in Reach: Create a Commons with Three Zones," *DN*, September 20, 2015. The op-ed also called for making all civil penalties returnable to the Midtown Community Court, which would enable "law enforcement to track repeat offenders and get them the help they need," and for a thorough study of pedestrian and vehicular congestion in Times Square and the Theater District to figure out what was choking traffic the most and better shape transportation policy in the district.

60  For a description of Times Square Commons, see Times Square Alliance, "Times Square at a Crossroads," in Committee on Transportation, Hearing Testimony, Int. No. 1109-A, March 30, 2016, https://legistar.council.nyc.gov/MeetingDetail. aspx?ID=463154&GUID=9076D9E3-3C35-48A2-8480-BEAD05A45608&Options=inf o%7C&Search, 368–383.

61  Jillian Jorgensen, "Leaders of Topless Task Force Say Times Square Plazas Will Stay—For Now," observer.com, https://observer.com/2015/09/leaders-of-topless-task-force-say-times-square-plazas-will-stay-for-now/#:~:text=For%20Now%20 %7C%20Observer-,Leaders%20of%20Topless%20Task%20Force%20Say,Plazas%20 Will%20Stay%E2%80%94For%20Now&text=New%20York%20City%20 won't,Elmos%E2%80%94at%20least%20not%20yet

62  Editorial, "Order in the Square," *DN*, September 19, 2015, 22.

63  Liam Stack, "A Fast Lane for Pedestrians? A City Dweller's Dream," *NYT*, November 6, 2015.

64  City Council, City of New York, Committee on Transportation, "Committee Report of the Human Services Divisions, Proposed Int. No. 1109-A," March 30, 2016, 4; New York City Department of Transportation, "Notice of Adoption of Rules related to Pedestrian Plazas," May 26, 2016, https://www.nyc.gov/html/dot/down loads/pdf/notice-of-adoption-plaza-rules.pdf

65  City Council, City of New York, Committee on Transportation, Hearing Transcript on proposed Int. No. 1109-A, March 30, 2016 (hereafter, Int. No. 1109-A hearing transcript), 189.

66  Int. No. 1109-A Hearing Transcript, 8, 242.

67  Int. No. 1109-A Hearing Transcript, 48, 45–47.

68  Int. No. 1109-A Hearing Transcript, 112–113.

69  Daniel Garodnick, author telephone interview, June 14, 2021.

70  Int. No. 1109-A Hearing Transcript, 54.

71  Elizabeth Reiner-Platt on behalf of the Sexton Law Committee of the New York Bar Association testified in the 2016 hearings on behalf of the rights of topless women on the basis of gender equality. The Council's proposed legislation was neutral on its face, but "the motivation for and history of the bill is focused overwhelmingly on the regulation of women," specifically the *desnudas*. No bill, she argued, was ever introduced to regulate seminude male performers such as the Naked Cowboy, when he appeared in Times Square. She was concerned that unequal treatment of men and women might result by the bill's requirement of a DOT activity permit for all events within the pedestrian area. Int. No. 1109-A Hearing Transcript, 238–240.

72  Daniel Garodnick and Corey Johnson, "Opinion: Rules for Times Square's Costumed Characters Working Like a Charm," *Crain's New York Business*, July 5, 2016, https://www.crainsnewyork.com/article/20160705/OPINION/160639988/rules-for-times-square-s-costumed-characters-working-like-a-charm

73  Tim Tompkins, author interview, April 9, 2021.

## CHAPTER 6

1  Sandy Isenstadt, *Electric Light: An Architectural History* (Cambridge, MA: MIT Press, 2018), 155.

2  Charles V. Bagli, "Bullish on Times Square Neon: Wall Street Muscles into Mecca of Commercial Glitter," *NYT*, August 20, 1998, B1, B6 at B6.

3  Times Square Alliance and Times Square Advertising Coalition, "Times Square Advertising Study," June 2017, https://www.timessquarenyc.org/sites/default/files/body-pdfs/TSAC%20one%20pager_2017_correct.pdf

4  Isenstadt, *Electric Light*, 176.

5  William Leach, "Introductory Essay: Commercial Aesthetics," in *Inventing Times Square: Commerce and Culture at the Crossroads of the World*, ed. William R. Taylor (New York: Russell Sage Foundation, 1991), 236.

6  Darcy Tell, *Times Square Spectacular: Lighting Up Broadway* (New York: Smithsonian Books with HarperCollins, 2007), 40. Also see Mike Wallace, *Greater Gotham: A History of New York City from 1898 to 1919* (New York: Oxford University Press, 2017), 428–430.

7  1920 advertisement, https://www.pinterest.com/pin/455215474832691856/

8  Copy for "New York at Night, Broadway at 47th Street" (Brown Brothers photographers White Rock sign), circa 1910, New-York Historical Society exhibition *Signs and Wonders*, 1997; author material.

9  *Report of the Mayor's Billboard Advertising Commission of the City of New York*, August 1, 1913, 7, https://babel.hathitrust.org/cgi/pt?id=mdp.39015013156933&view=1up&seq=5&skin=2021

10  Leach, "Introductory Essay: Commercial Aesthetics," 240.

11   Douglas Martin, "Douglas Leigh, The Man Who Lit Up Broadway, Dies at 92," *NYT*, December 16, 1999, B13; Tell, *Times Square Spectacular*, 105.

12   David W. Dunlap, "Times Square at 100: The Crossroads of the Crossroads," *NYT*, June 13, 2004, CY3; Isenstadt, *Electric Light*, 181.

13   Meyer Berger, "From White Way to Color Canyon," *NYT Magazine*, June 4, 1944, SM34; David Bird, "Times Sq. Landmark Returns in Puff of Smoke," *NYT*, August 15, 1972, 37; Tell, *Times Square Spectacular*, 115.

14   Christopher Gray, "Streetscapes: Douglas Leigh, Sign Maker; The Man Behind Times Square's Smoke Rings," *NYT*, October 25, 1998, 11:5.

15   "City Seen Powerless On Movie Marquees," *NYT*, October 28, 1965, 46.

16   Tell, *Times Square Spectacular*, 147, 150.

17   Ken Bloom, *Broadway: An Encyclopedic Guide to the History, People and Places of Times Square* (New York: Oxford/Facts on File, 1991), 348; Lawrence Van Gelder, "Lights Out for Times Square News Sign?," *NYT*, December 11, 1994, 60.

18   Philip H. Dougherty, "Japanese Light Up Times Square," *NYT*, March 2, 1982, D21.

19   Sama Kusumoto, "Personal Account: Japanese Enlightenment," *NYT*, March 24, 1991, 6:34.

20   As quoted in David W. Dunlap, "Column One: Changes—Curtain Coming Down," *NYT*, October 9, 1986, B1.

21   Sewell Chan, "Neo Nostalgia from Times Sq. to Be Sold by Sign Maker," *NYT*, May 15, 2006.

22   Tell, *Times Square Spectacular*, 126–127.

23   Public Art Fund, "Jenny Holzer: Messages to the Public," https://www.publicart fund.org/exhibitions/view/messages-to-the-public-holzer/#:~:text=Messages%20 to%20the%20Public%20formed,Spectacolor%20board%20at%20Times%20Square

24   Katerina Stathopoulou, "Deep Focus: The Timeless Relevance of Alfredo Jaar's 'A Logo for America,'" art21, April 2, 2020, https://art21.org/read/the-timeless -relevance-of-alfredo-jaars-a-logo-for-america/; Grace Glueck, "And Now, a Few Words from Jenny Holzer," *NYT*, December 3, 1989, SM42; Mary Houlihan, "Jenny Holzer's Art of Words: Whatever the Media She Likes to Let Language Do the Talking," *Chicago Sun Times*, October 19, 2008, D7.

25   "The Talk of the Town," *New Yorker*, February 14, 1997, 27; Philip H. Dougherty, "Advertising: An Addition to Times Square," *NYT*, October 11, 1976, 44.

26   Christopher Gray, "Streetscapes: George Stonbely: A Times Square Signmaker Who Loves Spectacle," *NYT*, January 30, 2000, RE9; https://en.wikipedia.org/wiki/ George_Stonbely.

27   Mark McCain, "The Attention-Getter of Times Square," *Boston Globe*, November 22, 1984, A76.

28   Dougherty, "Advertising: An Addition to Times Square"; McCain, "The Attention-Getter of Times Square."

29   Gray, "Streetscapes: George Stonbely."

30   Doug Stewart, "Times Square Reborn," *Smithsonian* 28, no. 11 (February 1998): 34–44.

31  Gregory F. Gilmartin, *Shaping the City: New York and the Municipal Art Society* (New York: Clarkson Potter/Publishers, 1995), 453; Hugh Hardy, author interview, January 9, 1997.

32  Gilmartin, *Shaping the City*, 234, 443.

33  New York City Zoning Code, revisions to section 81-732.

34  David W. Dunlap, "The Sign Makers Turn Up the Wattage," *NYT*, June 29, 1997, R1.

35  David W. Dunlap, "Signs Signal Both Profit and Controversy," *NYT*, February 6, 1994, 10:1.

36  Tama Starr and Ed Hayman, *Signs and Wonders: The Secrets of Mystical Marketing* (New York: Doubleday, 1998), 289.

37  Stuart Elliott, "Advertising: After More than 40 Years, Wrigley Is Set for a Flashy Return to Times Square," *NYT*, June 19, 2001, C6.

38  Steve Lohr, "Reinventing the Neon Jungle: Times Square Billboards Take On a High-Tech Cast," *NYT*, November 6, 1995, D1; Ann Carrns, "Seeing Dollar Signs in Times Square," *WSJ*, February 28, 1997, B12; also Charles Bagli, "Times Square, Plugged," *New York Observer*, March 20, 1995, 17.

39  Jay Levin, "Signs of Prosperity in Times Square," *Crain's New York Business*, October 19, 1998, 52.

40  Anthony Ramirez, "Neighborhood Report: Midtown; Bus Terminal Will Show How Big a Sign Can Get," *NYT*, February 9, 1997, 13:6; Karrie Jacobs, "Site Lines/Dressed to Shill: The Bus Terminal Gets a Madison Avenue Makeover," *New York*, July 27, 1998, 15.

41  Stuart Elliot, "Joe Boxer Sign in Times Square," *NYT*, September 8, 1995, D4; Lohr, "Reinventing the Neon Jungle."

42  Stuart Elliott, "The Media Business: Advertising; Selling Underwear, and Ideas: New Signs Are Turning Times Square into an Issue Forum," *NYT*, September 9, 1994, D15.

43  "Iconic Photos: Famous, Infamous and Iconic Photos," June 26, 2010, https://iconicphotos.wordpress.com/2010/06/26/ck-tom-hintnaus/, accessed December 10, 2021; Valerie Steele, "Calvinism Unclothed," *Design Quarterly*, Autumn 1992, 33; Michael Gross, "Calvin Klein," *Adweek Markets and Marketing Special Report*, May 1985, 49, as quoted in Steele, "Calvinism Unclothed," 33.

44  Associated Press, "Suggestive Ads for Klein Jeans Draw FBI's Eye: Some Call Campaign Child Pornography," *Baltimore Sun*, September 9, 1995, 3A; Alexandra Marks, "A Backlash to Advertising in Age of Anything Goes," *Christian Science Monitor*, February 22, 1999, 1.

45  Stuart Elliott, "Advertising: Will Calvin Klein's Retreat Redraw the Lines of Taste?," *NYT*, August 29, 1995, D1.

46  Bill Hoffman, "Attention Grabber Nixed—Billboard Too Hot for Times Square," *NYP*, June 10, 2005; "Sexy Ad Banned from Times Square," UPI, June 10, 2005.

47  Carol Campanile, "'Fake News' Billboard Pulled Down in Times Square," *NYP*, February 6, 2018.

48  Madison Gray, "Controversial Billboard depicting U.S. Soldier and Muslim Woman Hits Times Square," *Time*, January 29, 2014.

49  Vivian Marino, "Square Feet: The 30-Minute Interview," *NYT*, March 14, 2010, RE11; Jeffrey Katz, author telephone interview, December 17, 2021.

50   Anthony Ramirez, "Advertising: A Provocative Approach Helps an Environment Group Push Its Cause," *NYT*, June 27, 1995, D7.

51   Elliott, "The Media Business: Advertising; Selling Underwear, and Ideas."

52   Jeremy Male, author interview, January 12, 2022.

53   David Cole email to author, December 14, 2021; Andy Newman, "New M.T.A. Rules on Ads Anger Civil Libertarians," *NYT*, October 1, 1997, B3; Emma G. Fitzsimmons, "M.T.A. Bans Political Ads on Subways and Buses after a Court Order," *NYT*, April 30, 2015, A26.

54   Emily Steel, "Times Square's Biggest and Most Expensive Digital Billboard Is Set to Shine," *NYT*, November 16, 2014.

55   Steel, "Times Square's Biggest and Most Expensive Digital Billboard."

56   Samsung Newsroom U.S., "Serenity in the City that Never Sleeps: Samsung Smart LED Signage Brings a Digital Waterfall to Times Square," July 27, 2021, https://news.samsung.com/us/samsung-smart-led-signage-nature-times-square-nyc-tsq/

57   Caption from image in Ric Burns and James Sanders with Lisa Ades, *New York: An Illustrated History* (New York: Alfred A. Knopf, 1999), 710.

## CHAPTER 7

1   "Clinton: A Plan for Preservation," conducted by Weiner/Gran Associates for the Clinton Steering Committee, n.d. (1974), https://cbmanhattan.cityofnewyork.us/cb4/wp-content/uploads/sites/10/2020/06/clinton_preservation_plan_gran_sultan.pdf

2   "Clinton: A Plan for Preservation," 9 (unnumbered).

3   "Midtown 8th Ave. Shows New Vigor," *NYT*, December 30, 1956, R1; Arnold H. Lubasch, "A Mile of 8th Ave. Gaining Stature," *NYT*, May 29, 1966, R1; Carter B. Horsley, "Eighth Ave. Heading for Better Times," *NYT*, April 15, 1979, R1; David W. Dunlap, "Column One: 8th Ave. Scenes; Present to Future: Dowdy to Jaunty," *NYT*, December 11, 1986, B1; Iver Peterson, "Eighth Avenue Goes from Grit to Glitter," *NYT*, January 29, 1989, R1; Thomas J. Lueck, "Times Sq.'s Gleam Reaching 8th Avenue; A Seedy Strip Slowly Gives Way to Assaults of the Squeaky Clean," *NYT*, June 20, 1997, B1; Christopher Gray, "Streetscapes: Eighth Avenue, from 43d to 55th Street; Beyond Times Square's Glitz, a Motley Avenue," *NYT*, September 26, 1999, 11:9.

4   Lisa W. Foderaro, "If You're Thinking of Living in: Clinton," *NYT*, June 21, 1987, R11.

5   Claudia H. Deutsch, "Commercial Property/Times Square; Those Retail Feet Are Dancing North of 42d Street," *NYT*, March 10, 1996, 9:11.

6   Rick Lyman, "As the Great White Way Turns a Corner," *NYT*, May 8, 1998, E1.

7   J. A. Lobbia, "Hell's Kitchen Is Burning," *Village Voice*, September 8, 1998, https://www.villagevoice.com/1998/09/08/hells-kitchen-is-burning/

8   Peterson, "Eighth Avenue Goes from Grit to Glitter."

9   Times Square Alliance, "Sign of the Times: Eighth Avenue on the Rise," n.d. (ca. 2007), 2, 11.

10  Kathryn Brenzel, "Extell Plans Theater District Hotel, Avoiding Special Permit," *The Real Deal*, January 13, 2022, https://therealdeal.com/2022/01/13/extell-plans-theater-district-hotel-avoiding-special-permit/

11  Lisa W. Foderaro, "Residential 'Wall' Rises along West 42d," *NYT*, September 13, 1987, 632; Charles V. Bagli, "Once Scorned, Far West 42nd St. Is Now Much in Demand," *NYT*, April 26, 2000, B1.

12  Steve Cuozzo, "Hotel Plans Lined Up for 8th Ave.," *NYP*, June 10, 2008, 60.

13  Foderaro, "Residential 'Wall' Rises along West 42d."

14  Tracie Rozhon, "The 15-Year Story of 2 40-Story Towers: They Are to Rise, at Last, on 42d St. between 11th and 12th," *NYT*, June 27, 1999, RE1.

15  Joseph Berger, "Hell's Kitchen, Swept Out and Remodeled," *NYT*, March 19, 2006, 29.

16  Mary Clark, *Community: Journal of Power Politics and Democracy in Hell's Kitchen* (Middletown, DE: independently published, 2022), 25.

17  Michael R. Benson, "Clinton Frets over That Gleam in Developers' Eyes," *NYT*, December 22, 1985, RE5.

18  Benson, "Clinton Frets over That Gleam in Developers' Eyes," 8:5.

19  Martin Gottlieb, "Planners Considering Blockfront Towers," *NYT*, January 16, 1986, B1.

20  Joe Restuccia, author interview, February 11, 2022.

21  Clark, *Community*, 94; Paul Goldberger, "Clinton Renewal Proposal Raises Fears over Effects of 2 High-Rises," *NYT*, January 16, 1986, B1.

22  Clark, *Community*, 96; David W. Dunlap, "Koch, under Stiff Pressure, Kills Clinton Housing Plan," *NYT*, April 18, 1986, B1; Nathan Tempey, "Urban Removal: How a Utopian Vision for Hell's Kitchen Burned Out," https://gothamist.com/news/urban-removal-how-a-utopian-vision-for-hells-kitchen-burned-out

23  Goldberger, "Clinton Renewal Proposal Raises Fears"; Matthew L. Wald, "No Simple Way for City to End Housing Burden," *NYT*, December 3, 1983, 25.

24  Robert A. M. Stern, David Fishman, and Jacob Tilove, *New York 2000: Architecture and Urbanism between the Bicentennial and the Millennium* (New York: Monacelli Press, 2006), 457; Goldberger, "Clinton Renewal Proposal Raises Fears."

25  Stern, Fishman, and Tilove, *New York 2000*, 459.

26  Marvine Howe, "Neighborhood Report: Chelsea/Clinton, a Tradeoff: Trucks for Housing," *NYT*, March 6, 1994, 105.

27  JoAnn Macy quoted in Rachelle Garbarine, "Residential Real Estate: Affordable Apartments Open Way for Financing," *NYT*, June 20, 1997, B5; Joe Restuccia, as spoken to Rosa Goldensohn, "Podcast: Hell's Kitchen's Affordable Housing Guru Shares Decades of Wisdom," July 15, 2015, https://www.dnainfo.com/new-york/20150715/hells-kitchen-clinton/podcast-hells-kitchens-affordable-housing-guru-shares-decades-of-wisdom/. Other Restuccia quotes in this section come from the same podcast.

28  Restuccia, podcast.

29  William Zeckendorf Jr., *Developing: My Life* (New York: Andrea Monfried Editions, 2016), 148–149.

30  Paul Goldberger, "Plan for Old Garden Site: Impressive Restraint and a Sense of the City," *NYT*, November 26, 1985, B16; Kahn quote in Karl Sabbagh, *Skyscraper:*

*The Making of a Building* (New York: Viking, 1990), 44. The project was also documented on a Channel 4/PBS mini series based on the book.

31  Philip S. Gutis, "Community Boards Gaining Power: 59 Local Bodies Reshaping Their Neighborhoods," *NYT*, September 21, 1986, R1; Clark, *Community*, 91.

32  Clark, *Community*, 92.

33  Sabbagh, *Skyscraper*, 38; Restuccia, podcast.

34  David Reiss, "Housing Abandonment and New York City's Response," *NYU Review of Law and Social Change* 22 (1996–1997): 787; Restuccia, podcast.

35  Dan Margolis, director of the Community Housing Improvement Program, as reported by Malcolm Gladwell, "N.Y. Hopes to Help Homeless by Reviving Single Room Occupancy Hotels," *Los Angeles Times*, April 25, 1993, quoted in Brian J. Sullivan and Jonathan Burke, "Single-Room Occupancy Housing in New York City; the Origins and Dimensions of a Crisis," *City University of New York Law Review* 17 (2013): 119.

36  "The City banned the construction of new SRO units, restricted SRO occupancy to exclude families, mandated the reconversion of many of the new SRO units, altered building and zoning codes to discourage SRO occupancy, and provided tax incentives to encourage the conversion of all SRO units to (higher rent) apartments." Sullivan and Burke, "Single-Room Occupancy Housing," 122.

37  Sullivan and Burke, "Single-Room Occupancy Housing," 123; Anthony J. Blackburn, "Single Room Living in New York City," report prepared for the City of New York Department of Housing Preservation and Development, September 1996, 8; Sullivan and Burke, "Single-Room Occupancy Housing," 123; Anemona Hartocollis, "Sweeping Away the SRO Hotels," *Newsday*, January 14, 1990, 6; Peter Grant, "Court Decision Sparks Open Season on SROs," *Crain's New York Business*, July 17, 1989, 1.

38  Peterson, "Eighth Avenue Goes from Grit to Glitter."

39  Quoted in Dennis Hevesi, "In Hell's Kitchen, a Changing Skyline," *NYT*, May 12, 2002, L1; quoted in Berger, "Hell's Kitchen, Swept Out and Remodeled."

40  Rachelle Garbarine, "In Far West 50's, Project Will Bring New Rentals," *NYT*, May 26, 2000, B6.

41  Joyce Cohen, "If You're Thinking of Living in/Clinton: Gritty Gives Way to Gentrification," *NYT*, May 7, 2000, RE5; Rachelle Garbarine, "96 Apartments for Low- and Middle-Income Renters in Clinton," *NYT*, September 5, 2003, B6.

42  Manhattan Community Board 4, "Statement of District Needs, Fiscal Year 2004," July 2002, 4.

43  "City of New York Manhattan Community Board Four, letter to the Awards Committee, Preservation League of New York State, Re: The Emerson, 554 West 53rd Street, New York, New York 10019," n.d. [February 2009], https://cbmanhattan.cityofnewyork.us/cb4/wp-content/uploads/sites/10/downloads/pdf/agendas/2009_02/4%20EXEC%20Emerson%20Pres%20League%20Awards%202009.pdf

44  Hevesi, "In Hell's Kitchen, a Changing Skyline."

## CHAPTER 8

1  "141 Astor Lots Auctioned for $5,159,075," *New-York Tribune*, March 10, 1920, 7.

2  https://www.clintonhousing.org/what-we-do/building-profile.php?id=59

3   Julian E. Barnes, "A Bit Nervously Theater Row Packs Up," *NYT*, March 13, 2000, E1; Jesse McKinley, "Upscale March of Theater Row: A Centerpiece of Redevelopment," *NYT*, November 21, 2002, E1; Ralph Blumenthal, "42d St. Revival May Alter Face of Theater Row," *NYT*, October 31, 1998, 1.

4   McKinley, "Upscale March of Theater Row"; Tracie Rozhon, "Theater Below 42nd Street Rental Tower: Stage Stars and Stripes," *NYT*, October 21, 2001, RE1.

5   Ralph Blumenthal, "Transforming Theater Row: An Unlikely Urban Drama Heads for a Happy Ending," *NYT*, May 11, 2000, B1.

6   Anthony Bianco, *Ghosts of 42nd Street: A History of America's Most Infamous Block* (New York: William Morrow, 2004), 185, 188, 191; Blumenthal, "Transforming Theater Row."

7   As quoted in Bianco, *Ghosts of 42nd Street*, 190, citing Bruce Buckley, "Theater Manager Has Dream for 42nd," *Chelsea Clinton News*, October 9, 1975; Blumenthal, "Transforming Theater Row."

8   Justin Davidson, *Magnetic City: A Walking Companion to New York* (New York: Spiegel & Grau, 2017), 130.

9   Davidson, *Magnetic City*, 131, 117.

10  Sam Roberts, *A History of New York in 27 Buildings: The 400-Year Untold Story of an American Metropolis* (New York: Bloomsbury, 2019), 179.

11  Ada Louise Huxtable, "Architecture View: The Many Faces of 42d Street," *NYT*, March 19, 1979, D31. The second quote is from a similar piece, "Architecture View: Old Magic and New Dreams on 42d Street," *NYT*, November 6, 1977, D31.

## CODA

1   Adam Gopnik, "A City Comes Back to Life," *New Yorker*, June 7, 2021.

2   Corey Kilgannon, "If There Are No Crowds, Is It Still Times Square?," *NYT*, December 1, 2020, 1.

3   Office of the New York State Comptroller, "The Office Sector in New York City," Report 11-2022, October 2021.

4   New York City Independent Budget Office, "Focus On: The Preliminary Budget," April 2021; "Fiscal Outlook," January 2021.

5   Quoted in Nicole Gelinas, "Eye on the News: Will New York Come Back," *City Journal*, April 28, 2021, https://www.city-journal.org/richard-ravitch -discusses-new-yorks-comeback

6   Nicole Gelinas, "From the Magazine: New York's Year from Hell," *City Journal*, Autumn 2020, https://www.city-journal.org/government-can-ensure-new-york -recovery

7   "Renaissance Town: How, after 9/11, New York Built Back Better," *Economist*, September 8, 2021, https://www-economist-com.ezproxy.cul.columbia.edu/united -states/how-after-9/11-new-york-built-back-better/21804389

8   C. J. Hughes, "Who Owns the Block: As Goes Eighth Avenue, So Goes Times Square," *Crain's New York Business*, July 25, 2022, 4.

9   Patrick McGeehan and Nicole Hong, "City Places Bet Foreign Tourists Still Love N.Y.C.," *NYT*, October 20, 2021, A1; Times Square Alliance, Annual Report 2022, https://www.timessquarenyc.org/sites/default/files/resource-pdfs/TSA%20Annual%

20Report%202022%20FINAL.pdf; NYC & Company, "NYC Travel and Tourism Outlook," June 2022, https://assets.simpleviewinc.com/simpleview/image/upload/v1/clients/newyorkcity/2022_Travel_Tourism_Factsheet_June_Update_jm_bb67b6c9-a28c-47e3-b853-955c7c32cffe.pdf

10  See https://tsxbroadway.com/; Nicole Hong, "Times Square at Its Overcrowded, Dizzying Worst Is Exactly What N.Y.C. Needs," *NYT*, May 28, 2022.

11  https://www.jamestownlp.com/news/jamestown-launches-500-million-redevelopment-of-one-times-square-the-site-of-the-new-years-eve-ball-drop; Kim Velsey, "One Times Square, Long Empty, Will Now Bring the Billboards Inside," *Curbed*, May 6, 2022, https://www.curbed.com/2022/05/one-times-square-redevelopment-renovation-advertising.html

12  "Take a Look at Our New Times Square Restaurant Design," https://corporate.mcdonalds.com/corpmcd/en-us/our-stories/article/ourstories.new_restaurant.html; "New Times Square McDonald's—Big Mac with a View," https://www.tripadvisor.com/ShowUserReviews-g60763-d878353-r678990908-McDonald_s-New_York_City_New_York.html

13  Luis Ferré-Sadurni and Grace Ashford, "N.Y. Democrats to Pass New Gun Laws in Response to Supreme Court Ruling," *NYT*, June 30, 2022.

14  Reuters Staff, "Factbox: Attacks and Thwarted Plots Targeting New York's Times Square," June 7, 2019, https://www.reuters.com/article/us-new-york-crime-history-factbox/factbox-attacks-and-thwarted-plots-targeting-new-yorks-times-square-idUKKCN1T81UZ; Nicole Gelinas, "Eye on the News: Time's Up in Times Square," *City Journal*, October 11, 2021, https://www.city-journal.org/rising-violent-crime-in-times-square; Greg David, "Economy: Tourists Are Flocking Back to NYC, but Fear of Crime May Be Keeping Day-Trippers Away," *The City*, https://www.thecity.nyc/economy/2022/7/6/23197456/tourists-back-nyc-fear-crime-day-trippers-hotels-restaurants; Larry Celona, Tina Moore, Carl Campanile, and Gabrielle Fonrouge, "Metro: Times 'Scare': How NYC's Soaring Crime Is Bleeding into Crossroads of the World," *NYP*, June 29, 2021.

# INDEX

September 11 (9/11) terrorist attacks, 3,
    6, 160, 162, 188, 242, 257, 313, 315,
    333, 371, 372, 377
  National September 11 Memorial
    Museum Pavilion, 228
750 Seventh Avenue, 231, 271
Seven Times Square, 188, 400n41
Sex trade, 65–67, 95–100, 104–112
  burlesque, 65, 70, 73, *73*, 91, 120
  Clinton and, 65, 323, 344, 354, 358
  Eighth Avenue, 96, 109, *110*, 120, *137*,
    140, 157, *158*, 323, *329*, 335
  massage parlors, 65–66, 104, 108–112,
    120–121, 135, 360
  movies and, 76, 209
  peep shows, 65, *79*, 95–98, *97*, 104–
    106, 116, 121, *137*, 140, 156, 157,
    159
  pornography, 5, 8, 76, 95, 98–100,
    *100*, 105–106, 108, 111, 123, 156,
    157–159, *158*, 193, 202, 209, 287,
    307, 309, 326, 360
  prostitution, 5, 53, 92, 94, 96–100, *98*,
    108–111, 120–121, *121*, 138, 140,
    *153*, 159–160, 202, 203, 250, 283–
    284, 323, 344, 354, 358, 363
  sex shops, 65, 99, 104, *158*, 159, 185,
    189
  topless bars, 65, 95, 96, 111
SFX Entertainment, 189
Shanley's, 62, 63
Sheehy, Gail, 91, 96
Sheffield Apartments, 327–328
Sheraton Times Square, 380
Sherwood Equities, 299, 313
Shields, Brooke, 307
Show World Center, 157–159, *158*
Shubert Alley, 38
Shubert brothers, 30, 37–38, 60, 61, 72
Shubert Organization, 70, 148, 359
Shubert Theatre, 38, 58
Shuldiner, Joseph, 338
Siegel, Norman, 307
Signs. *See also* Billboards
  First Amendment and, 315
  ghost signs, 19, *20*, *103*
  "sign evil," 277, *279*
Silverstein, Larry, 333–334
Silver Towers, 333, *334*
Sindin, Simone, 349
Single-room-occupancy (SRO) struc-
    tures, 346–348
Sixth Avenue, 81, 85, 90, 221, 295
Skadden, Arps, Slate, Meagher & Flom,
    241, 271

Skyscrapers, 348. *See also* 42nd Street
    Development Project: office towers;
    Office buildings
  early (prewar), 21, 41, 62
  East Midtown, 9, 133, 369
  Far West Midtown, 370
  Times Square, 6, 88, 115, 178–179,
    187, *188*, 231, 291
Smith Travel Research, 379
Snøhetta, 228–229, *230*, 241
SnoreStop, 310, *313*
SoHo, 232, 378
Solomon Equities, 231
Sony, 168, 271, 285, 294
South Street Theatre, *362*
Special Clinton District, 205–206, 208,
    331, 332, 335, 336–337, 343, 349,
    402n58
Special Theater District, 87, 88, 331, *332*
  Theater Subdistrict, 331
Spectacolor light board, 106, 271, 291–
    294, *292*, 296, *296*, 319
Speculation, real estate, 2, 4–5, 11–22,
    24, 33–35, 53–54, 58–64
Spence, Chuck, 348
Stage 42, 359
Stanford, The, 142
Stanley Theatre, *101*
Starr, Tama, 284, 287, 295, 306, 314
Steele, Valerie, 307
Stern, Robert A. M., 87, 88, 149–150,
    151
Stern, William J., 187
Sternbergh, Adam, 214
Steyer, Tom, 310
Stonbely, George N., 269, 270, 289,
    292–295, *294*, 319
Stone, Jill, 102
Strand, The, 142, 324
Strand Theatre, *21*, 67, 69, 231
Street Deals, 196, 198
Studebaker building, *274*
Sturz, Herbert, 115–118, 121–122, *123*,
    125, 127, 129, 133, 202
Subway system, 4, 16, 31–33, *34*, 36, 40,
    70, 73, 99, 165, 175, 192, 216, 315,
    372, 398n11
  Times Square station, 4, 15, 16, 31, *34*,
    49, 74, 95, 99, 121, 125, 129, 132,
    152, 165, *166*, 371 (*see also* Hole,
    the)
Sullivan, Brian J., 347
Sullivan, Robert, 216
Swanson, Gloria, 83–84
Swormstedt, Ted, 287